# Concepts and Cases in

# Nursing Ethics

# CONCEPTS AND CASES IN

# NURSING ETHICS

*third edition*

edited by

## MICHAEL YEO, ANNE MOORHOUSE, PAMELA KHAN, and PATRICIA RODNEY

broadview press

Library and Archives Canada Cataloguing in Publication

  Concepts and cases in nursing ethics / edited by Michael Yeo ... [et al.]. — 3rd ed.

Includes bibliographical references and index.
ISBN 978-1-55111-735-5

    1. Nursing ethics.  2. Nursing ethics—Case studies.
I. Yeo, Michael Terrence  II. Title: Nursing ethics.

RT85.C653 2010          174.2          C2010-905115-7

Broadview Press is an independent, international publishing house, incorporated in 1985.

We welcome comments and suggestions regarding any aspect of our publications—please feel free to contact us at the addresses below or at broadview@broadviewpress.com.

| | |
|---|---|
| *North America* | PO Box 1243, Peterborough, Ontario, Canada K9J 7H5 |
| | 2215 Kenmore Ave., Buffalo, New York, USA 14207 |
| | Tel: (705) 743-8990; Fax: (705) 743-8353 |
| | email: customerservice@broadviewpress.com |
| *UK, Europe, Central Asia,* | Eurospan Group, 3 Henrietta St., London WC2E 8LU, UK |
| *Middle East, Africa, India,* | Tel: 44 (0) 1767 604972; Fax: 44 (0) 1767 601640 |
| *and Southeast Asia* | email: eurospan@turpin-distribution.com |
| *Australia and New Zealand* | NewSouth Books, c/o TL Distribution |
| | 15-23 Helles Ave., Moorebank, NSW, Australia 2170 |
| | Tel: (02) 8778 9999; Fax: (02) 8778 9944 |
| | email: orders@tldistribution.com.au |

www.broadviewpress.com

Broadview Press acknowledges the financial support of the Government of Canada through the Canada Book Fund for our publishing activities.

Copy-edited by Robert Clarke.

This book is printed on paper containing 100% post-consumer fibre.

PRINTED IN CANADA

# CONTENTS

# PREFACE

The preface to the second edition of this book began with the sentence: "Health care in Canada has changed dramatically in the five years that have passed since the first edition of this book." Some fourteen years have passed since the second edition, and to address the even more dramatic changes that have occurred since then we found that an even more significant revision of the text was necessary. To aid in this task, two additional editors and co-authors joined in the project: Patricia Rodney (University of British Columbia) and Pamela Khan (University of Toronto). They brought not only considerable expertise in current trends in health care and nursing ethics to this new edition but also new perspectives.

The overall format of the text remains the same, organized mainly around discussion of central concepts in nursing and health care ethics, with provocative cases that probe and illustrate each concept. Throughout, the analytic framework also remains much the same, but the analysis has been reworked in view of updated references from the literature and with reference to significant changes in the field of nursing ethics, the profession of nursing, health care, health policy, and society more generally. To do justice to these changes it was necessary to do more than tinker with the previous edition. Accordingly, there are two major changes in this edition.

- Most of the cases from the second edition have been replaced with new cases and case commentaries that better express and reflect the current and emerging practice environment of nursing.

- A new chapter has been added that addresses head-on the significant changes that have occurred in the sociopolitical context of health care since the last edition. Complementing this discussion, the chapter also highlights significant changes that have occurred in the field of nursing ethics, as nurse ethicists and theorists have been turning with increasing attention to the sociopolitical context of ethical issues in nursing and health care.

Indeed, given the extent of the revisions and additions, this edition is as much a rewrite of the previous edition as it is a revision. Even so, in important ways it still bears the traces of the earlier editions. And the voices of co-authors who contributed to the very first edition and were not involved in the preparation of this edition can still be heard. It is fitting here to acknowledge with abiding gratitude the work of these individuals: Trudy Molke (Beneficence); Jean Dalziel (Autonomy); Sandra Mitchell (Truthfulness), Irene Krahn (Confidentiality); Gail Donner (Justice); and Ann Ford (Integrity).

Putting this new edition together took longer (much longer) than originally anticipated. Alex Sager and Greg Janzen of Broadview Press were very understanding, supportive, and encouraging. Thanks are due also to Rob Clarke for his editorial assistance and his patient willingness to accommodate us as we set and missed various deadlines.

Michael Yeo

# INTRODUCTION

*The unexamined life is not worth living.*

— SOCRATES

The profession of nursing, like the health care system, is undergoing rapid development. New and diverse roles are emerging, and old roles are being redefined. Nurses are becoming more and more reflective about the meaning of nursing. What is nursing, and what ought nursing to be? Increasingly, it is recognized that such questioning is intricately bound up with ethics.

The aim of this book is to present a unified perspective on the ethical dimension of contemporary nursing. Its objective is to furnish nurses with a clearer understanding of the key terms and arguments in which ethical issues in nursing are interpreted, discussed, and analyzed. Such understanding will better equip nurses to face the challenges of their profession and to practise responsibly in their chosen fields and specialties.

The book is divided into eight main chapters. The first chapter is a brief primer on ethics to familiarize the reader with the main lines of thought in ethical theory. Chapter 2, new to this edition, surveys the situation of contemporary nursing in view of current political and economic developments.

Chapters 3 through 8 are devoted to the elucidation of six fundamental ethical concepts: beneficence, autonomy, truthfulness, confidentiality, justice, and integrity. Each of these concepts denotes a value, principle, or virtue highly prized in health care. Almost any ethical issue in nursing involves reference to one or more of them. Each of these chapters includes cases for discussion. Cases derived from actual incidents have been modified to preserve confidentiality. Each case is preceded by an introductory preamble, which puts the issue raised by the case in context, and is followed by a critical commentary in which ethical analysis is brought to bear.

The book is designed to be read from beginning to end, but each chapter is self-contained and stands on its own. An introduction at the beginning of each chapter elucidates the main problems and issues associated with the concept to which that chapter is devoted. Other related terms and concepts are introduced and analyzed whenever they help to clarify the matter under discussion. Where applicable, quotations are given from various codes of ethics in nursing. At the end of each chapter, a list of study questions is provided to stimulate further reflection and discussion. Those who wish to do further reading or research on selected topics will find the extensive footnotes and references a good starting point.

## What Is Nursing Ethics?

Various meanings can be assigned to the term "nursing ethics." Used in one sense, nursing ethics refers to the expressed ethical norms of the nursing profession: the values, virtues, and principles that are supposed to govern and guide nurses in everyday practice. These are typically phrased as moral injunctions such as "be truthful with patients" or "respect patient confidentiality." They may also be expressed as exhortations to adopt and practise particular virtues, such as caring or fairness. As publicly stated by the profession in codes of ethics, these norms serve not only to guide nurses in their practice and character formation but also to inform the public about what they can expect from professional practitioners.

Ethical norms thus expressed state the profession's ethical ideal: how nurses *ought* to conduct themselves. However, for a variety of reasons, nurses may or may not in fact so conduct themselves. The working environment in some institutions or settings may be less conducive to the realization of professional nursing values than it is in others. Ethical sensitivity and conscientiousness will vary somewhat from nurse to nurse and institution to institution. A sociologist or a psychologist studying moral behaviour among a group of nurses might form a very different picture of ethics in nursing than the one presented in a professional code of ethics. The phrase "nursing ethics," accordingly, can also be used descriptively to refer to the norms that do in fact guide the moral behaviour of nurses.

In yet another context, "nursing ethics" refers to the growing body of writing in books and professional journals that deals with the moral dimension of nursing wherein various ethical issues are analyzed, discussed, and debated. Used in this sense, nursing ethics is not a set of norms, actual or ideal, but a field or discipline in which such norms are explored and analyzed.

These three meanings are interrelated. Ideal ethical norms as stated in professional nursing codes shape the actual behaviour of practitioners. The nursing ethics literature builds from and modifies both the actual and ideal norms of the profession. Each of the three senses indicated can be situated in the broader context in which it has evolved and continues to evolve.

## Nursing Ethics and Bioethics

Nursing ethics has developed alongside the much broader phenomenon of bioethics. Bioethics may be defined as reasoned enquiry about the ethical dimension of interventions in the lives of human beings directed to or bearing on their health good, individually or collectively. Health care is an obvious example of such an intervention, and in this regard bioethics is sometimes used synonymously with "health care ethics."[1] Issues of research and experimentation also are included in the field of bioethics.

Several factors bear on the emergence of contemporary bioethics and have also influenced present-day nursing ethics. The three described below are especially noteworthy.

### 1. Technological Developments

Rapid scientific and technological developments have presented health professionals with new powers, and with these, countless ethical issues. The respirator is a good example. It enables the prolongation of life (or dying), but with this power difficult ethical questions arise. Under what conditions ought someone to be put on or removed from a respirator? Whose decisions are these to make? There has been

---

1  See Rodney et al., 2004, for a history of health care ethics.

considerable uncertainty and disagreement about what is morally (and even legally) right in these matters, as was learned from the landmark case of Karen Quinlan (Pence, 1990). In Canada, the issue of withdrawal of life-sustaining treatment was brought to a head in 1992 by the Nancy B. case (Roy, Williams, & Dickens, 1994).

The respirator is but one example of how "progress" in modern science and medicine generates difficult moral issues. Equally poignant examples can be drawn from reproductive technology, transplantation, and genetics, to name only some of the more topical ones. Contemporary health care, thanks in large part to technological developments that have outpaced the ethical consensus in our society, presents us with more and more confusing grey areas. Those engaged in bioethics, drawing upon moral philosophy, attempt to think critically and systematically about these difficult grey areas.

## 2. Research and Experimentation

The negative publicity about gross abuses in research involving human subjects that took place in Nazi Germany and of questionable research practices in North America generated considerable discussion about ethics in research (Beecher, 1959, 1966). Should some categories of people — for example, children, captive populations, mentally incompetent persons — be excluded from research? What measures and controls will best ensure the voluntariness of research subjects? How do we decide acceptable ratios of benefit to harm, and who should decide on these ratios? Many of the main concepts and principles of bioethics such as informed consent, autonomy, and beneficence have been defined and redefined against this background.

## 3. Authority, Consumerism, and Patients' Rights

Throughout the 1960s, the idea of consumer education and protection took hold in North America, and the rhetoric of rights became more and more prominent in discussions about matters ethical (Fleming, 1983). In this climate, increased scrutiny was directed toward the health care system as a locus of considerable power. "Patients" increasingly came to view themselves as "consumers." An important landmark occurred in 1973 when the American Hospital Association introduced a twelve-point "Patients' Bill of Rights," which was subsequently translated into policy in numerous American and Canadian institutions (Storch, 1982).

The rise of the patients' rights movement occurred concurrently with rising public distrust of the authority vested in religion, government, scientists, and professionals. Increased scrutiny was brought to bear on the practice of health professionals, and with this came higher standards of public accountability. Many ethical matters once trusted to the discretion of professional authorities came to be designated as public questions. A new ethic emerged and took shape around the watchword "autonomy." This was in part shaped by a growing cultural and political pluralism in which the values of individual rights and liberties ruled the day. The paternalism long entrenched in the health professions came to be widely criticized. Patients demanded to be more involved in decision-making regarding their health care. Broad legislative changes both reflected and shaped new public expectations about patient involvement in health care planning, the doctrine of informed consent being a prime example of this trend. What public consensus existed on health care ethics was strained as new ethical issues came to the fore and old ones took on a new complexion and urgency.

Social developments along these lines opened up the space of questioning within which contemporary bioethics developed. Professional philosophers and theologians brought their traditions and skills to bear on the many ethical questions and issues that were emerging, and health professionals became increasingly interested in moral philosophy and moral reasoning.

To date, the greatest amount of work in bioethics has been in the specific area of *medical ethics*. The relationship between nursing ethics, medical ethics, and more generally bioethics is a matter of some controversy (Fry, 1989; Twomey, 1989). To what extent is nursing ethics distinct from medical ethics? Certainly there are interconnections and lines of influence, but there are differences as well. Whatever distinctness contemporary nursing ethics has emerges out of the situation of contemporary nursing.

## Nursing Ethics and Nursing

Several features of nursing have helped to shape contemporary nursing ethics. To begin with the most obvious, nursing has been predominately a woman's profession and remains so today. Some authors, building from the premise that women (whether by nature, culture, or both) value such things as nurturing and caring more than men, argue that an "ethic of care" may be especially appropriate for nursing (Huggins & Scalzi, 1988; Crowley, 1989). This point of view, and the assumptions that inform it, is a matter of debate, as we shall see when we discuss the matter in greater detail in chapter 3. Regardless, there is evidence that nursing, by contrast with the "medical model," for example, has been more oriented around "caring" than "curing" (Watson, 1979; Gadow, 1985; Benner & Wrubel, 1989; MacPherson, 1989). Moreover, nursing has tended to work with a broader understanding of health than have most other health professions. This has implications for the kinds of ethical issues that arise and the way in which they are framed.

Gender is also significant as concerns the value that society and other health professionals have attached to the work of nursing, and it bears on such important matters as the drive for professionalism in nursing (Delamothe, 1988). Historically — and this is not unrelated to sexual difference — nursing has been in a position of subordination in the health care system. In this regard, it is instructive to recall the motto of the Mack Training School for Nurses, the first of its kind in Canada: "I see and am silent" (Coburn, 1987).

The experience of powerlessness — and this experience is by no means a thing of the past — has especially sensitized nursing to issues of power in health care (Rodney, 1988, 1989; Rodney & Starzomski, 1993; Tunna & Conner, 1993; Varcoe & Rodney, 2009; Storch et al., 2009). Yarling and McElmurry (1986) go so far as to claim that, under existing legal and institutional arrangements, many nurses do not have the freedom or power to practise ethically. Although this thesis is open to debate (see Bishop & Scudder, 1987), there can be no doubt that the situation of nursing vis-à-vis the distribution of power in the health care system informs and shapes many of the ethical issues nurses face in their daily practice. Potentially, current reform trends toward restructuring and reorganizing in health care may be empowering for nurses. However, if driven by the economic bottom line, health reform could exacerbate the problem of powerlessness.

Related to the distribution of power is the fact that many ethical issues arise because nurses often find themselves in institutional situations wherein they have multiple obligations (Storch, 1988). In the classic scenario, there may be a conflict between the nurse's commitment to the patient, on the one hand, and the "orders" of the physician, on the other. Although today the profession proclaims that the primary loyalty is to the patient, nursing still must struggle against the legacy of Florence Nightingale, who pledged the primary loyalty of the nurse to the physician (Storch, 1982). Notwithstanding the trend toward team care based on shared decision-making, the legal and institutional horizon of nursing is such that nurses sometimes must contend and live with the effects of decisions into which they may have had little or no input, and with which they may disagree. This reality is reflected in the nursing ethics literature, in which themes such as conscience and integrity figure prominently.

Another feature constitutive of present-day nursing ethics is what Storch calls "being there" (1988, p. 212). Nursing care is often less episodic than that provided by other health professionals. In a hospital setting, for example, physicians may come and go but nursing is there for the patient around the clock. Other health professionals tend to get unconnected snapshots of the patient whereas the nurse gets a full-length movie version. The contact between the nurse and the patient is such that many dimensions of the patient's being are disclosed in the relationship. As Gadow (1980) puts it, "the nurse attends the patient as a whole, not just as a single problem or system" (p. 81).

The duration and nature of his or her contact with the patient make it possible for the nurse to know the patient somewhat more intimately than do other health professionals. This puts the nurse "in the ideal position among health-care providers to experience the patient as a unique human being with individual strengths and complexities" (Gadow, 1980, p. 81). This experience bears on a number of ethical matters. For example, it is one thing to be less than fully truthful with someone whom one knows only superficially, and another to be so with someone with whom one has established a closer relationship.

## Models of the Nurse-Patient Relationship

The ethical landscape of nursing appears differently depending on how the relationship between nurse and patient is viewed. Smith (1980) distinguishes three typical roles nurses adopt in relation to patients: surrogate mother, technician, and contracted clinician. Curtin (1979) adds several other roles to this list: champion of the sick, health educator, physician's assistant, healer, and patient's advocate. Some of these are manifestly less acceptable than others, but all have some basis in the reality of nursing. The ethical question concerns the roles that nurses self-consciously and deliberately should adopt. Those most favoured in the nursing ethics literature are based on the contractual and advocacy model of the nurse-patient relationship, as described below.

### 1. The Contractual Model

Following the contractual or covenantal model, the nurse and the patient negotiate the moral parameters of the relationship and through dialogue make explicit what each expects from the other. Does the nurse or the patient have any special values likely to come into play in the course of the relationship? How involved does the patient want to be in the decision-making process? What family members or friends are to be consulted should the occasion arise? In the course of discussion, either the nurse or the patient may find that the other has unacceptable expectations or demands. If so, it is best that this be known in advance of any issues that might arise.

The contract or understanding thus negotiated subsequently comes to serve as a guide and reference point for whatever ethical decision-making might be required in the course of the relationship. It builds trust in the relationship because each person knows what to expect from the other (Cooper, 1988). It also empowers the patient by creating a sense of control at a time when he or she may be disoriented by illness and by being in a foreign environment (Ziemann & Dracup, 1989). The preference that many nurses have for the word "client" in place of "patient" is in keeping with the empowering spirit of the contractual model, emphasizing as it does the agency of the client/patient and the voluntary element of the relationship.

## 2. The Patient's Advocate Model

The role of patient or client's advocate has been adopted and endorsed by nursing to a far greater extent than by other health professions. One reason for this may be that nurses, because of their own experience, are better able to identify and empathize with the vulnerability and powerlessness of the patient.

Although widely embraced, the notion of patient advocacy is often vaguely understood. The term "advocate" itself is imported into health care from law. It came into vogue with the emergence of consumerism and the patients' rights movement in health care. To advocate in the context of health care is often taken to mean advocating on behalf of the patient's rights (Annas, 1974), and in particular his or her right to be informed about and involved in treatment decisions.

Conceived in terms of patients' rights, advocacy is often presented as a kind of foil or corrective to a perceived tendency in the health care system to deny the patient his or her rights. Kosik (1972) expresses this view of advocacy very clearly: "Patient advocacy is seeing that the patient knows what to expect and what is his right to have, and then displaying the willingness and courage to see that the system does not prevent his getting it" (p. 84).

The rights-based model of advocacy has been criticized on a number of counts. Many nurses conceive the scope of advocacy as defined by the patient's interests or good more broadly conceived (Curtin, 1979; 1983). Gadow (1980, p. 84), critical of viewing the patient abstractly as a bearer of rights, speaks of "existential advocacy" directed to the patient as a whole being. Existential advocacy steers a middle course between paternalism (unilaterally imposing upon the patient one's belief about what is good) and what she calls "consumer protection" (the nurse becoming an instrument in the service of what the patient wishes).

To Gadow's cogent critique of the rights-based, consumer-protection model of advocacy, an historical footnote can be added. The rights-based idea of advocacy developed as a corrective to widespread paternalism in the health care system. Thanks in part to the contribution of nursing, paternalism is probably less common in the contemporary health care system than it used to be, and less acceptable, but it is by no means a thing of the past, even in nursing.

These models, and others like them, have important limitations. For one thing, they are premised on a one-to-one relationship of individual nurse to individual patient. As such they do not address the reality that individual nurses typically work collaboratively with other nurses and health professionals in providing care to patients; and these collaborative relationships often complicate a nurse's relationship with patients. In some cases too, such as in public health, the nurse does not have a single person as a patient or client but rather a family or even a community. As well, these models do not fully capture the roles that nurses play in broader social contexts — that is, in situations in which nurses attempt to enhance the available quality of care and ensure equitable access to that care, or in which they work to have an impact on the general health of individuals and communities. For many nurses today, advocacy goes considerably beyond relationships with individual patients to include social and political action in the name of social justice and human rights (Kirkham and Browne, 2006).

## A Knowledge Base in Ethics for Nursing

Having described the context in which contemporary nursing ethics has developed, what does all this mean to the individual practising nurse? A helpful way of focusing this question is to ask what knowledge base in ethics is appropriate for today's nurse? There is room for debate around this question, but the nursing ethics literature reflects consensus around at least three main areas of knowledge and reflection: (1) moral beliefs and values; (2) relevant codes, policies, and laws; and (3) fundamental concepts of moral philosophy.

## 1. Moral Beliefs and Values

The Socratic injunction "know thyself" names the task at the entrance to the moral life. Through our upbringing and acculturation — the influence of family, peers, and so on — we acquire numerous beliefs about right and wrong and good and bad. Beliefs thus acquired are deeply constitutive of who we are as adults, and may manifest themselves in our actions without our ever having reflected upon them. We may not realize how these beliefs express themselves in our lives until challenged by others. The choice of the ethical life as expressed in the injunction "know thyself" commits one to bringing such unreflected beliefs to light and, having clarified them, to explicitly and responsibly embrace, reject, or modify them. As proclaims another famous Socratic dictum: "The unexamined life is not worth living."

The task of acquiring self-knowledge may also be expressed with reference to "values" rather than to "moral beliefs," and indeed this is the preferred language in nursing. Values clarification has been a major theme in the nursing ethics literature, and various techniques for education in values clarification have been developed (Steele & Harmon, 1979). In its essentials, values clarification is a process of becoming more aware and reflective about the values that have been inculcated in us through various influences. This enables us to decide in a self-conscious way what values we ought to prize and promote, and to assess how various practices stand in relation to these values. Flaherty (1985) states the challenge clearly: "The examined life is lived today by those nurses who are willing to question the prevailing customs and taboos of the situations in which they find themselves, including their own behaviour, to identify whether what they see is consonant with the standards of practice for which they stand accountable" (p. 104). Such an examination should also include consideration of how either personal or professional values may come into play in relation to the values of patients.

Intervention in the lives of others with respect to matters about which they care and value deeply carries tremendous responsibility. In nursing, such intervention is mandated and legitimized in the name of health and health care. Therefore, health is the most obvious value that matters in the health care context. However, beneficent concern for the health of the patient may come into conflict with several other, sometimes competing values, such as autonomy, truthfulness, confidentiality, and justice.

Where values are concerned — where things about which people care deeply are at stake — one whose professional promise is to benefit and respect the patient must acquire a certain facility in moving within the dimension of values. This means, first of all, becoming sensitive to the values dimension of nursing. At every step in the nursing process questions of value should be raised, if only to ask "Are there any questions of value to be considered here?" This is not to say that every nursing intervention, however routine, will raise an explicit ethical issue requiring an explicitly ethical decision. Indeed, few do. But every nursing act, as an intervention in the lives of others, has at least the possibility of promoting or transgressing some good or value.

The values dimension of nursing, then, is very complex. It encompasses full-blown ethical dilemmas — situations involving two or more conflicting values or principles such that one can be satisfied or realized only at the expense of not satisfying the other — but much more besides. Many situations raise or present ethical concerns but are not necessarily crises or dilemma situations. Whatever the situation, knowing what one values and being sensitive to the values of others is an essential condition of responsible and ethical practice.

## 2. Relevant Codes, Policies, and Laws

A knowledge base in ethics for nursing should also include codified ethics — codes, policies, and laws — as they relate to nursing practice. These include codes of ethics promulgated by professional associations in which one is a member or even a stakeholder. At the international level, there is *The ICN Code of Ethics for Nurses* (International Council of Nurses, 2006). At the national level, there is the Canadian Nurses Association (CNA, 2008) *Code of Ethics for Registered Nurses* and the American Nurses Association (ANA, 2001) *Code for Nurses with Interpretive Statements*. At the provincial or state level, there are such documents as *Practice Standards: Ethics* (College of Nurses of Ontario, 2009). Various professional organizations also publish helpful policy statements related to particular issues or addressed to nurses working in a specific context or area. For example, nurses actively engaged in research should be familiar with *Ethical Research Guidelines for Registered Nurses* (CNA, 2002). Nurses working in a variety of institutional contexts can find guidance in two statements produced collaboratively by the Canadian Healthcare Association, Canadian Medical Association, Canadian Nurses Association, and the Catholic Health Association of Canada: *Joint Statement on Resuscitative Interventions* (1995); and *Joint Statement on Resolving and Preventing Ethics Conflicts Involving Health Providers and Persons Receiving Care* (1999).

The nurse would also be well-advised to be familiar with any relevant policies issued by the institution in which he or she works and to measure these against personal and professional values. Indeed, it is wise to familiarize oneself with such policies before entering an employment contract, especially if one has intense convictions about issues likely to arise in the institution. At the broader level of society, morally responsible nursing requires the nurse to be familiar with whatever social norms and laws bear on his or her practice.

As important as they are, codes, policies, or laws cannot take the place of or eliminate the need for ethical decision-making. For one thing, they are bound to be vague or silent about many ethical issues that arise for nurses. Even when they are explicit, the answer that one was simply doing what was mandated by a code, policy, or law is never enough to satisfy the demands of ethical accountability when the moral appropriateness of a particular action is called into question. Ethics is largely about being able to give reasons in defence of what one decides, and this includes even the decision to abide by (or to reject) the injunctions of a given code, policy, or law.

Moreover, codified ethics are not absolute or infallible. To take the case of law, an action may be legal, yet unethical from one standpoint or other. Many people believe that this is so as concerns abortion in Canada and the United States at the present time. Similarly, something that is illegal may be ethically permissible or even required in some values systems.

Although ethical codes, policies, and laws do not settle an ethical issue in absolute terms, they do furnish a good starting point for reflecting on a given issue. They embody the collective wisdom of our profession, institution, or community. Although those who bring ethical analysis to bear on an issue may arrive at contrary conclusions, it would be arrogant to do so without having at least considered the codified ethics, policies, and laws on these matters. Moreover, given the authority that stands behind them, the consequences of ignoring or transgressing such official edicts can be very grave, and ought to be weighed in the deliberations of a prudent person. On the positive side, codes of ethics, policies, or laws, in addition to providing guidance, can give powerful support and backing for someone working in a setting in which other people are inclined to ignore ethical concerns.

## 3. Fundamental Concepts of Moral Philosophy

A knowledge base in ethics for nursing should also include some knowledge of moral philosophy. Moral philosophy is a highly specialized discipline, and there is disagreement about how much competence a nurse ought to have in this knowledge base. What ought the nurse to know by way of ethical theory? How well-versed should he or she be in the methods of moral reasoning? Should he or she know something about metaethics?

If ethical theory is not an essential component of nursing knowledge, it is certainly desirable at least for nurses to have some grounding in this subject. For this reason, this text includes a primer on ethical theory to provide the reader with some rudimentary knowledge of the main lines of theoretical enquiry.

Whatever might be obligatory as concerns knowledge of ethical theory, we believe that at the very least nurses should have facility in the use of fundamental concepts by means of which to identify, describe, and analyze ethical issues. The six concepts that form the skeletal framework of this book — beneficence, autonomy, truthfulness, confidentiality, justice, and integrity — have been chosen because they are foundational in nursing ethics. Fortunately, most of these concepts are already part of the ordinary language of nursing, and so education in this area is largely a matter of building on or deepening what one already knows. Ethics, after all, applies to everyone, and everyone has the basic equipment necessary for the conduct of a moral life.

However, the common-sense usage of moral concepts has many inadequacies. In the first place, these concepts are frequently assigned vague and even contradictory meanings. In moral disagreements people often talk at cross-purposes because they interpret terms and concepts differently. Secondly, moral analysis often comes quickly to a point where two or more positions, each of which expresses a competing value, are at odds. To take treatment refusal as an example, one person, appealing to autonomy, might insist on the patient's right to refuse whereas another, guided by beneficence, might insist on the duty to do what will benefit the patient. A more philosophical understanding of the fundamental concepts used in moral analysis and the tensions between them can help to sort out confusions, clarify disagreements, and promote creative problem-solving. This is desirable both with respect to the nurse's ongoing commitment to self-examination and his or her desire to do what is right.

Such an understanding can be pursued at different levels. The literature in nursing ethics and bioethics, for example, provides analyses that clarify these concepts considerably beyond their often imprecise and confused usage in everyday language and contains helpful discussions of the basic ethical issues that nurses face. At a more philosophical level, which may exceed what the nurse needs to know, moral theorists situate these concepts somewhat more systematically in the context of moral theories.

The three subject areas described above (moral beliefs and values; relevant codes, policies, and laws; and fundamental concepts of moral philosophy) constitute a reasonable knowledge base for ethics in nursing. However, it is important to realize the limits of becoming more reflective about this knowledge base. Acquiring knowledge is not the same thing as becoming virtuous, except insofar as acquiring knowledge can itself be said to be a virtue. That people are good at the process of values clarification; well-versed in relevant ethical codes, policies, and laws; and well-read in the nursing ethics literature and in moral philosophy does not mean that they will be good in the sense of acting with virtue. Someone can be well-informed about ethics but insensitive or even cruel. Conversely, someone may be very kind but ill-informed about ethical concepts and moral reasoning. Even so, becoming more reflective may at least complement the cultivation of the virtues thought to be desirable for nursing. At the very least, it can help nurses to become clearer about what virtues are desirable and why.

More directly, reflecting on the knowledge base for ethics in nursing will help the nurse to develop certain skills. Such reflection will help the nurse to:

- become more sensitive to the ethical dimension of nursing;

- become more conversant in the moral values and principles that are at issue or at stake in the scope of his or her nursing practice;

- recognize and identify ethical issues when they arise;

- analyze ethical issues more thoroughly (e.g., describe the main arguments that can be deployed on either side of a given issue, bring relevant concepts and principles to bear on options, and so on).

The moral life presents itself to us as a task and a challenge, and the task will vary somewhat depending on one's life situation. This book is specifically designed for people whose life situation is nursing and who face the special kinds of ethical issues that nurses tend to face. A good part of the moral task for nursing is to gain a better understanding of its ethical dimension. In this regard, this book will be both useful and informative.

The moral task for nurses, however, is not simply a matter of knowing but also of doing or even becoming, and whether good comes of this knowledge depends on the activity of the reader who at this very

moment is finishing this sentence. Writes Levine (1977): "Ethical behaviour is not the display of one's moral rectitude in times of crisis. It is
the day-by-day expression of one's commitment to other persons and
the ways in which human beings relate to one another in their daily
interactions" (p. 846).

## Ethical Analysis and the Nursing Process

In a field of human interaction where values are as pervasive as in
health care, it is virtually inevitable that conflicts of value will arise in
a nurse's practice. In any given situation, the beliefs and values of the
nurse, of the profession, of the patient, of the patient's family or friends,
of other health professionals, and of society in general may come into
play. Sometimes the values of all concerned will not be congruent, and
the nurse will be faced with an ethical conflict or issue.

The nature of ethics is such that there can be no mechanical formula
for resolving issues when they arise. However, familiarity with the values dimension of the situation, any codified statements that may bear
on it, and the main concepts of ethics and the ability to bring them to
bear on a given issue can be of considerable help. In this regard, a first
point to emphasize about ethical analysis — although hardly much of a
help to someone in the throes of an ethical issue — is that big problems
usually start off as small problems, and can be prevented, arrested, or
at least minimized by thoughtful intervention at an early stage. Thus, it
is important to become vigilant about proactively raising questions of
value in one's daily practice.

Whatever the nature of the ethical problem, three interrelated components of ethical analysis can be brought to bear: descriptive analysis,
conceptual analysis, and normative analysis (Martin & Schinzinger,
1989). *Descriptive analysis* is directed toward ascertaining the truth
and acquiring knowledge. What is going on in the situation? What
are the relevant facts of the matter? What do we know for sure, and
what do we need to know in order to make an informed decision? The
task here is to gather whatever data might bear on ethical choice and
practice. Such data may include facts about the health status and medical condition of patients, the perspectives of the main agents involved,

information about relevant policies and laws, the relationships of power among the stakeholders, and a wide range of other topics.

*Conceptual analysis* has to do with clarifying the meaning of key concepts involved in the analysis of a case or issue. In addition to the fundamental concepts around which this book is organized, numerous other concepts may also come into play. Sometimes these concepts are vague or ambiguous, such as "quality of life," "health," and "harm." Often, concepts are laden with values which skew the analysis of the issue toward one side or the other. In a discussion about abortion, for instance, the concept of "personhood" may load the dice in such a way as to prejudice the outcome. In an examination of euthanasia the concept of "killing" may function in a similar way. The task of conceptual analysis is to sort out the various meanings of key concepts and to unpack terms loaded with values and questionable assumptions.

*Normative analysis* is directed toward deciding what ought to be done. It involves sorting out the various moral values, duties, or principles that may bear on the choice at hand. What values or duties are in conflict, and on the basis of which criteria or arguments should they be weighed? Who among those involved in the case ought to participate in making decisions? What options are available, and, ethically speaking, what counts for and against the various options?

All of the above aspects of ethical analysis may be relevant to the solution of an ethical problem at hand and can be integrated into the nursing process. In addition, the nursing process itself can be adapted to furnish a useful framework for ethical analysis, as described below.

## 1. Assessment

One of the most important challenges of ethical analysis is to recognize in the first place that an ethical problem or issue has arisen in a particular situation, or even that an apparent problem or issue has an ethical dimension. Not infrequently ethical analysis does not get off the ground because those involved do not see the situation or problem as something that has to do with ethics or values. Reporting on their extensive nursing ethics study, Storch et al. (2009) indicate that "getting participants to recognize the ethical dimension of a situation" was often the "necessary first step." As an example they mention an instance in which a number of new physicians were not willing to wear identity badges; the nurses dismissed this issue as "not being about ethics" (p. 22). Greater familiarity with ethical concepts and typical issues related to those concepts will help nurses develop a sensitivity to the presence of ethical issues that might otherwise go unnoticed or not be identified as such. Ethical analysis can only begin when an issue has been identified as ethical, or as having an ethical dimension.

If an issue has been identified as ethical or having an ethical dimension, the first step is to work out a reasonable assessment or interpretation of the issue at hand. The emphasis here is on the word "reasonable," for it is quite likely that one already has a preconceived interpretation to begin with. That the situation presents itself as an "ethical issue" indicates at least some minimal interpretation.

One's initial interpretation of the ethical situation may be vague, incomplete, or even false. Interpretation in matters of value may be extremely complicated and subtle. Certain questions should be asked by way of testing and deepening one's initial interpretation of the issue. What exactly is the issue? Is it properly an ethical issue? What kind of ethical issue? What ethical concepts does it bring into play? What is the context in which it has arisen? In part this context may be defined by the mission statement of the institution, relevant policy statements, one's professional code of ethics, legalities, and so on. What bearing if any do they have on the issue? What are the relevant facts and how clearly are they understood? What values are at stake? Whose values? Who are the significant people involved? In what terms do they interpret the issue? Are you certain that you know how they view things? Do they understand your point of view? What are the main arguments on the different sides of the issue? What are the relationships of power among those involved, and in the roles they play? Are people free to express their views, and do they feel free? Or is there perhaps some degree of coercion in the circumstances of the situation?

Such questions must be raised in order to work out a responsible assessment or interpretation. The most reasonable way to answer them is likely to involve talking with others and putting questions to them.

The nursing literature on ethics may also be helpful. In the course of working toward an interpretation, one will often find that the issue is based on a misunderstanding or lack of communication.

By way of interpreting the issue, it is also extremely important that the nurse be as clear as possible about his or her values. In some instances, the nurse may learn that he or she is ambivalent about an issue that has arisen. Of course, it is always better for the nurse to have thought about and decided upon his or her values prior to being thrown into an issue. In part, the purpose of this book is to facilitate such an enquiry into one's values in a moment of quiet reflection. Even so, sometimes we only discover what our values really are (or perhaps discover that we are not as sure about things as we previously believed we were) when challenged with a real life issue.

## 2. Planning

Having arrived at a reasonable interpretation of the situation (or even in the course of doing so), a second step is to identify and plan options. What are the alternatives? Who supports which option and why? What are the main arguments for and against each? What bearing, if any, do law, institutional mission statements and policies, and professional codes have on the options? Have all of the relevant people been taken into consideration? How much input ought each of those involved to have? Who ought to be involved? Do they understand the options?

Having sorted out the options, the task then is to weigh them and choose the one that, all things considered, is morally best. Some options will be more promotive of certain values than others. Sometimes the scale will be loaded heavily on the side of one particular option, in which case the decision will be relatively easy. Other times two or more options evaluated in terms of conflicting values may approach being equal in weight, and the judgement between them will be difficult.

## 3. Implementation

Having decided on an option, or in order to decide, questions arise about how best to implement the option in a sensitive and effective way. Do relevant others understand why this particular option was chosen? Who should be involved in its implementation? What effects is it likely to have? To what extent can these consequences be managed and negative outcomes anticipated and warded off? Some adjustment of one's planned course of action may be necessary as one gets feedback from the implementation process (e.g., when unexpected complications arise).

## 4. Evaluation

Having implemented an option, in the interests of learning from experience and ensuring effective care, one is obliged to review the situation. How are things working out? To what extent are they working out as anticipated? How do those involved (and especially the patient) feel about how things turned out? Does the issue have any broader dimensions (e.g., implications for institutional policy) that should be addressed in light of what happened? Is there anything that can be done to prevent such issues from arising in the future? Questions about process should also be raised. Is the process by which the decision was made a good one? Could better procedural mechanisms be established to facilitate future decision-making?

Incorporating ethics into the nursing process is a good way of ensuring ethical practice, and using the nursing process as a framework for analysis is a good way of working through an ethical issue that has arisen. Other frameworks for moral reasoning and decision-making for nurses are available (e.g., Curtin, 1982, p. 61; Thompson & Thompson, 1985, p. 99), but not surprisingly they tend to agree in essentials. Appendices A and B include two such frameworks. Students will find it helpful to work through one or more of the issues presented in the text using these models.

Frameworks or models of this sort can indeed be useful, but a word of caution is in order. They are intended to aid decision-making and not to replace it. Decision-making requires judgement, and judgement guides the use of any framework as much as it may be guided by it. Hence, one should not be too rigid in following the direction of a given model. A good chef knows the importance of recipes, but knows as well how to add, subtract, and substitute ingredients as necessary.

## Strategies for Case-Based Teaching and Learning

The intended audience of this book includes not only practising nurses but also nurse educators and students. The case method adopted in this book has proven itself a useful and effective way to teach ethics. Cases help students to see how the tools and concepts of ethical analysis apply in concrete ways. Moreover, whereas ethics in the abstract can be somewhat dry, cases engage the interest of students and make for lively discussion.

The ways in which cases may be used in educational contexts are limited only by the imagination of the nurse educator, but two main strategies are particularly worth mentioning. One such strategy is role-playing. This involves having students assume the roles of the various characters in the case. Students enact the case and flesh out the limited information given with imagined dialogue. This brings the characters to life and helps students to gain a better appreciation of the complexities and of the different points of view. In this regard, it can be very eye-opening for a student to assume the role of a character with whom he or she is unsympathetic.

A second strategy is the classical debate format. This involves having students defend and argue for different sides of the issue. This may be especially appropriate when the issue is a genuine dilemma, and one about which the class itself is divided. Another variation on this strategy is for the instructor or one of the students to assume the role of "devil's advocate," defending the position that appears weaker or less popular.

In addition to these general strategies, a number of techniques can be used to facilitate discussion. Sometimes it is instructive to vary the facts of the case (e.g., change the setting from a hospital to a patient's home; modify details about the patient's medical condition; reverse sexes; and so on). Such variations may throw new light on the issue and help to clarify the values and concepts involved in the analysis.

Another technique is to invite students to imagine other cases that are similar, or other situations in which the same issue arises with a perhaps slightly different twist. This helps students to develop flexibility in applying the concepts and values under discussion.

It is also useful to invite students to relate the case, or the issue raised by the case, to their personal experiences. Ethical analysis, after all, is little more than a game if students do not integrate what they have learned into their own lives. Relating the cases and issues to personal experiences will help students to shape their lives and practices in light of what they are learning.

## References

American Nurses Association. (2001). *Code of ethics for nurses with interpretive statements*. Silver Spring, MD. <http://www.nursingworld.org/MainMenu Categories/ThePracticeofProfessionalNursing/EthicsStandards/CodeofEthics. aspx>.

Annas, G.J. (1974). The patient rights advocate: Can nurses effectively fill the role? *Supervisor Nurse* 5 (7), 20-25.

Beecher, H.K. (1959). *Experimentation in man*. Springfield, IL: Charles E. Thomas.

Beecher, H.K. (1966). Ethics and clinical research. *The New England Journal of Medicine* 274 (24), 1354-1360.

Benner, P., & Wrubel, J. (1989). *The primacy of caring: Stress and coping in health and illness*. Menlo Park, CA: Addison-Wesley.

Bishop, A.H., & Scudder, J.R. Jr. (1987). Nursing ethics in an age of controversy. *Advances in Nursing Science* 9 (3), 34-43.

Canadian Healthcare Association, Canadian Medical Association, Canadian Nurses Association, & Catholic Health Association of Canada. (1995). *Joint statement on resuscitative interventions*. Ottawa. <http://www.cna-nurses.ca/CNA/ documents/pdf/publications/PS21_Joint_Statement_Resuscitative_ Interventions_1995_e.pdf>.

Canadian Healthcare Association, Canadian Medical Association, Canadian Nurses Association, & Catholic Health Association of Canada. (1999). *Joint statement on resolving and preventing ethics conflicts involving health providers and persons receiving care*. Ottawa. <http://www.cna-aiic.ca/CNA/documents/pdf/ publications/prevent_resolv_ethical_conflict_e.pdf>.

Canadian Nurses Association. (2002). *Ethical research guidelines for registered nurses*. Ottawa.

Canadian Nurses Association. (2008). *Code of ethics for registered nurses.* Ottawa. <http://www.cna-aiic.ca/CNA/documents/pdf/publications/Code_of_Ethics _2008_e.pdf>.

Coburn, J. (1987). "I see and am silent": A short history of nursing in Ontario, 1850-1930. In D. Coburn, C. D'Arcy, G.M. Torrance, & P. New (Eds.), *Health and Canadian society: Sociological perspectives* (2nd ed., pp. 441-462). Markham, ON: Fitzhenry & Whiteside.

College of Nurses of Ontario. (2009). *Practice standard: Ethics.* Toronto. <http:// www.cno.org/docs/prac/41034_Ethics.pdf>.

Cooper, M.C. (1988). Covenantal relationships: Grounding for the nursing ethic. *Advances in Nursing Science* 10 (4), 48-59.

Crowley, M.A. (1989). Feminist pedagogy: Nurturing the ethical ideal. *Advances in Nursing Science* 11 (3), 53-61.

Curtin, L.L. (1979). The nurse as advocate: A philosophical foundation for nursing. *Advances in Nursing Science* 1 (3), 1-10.

Curtin, L.L. (1982). No rush to judgment. In L.L. Curtin & M.J. Flaherty (Eds.), *Nursing ethics: Theories and pragmatics* (pp. 57-63). Bowie, MD: Robert J. Brady.

Curtin, L.L. (1983). The nurse as advocate: A cantankerous critique. *Nursing Management* 14 (5), 9-10.

Delamothe, T. (1988). Nursing grievances V: Women's work. *British Medical Association Journal* 296 (30), 345-347.

Flaherty, M.J. (1985). Ethical issues. In M. Stewart, J. Innes, S. Searl, & C. Smillie (Eds.), *Community health nursing in Canada* (pp. 97-113). Toronto: Gage.

Fleming, J.W. (1983). Consumerism and the nursing profession. In N.L. Chaska (Ed.), *The nursing profession: A time to speak* (pp. 471-478). New York: McGraw-Hill.

Fry, S.T. (1989). Toward a theory of nursing ethics. *Advances in Nursing Science* 11 (4), 9-22.

Gadow, S.A. (1980). Existential advocacy: Philosophical foundations of nursing. In S.F. Spicker & S.A. Gadow (Eds.), *Nursing: Images and ideals* (pp. 79-101). New York: Springer.

Gadow, S.A. (1985). Nurse and patient: The caring relationship. In A.H. Bishop & J.R. Scudder Jr. (Eds.), *Caring, curing, coping: Nurse, physician, patient relationships* (pp. 31-43). Birmingham: University of Alabama Press.

Huggins, E.A., & Scalzi, C.C. (1988). Limitations and alternatives: Ethical practice theory in nursing. *Advances in Nursing Science* 10 (4), 43-47.

International Council of Nurses. (2006). *The ICN code of ethics for nurses.* Geneva. <http://www.icn.ch/icncode.pdf>.

Kirkham, S.R., & Browne, A.J. (2006). Toward a critical theoretical interpretation of social justice discourses in nursing. *Advances in Nursing Science* 29 (4), 324-339.

Kosik, S.H. (1972). Patient advocacy or fighting the system. *American Journal of Nursing* 72 (4), 694-698.

Levine, M.E. (1977). Nursing ethics and the ethical nurse. *American Journal of Nursing* 77 (5), 845-849.

MacPherson, K.I. (1989). A new perspective on nursing and caring in a corporate context. *Advances in Nursing Science* 11 (4), 32-39.

Martin, M.W., & Schinzinger, R. (1989). *Ethics in engineering* (2nd ed.). New York: McGraw-Hill.

Pence, G.E. (1990). *Classic cases in medical ethics: Accounts of cases that have shaped medical ethics, with philosophical, legal, and historical backgrounds.* New York: McGraw-Hill.

Rodney, P. (1988). Moral distress in critical care nursing. *Canadian Critical Care Nursing Journal* 5 (2), 9-11.

Rodney, P. (1989). Towards ethical decision-making in nursing practice. *Canadian Journal of Nursing Administration* 2 (2), 11-13.

Rodney, P., & Starzomski, R. (1993). Constraints on the moral agency of nurses. *Canadian Nurse* 89 (9), 23-26.

Rodney, P., Burgess, M., McPherson, G., & Brown, H. (2004). Our theoretical landscape: a brief history of health care ethics. In J. Storch, P. Rodney, & R. Starzomski (Eds.), *Toward a moral horizon: Nursing ethics for leadership and practice.* Toronto: Pearson-Prentice Hall, 56-76.

Roy, D.J., Williams, J.R. & Dickens, B.M. (1994). *Bioethics in Canada.* Scarborough, ON: Prentice-Hall.

Smith, S. (1980). Three models of the nurse-patient relationship. In S.F. Spieker & S.A. Gadow (Eds.), *Nursing: Images and ideals* (pp. 176-188). New York: Springer.

Steele, S.M., & Harmon, V.M. (1979). *Values clarification in nursing.* New York: Appleton-Century-Crofts.

Storch, J.L. (1982) . *Patients' rights: Ethical and legal issues in health care and nursing.* Toronto: McGraw-Hill Ryerson.

Storch, J.L. (1988). Ethics in nursing practice. In A.J. Baumgart & J. Larsen (Eds.), *Canadian nursing faces the future: Development and change* (pp. 211-221). St. Louis: C.V. Mosby.

Storch, J., Rodney, P., Pauly, B., Fulton, T.R. et al. (2009). Enhancing ethical climates in nursing work environment. *The Canadian Nurse* 105 (3), 20-26.

Thompson, J.E., & Thompson, H.O. (1985). *Bioethical decision-making for nurses.* Norwalk, CT: Appleton-Century-Crofts.

Tunna, K., & Connor, M. (1993). You are your ethics. *The Canadian Nurse* 89 (5), 25-26.

Twomey, J.G. Jr. (1989). Analysis of the claim to distinct nursing ethics: Normative and non-normative approaches. *Advances in Nursing Science* 11 (3), 25-32.

Varcoe, C., & Rodney, P. (2009). Constrained agency: The social structure of nurses' work. In B.S. Bolaria & H. Dickinson (Eds.), *Health, illness, and health care in Canada* (4th ed., pp. 122-150). Toronto: Harcourt Brace.

Watson, J. (1979). *Nursing: The philosophy and science of caring*. Boston: Little, Brown, and Company.

Yarling, R.R., & McElmurry, B.J. (1986). The moral foundation of nursing. *Advances in Nursing Science* 8 (2), 63-73.

Ziemann, K.M., & Dracup, K. (1989) . How well do CCU patient-nurse contracts work? *American Journal of Nursing* 89 (5), 691-693.

# 1 A PRIMER IN ETHICAL THEORY

*It is the mark of an educated mind to expect that amount of exactness in each kind which the nature of the particular subject admits.*

— ARISTOTLE

## Morality and the Sense of "Oughtness"

Morality is rooted in our sense of *oughtness*. When we judge that some action, decision, or policy is right or wrong, or good or bad, we do so from the point of view of what ought and ought not to be.

Consider the following sorts of moral judgements a nurse might make:

Mr. A. has a *right* to be involved in deciding his plan of care.

Nurse B. *needs to be* more caring in the way she talks with patients.

It's our *duty* to provide care to Ms. C. without bias, even though she did incur her injury in a bank robbery in which she killed two innocent bystanders.

If you have reason to believe that Nurse D. is being abusive with patients, you *must* do something to correct the situation, even if it means jeopardizing your friendship with him.

Each of these judgements has to do with how someone *ought* to act, although some of them do not express this directly. For example, the assertion that Mr. A. has a right to be involved in deciding his plan of care means that his caregivers *ought* to involve him. To say that Nurse B. needs to be more caring means that she *ought* to be so.

The *moral* ought expressed in the above statements is different from other senses of the term "ought." Sometimes we use ought in a non-moral sense, as in the sentence "*You* ought to get to bed early *if* you want to be alert for the exam tomorrow." In this case, what you ought to do is conditional upon some end or goal that you may wish to achieve. "*If* you want to be alert, *then* you ought to go to bed early." Ought in this sense has to do with the means to an assumed end.

By contrast, the moral ought does not have any "ifs" attached to it. It is not that you ought to respect the patient's wishes *if* you wish to be liked by him or her, or *if* you wish to avoid getting into trouble, or anything of the sort. Those may be good reasons for doing so, but they are not moral reasons. The moral ought enjoins you to respect the patient's wishes simply because you have a responsibility, obligation, or duty to do so. Oughtness in the moral sense is not optional or conditional upon non-moral ends or goals.

This sense of oughtness is common to all moral experience. The language in which we articulate and codify it includes such terms as rights, duties, responsibilities, values, obligations, and virtues — all of which are rooted in our sense of what ought and ought not to be.

Whatever the terms we use to express them, moral judgements and evaluations ultimately amount to claims about how someone *ought* to act. They embody *moral ideals*. These ideals are the basic elements of morality and govern moral life in two main ways. Firstly, they *guide* us in our conduct and decision-making. They give us something to aim for, targets to strive toward. Secondly, we use them to *evaluate* conduct and decision-making, whether our own or that of someone else. For example, to say that a nurse who deceives a patient about a prognosis has acted wrongly is to evaluate his or her conduct negatively in light of some such ideal as "Nurses ought to be truthful with their patients."

## Ethical Analysis

Morality is pervasive in our lives. If you think back on any given day of your life, chances are that you will have made several moral judgements or moral choices during that day, whether at work, at home, or even at play on the golf course.

Most of the time, we get by without making the moral dimension of what we do explicit. Sometimes we do not even recognize that a situation in which we are actors has a moral dimension. Moreover, in many situations we do recognize as morally charged, what is morally required is relatively obvious.

However, in many instances, especially in health care, moral issues arise very explicitly and are not easily resolved. Several factors contribute to moral complexity.

One factor is that people sometimes disagree about moral ideals. For example, not everyone would endorse the ideal that the public ought to be actively involved in deliberations about options for health reform. Some believe that the public is not sufficiently knowledgeable about the subject to make wise decisions, or is prone to choosing with its heart rather than its head. According to this point of view, it is better that public involvement be kept to a minimum — managed for public relations purposes perhaps — and that experts make the decisions.

A second complicating factor is that, even among those who agree about a particular ideal, there may be disagreement about how it should be applied in a given situation. For example, some would argue that the ideal of public participation means that the public ought to be involved in details regarding the amalgamation of several health services, whereas others would argue it is enough that the amalgamation proceed consistently with public values broadly construed.

A third complicating factor is that moral ideals sometimes conflict with one another. In some situations it may be difficult or impossible to satisfy all relevant principles at the same time. Suppose, for example, that a health agency is committed both to the ideal of public participation and to the ideal that resources should be allocated in such a way as to yield maximum benefit for every dollar expenditure. If the public preferred an allocation option deemed to be inefficient or not maximally promotive of achieving benefits, these two ideals would be in conflict.

Problems of the sort identified above indicate the need for careful reflection and analysis about moral matters. This is the province of ethics. If *morality* can be conceived as a set of principles or ought statements — a list of do's and don'ts — *ethics*, by contrast, is reflective analysis about or using those ideals or principles.

Ethics — careful and systematic reflection and analysis about moral ideals and how they bear on practical issues — is important and useful for a number of reasons:

- Moral ideals or principles as we live them day to day are sometimes vague, or even confused. Ethics helps us to identify, articulate, and clarify them and sensitizes us to the pervasiveness of moral issues in our lives. It helps us to be explicit about our moral choices.

- People often endorse moral ideals or principles without justification for them. Ethics helps us to deepen our understanding of moral ideals and principles and the reasons that can be given against and in support of them and their application in a given case.

- In some situations, moral ideals or principles conflict with one another. Ethics helps us to understand the basis of such conflict and what is at stake in a given issue.

- Working through a process of ethical analysis helps ensure that all relevant considerations are entertained prior to making a decision, and that the decision subsequently reached will be a *morally principled and rationally defensible decision.*

## Accountability and Morally Principled Decisions

One of the defining features of the health professions is the trust on which relationships with patients is based. This trust increases the burden of responsibility for health professionals and makes it all that much more important for them to be explicit about their moral choices and the principles and values informing those choices.

When we act in trust, we act on behalf of someone or some group and are accountable to them for what we do, even if we are additionally accountable to others in our institutional or employment setting.

Power, knowledge, and vulnerability are not evenly balanced in the patient-professional relationship. People acting in positions of trust have considerable power to cause harm or good.

Morality, especially in a pluralistic society such as ours, is something about which reasonable people may disagree. Almost always people will agree that some decisions are clearly "wrong." In many cases, however, it is not clear which, from among several live options, is the "right" decision.

However, if the plurality of points of view in our society means that not every decision has a morally right answer, this does not mean that anything goes. Being morally accountable does not mean that one will always make what others, and in particular those to whom one is accountable, believe is the "right" decision. But it does mean being able to defend and justify whatever decision one makes.

Thinking about moral decision-making from the standpoint of defending and justifying one's decision to others helps us to focus the task of ethics. Ethics is in the service of being accountable for our choices. When pressed to defend a decision or a policy, answers such as "I didn't really notice that there was a moral issue there at all" or "I just went on my gut feeling" are not good enough. The person to whom we are giving an account for our decision is likely to ask us such questions as "Did you consider and weigh the moral ideal or principles at stake?" and "Did you think about the alternatives and consequences?"

Given the realities of busy schedules and decisions that have to be made immediately, often we do not have the time to be as thorough in ethical analysis as we might otherwise like to be. However, although the real-world pressures on decision-making are formidable, they are no excuse for failing to make morally defensible decisions. The person to whom an accounting is owed is unlikely to be satisfied by the answer "1 didn't have time to think about that."

Ethical analysis and reflection should not be viewed just as something that one brings into play only in the thick of some crisis or other. The best occasion for ethical analysis and reflection is not in the middle of an issue but in an atmosphere of relative calm. In such moments, one can clarify the moral principles relevant to the role one plays and explore how they bear on the typical sorts of issues one is likely to face in the discharge of one's responsibilities. If one has given sufficient thought to ethics, one will not be starting from ground zero when one finds oneself in the thick of a moral issue. The relevant moral principles will be more readily apparent and their application to options and alternatives will be clearer.

Ethical analysis is no guarantee that we will make the right decision (there may not be one), but it will at least help us to make morally principled decisions, decisions we can justify with reference to the moral ideals and principles at stake and defend if called upon to give an accounting.

## Ethical Theory

Ethical analysis is a matter of examining our opinions about right and wrong and probing the moral ideals that bear on moral judgement and evaluation. This typically involves such things as identifying the principles or values relevant to a given issue and evaluating options for action in light of these principles or values.

As described above, ethical analysis is integral to moral life. All of us engage in it at least to some degree. Theorizing about ethics, by contrast, takes ethical analysis to a greater depth. It probes the foundation of morality.

Ethical theory attempts to systematize moral intuitions, values, and principles in a consistent framework or to root them in a common ground. Ethical analysis tends to focus on a particular moral issue of concern, whereas ethical theory operates at a more abstract or general level. Ethical theories purport to say something about how in general or as a rule we *ought* to behave and to furnish reasons why we should act one way rather than another. They systematize our intuitions and unreflective feelings about "oughtness."

The challenges of acquiring facility in ethical theory are considerable. It is a highly specialized and technical area within the general domain of philosophy. Many of the key works are written by and for philosophers and presuppose considerable knowledge about the main ideas and lines of debate in philosophy.

In addition, the field is fraught with controversy. Ethical theorists disagree among themselves about the nature of ethical theory, its practical relevance, the relationship between ethical theory and moral action, which ethical theory is most worthy of our assent, and about a host of other issues.

It would be impossible to do justice to these theoretical debates in a few pages, but the summary below will at least acquaint you with the main lines of thought. For those who wish to research the subject further, there are many good survey texts available (e.g., Denise & Peterfreund, 1992; Moore & Stewart, 1994; Giersson & Holmgren, 2000; Graham, 2004; LaFollette 2007). Additionally, different ethical theories point to quite different and sometimes quite contrary conclusions about what to do in a given ethical situation. Given these difficulties, some nursing ethicists not surprisingly question the usefulness of ethical theories for nursing ethics (Peter & Liaschenko, 2003; Allmark, 2005).

## Theories about Morality

Before introducing the main ethical theories of relevance to nursing ethics, it is important to say a few words concerning certain *theories about morality* (as opposed to ethical theories) that raise doubts about the validity of ought judgements and moral ideals. These theories call into question the very possibility of ethical theory, and indeed the possibility of valid moral judgements. Four such theories are briefly outlined below.

### 1. Egoism

Egoism is the view that the only motive for human behaviour is self-regard or self-interest. It takes this to be a general truth about human nature or human psychology.

Egoism does not say that what people do is always *in fact* in their own best interests. That would obviously be false. People occasionally do things that are manifestly self-destructive. The egoist claims that in such cases the person is nonetheless motivated by self-interest, but mistaken about where his or her interests lie, or unable to subordinate immediate gratification to long-term gains. The bottom line for the egoist is that we are self-interested in everything we do, but not necessarily wise about what our best interests are or disciplined enough to act consistently with them.

The main fact about human behaviour that seems to contradict egoism is that we do sometimes do things that appear to be motivated by selfless moral ideals or concern for others. Sometimes we do something just because we believe it is our duty, perhaps even at considerable personal expense. We make sacrifices to help someone else out. How can egoism be upheld in the face of such examples?

The egoist grants that in some cases it *appears* that people are acting selflessly, but advances that this is really a deception. According to the egoist, someone who acts in a way that is apparently selfless is really acting on the basis of some hidden, self-serving motive, even if only the desire to feel good about seeming to act selflessly.

It is impossible to disprove such a sweeping claim about human psychology and motivation. However, it is also impossible for the egoist to prove it. The egoist's thesis is a postulate that can be neither confirmed nor refuted by experience. As such it does not undermine the "oughtness" that is crucial to the very possibility of morality. In order to establish morality on a solid foundation, it is enough to establish that we do indeed experience a sense of "oughtness" and are able to distinguish experientially between moral motives or reasons and those that are merely in the service of our self-interest.

Moreover, if the demands of morality and the demands of self-interest — duty and inclination — sometimes conflict, they do not always. Although morality requires a willingness to subordinate self-interest to duty, in many and perhaps even most moral situations there is a convergence between our obligations and our interests.

## 2. Emotivism

Emotivism is the belief that moral beliefs and ideals are a kind of reflex of our psychological makeup. They merely express personal preferences, likes and dislikes. In this respect, they are akin to judgements of taste: e.g., "I like peas"; "She finds broccoli disgusting." Such expressions of preference tell us something about the likes and dislikes of the person making them, but nothing about the nature of peas or broccoli.

For emotivists, the same is true of moral ideals and judgements. Someone who expresses a moral belief about the rightness or wrongness of some action or practice (e.g., abortion, assisted suicide, etc.) is merely telling us about his or her preferences, and nothing about the objective nature of the action or practice. To say that assisted suicide is wrong is just a confused way of speaking. Just as someone who says that "Peas are good" really means and says nothing more than "I like peas," someone who claims that assisted suicide is wrong really means and says nothing more than "I do not like assisted suicide" or "I feel that it is wrong." In both cases, according to the emotivist, what at first glance appears to be an objective statement is a disguised statement of preference. The belief merely reflects or expresses the subjective preference of the person holding it and contains no information about the objective state of affairs.

In defence of emotivism, it is true that moral judgements vary from person to person and sometimes reflect, in an obvious way, the psychological makeup and conditioning of the one doing the judging. Moreover, such information as they contain is clearly not objective, or at least not in the same way that factual information is. To say that abortion terminates the life of the fetus, or that the procedure involves risks of such and such a kind, is a statement of fact. It tells us something about the act or practice, and what it claims can be proved or disproved by scientific study. To say that abortion is wrong (*or* right), however, tells us nothing objective, or at least nothing that could be proved or disproved in the manner of a factual claim. However, it does tell us something about the person making the claim, and for the emotivist that is all the information it contains.

The emotivist is certainly right that value judgements sometimes vary from person to person and that they do not have the same status as factual claims. However, this does not warrant the conclusion that value judgements are therefore merely subjective, or nothing more than expressions of preferences.

The critical feature of moral ideals and value judgements that emotivism fails to account for is that they are amenable to rational discussion and persuasion in a way that mere preferences or judgements of taste are not. We expect and even demand that people give reasons to support their moral judgements. We debate and argue about moral ideals. We seek to persuade others about the reasonableness or unreasonableness of a particular moral belief. It is true that people do not always come to agreement in the course of such persuasion and argumentation, but they sometimes do. And even when they don't, they do not therefore abandon rationality as the standard by which moral beliefs are to be arbitrated.

### 3. Relativism

Relativism holds that moral ideals and beliefs can be reduced to the conditions under which they originate. They are a product of upbringing and conditioning, at best conventions that have developed within a particular society or group. As such, they are not true always and everywhere for everyone but relative to time, place, and person. What is right for one time, culture, or person, may not be right for another.

Cultural relativism is the doctrine that moral beliefs a) are rooted in particular cultures, and vary from one culture to another, and b) have scope or validity only in the culture from which they derive.

The first claim is undoubtedly true. Anthropologists debate whether or to what extent some moral beliefs are invariable or constant across all cultures, but examples that they do vary from one culture to another can be produced at great length. It is also well-known that societies inculcate moral ideals and beliefs in their members through various types of conditioning, including education, religion, and media.

The second claim, however, is very questionable and warrants careful analysis. Against the thesis that at least some moral beliefs are true and binding always and everywhere and for everyone, the relativist asserts that moral beliefs have only local validity, to the extent that they have any validity at all. There is no universal standard by means of which to evaluate moral beliefs. Something that is morally permissible in one society may be forbidden in another, and there are no grounds upon which one could say that one of these cultures is right and the other is wrong.

One implication of this view is that it is inappropriate to pass moral judgement on or otherwise seek to modify the moral beliefs of someone from another culture. An example currently the subject of controversy may help focus the issue. Female genital mutilation is practised today in certain parts of the world and thought to be morally acceptable there (although many people in these cultures do not agree with the practice). In North American society, on the other hand, the practice is generally thought to be abhorrent.

For the relativist, it makes no sense to ask which point of view is really right or best. There is no standard outside of the plurality of cultures and points of view from which to judge the morality of practices within those cultures. There are no moral absolutes. The relativist would argue that although North Americans may be justified, within their own value system, in condemning female genital mutilation in North American society, there are no grounds upon which to condemn the practice for or in other cultures. Relative to North American moral standards, the relativist would say, the practice is wrong. Relative to the standards of certain other cultures, however, the practice is acceptable. For North Americans to condemn this practice in other cultures, the relativist argues, would be to falsely promote their merely local beliefs to absolute status, and in effect to impose these culturally specific beliefs on others without justification.

History does indeed record many examples in which one culture arrogantly imposes its will upon another under the pretence that its own beliefs have privileged status. In this regard, relativism may promote a spirit of humility and toleration for others with different points of view, and that is a good thing. Toleration is especially important in nursing, where the commitment to respect the autonomy of patients means respecting (but not necessarily agreeing with) the patient's values when those values conflict with one's own.

However, as a general theory about morality, relativism is untenable, and for reasons similar to those pertaining to emotivism. The thesis that an ought statement holds true (to the extent it holds true at all) only for those people who have been brought up or conditioned to accept it is incompatible with the sense that at least some moral judgements have in our ordinary experience, and indeed regardless of our culture and upbringing. For example, when we say that it is wrong to deceive people about their medical condition, we do so in the belief that there are good reasons why it is wrong, and that these reasons ought to be persuasive for everyone and anyone. Whether they actually are is a different matter, but in any event this sense of universal validity is bound up with at least some moral judgements. Moreover, notwithstanding the great diversity among cultures with respect to moral beliefs, there are many principles that virtually all societies endorse. These principles have received their expression in various documents, such as the *Universal Declaration of Human Rights* (United Nations, 1948).

### 4. Might Makes Right

According to the "might makes right" view, moral norms and rules merely express and serve the will of those in a position of power to make and enforce them. Ultimately, morality reduces to power. As a well-known parody of the Golden Rule puts it, "Those who have the gold make the rules."

This view holds some plausibility as a description of how things often happen in the real world. Most of us can probably recall moral situations in which, at the end of the day, the interests and values of those in a position of power prevailed just because they were able to assert their power. Nurses, who historically have not wielded much power in hospitals, sometimes complain about how much control hospital administrators and physicians have over decision-making, and how this power sometimes expresses itself and prevails when it comes to making moral rules and settling moral conflicts.

However, to acknowledge that "right" is often decided by "might" is not to justify this, or to accept that this is how things *ought* to happen. Indeed, it is our strong belief that right ought not to be decided by might but rather by good reasons, and that we should feel indignant when right is decided by might, and might alone.

This world is far from perfect, and the institutional arrangements under which nurses practise are often less than ideal. It would be naive to underestimate the reality and force of power and politics, especially in a field as rife with conflict and competing interests as health care. However, it is important to realize that the demand for moral justification can never be satisfied by appeals to power, or to the way things tend to happen.

Moral justification requires reason. Power or might is indeed something to be reckoned with, but it is never by itself a moral justification.

## Ethical Theories

Each of the theories about morality sketched above contains some elements of truth. Self-interest is undoubtedly an important factor in motivation. Moral judgements are deeply rooted in our emotional life. There is a great deal of relativity in morals from one culture to another, and even from one person to another. History records many examples in which moral rules reflect and entrench the interests of those who have the power to make the rules.

However, these theories fail to account adequately for what is most fundamental to morality, namely, our experience of "oughtness." In at least some instances, we feel ourselves torn between the pursuit of self-interest, on the one hand, and our sense of duty, on the other. We are sometimes able to distinguish mere emotional response to an issue from what upon reflection we take to be a more properly moral response backed up by good reasons. About some things at least, we reserve the right to criticize the conventions and moral rules deemed authoritative in a given society, whether our own or that of someone else. And notwithstanding that all too frequently it happens that right is decided by might, we nonetheless pass moral judgement on this state of affairs and assert that things ought not to be such.

In the final analysis, our sense of oughtness is incompatible with the view that right and wrong are reducible to self-interest, preferences, cultural differences, or power. To satisfy this sense of oughtness, it is not sufficient simply to assert moral judgements. We expect moral judgements to be justified. We demand *reasons* in support of moral claims.

It is in the search for deep reasons upon which to ground moral claims that ethical theory comes into play. Ethical theory begins from the fact that moral judgements and evaluations have a quality of ought-ness, which binds people regardless of their interests, emotional feelings, opinions inculcated by societal conditioning, or power to enforce their will upon others. Ethical theories seek to articulate deep reasons or rationales for judgements about how we ought and ought not to act.

There are many varieties of ethical theories. For our purposes, it will be helpful to group them under six main headings: deontology, consequentialism, virtue ethics, the ethic of care, feminist ethics, and relational ethics.

## 1. Deontology

The word "deontology" derives from the Greek word for duty. Deontologists conceive of morality as a system of moral duties, principles, rules, or imperatives. The task of the moral agent is to discern what his or her duties are, and to act consistently with and in the spirit of those duties.

But how do we know what our duties are? Immanuel Kant (1724-1804), the most prominent deontologist, believed that all our duties derive from a fundamental imperative binding on any rational being. He called this the "categorical imperative," which he formulated as follows: "I ought never to act except in such a way *that* I *can also will that my maxim should become a universal law*" (1785/1964, p. 70).

This is less complex than it sounds at first hearing. Think of the categorical imperative as a kind of test. Faced with a decision, Kant is saying, formulate the rule (in his terms, "the maxim") on the basis of which you are proposing to act. Then ask yourself whether it would be reasonable if anyone and everyone acted on the basis of this same rule. If it would not be reasonable to "universalize" this rule — to apply the same rule to anyone and everyone — it fails the test and is not an appropriate rule for moral action.

An example will help to clarify this. Suppose you are considering telling a lie in order to cover up a mistake you made with a patient. The maxim or rule here might be expressed as follows: "It is permissible to lie in order to conceal one's error." If everyone were licensed to lie in order to cover up their mistakes (if the rule were made universal law), the fundamental trust upon which the health care system is based would be undermined. Such a rule would not pass the test of "universalizability" and therefore would not be morally defensible. The rule that one should tell the truth, on the other hand, does pass the test.

Kant emphasized that the categorical imperative is not imposed upon us from without. No one has to tell us what our duty is, or can rightfully impose a moral duty upon us. Insofar as we are beings of reason, each of us is able to comprehend directly what our duty is. To yield to the categorical imperative is not to yield to the will of another but rather to yield to the law of universal human reason, the law of our own reason. This point is of crucial importance for understanding Kant's concept of autonomy.

For Kant, autonomy meant submitting oneself to a law that one gives oneself. The moral law, the categorical imperative, is self-given, since one "discovers" it as the law of one's reason (which is the same for everyone). To be autonomous is to act in accordance with the demands of reason.

When the notion of autonomy is invoked in health care ethics, it usually means the patient's right to make his or her own decisions, particularly in the matter of treatment options. This is related to Kant's usage insofar as it is based on the belief that each adult person is responsible for his or her own life, and no one can rightfully usurp this responsibility. However, for Kant autonomy entailed something more than the *right* to make decisions for oneself. It also entailed the *duty* to decide in accordance with the demands of reason.

Thus for Kant autonomy does not mean doing what one desires, or succeeding in having one's will prevail. The person driven by desire is no more autonomous in Kant's sense than is the person under the compulsion of another's will. It is not doing what we desire that makes us autonomous but rather doing what, on the basis of reason, we know to be the right thing.

Desire provides a powerful motivation for human behaviour but it is not a moral motive. The moral question "What is the right thing to do?" is not reducible to the question "What will best satisfy my desires or interests?" The right thing to do — what duty requires of us — is right regardless of whether it happens to coincide with our desires or interests (i.e., it is "categorically" right). What makes something right is its conformity with the categorical imperative, its quality of being morally binding for beings governed by reason.

In some instances at least, what duty requires of us may not match our desires or self-interests. Even when they do coincide, it is still important for Kant that duty, and not desire, be the motive for our action. Accordingly, he distinguished between *acting from duty* (motivated by willingness to do one's duty, just because it is one's duty), and *acting in accordance with duty* (doing the right thing, but not necessarily for a moral reason). Our moral worth involves doing the right thing (what duty requires), and for the right reason (just because it is our duty).

Much of what Kant says, although expressed in a terminology that is difficult for the non-philosopher to understand, rings true to our common and philosophically untutored experience of morality. Indeed, Kant claimed that the categorical imperative expresses in a formal way the moral grounds upon which people act whenever they do act morally. Someone who asks "But what if everyone acted that way?" is expressing the basic logic of the categorical imperative. The same is true when someone asks "What if the roles were reversed and John did to me what I am considering doing to him?"

Kant's categorical imperative can be employed as a test for determining and assigning *moral rights* as well as duties. To determine whether a claimed moral right is indeed morally valid one asks whether the right in question is universalizable. Moral claims expressed in terms of duties can also be translated in terms of moral rights. The statement that Nurse L. has a duty to tell the truth can be otherwise expressed as a claim about what is owed to other people (e.g., Mr. Smith has a *right* to know the truth).

A standard criticism of Kant's theory is that he does not adequately address the problem of moral conflict. The main conflict Kant focuses on is between duty and inclination or self-interest. The most vexing moral conflicts in nursing ethics, however, are not between duty and self-interest but rather between one duty and another, or one right and another. What do we do in a situation when more than one duty comes into play, each of them pulling us in an opposite direction? Kant offers no guidance here because he believed that the categorical imperative furnished a clear and unambiguous test to determine our duty and that, if the test were properly done, there could be no conflict of duties. On this point, Kant's theory appears not to fit well with our moral experience.

In response to this limitation, commentators otherwise sympathetic to Kant have modified his theory to allow for a plurality of duties. This theory is called "pluralistic deontology," in contradistinction to Kant's theory, which reduces all duties to a single source or principle (the categorical imperative).

W.D. Ross is the most famous exponent of this view. Ross (1930) identified seven independent duties (non-maleficence, beneficence, fidelity, reparation, gratitude, self-improvement, and justice), each of which carries some moral weight. Although Kant would no doubt endorse the duties on this list, he would claim that ultimately they can be reduced to a single principle. Ross, on the other hand, believed them to be irreducible. Ross thus allows for the possibility of a genuine conflict between moral duties, which conflict cannot be resolved by reference to any overarching principle such as the categorical imperative.

Another problem critics find with Kant's theory is its rigidity. For Kant, moral rules are binding regardless of the consequences that following these rules might have in a given instance. This is captured in the phrase "Do the right thing though the world should perish."

To illustrate this, consider the issue of disclosing potentially harmful information to a patient about his or her prognosis. Some might argue that whether telling the truth is the right thing to do will depend upon whether on balance the truth will do the patient more harm than good. For Kant, however, the question of rightness in this and other situations is to be decided independently of the projected consequences of the action. And Kant would say that the right thing to do is to tell the truth. His advice, so to speak, would be "Do the right thing, though the patient should perish."

## 2. Consequentialism

Whereas for Kant the test or standard of moral rightness is conformity to the law of reason or the categorical imperative, for consequentialists moral rightness depends on the consequences of action. Moral decision-making is a matter of projecting the consequences of various action alternatives and selecting the one that on balance will produce the most good. The moral imperative here is to maximize good consequences and minimize bad ones.

This raises the obvious question of how we measure and assess the goodness of consequences. For utilitarianism, the most prominent consequentialist theory, the highest good is happiness. However, it is not the happiness of the individual decision-maker that should guide decision-making, or at least not his or her happiness alone. Rather it is the happiness of everyone potentially affected by one's decision that counts. Therefore in our actions we should strive to produce the greatest amount of happiness possible for everyone concerned. John Stuart Mill (1806-63) referred to this as the principle of utility, which he articulated as follows: "The creed which accepts as the foundation of morals, Utility, or the Greatest Happiness Principle, holds that actions are right in proportion as they tend to promote happiness, wrong as they tend to produce the reverse of happiness" (1863/1961, p. 194).

Utilitarianism thus yields a simple formula for making moral decisions. The first step is to project the consequences of each action alternative available to us. The second is to calculate how much happiness, or balance of happiness over unhappiness, will be produced by each action and its projected consequences. The third step is to select that action which, on balance, will produce the greatest amount of happiness for the greatest number of people.

Critics point out several problems with utilitarianism. One problem has to do with the difficulties of accurately predicting the consequences of our actions. A more serious problem has to do with how we determine how these consequences measure up in terms of happiness. How do we measure happiness?

Probably the most serious criticism of utilitarianism is that, in principle at least, it could sanction actions generally thought to be immoral. For example, on utilitarian grounds, it would be acceptable, if not obligatory, to sacrifice the happiness of a few persons in order to maximize overall happiness for the collective. A rather gruesome example will help to illustrate this point.

Suppose there are ten candidates waiting for various transplants, and a serious shortage of donors and available body parts. Some of these people are expected to die if they do not get their transplants right away. An enterprising person suggests kidnapping a homeless person to harvest his or her organs and distribute among the ten. This idea sounds morally repulsive to us, since it would violate moral rights and duties thought to be sacrosanct. However, for the utilitarian the fact that such an action would run counter to deep intuitions and fundamental moral principles would not be sufficient to rule it out. Following the greatest happiness principle, he or she would project the consequences of both kidnapping and not kidnapping the homeless person and try to determine how much happiness, on balance, would result from each course of action. If the kidnapping option won this contest, it would be mandated by utilitarianism.

In response to such concerns, philosophers have distinguished between act and rule utilitarianism. Act utilitarianism enjoins us to perform the utilitarian calculation for each action considered separately. Rule utilitarianism, on the other, enjoins us to perform the calculation not for particular actions but rather with reference to general moral rules, such as the rule that one ought not to abduct and kill innocent human beings. If the rule is overall promotive of human happiness, then one should follow the rule, without regard to consequences in particular cases.

Rule utilitarians further argue that the rules of ordinary morality are for the most part promotive of the greatest possible happiness and therefore should be adhered to. Given this qualification, rule utilitarianism is much more compatible with ordinary morality, and indeed with deontological ethics, than is act utilitarianism.

## 3. Virtue Ethics

Despite their differences, deontology and consequentialism are alike in their focus on moral rules or decision-making principles. Moral life is conceived of as rule or principle-governed behaviour, whether the rule in question be the greatest happiness principle, the categorical impera-tive, or some collection of irreducible moral principles.

Virtue ethics, on the other hand, views moral life as having less to do with rules or principles for determining right action than with habits and dispositions. The emphasis is on moral character: not on actions or decisions as such, but rather on the kind of person one is and should be.

Aristotle (384-322 BC) is the philosophical father of virtue ethics. In the *Nichomachean Ethics* (1934) he roots virtue in a theory of the human good, grounding this in turn in a conception of human nature. What is good for human beings — that towards which we should strive — has its basis in the kind of beings we are by nature. Virtues are those habits and character traits the perfection of which enables us to realize and fulfill our natures.

For Aristotle, what sets us apart as human beings and is definitive of our uniquely human nature is reason. Thus the highest virtues are those having to do with the cultivation and employment of reason. Aristotle also believed that we are by nature social beings. As such we require the society of others to develop and fulfill our natures most perfectly. Accordingly, the virtues proper to us are ones that contribute not only to our own good and excellence, considered individually, but also to the good and excellence of the community. In keeping with this, Aristotle focuses on moral education. The ideal of moral education is to inculcate in the young and impressionable the habits and disposi-tions — i.e., virtues — that will enable them individually to reach their highest potential and at the same time contribute to the overall good of the community.

Virtue ethics has enjoyed a renaissance in contemporary ethical theory (e.g., Foot, 1978; Dent, 1984). In large part, this is a reaction against the dominant deontological and utilitarian theories. Macintyre (1984) provides a scathing critique of dominant moral theory in its attempt to ground ethics in universal moral principles and to represent moral life as a matter of following rules. Moral rules or principles thus derived, he argues, are either too general to provide guidance in partic-ular situations, or, if sufficiently particular, too controversial to win the agreement of all persons concerned.

Macintyre argues that moral life cannot be represented adequately in the absence of a concrete conception of the human good. And this good is not something that can be reduced to an abstract rule or principle, true always and everywhere for everyone. Rather the human good is embodied in moral communities and traditions. Who we are and what we ought to strive for cannot be decided in abstraction from the traditions that have shaped us and the communities in which our possibilities are delimited.

Hauerwas (1977) reasons along similar lines, arguing that attempts to ground the moral life in moral systems designed in accordance with universal principles are bound to fail. Such systems are at best pale imitations of concrete moral life. Living a moral life is less a matter of adhering to the right moral system or following the right moral rules than it is of responding thoughtfully to the myths and stories that have shaped us, and responding to moral situations in light of these stories.

Virtue ethics holds many attractions for contemporary bioethics, and indeed both Macintyre and Hauerwas have written about bioethics. Bioethicists sympathetic to or working within this approach (e.g., Pellegrino, 1974, 1977; Putman, 1988) remind us that the health professions are moral traditions. As such they embody concrete norms about the good. To enter a health profession is to enter a moral community, the ends and ideals of which are embodied in long-standing traditions. To be a "good" nurse or a "good" doctor is to have the kind of character proper to the ends of nursing or of medicine. In this vein, Pellegrino and Thomasma (1988) champion beneficence, or care for the good of patients, as the paramount virtue proper to those in the helping professions.

Virtue ethics has obvious applications concerning the education of health professionals, and it has received considerable attention specifically in the nursing ethics literature (e.g., see Armstrong, 2006). Still, its relevance to the myriad problems in contemporary bioethics is less clear. Should the dying patient's feeding tube be removed? On what grounds should those in line for a transplant be prioritized? Should consent always be sought for DNR-orders? About such questions virtue ethics offers little guidance (of course, the same might also be said of competing theories).

The emphasis on particular traditions and communities raises yet other concerns. If everyone were shaped by the same tradition and belonged to the same moral community, a concrete conception of the human good might be workable. But contemporary society is not like that at all. We are a mosaic of people from sometimes very different traditions and communities, with sometimes very different conceptions of the good life. Given this reality, it seems unlikely that we could achieve consensus on a concrete conception of the good life. However, the prospect of consensus on moral rules and principles that would traverse our differences seems much more of a live option.

## 4. The Ethic of Care

The ethic of care is like virtue ethics in many respects, and could even be classified as being one kind of virtue ethics. However, given its importance for nursing, and its affinities with other strains in contemporary theorizing about bioethics that cannot be thus classified, it warrants independent consideration.

The ethic of care emerged out of the work of Carol Gilligan (1982), which in turn was responsive to Lawrence Kohlberg's (1981) work on moral development. Kohlberg posited a stage theory of moral development. At the first and most primitive stage of moral development — the pre-conventional — moral decision-making is guided by the fear of punishment and the desire to satisfy one's own desires. At the next stage — the conventional stage — moral decision-making is guided by the desire to please others, deference to authority, and a slavish obedience to the moral conventions dominant in one's social environment. The pinnacle of moral development — the post-conventional stage —is marked by autonomy and independent thinking. Decision-makers at this level are guided by the independent use of reason, and such moral principles as reason suggests to be universally valid for all people.

Gilligan was troubled by the fact that girls tended to score differently than boys on Kohlberg's moral development scale. If one accepted Kohlberg's hierarchy, one would have to say that they scored lower. Gilligan granted that females do indeed approach moral problems differently than males (although she describes this difference differently than did Kohlberg). However, rather than viewing this difference as a deficiency, she called into question Kohlberg's value assumptions about the importance of autonomy, and posited what is different in female moral reasoning as something positive rather than as a stage to be gotten beyond.

Gilligan elaborated this difference in her own research, in which she "found that girls and women tend to approach ethical dilemmas in a contextualized, narrative way that looks for resolution in particular details of a problem situation; in contrast, boys and men seem inclined to try to apply some general abstract principle without attention to the unique circumstances of the case" (Sherwin, 1989, p. 58). The contextual approach common to girls and women she called the "ethic of care." The principle approach more common to boys and men she called "the ethic of justice."

The justice orientation is very similar to the preoccupation with moral rules and principles shared by deontology and utilitarianism. The care orientation, by contrast, is focused less on rules than on virtues such as kindness and concern. It emphasizes not abstract rules or principles that would apply always and everywhere but rather the particular context in which the moral issue arises, and the network of individuals connected by the issue. It values independence or autonomy less than it does relatedness with others, and sensitivity and concern for their needs.

Gilligan's work has generated much interest and controversy in a variety of fields, especially feminism, and has been complemented and developed by others. Noddings (1984), for example, has developed a theory of caring based on receptiveness, responsiveness, and relatedness.

Caring has long been a central element of nursing and has figured prominently in nursing theory (e.g., Watson, 1985; Benner & Wrubel, 1989; Fry & Johnstone, 2002; Tschudin, 2003). This caring focus and the fact that nursing remains today largely a "woman's profession" make the ethic of care an especially relevant subject matter for nursing ethics (Gadow, 1985; Brody, 1988; Fry, 1989). Gilligan advanced that the care ethic is different from, but not (as Kohlberg's theory would imply) subordinate to, the justice ethic. She celebrated this ethic as the distinct voice of women, which hitherto had been suppressed by the dominant male ethic and relegated to second-class status. Huggins and Scalzi (1988) caution, "If an ethical base for nursing practice is built on the ethic of justice, and the nurse's orientation is the ethic of care, there will continue to be a denial of the nurse's own voice" (p. 46). Should nursing ethics embrace the ethic of care?

Many of the concerns expressed about virtue ethics apply also to the ethic of care. In addition, the ethic of care has generated other controversies, within and outside nursing (e.g., see Sherwin, 1992b; Nelson, 1992; Noddings, 1992; Vezeau, 1992; Tronto, 1993). One concern of particular significance for nursing is that the ethic of care reproduces and reinforces clichés about gender roles that have been used to promote and justify occupational segregation. Women (especially mothers and nurses) do the caring, while the men do the "really important" work, like managing, and building, and fixing ... and curing. Given the way our society values caring compared to the supposedly more masculine traits, buying into the ethic of care could contribute to the undervaluation of nursing in the health care system.

A less strategic and more principled concern about the ethic of care has to do with how this approach is understood vis-à-vis other approaches. It makes a great deal of difference whether the ethic of care is championed as competing with or complementing the ethic of justice. It is certainly true that caring has been the central value or virtue in the nursing profession, and few would find reason to quarrel with this focus. However, justice-oriented virtues such as autonomy, fairness, and impartiality have also had an important place in nursing and nursing ethics. To the extent that the ethic of care is understood as being in competition with these virtues, and incompatible with a concern for universal moral principles, its suitability for nursing and nursing ethics is very questionable.

## 5. Feminist Ethics

Like the ethic of care, feminist ethics holds obvious interest for nursing — especially given the historical tendency of the nursing profession to be gendered. An historical overlap exists between the two approaches because much early work in feminist ethics adopted, or was at least sympathetic to, the ethic of care approach. Today the ethic of care is but one of many strands in feminist ethics. As Ellenchild Pinch (1996) points out in her review of feminism and bioethics, the wide variety of feminist theories range from liberal to Marxist feminism, including strains as diverse as eco-feminism and psychoanalytical feminism. Much of this theorizing challenges the ethic of care (for example, for reinforcing gender stereotypes).

Although contemporary feminist ethics draws from diverse feminist theories and encompasses a broad range of diverse perspectives, certain tendencies do stand out. In general they can be grouped under three main overlapping features: attentiveness to issues of difference; attentiveness to power dynamics; and attentiveness to context and relatedness.

A key insight of feminism is that gender makes a difference in the construction of roles and identities in society, and accordingly in how individuals and groups are treated. This difference remains despite significant gains made in equality in the last century. Feminist ethics is based on the understanding that society remains "patriarchal" in many ways. The interests and perspectives of men are often privileged and those of women are muted, sometimes in ways that are quite subtle and taken for granted as if they were "natural." Thus, in assessing the ethics of a situation — whether a clinical matter or a matter of public policy — feminist ethicists are on the lookout for gender prejudices embedded in cultural norms and institutional policies. They are especially alert to the potential for direct or indirect sexual discrimination and issues of sexual equality. Is one or another individual or group being disadvantaged based on sex, perhaps due to prejudices that are not recognized as such? Indeed, many feminist bioethicists believe that mainstream ethics, or what O'Brien (1981, p. 6) calls "malestream" ethics, is permeated by prejudices that privilege males. Rawlinson (2001) views feminist bioethics as the "project of beginning from women's experiences and bodies in formulating the problems, principles and concepts of ethics" (p. 413). In this thought she echoes earlier work by Warren (1989, p. 82), who looked to diversity, relationships, and ordinary experience as a ground for ethical theorizing.

Much early work in feminist ethics focused on matters traditionally defined as "women's issues," such as reproduction, and on gender difference, but as feminist ethics developed, the range of issues that it covered expanded (Wolf, 1996). Its scope today recognizes that dynamics similar to sexism are at work alongside other differences, such as those related to sexual orientation, race, ethnicity, class, and disability — which also relate to cultural and institutional prejudices. Feminist analysis concerning the pernicious effects of gender prejudices and unjustifiable differential consideration and treatment can thus be applied in these other instances. Feminist ethics today tends to bring all such differences and their effects under scrutiny in the assessment and analysis of ethical issues.

These various differences are in turn closely connected to the second main feature of feminist ethics: attentiveness to power dynamics. Women, gay people, racial or ethnic minorities, people with disabilities, and people who live in or near poverty are all subject to the dominant prejudices of our culture. By and large these are the prejudices of those who have held power and whose interests are served by the resulting discrimination. Accordingly, feminist ethics is especially attentive to how the dynamics of power have a bearing on ethical issues, sometimes in quite subtle ways. Who holds what power in a given situation? Who is most vulnerable? For those who tend to be less privileged, what is the likely impact of actions or policy aimed at distributing or redistributing power?

Along these lines, feminist ethics counteracts or corrects a tendency to privilege the values and interests of the dominant culture by foregrounding the values and interests of those who tend to be less powerful and more vulnerable. In attending to questions about power and its distribution, feminist ethics tends to be overtly political. Indeed, most feminist ethicists would consider themselves to be political activists, addressing and often challenging dominant norms — including norms that are more or less explicit in mainstream ethics — in the name of "social justice" (Kirkham & Browne, 2006).

The entrenched prejudices and dynamics of power emphasized by feminist ethics come into play through a wide range of ethical issues. "Oppression" and "exploitation" cut across different ethical issues, which brings us to the third feature of feminist ethics: sensitivity to context and relatedness (Sherwin, 1992a, 1992b; Liaschenko, 1993; Peter & Liaschenko, 2003). Ethical issues invariably occur in contexts, and feminist ethics tends to consider the contexts of the prejudice and power dynamics — contexts often neglected by, if not embedded in, mainstream ethics. Indeed, recent work in feminist ethics turns to the global and international context of ethics (Tong, Anderson, & Santos, 2001; Tong, Donchin, & Dodds, 2004; Sherwin, 2008).

This emphasis on context and relatedness also tends to determine how ethical issues are constructed, and how the individuals involved are seen. Feminist ethicists believe that mainstream ethics considers ethical issues in isolation and devoid of relatedness to context; that it conceptualizes individuals as if they were in isolation from the broader world around them, from their relationships in that world. The concept of "autonomy" as it has been conceptualized and foregrounded in mainstream ethics has been the subject of much criticism in this regard. One prominent current of thought in feminist ethics advances an alternative concept of "relational" autonomy that takes into account relationships, relatedness, and context (Sherwin, 1998; McLeod and Sherwin, 2000; Donchin, 2001, 1995; MacDonald, 2002).

A strength of feminist ethics is that it expands and enlarges the scope of attention and consideration in the assessment and analysis of ethical issues. It brings to light contextual dimensions of prejudice, power, and relatedness that might otherwise be neglected or unnoticed. In expanding and enlarging the scope of attention and consideration, it also expands and enlarges the field of action. It looks to address not just one or another issue at hand, but also the cultural and political context in which the issue arises. As a style or method of analysis, feminist ethics can contribute a great deal to enriching our understanding of ethical issues.

Feminist ethics is not just a mode of analysis that attends to and brings to light dimensions of ethical issues that might otherwise go unnoticed. It tends also to assume and promote a set of definite ethical and political commitments. From this normative standpoint it challenges prevailing norms and policies and seeks to bring about social change. To be sure, the precise content of these ethical and political commitments will vary to some degree, but most feminist ethicists agree that the project entails a set of political commitments and calls for overtly political action to address the broader contextual dimensions of power and prejudice. In this respect, feminist ethics is different from the other ethical theories, which not only tend to focus on ethical issues more or less in isolation, but also tend to be politically neutral, or at least less overtly political, on questions of broader social change.

Although the overtly political activism of feminist ethics can provide an advantage when it comes to dealing with issues and cases, it can also be a disadvantage. To the extent that feminist ethics entails a set of value or even political commitments, it risks alienating those who do not, for one reason or another, share those commitments. For example, Sherwin (2008) advocates the development of "an ethics that can help guide us away from the treacherous path humanity is now following" (p. 8). In speaking of "an ethics" here, she is referring not so much to a way of analyzing ethical issues as to a specific set of value commitments. To be sure, she leaves the content of this "ethic" unspecified. Still, whatever specific value commitments it would include, it is evident that this "ethics" must be different from the "ethics" currently held by many or most people because she exhorts that "humans must undertake massive changes in established patterns of behaviour on several fronts" and warns about "massive behavioural norms that will require revision if we are to head off the multiple threats facing us" (p. 8). What she envisages is a fairly large-scale and radical political program; understandably, those who follow "established patterns of behaviour" deemed to require "massive change" or who hold "behavioural norms" deemed to "require revision" may be reluctant to sign on to such a program.

To the extent that feminist ethics involves advocacy for, and political action toward, a particular ethics, it faces the same sort of challenge confronted by sectarian ethics. Christian ethics, for example, insofar as it entails or embodies a set of definite commitments (albeit, typically not overtly political), is especially attractive for people who share those commitments, but what of those who do not? Even if a political program championed by feminist ethics were to be widely embraced within the nursing profession, what of those patients who do not agree with this political program? Just as the patient population encompasses a broad range of religious views, including atheistic views about religion, so too does it encompass a broad range of political views, including some that might be inconsistent with or antagonistic toward a specific program of feminist ethics.

## 6. Relational Ethics

A relatively recent development in ethical theorizing, relational ethics emerged in the 1990s out of a University of Alberta research project that spawned a full-length book on the subject (Bergum & Dossetor, 2005). Vangie Bergum, a nurse ethicist, has been a leading figure in its articulation and development.

The core features of relational ethics prove challenging to identify, not only because the approach is new and developing, but also because its main precepts, quite deliberately, leave a good deal of room for interpretation. Relational ethics has obvious affinities with the ethics of care and with the stream of thinking about relational autonomy in feminist ethics. It is also significantly different from these theories and the others outlined in this chapter.

Bergum (2004) contrasts relational ethics with other theoretical approaches:

> When ... we view ethical action from the perspective of relationship, we move away from direct attention to epistemology (traditionally defined in terms of ethical theory and principles), virtues (behaviors such as telling the truth and being compassionate), or problems (such as euthanasia, stem cell research, or disparities of health and illness, wealth and poverty). Rather, we attend to the moral space created by one's relation to oneself and to the other. (p. 486)

Although Bergum contrasts relational ethics with these other approaches, this does not suggest antagonism to them. Relational ethics does not so much supplant or replace the other approaches as it supplements them. The key difference is one of "attention," as she puts it: relational ethics puts relationships, rather than principles, virtues, or problems, in the foreground of analysis. Whatever principles, virtues, or problems may be in play, the nurse is always situated in a network of relationships. This lived reality is the starting point for reflection and analysis. Thus relational ethics enjoins nurses to "attend to the quality of relationships in all nursing practices, whether with patients and their families, with other nurses, with other health care professionals, or with administrators and politicians" (Bergum, 2004, p. 487). She elaborates four main themes in light of which the quality of relationships can be brought into view: environment, embodiment, mutual respect, and engagement (p. 488).

According to Austin, Bergum, and Dossetor (2003), the project of relational ethics is "to create an ethics for health care that is grounded in our commitments to each other" (p. 46). To be sure, these commitments are multiple, open to interpretation and debate, and sometimes conflicting. Regardless, they are inscribed in whatever situation and network of relationships we experience. Relational ethics would have us begin our analysis of ethical situations by bringing to light and reflecting upon commitments already made by those involved, including ourselves, and the relationships informed and bonded by those commitments.

Commitments are a more concrete focus of attention than are principles or virtues. When we look, for instance, to the principles or virtues relevant to a given situation, in the first instance we do not necessarily have to look to ourselves and to the lived reality of others in that situation. But when we start with our commitments, we must above all and firstly look to ourselves, and to the network of relationships in which we find ourselves, and to the lived reality of others as they likewise find themselves in networks of relationships with attendant commitments. The starting question is not so much "What principles apply?" or "What should I do?" but rather "Who am I?" and "What relationships and commitments already inform the person that I am in this particular situation?"

The emphasis on relationships and on the commitments informing these relationships means that, essentially, relational ethics is about persons — oneself and others as embodied in networks of relationships — and about already having commitments and having been shaped and formed by those commitments. This is perhaps what Bergum (2004) means when she says, "Relational ethics is really about understanding and knowing ourselves as we engage others" (p. 502). Doane (2004) captures this emphasis well in saying that relational ethics is about the "re-personalization of ethics" (p. 434).

Relational ethics connects well with the older traditions in ethics and philosophy in focusing attention and reflection upon who we are already or who we find ourselves to be, and in its project of coming to understand ourselves and others better in view of the concrete commitments that inform the network of relationships in which we find ourselves. Such attention does not preclude attention to and reflection upon principles, virtues, problems, or dynamics of power. It is a question, rather, of where we begin: relational ethics would have us begin with who we are, or who we find or even discover ourselves to be.

Relational ethics does not furnish us with moral rules or prescriptions for action. If we expect ethics to provide definite guidance for action, this limitation might count as a weakness. But from the standpoint of relational ethics this expectation itself would be considered questionable, at least at the outset of ethical analysis and reflection. To ask, "What does relational ethics say is the right thing to do in this or that circumstance?" would be to miss its point. For relational ethics, the answer to the question "What should I do" will always be something like: "Begin where you are, and with who you are, reflecting upon the bonds and commitments that are already inscribed in the network of relationships in which you find yourself."

## Conclusion

This summary account of contemporary ethical theory is necessarily sketchy and incomplete. To do justice to these theories much more would need to be said. A comprehensive account would also include more about other streams in contemporary moral theory, such as narrative ethics, discourse ethics, communitarian ethics, and principlism, which has been specifically tailored to nursing in a textbook by Edwards (1996).

Even so, this sketch of the main lines of thought in contemporary ethical theory should be sufficient for the reader to get a reasonable sense of the range of opinion in the field and of the main ideas and issues. It should be a good starting point for further reading and reflection. See Brown et al. (2004) for a concise history of health care ethics, and Rodney et al. (2004) for a concise history and overview of theoretical strands in nursing ethics.

In presenting this brief sketch of ethical theory, we are not suggesting that nurses should pick one from among them. Indeed, McCarthy's (2006) call for a "pluralistic view of nursing ethics" has merit, suggesting the advantage of accommodating the very diverse range of perspectives that exist in contemporary nursing and among nurses. The final judgement about the strengths and weakness of the various theories discussed rests with the reader, whose task it is to assess them rationally in light of his or her own moral experience. Ultimately, each of us must come to terms in our own way with questions concerning who we are, what we are all about, and what we are committed to. Thinking through the theories described here will help. Keep in mind too that ethical theory is not the only pathway to insight about ourselves. For instance, the fine arts — including novels, poetry, music, and film — are another important way to travel down that road.

## References

Allmark, P. (2005). Can the study of ethics enhance nursing practice? *Journal of Advanced Nursing* 51 (6), 618-624.

Aristotle (1934). *Nichomachean ethics* (2nd ed.), H. Rackham (Trans.). Cambridge: Harvard University Press.

Armstrong, A.E. (2006). Towards a strong virtue ethics for nursing practice. *Nursing Philosophy* 7, 110-124.

Austin, W., Bergum, V., & Dossetor, J. (2003). Relational ethics: an action ethics as a foundation for health care. In V. Tschudin (Ed.), *Approaches to ethics: Nursing beyond boundaries*. New York: Butterworth-Heinemann, 45-52.

Baier, A.C. (1985). What do women want in a moral theory? *Nous* 19, 53-63.

Benner, P., & Wrubel, J. (1989). *The primacy of caring: Stress and coping in health and illness*. Menlo Park, CA: Addison-Wesley.

Bergum, V. (2004). Relational ethics in nursing. In J. Storch, P. Rodney, & R. Starzomski (Eds.), *Toward a moral horizon: Nursing ethics for leadership and practice*. Toronto: Pearson-Prentice Hall, 485-503.

Bergum, V., & Dossetor, J. (2005). *Relational ethics: The full meaning of respect*. Hagerstown: University Publishing Group.

Brody, J.K. (1988). Virtue ethics, caring, and nursing. *Scholarly Inquiry for Nursing Practice: An International Journal* 2 (2), 87-96.

Brown, H., Rodney, P., Pauly, B., Varcoe, C., & Smye, V. (2004). Working within the landscape: nursing ethics. In J. Storch, P. Rodney, & R. Starzomski (Eds.), *Toward a moral horizon: Nursing ethics for leadership and practice*. Toronto: Pearson-Prentice Hall, 126-153.

Denise, T.C., & Peterfreund, D. (1992). *Great traditions in ethics* (7th ed.). Belmont, California: Wadsworth Publishing Company.

Dent, N.J.H. (1984). *The moral psychology of the virtues*. Cambridge: Cambridge University Press.

Doane, G. (2004). Being an ethical practitioner: The embodiment of mind, emotion and action. In J. Storch, P. Rodney, & R. Starzomski (Eds.), *Toward a moral horizon: Nursing ethics for leadership and practice*. Toronto: Pearson-Prentice Hall, 433-446.

Donchin, A. (1995). Reworking autonomy: Toward a feminist approach. *Cambridge Quarterly of Healthcare Ethics* 4, 44-55.

Donchin, A. (2001). Understanding autonomy relationally: Toward a reconfiguration of bioethical principles. *The Journal of Medicine and Philosophy* 26 (4), 365-386.

Edwards, S.D. (1996). *Nursing ethics: A principle-based approach*. Basingstoke: Macmillan Press.

Ellenchild Pinch, Winifred J. (1996). Feminism and bioethics. *MedSurg Nursing* 5 (1), 53-57.

Foot, P. (1978). *Virtues and vices*. Oxford: Basil Blackwell.

Fry, S. (1989). The role of caring in a theory of nursing ethics. *Hypatia* 4 (2), 88-103.

Fry, S.T., & Johnstone, M. (2002). *Ethics in nursing practice* (2nd ed.). Oxford: Blackwell Publishing.

Gadow, S. (1985). Nurse and patient: The caring relationship. In A.H. Bishop & J.R. Scudder, Jr. (Eds.), *Caring, curing, coping: Nurse, physician, patient relationships* (pp. 31-43). Birmingham: University of Alabama Press.

Giersson, H., & Holmgren M. (2000). *Ethical theory: A concise anthology*. Peterborough: Broadview Press.

Gilligan, C. (1982). *In a different voice*. Cambridge: Harvard University Press.

Graham, G. (2004). *Eight theories of ethics.* New York: Routledge.

Hauerwas, S. (with D. Burrell). (1977). From system to story: An alternative pattern for rationality in ethics. In S. Hauerwas, R. Bondi, & D.B. Burrell (Eds.), *Tragedy and truthfulness* (pp. 15-39). Notre Dame, Ind.: University of Notre Dame Press.

Huggins, E.A., & Scalzi, C.C. (1988). Limitations and alternatives: Ethical practice theory in nursing. *Advances in Nursing Science* 10 (4), 43-47.

Kant, I. (1785/1964). *Groundwork of the metaphysics of morals,* H.J. Paton (Trans.). New York: Harper and Row Publishers.

Kirkham, S.R., & Browne, A.J. (2006). Toward a critical theoretical interpretation of social justice discourses in nursing. *Advances in Nursing Science* 29 (4), 324-339.

Kohlberg, L. (1981). *Essays on moral development.* New York: Harper and Row Publishers.

LaFollette, H. (2007). *Ethics in practice: An anthology.* Oxford: Blackwell Publishing.

Liaschenko, J. (1993). Feminist ethics and cultural ethos: Revisiting a nursing debate. *Advances in Nursing Science* 15, 71-71.

MacDonald, C. (2002). Nurse autonomy as relational. *Nursing Ethics* 9 (2), 194-202.

Macintyre, A. (1984). *After virtue* (2nd ed.). Notre Dame, Ind.: University of Notre Dame Press.

McCarthy, J. (2006). A pluralist view of nursing ethics. *Nursing Philosophy* 7, 157-164.

McLeod, C., & Sherwin S. (2000). Relational autonomy, self-trust, and health care for patients who are oppressed. In C. MacKenzie & N. Stoljar (Eds.), *Relational autonomy: Feminist perspectives on autonomy, agency and the social self.* Oxford: Oxford University Press, 259-279.

Mill, J.S. (1863/1961). *Utilitarianism.* In Max Lerner (Ed.), *Essential works of John Stuart Mill.* New York: Bantam Books.

Moore, N.B., & Stewart, R.M. (Eds.) (1994). *Moral philosophy: A comprehensive introduction.* Toronto: Mayfield Publishing Company.

Nelson, H.L. (1992). Against caring. *The Journal of Clinical Ethics* 3 (1), 8-15.

Noddings, N. (1984). *Caring: A feminine approach to ethics and moral education.* Berkeley: University of California Press.

Noddings, N. (1992). In defense of caring. *The Journal of Clinical Ethics* 3 (1), 15-18.

O'Brien, M. (1981). *The politics of reproduction.* Routledge and Kegan Paul.

Pellegrino, E.D. (1974). Educating the humanist physician: An ancient ideal reconsidered. *Journal of the American Medical Association* 22 (11), 1288-1294.

Pellegrino, E.D. (1977). Rationality, the normative and the narrative in the philosophy of morals. In S. Hauerwas, R. Bondi, & D.B. Burrell (Eds.), *Tragedy and truthfulness* (pp. 153-168). Notre Dame, Ind.: University of Notre Dame Press.

Pellegrino, E.D., & Thomasma, D.C. (1988). *For the patient's good.* New York: Oxford University Press.

Peter, E., & Liaschenko, J. (2003). Whose morality is it anyway? Thoughts on the work of Margaret Urban Walker. *Nursing Philosophy* 4 (3), 259-262.

Putman, D.A. (1988). Virtue and the practice of modern medicine. *The Journal of Medicine and Philosophy* 13 (4), 433-443.

Rawlinson, M.C. (2001). The concept of a feminist bioethics. *The Journal of Medicine and Philosophy* 26 (4), 405-416.

Rodney, P., Burgess, M., McPherson, G., & Brown, H. (2004). Our theoretical landscape: A brief history of health care ethics. In J. Storch, P. Rodney, & R. Starzomski (Eds.), *Toward a moral horizon: Nursing ethics for leadership and practice.* Toronto: Pearson-Prentice Hall, 56-76.

Ross, W.D. (1930). *The right and the good.* New York: Oxford University Press.

Sherwin, S. (1989). Feminist ethics and medical ethics: Two different approaches to contextual ethics. *Hypatia* 4 (2), 57-72.

Sherwin, S. (1992a). Feminism and medical ethics: Two different approaches to contextual ethics. In H. Besquaret Holmes and L. Purdy (Eds.), *Feminist perspectives in medical ethics* (pp. 17-31). Indianapolis, IN: Indiana University.

Sherwin, S. (1992b). *No longer patient: Feminist ethics and health care.* Philadelphia: Temple University Press.

Sherwin, S. (1998). A relational approach to autonomy in health care. In S. Sherwin (Ed.), *The politics of women's health: Exploring agency and autonomy.* Pittsburgh, Penn.: Temple University Press, 19-47.

Sherwin, S. (2008). Whither bioethics? How feminism can help reorient bioethics. *International Journal of Feminist Approaches to Bioethics* 1 (1), 7-27.

Tong, R., Anderson, G., & Santos, A. (Eds.). (2001). *Globalizing feminist bioethics: Crosscultural perspectives.* Boulder, Col.: Westview.

Tong, R., Donchin, A., & Dodds, S. (Eds.). (2004). *Linking visions: Feminist bioethics, human rights, and the developing world.* Lanham, Md.: Rowman & Littlefield.

Tronto, J.C. (1993). *Moral boundaries: A political argument for an ethic of care.* New York: Routledge.

Tschudin, V. (2003). *Ethics in nursing: The caring relationship* (3rd ed.). Edinburgh: Butterworth-Heinemann.

United Nations (1948). *Universal declaration of human rights.* UN General Assembly Resolution 217 A(III). Geneva.

Vezeau, T.M. (1992). Caring: From philosophical concerns to practice. *The Journal of Clinical Ethics* 3 (1),18-20.

Warren, V.L. (1989). Feminist directions in medical ethics. *Hypatia* 4 (2), 73-87.

Watson, J. (1985). *Nursing: Human science and human care.* Norwalk, Conn: Appleton-Century-Crofts.

Wolf, S.M. (Ed.). (1996). *Feminism and bioethics: Beyond reproduction.* New York: Oxford University Press.

# 2 CONTEMPORARY CANADIAN CHALLENGES IN NURSING ETHICS

*Nurses' practice is influenced by social, cultural, and historical realities worldwide, and Canadian nursing practice is no exception to this fact. These influences underlie the context within nurses' practice, a context that affects their everyday lives as nurses.*

— JANET L. STORCH, "CANADIAN HEALTHCARE SYSTEM"

*In recent years important and dramatic changes have occurred in the sociopolitical context in which nursing practice takes place. Increasingly nursing theorists and ethicists have turned their attention "upstream" of the issues that arise in daily practice (Butterfield, 1990; Starzomski & Rodney, 1997).*

*In this chapter we examine pressing challenges on the sociopolitical horizon for nurses today and into the future. We consider how nursing has met those challenges and highlight the resources that are available, both within and outside the profession, to address the issues.*

Since the 1990s — as nursing students and registered nurses today know all too well — the working world of nurses has changed dramatically. In particular, nurses face increasingly complex health problems on the part of patients, families, and communities; and they must do their work in a climate of continuing cost constraint measures. As a result, nurses today find it more difficult than ever before to provide excellent care and consequently experience greater, or more intense, ethical (or moral) distress.[1]

In the new millennium, for a number of different reasons, nurses thus face many new challenges. But in the past decade they have also made considerable achievements, and they continue to bring incalculable strengths to health and health care for Canadians. Opportunities are certainly there for nurses who want to make a difference to the quality of their professional lives and the quality of their patients' lives.

## The Lived Experiences of Nurses Today

We begin here by offering three stories that illustrate what we see as some of the significant challenges in health care for nurses.[2] Through narratives the lived experiences of nurses and others who face ethical issues can be brought to life (Brown & Rodney, 2007; Nisker, 2004).

### 1. Susan's Story

Susan is a recent nursing graduate. She had always wanted to work with children, and so after graduation she accepted a position on a pediatric unit.

One day she goes home from work feeling quite distraught. She is not able to fully comprehend or accept what she had found herself doing during the previous night's shift. On her ward a six-year-old boy with cancer kept crying and crying. He cried so much he kept the other children awake. His parents might have been able to help, but they could not come to the hospital because they had to be at home, caring for their other children. Susan gave the boy as much time as she could, but she also had to be leaving his side to go and care for the other children. Finally, and quite reluctantly, she gave the boy a sedative. She knew that if she had been able to stay with him constantly, he would not have needed the sedative.

When Susan was a student she had promised herself that she would always find time for ill children who needed nursing care. "What is happening to me?" she now wonders. "I am becoming the person I never wanted to be, and so fast."

## 2. Jacques's Story

Jacques works in an emergency department. He has been a nurse for fifteen years and has seen a lot of changes. When he graduated with a diploma he immediately got a job at the hospital where he had trained. Then, during the 1990s, when hospitals were merged and closed, he found himself out of work for the first time. He used that time to complete his undergraduate degree in nursing. When he was ready to return to nursing work, the pendulum had swung: there was now a shortage of nurses. He quickly found a position as nursing manager of the emergency department.

Today Jacques encounters "situation normal": ambulance crews are lined up, waiting to unload their patients, and the hallways are lined with patients on stretchers. The waiting room is full. He looks down the corridor and sees Mrs. Le Blanc, an elderly patient with early dementia. She had taken a fall at home and fractured her hip. Her son is sitting beside her, looking exhausted. Mrs. Le Blanc, who her son says is usually very gentle, had started to be aggressive and uncooperative. Jacques knows that the emergency room environment and her accident have triggered her behaviour. The surgical unit cannot speed up her transfer. She will have to wait at least another five hours.

Jacques thinks to himself, "This could be my parent. Can I keep working under these conditions?"

## 3. Sandeep's Story

Sandeep works for a community-based nursing organization as a case manager. Her expertise is working with chronically ill persons in the community. She visits Ashley, a young woman with multiple sclerosis who lives in her parents' home in a basement apartment. During the visit she sees that Ashley needs more help with her activities of daily living. Ashley's parents cannot provide the extra help needed because of their own health problems. Sandeep explains that the home-care program cannot increase the hours sufficiently to meet Ashley's needs. She offers Ashley and her parents the names of agencies that can provide additional hours, but the family will have to pay for this help. They can afford some hours, but not enough. Reluctantly, Sandeep informs Ashley and her parents that another alternative is to have Ashley live in a long-term care facility. Ashley and her parents stoically refuse to consider applying to a long-term care facility. They correctly point out that it is more cost-effective for her to stay at home, and of course the quality of her life would be better at home.

Sandeep reflects, "Why do I have to tell these people such bad news? Why can't we do what is best for Ashley, her family, and all of us? I feel powerless."

These stories have a common theme of ethical or moral distress. In each case the nurses knew what ought to be done. In the end, for reasons beyond their control, they found that they could not honour their values and provide appropriate care. They felt powerless to change the situation, unable to make a difference in their place of employment or change the policies that had led to the difficult situations.

Decisions made at institutional, regional, provincial, territorial, and national levels were, to a significant extent, shaping the practice that these nurses were experiencing. At the same time, though, Susan, Jacques, and Sandeep did have significant resources to draw on — resources that the study of nursing ethics can make both more visible and enhance.

**Some Historical Background**

Susan, Jacques, and Sandeep — and their patients and their patients' family members — are dealing with ethical issues at the individual (micro) level, and these issues have their origins in health policy at multiple levels. These kinds of ethical issues, which are part of everyday practice, have their roots firmly fixed in the history of health care in Canada.[3]

*1. History of Funding Changes*

*The Canada Health Act* articulates the principles underlying Canadian health care, including matters of public administration, comprehensiveness, accessibility, universality, and portability (Feld-berg & Vipond, 2006; Storch, Rodney, & Starzomski, 2009). In response to the proliferation of biotechnology, the aging of the population, increases in chronic illness, and other challenges, provincial and territorial governments in the 1990s sought ways of reducing their health care spending.[4] The federal government reduced transfer payments for health care and other services — which only compounded problems for the provincial governments, which were also trying to reduce deficits (Armstrong & Armstrong, 2003; Commission on the Future of Health Care in Canada, 2002). Working within the *Canada Health Act*, provincial governments responded to the financial pressures by cutting back on their health care budgets in several ways. Some provinces shortened the list of services covered by the publicly funded health care system. Another strategy was to limit access to the public system. For example, refugees and foreign students were not eligible for health care provided by the publicly funded system. They placed restrictions on ordering tests and procedures, and introduced ways of providing care based on research that would purportedly lead to more efficient and effective use of services. As gaps in service increased, private health care providers filled the need, and more onus was put on families to fill gaps in care, especially home care (Raphael, Bryant, & Rioux, 2006; Canadian Centre for Policy Alternatives, 2000; Health Council of Canada, 2008; Lynam et al., 2003; Pauly, 2004; Perry, Lynam, & Anderson, 2006; Peter, 2004).

These changes in Canada and other Western countries were in part inspired by a belief in the "free" market and the rights of supposedly autonomous individuals to "choose" the best health care (Browne, 2001; Peter, 2004; Stein, 2001; Varcoe & Rodney, 2009). Yet, as the stories of Susan, Jacques, and Sandeep illustrate, the resources available to families do not always match needs, and getting access to appropriate health care can mean navigating a labyrinth of patchwork services. The contexts in which patients and their families live also have a significant impact. For example, in Jacques's narrative, how much worse would the situation of Mrs. Le Blanc and her family have been if none of them could speak English (or French in francophone health care settings)? In Sandeep's narrative, how much worse would the situation of Ashley and her family have been if they lived in an isolated rural area where home-care resources are even more scant than they are in an urban setting?

## 2. Impact on Patient/Family/Community Care and Nursing Practice

The changes in funding had major consequences for the public and nurses. The health care "reform" of the 1990s and early years of the new century resulted in a steady erosion of the acute, chronic, long-term, and preventative health care services available to people across Canada. Governments studied and implemented ways of providing service in a more efficient and cost-effective manner. Key initiatives included merging organizations, closing hospitals, and increasing outpatient and community care. With few exceptions, in large and small communities, hospital closures or mergers occurred in the face of community opposition and considerable evidence that necessary resources were being diminished or not delivered. In Calgary, for example, a hospital was literally blown up. There have also been sites of resistance. The francophone hospital near Ottawa successfully challenged the Ontario government's Health Services Restructuring Commission and maintained the only Ontario francophone teaching hospital.

As the Commission on the Future of Health Care in Canada (2002) pointed out, health care reform measures have had serious repercussions for

> elderly people who are discharged from hospital and cannot find or afford the home or community services they need. Women — one in five — who are providing care to someone in the home an average of 28 hours per week, half of whom are working, many of whom have children, and almost all of whom are experiencing tremendous strain. Health professionals, who are increasingly stressed, while performing tasks ill suited to their abilities and training. Patients, who are forced to navigate a system that is a complex and unfriendly mystery, in order to find the right specialist, the nearest facility, and the best treatment. (pp.xviii-xviv)

The financial crunches caused by health care reform have led to major organizational changes in nurses' working lives. Ways of providing patient care changed. Employers struggling to manage their budgets looked at reducing costs by doing away with full-time positions and instead employing part-time or casual nurses who do not receive benefits. The term "casualization" of nursing entered our vocabulary. By the mid-1990s and continuing thereafter, nurses were experiencing layoffs and redundancies. More nurses had casual positions, perhaps even holding several different jobs at different hospitals, clinics, or offices. Typically they did not have security or consistent schedules or benefits, and they faced increased workloads. Many health care professionals, especially nurses (like Jacques), became unemployed. New graduates found it hard to find steady employment. Many nurses moved to the United States to find full employment. Others left the profession (Canadian Health Services Research Foundation, 2001, 2006c). At the same time, across the country provincial governments cut back on the number of seats for registered nursing students in nursing programs. Although the number of graduates across the country later began to rise, Canada would consistently graduate fewer nursing students than it had done thirty years earlier, despite a 39 per cent increase in the Canadian population over the same time period (Canadian Nurses Association [CNA], 2008a). Confounding this problem has been a lack of systematic monitoring of nursing workforce demographics across the provinces (Ross, 2003).

All of these factors and conditions contributed to a serious shortage of registered nurses. Novice nurses leave the profession early in their careers, and experienced nurses retire early. Even though enrolment in nursing schools has more recently increased, the need for nurses cannot be met. Provincial governments and employers have recruitment and retention strategies to recruit and retain registered nurses, including employment recruitment trips to major U.S. cities to invite Canadians to return home. There are aggressive international nurse recruitment programs,[5] and foreign-educated nurses are being assisted to become eligible to work in Canada. Although there are long wait lists of applicants, and nursing enrolments in schools of nursing are high, the gap is continuing to widen. The retirement age for nurses is early — the majority retire before the age of fifty-five. Soon a generation of nurses educated in the 1970s will be leaving the profession through retirement.

Another fiscal strategy that gained momentum in the early 1990s and continued to accelerate with the nursing shortage was the reduction of registered nurse staffing ratios (Aiken et al., 2002). Registered nurses and licensed practical nurses have been increasingly replaced with unregulated workers (McGillis Hall et al., 2003; Pan-Canadian Planning Committee on Unregulated Health Workers, 2008). Unregulated workers are paid a lower salary than are registered nurses or licensed practical nurses. These employees are asked to provide personal care, assist patients with meals, clean rooms, and communicate with patients and their families. At the same time, licensed practical nurses are being asked to increase their scope of practice to include tasks (such as medication administration) in acute care that have traditionally been part of registered nursing practice. While the preparation and scope of practice for licensed practical nurses mean that such tasks are appropriate in the provision of care to stable patients, these changes are taking place in settings with significant registered nurse shortages and rising patient acuity.

As a consequence of these pressures on the system, frail persons are often not receiving adequate care in acute care, community, or long-term care institutions. Families are overburdened with caring for family members of all ages. Women, the traditional caregivers, have too often been expected to absorb "downloaded" caregiving. The goals of community care are laudable: promoting health, maintaining independence, and fostering quality of life. Yet the underfunding of community care has undermined these goals (Armstrong & Armstrong, 2003; Canadian Centre for Policy Alternatives, 2000; Commission on the Future of Health Care in Canada, 2002; Health Council of Canada, 2008; Lynam et al., 2003; Perry, Lynam, & Anderson, 2006; Peter, 2004; Raphael, Bryant, & Rioux, 2006). For the people and communities marginalized because of gender, race, class, age, substance use, homelessness, or rural and remote isolation, the problems can be even more severe (Anderson, 2006; Browne, 2007; Browne & Smye, 2002; Pauly, 2008). The vulnerable — people such as those with mental illnesses or people in

Aboriginal communities — are particularly at risk. Public health and health promotion programs (for example, teaching healthy parenting) have taken second place to reacting to more immediate problems (for example, immunizations for potential disease outbreaks).[6]

While the financial pressures in health care over the past two decades fast-tracked changes that might be beneficial, such as an increase in same-day surgery and outpatient (ambulatory) clinics and an increase in community care, acute care and long-term care beds were closed and service delivery methods were altered. Shorter and fewer admissions were combined with an expansion of community care requirements. Health care "at the right place by the right people" became a catch phrase. At the same time, the investment in community care that would make the changes work did not happen to the extent needed. In acute care and other facilities, the funding for health care staff, equipment, and medications needed by patients outside hospital walls was (and remains) inconsistent across the country. As Sandeep's story illustrates, much of the cost for health care has become the responsibility of patients and their families.

The effect on patient care is becoming increasingly apparent to the Canadian public. The media have reported widely on the deterioration in patient care. Systemwide problems of gridlock, illustrated by serious backlogs in emergency departments (similar to those experienced by Jacques), are being reported (Canadian Medical Association & Canadian Nurses Association, 2004). Images of emergency rooms being busy — and packed with patients waiting for assessment and transfer to an inpatient bed — are familiar to the public either through firsthand experience or news stories. For nurses such as Susan, Jacques, and Sandeep, the continuum of care has too often become a downward spiral that they are living daily. Reversing this spiral requires an understanding of some of the current health care reform responses now occurring across Canada.

**Health Care Reform Responses**

The health care reform initiatives that began to be taken in the early 1990s continued through the following decade and more, largely in response to the significant problems created by the initial reforms' cutbacks. By the late 1990s some of the federal funding had been restored, but the recent changes and the consequences for the public and health care professionals nevertheless fuelled a demand to look at ways of "fixing" the system. Patient and consumer groups and nursing professional organizations lobbied governments and informed the public that standards of care were being undermined. Participants at federal and provincial summits agreed that medicare must be preserved, and provinces insisted that the federal government increase funding for health care. As the century closed, the federal and provincial governments started to discuss how medicare could be maintained. The challenge for the Canadian health care system became a question of whether to reform the publicly funded system or introduce major changes that would involve a greater role for private health care. At the same time the majority of Canadians consistently reported that they valued Canada's publicly funded health care system and wanted to maintain this national treasure (Commission on the Future of Health Care in Canada, 2002; Health Council of Canada, 2008; Kenny, 2002; Standing Senate Committee on Social Affairs, Science and Technology, 2002; Storch, 2010).

In the opening years of the century three important reports examined the problems of the health services sector in depth and suggested different ways of responding to the problems. The first of these reports, *A Framework for Reform: Report of the Premier's Advisory Council on Health* (2001), came out of the province of Alberta under the Advisory Council chairmanship of Don Mazankowski. Among its other recommendations, the report called for delisting medical services, initiating user fees, setting higher health care insurance premiums, and fostering a greater contribution from private health care. The second report, *The Health of Canadians: The Federal Role*, was issued by Ottawa's Standing Senate Committee on Social Affairs, Science and Technology (2002), under the chairmanship of Michael J.L. Kirby. Its main recommendation was the introduction of a tax dedicated to health care that would raise $5 billion annually. These funds, the writers argued, would cover the need for a larger number of health care providers and more equipment and hospital beds; they would repair the damage done to the system in recent years and expand health services in general. The key recommendations included guarantee of care in a timely manner, a cap on individuals' pharmaceutical bills, a post-acute care home-care program funded fifty-fifty by the federal and provincial governments, and the establishment of an independent health care commissioner to monitor reforms and changes in payment plans for physicians.

A month after that report appeared, the "Romanow Report" was issued by the Commission on the Future of Health Care in Canada (2002), chaired by Roy J. Romanow, a former premier of Saskatchewan. This third study had been initiated by Prime Minster Jean Chrétien, who recommended that the Privy Council establish a commission with the mandate to recommend ways of maintaining the long-term viability of a universally accessible, publicly funded health system providing high quality care. The Commission was to investigate ways of providing care and treatment, and also to consider how to dedicate resources to health promotion. The Commission's mandate was to conduct an extensive review of evidence, listen to Canadians from all walks of life (including experts from a wide variety of backgrounds), and propose ways of strengthening the quality, effectiveness, and continued viability of Canada's health care system, along with ways of placing it on a sustainable footing.

The Romanow Report included an extensive research and policy review (Commission on the Future of Health Care in Canada, 2002). The Commission invited direct input from professionals and the public in many ways, including written submissions, email letters, phone calls, and presentations at a series of hearings held across the country. The Canadian Nurses Association and provincial nursing organizations made submissions in strong support of the *Canada Health Act*. These submissions included recommendations for the reform of how care is delivered, including greater access to home-care and pharmaceuticals. In their submission, the nurses presented themselves as key players in health care reform, emphasizing the importance of establishing a better interdisciplinary teamwork focused on patient/population needs rather than disciplinary hierarchies. For instance, nursing associations and nurse researchers promoted the formation of more interdisciplinary primary health care centres in which individuals and families could be seen for preventative, curative, and restorative health care by a well-coordinated network of dietitians, nurses, nurse practitioners, physicians, physiotherapists, and social workers (Rodney, 2002).

A guiding principle of the Romanow Commission was to be open and transparent. It documented its process for preparing an interim and final report, and all of the reports, research, and information received were made public. Under Romanow's leadership, members of the Commission sought to be inclusive by committing to make "every reasonable effort" to have participation from the public, stakeholders, and experts. Its website had twenty million visits — a figure that provides a strong indication of interest in the Commission and its accessibility.

Unfortunately, the Kirby and Romanow reports led to only limited progress on the issues presented. A series of federal-provincial meetings (commencing in 2003) resulted in an Accord on Health Care Renewal, which called for a slight increase in federal spending on health care and an improvement in provincial accountability for health care spending (Health Council of Canada, 2008). These meetings also resulted in the formation of a new government body with the potential to address many of the challenges to health care. A major recommendation of the Romanow Report was the creation of an interprovincial/federal Health Council of Canada, which was formed in 2003 and is supposed to assist in improving federal transfer funding as well as provincial accountabilities and transparency.[7] A 2008 report from the Health Council on the progress made between 2003 and 2008 indicated that, while some progressive innovations in health care delivery had been fashioned, many areas still showed a lack of progress, and various barriers had still not been addressed (Health Council of Canada, 2008). By 2010 the increased funding for health care from the federal government had still not returned to the levels of the early 1990s.

In the meantime, strong currents across the country pushed in the privatization direction of the Mazankowski Report (Premier's Advisory Council on Health, 2001). Canada has always had some privatized components of health care — for example, dental care, pharmaceuticals outside of hospitals, and many home-care and long-term care services (Commission on the Future of Health Care in Canada, 2002;

Feldberg & Vipond, 2006; Pauly, 2004). Furthermore, private insurance companies have always marketed insurance plans to people who need to supplement their coverage or to those who are living in Canada but are not covered by the public system. Many provincial governments have continued to introduce other private health care elements. For example, in Ontario, for-profit health care organizations were permitted to place tenders for provision of health care and community support. Established not-for-profit organizations could not compete with the lower private tenders who paid employees much less (Canadian Centre for Policy Alternatives, 2000). In British Columbia a public-private partnership (P3) resulted in the building of a new hospital in Abbottsford, which opened in 2008. Many private suppliers of goods and services are from the United States, and thus some commentators warn that the door has been increasingly opened for the Americanization of the Canadian health case system (Armstrong & Armstrong, 2003; Canadian Centre for Policy Alternatives, 2000; Raphael, Bryant, & Rioux, 2006; Storch, 2010).

A recent court case originating in Quebec in response to long-standing and widespread concerns about growing surgical wait lists across the county has shown that fears of the increasing privatization of Canadian health care are not groundless. In June 2005 the Supreme Court of Canada ruled in the case of *Chaoulli v. Quebec* that prohibitions on the purchase of private health insurance for services covered by the public health system were unconstitutional, given excessive waiting times in the public system. This constitutional challenge was brought by Dr. Jacques Chaoulli, who wanted to offer private health services, and George Zeliotis, a Quebec patient who had been on a waiting list for hip replacement surgery (Yeo, Emery, & Kary, 2009). Commentaries on this landmark case continue to proliferate. They range from those who believe that the Supreme Court's decisions enshrine the right to timely access to health care to those who warn that it signals the death knell for medicare in Canada.

While the privatization goals of effective and efficient health care delivery are laudable (and shared by those who promote a fully public system), researchers and policy analysts argue that privatization causes major inequities in the access to and quality of health care services (Armstrong & Armstrong, 2003; Raphael, Bryant, & Rioux, 2006; Storch, 2010). Given that income is a major determinant of health, those who are impoverished will be most at risk of ill health and will also have the most trouble getting access to the health care that they need (Heymann & Hertzman, 2007; Hertzman & Siddiqi, 2008; Raphael, 2006; Marmot, 2004).

## Vulnerabilities of the Nursing Profession

For a number of reasons — the root causes of which are complex and multifaceted — nurses and those they care for have experienced severe setbacks in the continuing and major reorganizations of health care, especially in the areas of nursing education and employment conditions.[8]

### 1. Nursing Education

Traditionally, nursing education from the 1960s through to the early 1990s focused primarily on the one-to-one relationships that nurses had with patients and families. For example, nursing students learned about the metaparadigm concepts of nursing, person, and health (Meleis, 1997), with little or insufficient attention paid to the immediate working environment, the persons they are providing care for, and the determinants of health and access to health care (Starzomski & Rodney, 1997). At the same time the foundation of education in nursing ethics was largely limited to the four principles of biomedical ethics: autonomy, beneficence, nonmaleficence, and justice (Rodney, Burgess et al., 2004). The application of these principles — as we shall see in the following chapters — provided a good starting point for helping nurses to understand and think through their individual ethical concerns with patients and families. Yet as ethics and nursing ethics developed, to understand and respond to the ethical problems in their working world nurses also needed to consider other dynamics.

Too often, using principles alone led to a reductionist application and the problems studied were limited to "quandary" life and death problems with individual patients, with not enough attention paid to "everyday" nursing concerns (Chambliss, 1996; Gadow, 1999; Storch, 2004; Warren, 1992). Cases discussed were predominantly about major life and death issues. Who will get the last bed in the ICU? Who will get the one organ available for transplantation? Furthermore, even though nurses learned about how dying patients ought to be engaged in informed choices about their treatment and care, often not enough attention was placed on helping nurses understand why patients may be denied the opportunity to direct their care. For example, there was a lack of study of the role of interdisciplinary conflict in the workplace and how to deal with such situations. At the same time it has become increasingly clear that health care team and family conflicts contribute to the silencing of patients and their family members as well as the silencing of nurses and other members of the health care team (McPherson et al., 2004; Solomon et al., 1993; Standing Senate Committee on Social Affairs, 2000).

In their work nurses constantly confront ethical issues. Is the consent really informed and given freely? Why must I follow an order that is not in the patient's best interest? How can I make sure the patient's voice is not lost in the system? In earlier years most nurses learned that patients' wishes regarding treatment decisions ought to be respected, yet they did not learn enough about how to "make it happen."

Another consequence of the individualistic focus was that nurses were ill-prepared to widen their understanding of specific ethical issues. For one, they found it hard to change their focus to include what it means to respect patients' autonomy in the context of their family and the competing needs of other patients. Second, it was even harder to look for the causes of the ethical problems "at the bedside," particularly causes related to the environment in which health care is delivered and the larger sociopolitical environment in which the determinants of health and access to health care are located. For instance, the problem of errors being made in health care delivery has gained much attention recently, and organizations have implemented programs designed to create safer practices. The focus is on developing policies, protocol checks, and communication tools. Yet until the sector addresses the root causes of why mistakes are made (such as fatigue, excessive workload, and interdisciplinary team conflict), these programs will have limited success (Institute of Medicine, 2004; Storch, 2005).

Recent research is also making it increasingly clear that patients marginalized because of factors such as gender, race, class, age, substance use, homelessness, and rural isolation experience serious health challenges and are often stigmatized in their attempts to get access to appropriate treatment and care. Yet nurses are sometimes complicit in labelling patients and their families as "difficult," non-compliant," or "drug-seeking," for instance (Browne, 2007; Pauly, 2008; Varcoe, 2004). Nurses need to adopt a language that takes them beyond the individualistic focus that perpetuates such stereotypes, and move toward a language rooted in community and justice.

In philosophical terms, then, we can say that an individualistic focus in ethics is necessary but not sufficient. At the micro level we certainly need to serve individual patients, but we also need to address their family members and their cultural/community context. We need to have an ethical awareness and expertise that extends to organizational (meso) issues, as well as to regional, provincial, national, and even international (macro) issues (McPherson et al., 2004; Raphael, Bryant, & Rioux, 2006; Storch, Rodney, & Starzomski, 2009; Yeo, 1993).

## 2. Employment Conditions

Employment conditions are a second major area of vulnerability for nurses. This is often termed the quality of work life issue, and for nurses it is a matter that creates many ethical problems. For the most part, nurses have not been well prepared to analyze and respond effectively to the systemwide changes that have occurred in recent years. Research tells us that nurses' ability to deliver care has been seriously challenged by the increased acuity/complexity of patients in all areas of care delivery, registered nurse staffing cutbacks and shortages, casualization of nursing positions, reductions in clinical nursing leadership, intradisciplinary and interdisciplinary team conflict, and unilateral organizational decision-making (Aiken et al., 2002; Canadian Health Services Research Foundation, 2001, 2006; Dunleavy, Shamian, & Thomson, 2003; Rodney & Street, 2004). Nurses and other health care providers feel that they are unable to provide adequate care to patients or alter the contextual factors that compromise patient safety and well-being. Furthermore, research indicates that the erosion in nurses' conditions of work are reflected in increased morbidity and mortality of patients in acute care.[9]

To a significant extent, these problems have arisen because until recently nurses have not learned how to respond proactively to stated (and unstated) policies and practices such as replacing registered nurses and licensed practical nurses with unregulated workers, or not replacing nurses who are ill and unable to work. Nurses historically have taken a passive role when facing extremely difficult conditions. Some commentators propose that this traditional response is related to nursing as a female-dominated profession, and to how many nurses are not especially well prepared, or even disposed, to deal with conflict (Chambliss, 1996). Others argue that nurses are oppressed, and until they break out of an oppressed relationship with employers and other health care groups they cannot influence their working conditions to provide care based on their professional values (David, 2000; Rodney, Brown, & Liaschenko, 2004; Varcoe & Rodney, 2009). Many nurses in direct care roles believe that there is a high price to be paid when they speak up and "rock the boat." The lessons of when and how to do so in an effective way have not, until recently, been learned, and these kinds of actions have not been rewarded in practice.[10]

Furthermore, nurses are sometimes complicit in censoring their colleagues who speak up about practice concerns, labelling them as "bleeding hearts" or "troublemakers" (Varcoe, 2001; Varcoe & Rodney, 2009). This dark side (Corley & Goren, 1998) of nursing practice has confounded an already difficult work environment and worsened individual nurses' moral distress. Indeed, the stories of Susan, Jacques, and Sandeep suggest a concern that they too will become complicit in ethical problems based in their practice. They need support at many levels. For nurses such as Susan, Jacques, and Sandeep a requisite of providing high-quality and ethical care is to be able to address the challenges they experience, including a heavy workload, lack of respect, and lack of control over their work environments. Yet often a disconnect exists between nursing organizations and organizational leaders, and nurses at the grassroots level. Nursing leaders need to continue to engage members in the advocacy work of health care organizations. Nursing educators have an obligation to help nursing students see the links between policy and their clinical practice and employment conditions that will allow them to provide ethical, compassionate, and competent care.

**Strengths of the Nursing Profession**

It takes time, energy, support, and moral courage to reflect and take action to address unethical situations and systemwide problems. Fortunately, the nursing profession overall, and individual nurses such as Susan, Jacques, and Sandeep, have significant strengths they can draw from to address the various challenges.

*1. Education*

For one, nurses today have benefited from a more comprehensive system of education. In almost all jurisdictions across Canada, nurses are prepared at a baccalaureate level as they enter practice (Dick & Cragg, 2006). This preparatory education emphasizes the development of competencies such as team communication, conflict resolution skills, critical thinking, research utilization, and ethical decision-making. A mastery of these competencies means that students graduate with a strong basis for the promotion of ethical practice. Indeed, the authors of this chapter can attest to the insight and commitment of students entering the nursing profession. Furthermore, huge cohorts of diploma-prepared nurses with expertise in practice have gone on to acquire baccalaureate degrees, which gives them the opportunity to reflect on and enhance their professional development. Thus, nurses such as Jacques can use their access to academic education to make changes in how they practise and to provide leadership for their colleagues in nursing and other disciplines. In Jacques's situation, he has shown moral sensitivity (Nortvedt, 2004) in refusing to accept the "situation normal" in his emergency department, and his continuing education has provided him with the skills needed to take his concerns to management.

While interdisciplinary education is not yet well-established in health care, new students in nursing and nurses returning to obtain a baccalaureate degree have increasing opportunities to learn from and with their colleagues in other disciplines. Palliative care and ethics education are two areas that have made apparent progress on this front. In palliative care, professional preparatory educational programs and continuing educational programs are helping students/providers from a variety of disciplines to learn about compassionate care at the end of life, including how to work better with each other, patients, and their family members. For example, British Columbia's well-established five-day-long interdisciplinary palliative care program (a continuing education event) has been running twice a year for twenty years. It has been extremely well received by nurses and other health care providers.

Significant progress has also been made over the past ten years in ethics-specific education, which has become a requirement for most health care professions, including nursing. This education is increasingly emphasizing interdisciplinary teamwork and conflict resolution in addition to traditional ethical theory. Institutional ethics committees also play a key role in the continuing education of health care providers and have proved to be an important resource for health care agencies in the areas of ethics education, case consultation, and policy formulation (McPherson et al., 2004). Overall, ethics committees and ethics consultants seek to improve the moral climate of health care agencies (American Society for Bioethics and Humanities, 1998; McPherson et al., 2004; Storch, Rodney, & Starzomski, 2009).[11]

*2. Research and Leadership*

A significant aspect of the advances in nursing education over the past two decades has been graduate nursing education. A large — and growing — cohort of nurses across the country is now prepared at masters and doctoral levels in nursing and other related fields (Thorne, 2006). This means that nurses are now more prepared to study the ethical problems in their practice and to participate in generating solutions. Nurses are therefore having an influence in the field of bioethics more generally. For example, Dr. Elizabeth Peter of the University of Toronto Joint Centre for Bioethics has had a significant influence in bringing forward ethical concerns about home health care delivery (Peter, 2004).

Increased access to graduate education in nursing has been generating a cohort of nurses who are much better prepared to take up the challenges in practice and to advocate for better conditions of work for nurses and better health care for patients, families, and communities. A number of nurse researchers and their colleagues in other disciplines, for example, have had a significant influence on health policy by documenting the increased morbidity and mortality associated with nurse staffing cutbacks and by recommending solutions (e.g., Aiken et al., 2002; Canadian Health Services Research Foundation, 2001, 2006a, 2006b, 2006c; Laschinger et al., 2000; Lankshear, Sheldon, & Maynard, 2005; Storch, 2005). Furthermore, there is a significant — and growing —body of research led by nurses exploring ethics in nursing practice, including research directed at improving the ethical practice of nurses and other health care providers (e.g., Austin, 2007; Corley et al., 2005; Rodney et al., 2006; Storch, 2005; Storch et al., 2009; Wolf & Zuzelo, 2006). Such bodies of research can go a long way in supporting the ethical practice of nurses.

## 3. Professional Organizations

Throughout Canadian history, professional nursing organizations have taken a strong position against the privatization of health care (Pangman & Pangman, 2010; Storch, 2010).[12] Policy statements, lobbying, and public relations activities have been directed at educating policymakers, politicians, and the public, arguing that publicly funded health care is ethically superior to for-profit health care. Nurses have engaged in the debate about public vs. private health care because they want to provide a high quality of care and meet their professional ethical standards in a system based on fairness and equity.[13]

Nursing organizations take an active role in advocating for the welfare of nurses, and the reform of the health care system to benefit patients, families, and communities. This action has been taking place at the national level through the Canadian Nurses Association, Canadian Federation of Nurses Unions, Health Canada's Office of Nursing Policy, and national specialty certification organizations. For example, the Canadian Nurses Association has influential position papers on important topics such as the nursing shortage, primary health care, and climate change. Action at the provincial level has involved professional associations and colleges, unions, and special interest groups. For example, the outbreak of SARS (Severe Acute Respiratory Syndrome) in Ontario in 2003 had a significant influence on subsequent pandemic planning across Canada, and the Registered Nurses Association of Ontario subsequently documented and analyzed practice concerns. The College and Association of Registered Nurses of Alberta became engaged in a campaign to respond to the most recent round of fiscal and resource constraints in Alberta.

The Canadian Nurses Association's continuing work on a national *Code of Ethics for Registered Nurses* (2008) is an important source of strength. Codes of ethics set the standards by which the profession and the public can evaluate (and potentially discipline) individual members. They also provide guidance for individual members about their own conduct (Storch, Rodney, & Starzomski, 2009; Oberle & Raffin Bouchal, 2009). The major changes in context between revisions are provided to explain the changes, additions, and other modifications in the Code (Storch, Rodney, & Starzomski, 2009).[14] Although codes of ethics cannot address all issues, and cannot provide complete guidance to address the complexity of issues at micro, meso, and macro levels, they do play a noteworthy role in providing a standard for ethical behaviour, and in facilitating greater sensitivity to ethical issues (CNA, 2008a; Oberle & Raffin Bouchal, 2009; Storch, Rodney, & Starzomski, 2009). The ongoing work by the CNA and its affiliated provincial associations and colleges on the *Code of Ethics for Registered Nurses* provides nurses such as Susan, Jacques, and Sandeep with a significant resource to promote their ethical practice.

## Toward Stronger Nursing Voices

A broad range of ethical principles/concepts thus provide guidance at all three levels of micro, meso, and macro. At the micro level, for example, we can work to respect patients' autonomous choices and provide care to help them and their families respond to their health and illness experiences. At the meso level we can promote trust and care between patients, family members, and health care providers as they face difficult decisions at times of transition or crisis; and we can protect nurses' integrity by ensuring that they can participate as full members of the health care team. At the macro level we can argue for a just allocation of resources so that health care agencies are able to provide adequate treatment and care for all patients and their families, and nursing organizations can become even more politically active in health policy reform.

Operating at meso and macro as well as micro levels requires a different kind of ethical expertise — expertise that is as much political as ethical. Thus, nursing needs to pay more attention to the sociopolitical context in which nursing ethics is located. The challenge for nurses is to advocate for health care based on ethical concepts such as beneficence, autonomy, truthfulness, confidentiality, justice, and integrity.

## Notes

1     Ethical or moral distress is what individuals experience when their moral reasoning tells them what the right thing to do is, but situational constraints — and sometimes their own angst — block them from moving from choice to action. Ethical and moral distress is accompanied by feelings of anger, frustration, guilt, and powerlessness (Canadian Nurses Association, 2008a; Jameton, 1984; Webster & Baylis, 2000). This concept is explained in detail in chapter 8.

2     These stories are fictionalized composites of situations that we have encountered in our clinical practice and research.

3     For a comprehensive overview of the history of health care in Canada, including the origins of cost constraint problems, see Feldberg and Vipond (2006), Storch (2010), and Pangman and Pangman (2010).

4     The health care reforms of the 1990s were influenced by shifts in the political ideologies of Canadian, U.S., and British governments in the late 1980s. These administrations moved toward a commitment to strengthen markets within and between countries and reduce health and social welfare spending (Armstrong & Armstrong, 2003; Raphael, Bryant, & Rioux, 2006; Canadian Centre for Policy Alternatives, 2000; Commission on the Future of Health Care in Canada, 2002; Kenny, 2002; Raphael, 2007; Stein, 2001). The formation of the North American Free Trade Agreement (NAFTA) in 1994 played an important role in health care changes in the 1990s and beyond.

More recently we have been facing another wave of challenges in health care delivery associated with the fiscal recession. The situation in Alberta is particularly acute. For example, on August 28, 2009, the College and Association of Registered Nurses of Alberta expressed serious concern that the Alberta Health Services "announced plans to cut staff by enticing nurses and other professionals into early retirement in order to address the health system's budget deficit." See <http://www.nurses.ab.ca/Carna/index.aspx?WebStructureID=4073>.

5    The ethics of recruiting nurses from developing countries, where nurses are desperately needed, is problematic. This is an area in need of more ethics research and policy work.

6    For a comprehensive historical review of health promotion in nursing, see MacDonald (2002).

7    The areas of reform that this Council was to oversee include primary health care, home-care, catastrophic drug coverage, wait times for diagnostic tests and medical procedures, electronic health records and other information technology for health care, patient safety, the supply of health care providers, the scientific basis for decisions about resources in health care, innovation and research, public health initiatives, and Aboriginal health (Health Council of Canada, 2008).

8    While our focus in this chapter — and in this text overall — is on registered nurses, we wish to acknowledge that *all* health care provider groups (care aides, dietitians, licensed practical nurses, occupational therapists, pastoral care workers, physicians, practical nurses, rehabilitation therapists, respiratory therapists, social workers, surgeons, and so on) have been adversely affected.

9    Most of the research has been done in acute care. It is likely that problems with increased morbidity and mortality are also being experienced in long-term and community care.

10   One tragic case occurred in Winnipeg in the early 1990s, when infants undergoing cardiac surgery experienced an unacceptably high mortality rate and operating room nurses' concerns went unheeded. See Ceci (2004) for an insightful analysis of the situation.

11   By moral climate we mean the structural and interpersonal resources in an organization, as well as the implicit and explicit values that permeate that organization (Rodney et al., 2006).

12   For comprehensive reviews of the nature of Canadian nursing associations, colleges, and unions, see Brunke (2010), Pangman and Pangman (2010), Ross (2003), and Villeneuve (2010).

13    For more on the principle of fairness, see chapter 7.
14    The CNA Code was revised for 2008. Revisions to codes of ethics also in-
      volve attempts to build consensus, with some resultant levels of compro-
      mise. In the latest version of the *Code of Ethics* (CNA, 2008a), for instance,
      there was considerable debate around splitting the Code into regulatory vs.
      aspirational values statements. The current version of the Code reflects that
      split.

## References

Aiken, L.H., Clarke, S.P., Sloane, D.M., Sochalski, J., & Silber, J.H. (2002). Hospital
    nurse staffing and patient mortality, nurse burnout, and job dissatisfaction.
    *JAMA* 288 (16), 1987-1993.

American Society for Bioethics and Humanities (1998). *Core competencies for
    health care ethics consultation.* Glenview, IL.

Anderson, J.M. (2006). Reflections on the social determinants of women's health.
    Exploring intersections: Does racialization matter? *Canadian Journal of Nurs-
    ing Research* 8 (1), 7-14.

Armstrong, P., & Armstrong, H. (2003). *Wasting away: The undermining of Cana-
    dian health care* (2nd ed.). Don Mills, ON: Oxford University Press.

Austin, W. (2007). The ethics of everyday practice: Healthcare environments as
    moral communities. *Advances in Nursing Science* 30 (1), 81-88.

Brown, H., & Rodney, P. (2007). Beyond case studies in practice education: Cre-
    ating capacities for ethical knowledge through story and narrative. In L.E.
    Young & B. Paterson (Eds.), *Teaching nursing: Developing a student-centered
    learning environment* (pp. 141-163). Philadelphia, PA: Lippincott, Williams, &
    Wilkins.

Browne, A.J. (2001). The influence of liberal political ideology on nursing science.
    *Nursing Inquiry* 8, 118-129.

Browne, A.J. (2007) Clinical encounters between nurses and First Nations women
    in a Western Canadian hospital. *Social Science & Medicine* 64 (10), 2165-2176.

Browne, A.J. and Smye, V. (2002). A postcolonial analysis of health care discourses
    addressing Aboriginal women. *Nurse Researcher* 9 (3), 28-41.

Brunke, L. (2010). Canadian provincial and territorial professional associations
    and colleges. In M. McIntyre & C. McDonald (Eds.), *Realities of Canadian
    nursing: Professional, practice, and power issues* (3rd ed.; pp. 147-165). Phila-
    delphia: Wolters Kluwer/Lippincott Williams & Wilkins.

Butterfield, P. (1990). Thinking upstream: Nurturing a conceptual understanding
    of the social context of health behavior. *Advances in Nursing Science* 12 (2), 1-8.

Canadian Centre for Policy Alternatives (2000). *Public pain, private gain: The privatization of health care in Ontario: A report to the Ontario Health Coalition.* Ontario.

Canadian Health Services Research Foundation. (2001). *Commitment and care: The benefits of a healthy workplace for nurses, their patients and the system.* Ottawa.

Canadian Health Services Research Foundation (2006a). *Looking forward, working together: Priorities for nursing leadership in Canada.* Ottawa.

Canadian Health Services Research Foundation (2006b). *Staffing for safety: A synthesis of the evidence on nursing staffing and patient safety.* Ottawa.

Canadian Health Services Research Foundation (2006c). *What's ailing our nurses? A discussion of the major issues affecting nursing human resources in Canada.* Ottawa.

Canadian Medical Association & Canadian Nurses Association (2004). The taming of the queue: Toward a cure for health care wait times. Discussion paper. Ottawa.

Canadian Nurses Association (2008a). *Code of Ethics for Registered Nurses.* Ottawa.

Canadian Nurses Association (2008b). *News release: Canada's health system faces another year of nursing student graduate shortfalls.* June 18. Ottawa.

Ceci, C. (2004). Gender, power, nursing: A case analysis. *Nursing Inquiry* 11 (2), 72-81.

Chambliss, D.F. (1996). *Beyond caring: Hospitals, nurses, and the social organization of ethics.* Chicago: University of Chicago Press.

Commission on the Future of Health Care in Canada (2002). *Building on values: The future of health care in Canada.* Ottawa.

Corley, M.C., & Goren, S. (1998). The dark side of nursing: Impact of stigmatizing responses on patients. *Scholarly Inquiry for Nursing Practice* 12 (2), 99–118.

Corley, M.C., Minick, P., Elswick, R.K., & Jacobs, M. (2005). Nurse moral distress and ethical work environment. *Nursing Ethics* 12 (4), 381-390.

David, B.A. (2000). Nursing's gender politics: Reformulating the footnotes. *Advances in Nursing Science* 23 (1), 83–93.

Dick, D.D., & Cragg, B. (2006). Undergraduate education: Development and politics. In M. McIntyre, E. Thomlinson, & C. McDonald (Eds.), *Realities of Canadian nursing: Professional, practice, and power issues* (2nd ed.). Philadelphia: Lippincott.

Dunleavy, J., Shamian, J., & Thomson, D. (2003). Workplace pressures: Handcuffed by cutbacks. *Canadian Nurse* 99 (3), 23-26.

Feldberg, G., & Vipond, R. (2006). Cracks in the foundation: The origins and development of the Canadian and American health care systems. In D. Raphael,

T. Bryant, & M. Rioux (Eds.). *Staying alive: Critical perspectives on health, illness, and health care*. Toronto: Canadian Scholars' Press.

Gadow, S. (1999). Relational narrative: The postmodern turn in nursing ethics. *Scholarly Inquiry for Nursing Practice* 13 (1), 57–69.

Health Canada (2002). Canada's health care system. Ottawa. <http://www.hc-sc. gc.ca/>.

Health Council of Canada (2008). *Rekindling reform: Health care renewal in Canada: 2003-2008*. Toronto.

Hertzman, C., & Siddiqi, A. (2008). Tortoises 1, hares 0: How comparative health trends between Canada and the United States support a long-term view of policy and health. *Healthcare Policy* 4 (2), 16-24.

Heymann, J., & Hertzman, C. (2007). Healthier societies: An introduction. In J. Heymann, C. Hertzman, M.L. Barer, & R.G. Evans (Eds.), *Healthier societies: From analysis to action*. Oxford: Oxford University Press.

Institute of Medicine (2004). *Keeping patients safe: Transforming the work environment of nurses*. Washington, D.C.: National Academies Press.

Jameton, A.L. (1984). *Nursing practice: The ethical issues*. Englewood Cliffs, N.J.: Prentice-Hall.

Kenny, N.P. (2002). *What good is health care? Reflections on the Canadian experience*. Ottawa: CHA Press.

Lankshear, A.J., Sheldon, T.A., & Maynard, A. (2005). Nurse staffing and healthcare outcomes: A systematic review of international research evidence. *Advances in Nursing Science* 28 (2), 163-174.

Laschinger, H.K.S., Finegan, J., Shamian, J., & Casier, S. (2000). Organizational trust and empowerment in restructured healthcare settings: Effects on staff nurse commitment. *Journal of Nursing Administration* 30 (9), 413–425.

Lynam, M.J., Henderson, A., Browne, A., Smye, V., Semeniuk, P., Blue, C., Singh, S., & Anderson, J. (2003). Healthcare restructuring with a view to equity and efficiency: Reflections on unintended consequences. *Canadian Journal of Nursing Leadership* 16 (1), 112–140.

MacDonald, M. (2002). Health promotion: Historical, philosophical, and theoretical perspectives. In L.E. Young & V. Hayes (Eds.), *Transforming health promotion practice: Concepts, issues, and application*. Philadelphia: FA Davis.

Marmot, M. (2004). Social causes of social inequalities in health. In S. Anand, F. Peter, & A. Sen (Eds.), *Public health, ethics, and equity*. Oxford: Oxford University Press.

McGillis Hall et al. (2003). Nurse staffing models as predictors of patient outcomes. *Medical Care* 41 (9), 1096-1109.

McPherson, G., Rodney, P., Storch, J., Pauly, B., McDonald, M., & Burgess, M.

(2004). Working within the landscape: Applications in health care ethics. In J. Storch, P. Rodney, & R. Starzomski (Eds.), *Toward a moral horizon: Nursing ethics for leadership and practice*. Toronto: Pearson-Prentice Hall.

Meleis, A.I. (1997). *Theoretical nursing: Development and progress*. 3rd ed. Philadelphia: Lippincott.

Nisker, J. (2004). Narrative ethics in health care. In J. Storch, P. Rodney, & R. Starzomski (Eds.), *Toward a moral horizon: Nursing ethics for leadership and practice*. Toronto: Pearson-Prentice Hall.

Nortvedt, P. (2004). Emotions and ethics. In J. Storch, P. Rodney, & R. Starzomski (Eds.), *Toward a moral horizon: Nursing ethics for leadership and practice*. Toronto: Pearson-Prentice Hall.

Oberle, K., & Raffin Bouchal, S. (2009). *Ethics in Canadian nursing practice: Navigating the journey*. Toronto: Pearson-Prentice Hall.

Pan-Canadian Planning Committee on Unregulated Health Workers (2008). Valuing health-care team members: Working with unregulated health workers: A discussion paper. Ottawa: Canadian Nurses Association.

Pangman, V.C., & Pangman, C. (2010). *Nursing leadership from a Canadian perspective*. Philadelphia: Wolters Kluwer, Lippincott Williams & Wilkins.

Pauly, B.M. (2004). Shifting the balance in the funding and delivery of health care in Canada. In J. Storch, P. Rodney, & R. Starzomski (Eds.), *Toward a moral horizon: Nursing ethics for leadership and practice*. Toronto: Pearson-Prentice Hall.

Pauly, B. (2008). Harm reduction through a social justice lens. *International Journal of Drug Policy* 19, 4-10.

Perry, J., Lynam, M.J., & Anderson, J.M. (2006). Resisting vulnerability: The experience of families who have kin in hospital—a feminist ethnography. *International Journal of Nursing Studies* 43 (2),173-184.

Peter, E. (2004). Home health care and ethics. In J. Storch, P. Rodney, & R. Starzomski (Eds.), *Toward a moral horizon: Nursing ethics for leadership and practice*. Toronto: Pearson-Prentice Hall.

Premier's Advisory Council on Health (2001). *A framework for reform: Report of the Premier's Advisory Council on Health* (Mazankowski Report). Calgary.

Raphael, D. (2006). Social determinants of health: An overview of concepts and issues. In D. Raphael, T. Bryant, & M. Rioux (Eds.), *Staying alive: Critical perspectives on health, illness, and health care*. Toronto: Canadian Scholars' Press.

Raphael, D. (2007). *Poverty and policy in Canada: Implications for health and quality of life*. Toronto: Canadian Scholars' Press.

Raphael, D., Bryant, T., & Rioux, M. (Eds.) (2006). *Staying alive: Critical perspectives on health, illness, and health care*. Toronto: Canadian Scholars' Press.

Rodney, P.A. (2002). Verbal brief to the "Romanow Commission on the Future of Health Care in Canada" on "Nursing Research and Health," Victoria, B.C. March.

Rodney, P., Brown, H., & Liaschenko, J. (2004). Moral agency: Relational connections and trust. In J. Storch, P. Rodney, & R. Starzomski (Eds.), *Toward a moral horizon: Nursing ethics for leadership and practice*. Toronto: Pearson-Prentice Hall.

Rodney, P., Burgess, M, McPherson, G., & Brown, H. (2004). Our theoretical landscape: A brief history of health care ethics. In J. Storch, P. Rodney, & R. Starzomski (Eds.), *Toward a moral horizon: Nursing ethics for leadership and practice*. Toronto: Pearson-Prentice Hall.

Rodney, P., Doane, G.H., Storch, J. & Varcoe, C. (2006). Workplaces: Toward a safer moral climate. *Canadian Nurse* 102 (8), 24-27.

Rodney, P. & Street, A. (2004). The moral climate of nursing practice: Inquiry and action. In J. Storch, P. Rodney, & R. Starzomski (Eds.), *Toward a moral horizon: Nursing ethics for leadership and practice*. Toronto: Pearson-Prentice Hall.

Ross, E. (2003). From shortage to oversupply: The nursing workforce pendulum. In J. Ross-Kerr & M.J. Wood (Eds.), *Canadian nursing: Issues and perspectives*. Toronto: Mosby.

Solomon, M.Z., O'Donnell, L., Jennings, B., Guilfoy, V., Wolf, S.M., Nolan, K., Jackson, R., Koch-Weser, D., & Donnelley, S. (1993). Decisions near the end of life: Professional views on life-sustaining treatments. *American Journal of Public Health* 83 (1), 14–23.

Standing Senate Committee on Social Affairs, Science, and Technology (2000). *Quality end-of-life care: The right of every Canadian*. Ottawa: Senate Subcommittee.

Standing Senate Committee on Social Affairs, Science and Technology (2002). *The Health of Canadians: The Federal Role: Final Report* [Kirby Report]. Ottawa.

Starzomski, R. & Rodney, P. (1997). Nursing inquiry for the common good. In S.E. Thorne & V.E. Hayes (Eds.), *Nursing praxis: Knowledge and action*. Thousand Oaks, Cal.: Sage.

Stein, J.G. (2001). *The cult of efficiency*. Toronto: Anansi.

Storch, J.L. (2004). Nursing ethics: A developing moral terrain. In J. Storch, P. Rodney, & R. Starzomski (Eds.), *Toward a moral horizon: Nursing ethics for leadership and practice*. Toronto: Pearson-Prentice Hall.

Storch, J.L. (2005). Patient safety: Is it just another bandwagon? *Nursing Leadership* 18 (2), 39-55.

Storch, J. (2010). Canadian healthcare system. In M. McIntyre & C. McDonald (Eds.), *Realities of Canadian nursing: Professional, practice, and power issues*. 3rd ed. Philadelphia: Wolters Kluwer/Lippincott Williams & Wilkins.

Storch, J., Rodney, P., Pauly, B., Fulton, T.R., Stevenson, L., Newton, L., & Schick Makaroff, K. (2009). Enhancing ethical climates in nursing work environments. *Canadian Nurse* 105 (3), 20-25.

Storch, J., Rodney, P., & Starzomski, S. (2009). Ethics in health care in Canada. In B.S. Bolaria & H. Dickinson (Eds.), *Health, illness, and health care in Canada.* 4th ed. Toronto: Nelson Education.

Thorne, S. (2006).Graduate education. In M. McIntyre, E. Thomlinson, & C. Mc-Donald (Eds.), *Realities of Canadian nursing: Professional, practice, and power issues.* 2nd ed. Philadelphia: Lippincott.

Varcoe, C. (2001). Abuse obscured: An ethnographic account of emergency unit nursing practice in relation to violence against women. *Canadian Journal of Nursing Research* 32 (4).

Varcoe, C. (2004).Widening the scope of ethical theory, practice, and policy: Violence against women as an illustration. In J. Storch, P. Rodney, & R. Starzomski (Eds.), *Toward a moral horizon: Nursing ethics for leadership and practice.* Toronto: Pearson-Prentice Hall.

Varcoe C., & Rodney, P. (2009). Constrained agency: the social structure of nurses' work. In B.S. Bolaria & H.D. Dickinson (Eds.), *Health, illness, and health care in Canada.* 4th ed. Toronto: Nelson Education.

Villeneuve, M.J. (2010).The Canadian Nurses Association and the International Council of Nurses. In M. McIntyre & C. McDonald (Eds.), *Realities of Canadian nursing: Professional, practice, and power issues.* 3rd ed. Philadelphia: Wolters Kluwer/Lippincott Williams & Wilkins.

Warren, V.L. (1992). Feminist directions in medical ethics. *HEC Forum* 4 (1), 19-35.

Webster, G., & Baylis, F. (2000). Moral residue. In S. B. Rubin and L. Zoloth (Eds.), *Margin of error: The mistakes in the practice of medicine.* Hagerstown, Md.: University Publishing Group.

Wolf, Z.R., & Zuzelo, P.R. (2006). "Never again" stories of nurses: Dilemmas in nursing practice. *Qualitative Health Research* 16 (9), 1191-1206.

Yeo, M. (1993). Ethics and economics in health care resource allocation. Working Paper no. 93-07. Ottawa: Queen's–University of Ottawa Economic Projects.

Yeo, M., Emery, J.C.H., and Kary, D. (2009). The private insurance debate in Canadian health policy: Making the values explicit. SPP Research Paper: The Health Series, The School of Public Policy, University of Calgary, vol. 2, Issue 3, June. <http://iapr.ca/files/iapr/MakingValuesExplicit.pdf>

# 3 BENEFICENCE

*The road to Hell is paved with good intentions.*

—AN OLD PROVERB

*One act of beneficence, one act of real usefulness, is worth all the abstract sentiment in the world.*

— ANN RADCLIFFE

---

*Caring about and for the well-being of others is the mainspring of nursing. In nursing ethics, this orientation toward the good of patients is called "beneficence." Beneficence is simple enough in principle, but it is often very complicated in practice. For example, sometimes it is difficult to know what is best for the patient. How ought personal, cultural, and familial perceptions and definitions of health be assessed, and, in situations of conflict, reconciled? What is an ethical balance between respect for the patient's rights and liberties and the nurse's knowledge or perceptions of what is good for the patient? How forceful or coercive should health professionals be in advancing their views of what is good for the patient? What is required in situations where doing what is best for the patient involves some element of personal risk or sacrifice on the part of the nurse?*

---

## Beneficence and Benefiting Others

Beneficence (from the Latin *bene* for "well" or "good" and *facio* for "to do") denotes promoting someone else's good or welfare.[1] The same root forms the word "benefit." *Beneficence,* as an ideal or principle of conduct, requires us to act in a way that *benefits* others. Such benefit might take the form of preventing or removing some harm, or more directly acting to produce a good.

The same knowledge, skills, and powers that health professionals use to produce benefit can also produce harm. This double edge is captured in the Greek word for drug (*pharmakon*), which can mean either remedy or poison. The same drug that is beneficial in one context may under certain circumstances be a harm. The same can be said of many different interventions.

Because health professionals are in a position to produce harm as well as benefit, it is important to supplement beneficence with *nonmaleficence*, which pertains to the noninfliction of harm (Beauchamp & Childress, 2001). Nonmaleficence is the value expressed in the classic dictum *primum non nocere*, that is, "first, do no harm." This injunction exhorts health professionals to exercise due care and caution in going about their business of working to produce benefit for their patients. A medication error, a slip of the hand, or an unguarded disclosure of information may cause a great deal of harm.

Beneficence has always been highly valued in the health professions — the so-called "caring" professions — and certainly in nursing. The first nurses in Canada belonged to religious orders that established hospitals in Quebec City and Montreal in the seventeenth century (Jamiesan, Sewall, & Suhrie, 1966). These Augustinian and Ursuline sisters cared for the settlers as well as the native peoples in much less than ideal circumstances. They often risked their health in their work as they practised the tenets of Christianity — doing good and benefiting others. The religious dimension is much less prominent today, but beneficence remains at the heart of contemporary nursing.

Beneficence is closely linked in meaning with caring. The caring orientation of nursing has been described and analyzed by numerous authors (Watson, 1979, 1994, 2005; Benner, 2001; Benner & Wruebel, 1989) and is sometimes contrasted with the curative orientation of medicine.[2] Nursing's emphasis on caring is evidenced in the various codes of ethics that govern the profession, and is incorporated into various definitions of nursing.

## Beneficence, Self-Concern, and Duty

In the earlier days of nursing, many people (almost always women) entered nursing with a sense of vocation. Selfless dedication and sacrifice were expected of these nurses. The culture of religious orders and military life were combined. As the profession of nursing developed in the last century, and with advances in the status of women in society and in labour and human rights legislation, nurses gained a legal right to fair employment conditions. Today many students enter the profession for reasons that are not solely altruistic. In addition to the rewards of being in a caring profession, nursing has an appeal because of the salary and benefits and employment opportunities. Increasingly men have entered the profession.

To varying degrees, most of us want to benefit others. For many people, and in particular those working in the "helping professions," caring comes naturally. To the extent that nurses care *about* their patients, caring *for* them may be less a burden than a joyful fulfillment or expression of deep desires and commitments. In many instances, helping others makes us feel good about ourselves. Many nurses report tremendous job satisfaction from making a positive difference in someone's life. Conversely, patients whose condition is such that little can be done to benefit them are among the most trying, partly because practitioners sometimes feel helpless in their presence.

Although caring for and benefiting patients is often in the service of the nurse's immediate desires and interests as well, it is not always so. In some instances, meeting the patient's needs may require hard work, personal risk, or sacrifice. Some tasks nurses may be expected to perform for the benefit of the patient may be very demanding, or unpleasant. There is some element of risk in caring for a person with an infectious disease. Working overtime to meet patient needs in emergency situations or when a unit is short-staffed may be a considerable inconvenience for the nurse. In such cases, caring for others is to some degree at odds with self-concern, or with caring for and about oneself.

Such conflict shows that, although desiring to do what will benefit others is a big part of beneficence, beneficence must be rooted in something else besides, or in addition to, desire. When the nurse finds satisfaction or gratification in caring for the patient, beneficence is easy. The situation is different when there is some degree of conflict between the nurse's own desires or self-concern and what is required to benefit the patient. Perhaps the nurse would *rather not* attend to the homeless man — dirty, lice-ridden, and reeking of the street — brought into the emergency. Meeting his needs may be very unpleasant. Perhaps the nurse would *prefer not* to care for the person with an infectious disease. Even with precautions, there is some element of personal risk in the procedure, and a mistake could have very grave consequences. Perhaps the nurse really *does not want* to work overtime to cover for colleagues away with flu. There may be other things he or she would rather be doing.

If, in such instances, beneficence enjoins the nurse to attend to the homeless man, or draw the blood sample, or work overtime, it cannot be because this is what the nurse in the first instance desires. Rather, it is because in some sense and to some degree these acts of caring are required as a matter of duty. If, as is often the case, what duty requires is at the same time what the nurse desires, then so much the better. However, beneficence sometimes requires us to do for reasons of duty what otherwise we would prefer not to do. The call of duty may spur us into action when concern for ourselves pulls us in another direction. Leading a moral life — a life responsive to the demands of duty — is a task that involves some measure of self-sacrifice, effort, and striving, even if in many or perhaps most instances what we desire to do and what we ought to do coincide.

How then do we know what our duties are? The grounds upon which our duties may be established are several.[3] In the context of professional ethics, it is often argued that our duties in some sense derive from the phenomenon of promising, as when we speak of "professional promise." According to this view, the duties of a professional emerge from a kind of contract between a profession and society, or between a given professional and a given patient. In the case of nursing, society confers certain rights and privileges on nurses, who in return implicitly promise to aim at certain standards of conduct, including those expressed in the profession's codes of ethics. The individual who enters the profession and assumes the role of nurse in our society thereby assumes as well certain duties that go with this role, the duty to act for the benefit of the patient being foremost among these. Such a duty is called a "fiduciary duty," meaning that it derives from a trust that professionals will use their skills and powers in the service of their patients. Nurses have been empowered and entrusted to act for the benefit of patients; patients expect them to do so.

By whatever means duty is grounded, it is sometimes difficult to decide precisely what and how much duty requires of us, especially with regard to beneficence.[4] Aside from what we might wish or desire to do, or what we might be inclined to do out of self-concern, what is entailed by a duty to benefit others? To what extent is it enough to avoid causing others harm, and to what extent are we required to produce positive benefits for others? How much sacrifice, effort, and striving does duty require of us? The answers to these questions will depend on the specific context and relationships in which one exists.

Although we admire persons who devote themselves passionately to the service of others even to the point of self-sacrifice, the hero sets an unreasonable standard of duty for nursing. Jameton (1984) points out that "in the name of idealism, nurses have traditionally been called upon to work long hours at low wages," and cautions that "nurses in particular should be wary of self-sacrifice" (p. 215). Yet we also disapprove of the nurse who acts only according to the bare letter of his or her job description or refuses to make any sacrifice for the good of the patient. Somewhere between these two extremes a reasonable mean must be found. How much giving does beneficence require of the nurse?

Under ideal circumstances there would be no conflict between concern for others and concern for self: caring for others would coincide with self-development, fulfillment of personal goals, and so on. Unfortunately, the world in which we live is less than ideal. Sometimes the nurse is called upon to do something in the service of the patient's good that requires a measure of self-sacrifice or selflessness.

Such a situation might arise when the need for care exceeds the supply of available practitioners. As a result of understaffing, a nurse may feel called upon to work harder or for longer periods of time than would otherwise be reasonable. To be sure, such understaffing may itself be a problem that needs to be addressed. Mindful of the possibility of exploitation, a nurse working in such situations should of course address the problem at the root level. Still, in the interim at least, the nurse is faced with a problem that requires immediate attention. In order to fill the pressing needs of patients, he or she may have to make some sacrifice. How much sacrifice is enough to satisfy the requirements of beneficence?[5]

Another situation in which the requirements of beneficence are unclear is when caring involves an element of personal risk. For instance, nurses may be unsure about the efficacy of the safety precautions instituted by the facility in which they work. Are they obliged to risk their own health or that of their families in order to provide care?[6] Nursing care is sometimes required in situations in which there is risk of physical and verbal abuse from patients. Patients are entitled to good nursing care, but what about when this entitlement comes into conflict with the nurse's own well-being? Acting as an advocate for the patient may in certain instances put the nurse at odds with his or her employer or with other health professionals. Does beneficence require the nurse to advocate for the patient's good even to the point that this involves a risk to job security?

Every nurse must strike some reasonable balance between the duty or wish to promote the good of patients, on the one hand, and self-concern, on the other. No formula can stipulate in advance what this balance should be. Ultimately, what constitutes a reasonable balance is a matter between the nurse and his or her conscience.

At the same time nurses need to make sure that managers and employers do not exploit their commitment to the well-being of their patients and normalize working situations that are stressful and put them at risk. Fatigue and stress are not only harmful to the nurses concerned, but also increase the risk of injuries, errors, and burnout. Nurses need to work together and through their professional organizations to ensure that the environments they work in do not unduly require sacrifice of them or put both themselves and their patients at risk. Managers and employers have a responsibility to reduce risks for all staff.

In the past nurses were expected to suffer indefinitely and in silence. More recently they have been rightly able to challenge unsafe employment conditions and the risk of harm caused by the public or patients. In some areas of nursing, nurses know and accept a variety of risks, ranging from acquiring an infection to verbal and even physical abuse. But there are ways of minimizing risk, and limits to the risks they can be expected to accept. For example, when they care for persons with communicable diseases, nurses should be provided with infection-control equipment. If that aid is not available, they can refuse to work until they are guaranteed the safest conditions possible (CNO, 2005).

## Problems Determining What Is Beneficial

Willingness to benefit others is one thing; knowing how and being able to benefit them is something different. *Good intentions* constitute an important aspect of beneficence, but so too does the ability to produce *good outcomes.* These two aspects of beneficence — the motivational or psychological and the consequential—are reflected in the notion of care.

On the one hand, caring can be conceived psychologically, as pertaining to someone's attitudes or dispositions. In this sense, caring applies to persons and the spirit in which they act in relation to others. Thus we praise someone for being concerned about and empathizing with others. We admire caring people for the good wishes or intentions upon which they act, sometimes even when their good intentions lead to bad results. Although caring in this sense may in itself be beneficial to others — just knowing that someone cares can have a therapeutic value — such benefits may be limited. Caring intentions may not be enough.

On the other hand, caring can also be conceived as applying not to persons as such, but rather to skills and abilities. In this sense, caring means *knowing how* to benefit someone and putting one's skills and abilities to work for his or her benefit. *Nursing care* refers to the kinds of things that the nurse, informed by nursing *knowledge,* might do to benefit the patient. A mother might indeed care for her sick child in the psychological sense described above, but, lacking the knowledge of how to benefit, may be unable to care in this second sense. Conversely, someone may know how to care in the sense of being able to secure a good outcome without caring in the sense of being genuinely concerned about the good of the other.[7] Moreover, as Benner and Wrubel (1989) point out, "the same act done in a caring and noncaring way may have quite different consequences" (p. 4).

Ideally, nursing care should combine both these senses of caring. Good nurses both care about their patients and use their nursing knowledge, skills, and abilities to care for them in ways that will produce benefit. "A caring relationship," Benner and Wrubel (1989) advance, "sets up conditions of trust that enable the one cared for to appropriate the help offered and to *feel* cared for" (p. 4). This trust includes both the feeling that the caregiver really does care, and the confidence that he or she has the knowledge and ability necessary to make a positive difference. The caring relationship is diminished if either of these conditions are not met.

In some cases, caring people possessing knowledge and skills to benefit others may be unsure about how best to produce benefit. There may be different or conflicting kinds of benefits to be considered. Benefits may be mixed with burdens or harms, and predicted outcomes may be more or less uncertain or probable. Judgements about how best to benefit the patient may be complicated by considerations of risk and burden as weighed against benefit. For example, in many cases it is uncertain whether cardio-pulmonary resuscitation is really in the patient's best interests. Often, there is uncertainty, and perhaps disagreement, about the benefit of treatment for patients who are severely damaged. What does beneficence require as concerns treatment decisions for a severely handicapped newborn who, even in the best case scenario, will emerge from surgery profoundly retarded, with limited motility, and unlikely to live beyond early childhood? Considering the burdens, would treatment really be a benefit? What about the burdens for others (e.g., the family, society)?

Treatment decisions in the grey zone where benefit to the patient is uncertain or disputed pose deep and difficult questions about the values, goals, and limits of health care. On the one hand, everyone will agree on the importance of *quality of life*, even if they disagree about what precisely it means or how to measure it. One of the reasons we value health care as we do is because it makes a difference in our quality of life.

On the other hand, however, *sanctity of life* is also an important value in health care. The respect given patients should not depend on their health status or quality of life. The low-weight neonate is to be treated with the same respect as the healthy newborn.

Thus interpreted, both quality of life and sanctity of life are important values in health care. It is important for health professionals to consider the impact of their interventions on the patient's quality of life. It is also important for health professionals to demonstrate respect for human life, regardless of its quality. Problems arise, however, insofar as how different individuals interpret, apply, and prioritize these values in specific contexts vary. For example, some health professionals interpret sanctity of life to mean that life should be preserved regardless of its quality. Others believe that, in cases where quality of life falls below a certain threshold, it is pointless — and even positively wrong — to preserve life. Such persons may claim that they too value sanctity of life, but argue that respect for human life does not entail that life ought always to be preserved.

The difficulties of determining what is beneficial are compounded by the fact that the scope of beneficence can be understood either in very broad or very narrow terms, depending on how broadly or narrowly benefit to the other is construed. Since the patient becomes the nurse's responsibility based on the expectation and trust that he or she will act on behalf of the patient's health interests, it seems reasonable to qualify the kind of caring specific to nursing in terms of health. Others may act beneficently toward patients in different ways — an accountant caring for their financial well-being, a priest for their spiritual well-being, and so on — but the nurse's care is primarily oriented toward their health. This, after all, is what nursing experience and knowledge prepare and qualify nurses to do.

For the moment, let us restrict the scope of beneficence to acting on behalf of the patient's good insofar as this good is identified with health (later we will give reasons to question this restriction). Even so, several problems arise. The concept of health, after all, is subject to different interpretations, and definitions of health cover a wide range of meaning. At one extreme are those who hold a narrow conception of health, defining it as the absence of disease or infirmity and restricting it to a biological or medical level. At the other extreme are those who hold a broader conception of health, extending it to include matters of lifestyle and to incorporate psychosocial considerations. The World Health Organization (WHO) definition of health as "a state of complete physical, mental, and social well-being" (Callahan, 1973, p. 77) is the most famous example of a broad conception of health.[8] As a rule, nursing tends to favour broad definitions of health.[9]

Cultural factors may also shape our conceptions of health. The meaning of "health" is to some degree relative to culture. What counts as "normal" body weight? What constitutes a balanced diet? How ought mothers to relate to their newborns? What are the characteristics of a healthy family? To some extent, the answers to such health questions vary from culture to culture. Different people, because of cultural or experiential differences, have varying opinions about what is healthy and what enhances their quality of life, especially when health is interpreted more broadly than physical health. These varying opinions about health and health benefits may cause conflict among health professionals, patients, and their families.

Differences concerning the understanding of health and the means by which it is maintained and restored have a bearing on what it means to act beneficently in the name of someone's health. Consider the controversial example of electroconvulsive therapy; or, shifting to a very different context, consider the debates about "therapeutic" abortion. Both of these "therapies" are legitimized in terms of health; disputes about them underscore the fact that what exactly counts as a health benefit may be far from self-evident.

Matters are further complicated if we question the initial restriction of beneficence to caring about health-related matters. Health, after all, is one good among others, albeit an important one. Many people prize other things above health, such as devotion to a political or religious cause, personal ambition, or the acquisition of wealth. They may even be quite willing to sacrifice their health for such things. How does one assess the value of health relative to other values?

Beneficence *can be* interpreted to incorporate the good of others conceived more broadly than in terms of health. Nurses *also* care about the ability of patients to act in accordance with their own values. They *also* care about the right of patients to be told the truth. However, in the literature and in common usage, the scope of beneficence tends to be restricted to the good of the patient as defined in terms of health.[10] Understood in this way, beneficence may come into conflict with other important values, and in particular with autonomy and truthfulness. It is in these terms that the issue of paternalism is usually expressed.

## Paternalism

The issue of paternalism comes to the fore when we shift from the question of *what standards* to use in determining the good of another to the question of *whose standards* ought to be accepted as authoritative. In particular, how much weight ought to be given to respecting the patient's rights or liberties when doing so is thought to be incompatible with the patient's good health? How much ought nurses to value the self-determination of patients to act on their own judgement when this seems contraindicated by nursing knowledge? How forceful or coercive should nurses be in imposing a plan of care in the name of the patient's own good? Which is more important, the patient's good as conceived in terms of health or the patient's autonomy? A generation ago, the answer to these questions would have been in favour of what the doctor or health care team thinks best. In theory those days have passed, but in some places this traditional approach prevails among nurses as well as physicians.

Nurses are expected to act as advocates for their patients. How is this possible in situations where the nurse's beliefs and values differ from those of the patient? Should nurses advocate only when the patient's views and wishes reflect their own, or are they expected to advocate even against their own values? Should nurses be expected to carry out treatments with which they are not in complete agreement?

One of the most profound changes in contemporary health care has been a shift in the locus of decision-making from health professionals to patients. Concurrent with this, there has been an increasing emphasis on values such as patient autonomy and the right to know the truth. Issues of paternalism may arise whenever one of these values comes into conflict with the beneficent concern to do what is best for the patient. Examples are legion. Anticipating that disclosure may not benefit the patient, or may even be contra-therapeutic, a nurse may be torn about whether to give a patient certain information. There may be some uncertainty as to how to proceed with a patient who expresses a choice that appears unwise in terms of health benefits (for example, a Jehovah's Witness's refusal of a blood transfusion). The nurse may be ambivalent about helping a patient with heart disease who needs assistance to smoke.

Such is the classic scenario for paternalism. Paternalism, according to Gerald Dworkin's (1971) well-known definition, is the "interference with a person's liberty of action justified by reasons referring exclusively to the welfare, good, happiness, needs, interests, or values of the person being coerced" (p. 108). In somewhat more blunt language, Jameton (1984) defines paternalism as "making people do what is good for them" as well as "preventing people from doing what is bad for them" (p. 90). The paternalistic person, acting in the name of beneficence, takes steps that he or she believes will promote the good of the other, perhaps even though the other disagrees or protests.

Because of their orientation toward benefiting the patient, health professionals have been inclined to paternalism, often making decisions without their patients' authorization or even consultation in the wellintended belief that they know what is best. Such paternalism used to be much more acceptable in our society than it is today. With the increasing value that our society has placed on liberty and individual rights, paternalism has become a derogatory term in the field of health care. Some writers, drawing from the tradition of beneficence in health care, argue that the critique of paternalism has gone too far, that we have been swept away by the rhetoric of autonomy and need to reassess our values (Pellegrino & Thomasma, 1988).

Even those who highly prize freedom or autonomy grant that paternalism may be justified under certain conditions. The most obvious example is in the parent-child relationship. Indeed, the term paternalism derives from this relationship (*pater* being the Latin word for father); it means to relate to someone as a father relates to a child. Paternalistic caring may be justified in the case of children, depending on the decision to be made and the child's experience and development in reasoning. A five-year-old child can decide whether or not to have a hamburger or a sandwich, but the question of whether or not to have an immunization is most likely beyond his or her maturity. Still, nurses should not necessarily be guided by the traditional view that children are not mature enough to know what is good for them, that they cannot be trusted to make their own decisions in matters of importance. Some children and adolescents may reach the standard of a mature minor — that is, they understand and appreciate the information necessary to make an informed decision. Ontario and many other jurisdictions have eliminated the age of consent for treatment. When adolescents decide they do not want aggressive treatment for cancer, and their parents want treatment to continue, nurses and colleagues have an obligation to determine if the patient meets the criteria of a mature minor. If so, the child can make this important treatment decision. Clearly, these situations can be difficult for all involved.

It is questionable to interfere with the liberty of adults for their own good, because adults are sufficiently mature or competent to make their own decisions based on what they value and what they believe to be good. Nevertheless, under certain conditions adults may be sufficiently like children as to warrant paternalistic intervention (e.g., when, because of cognitive impairment or some other deficiency, they are deemed incompetent). If people are incompetent, we generally accept the legitimacy of others making decisions for them. Even so, determining whether someone is incompetent to make certain choices may be very difficult. (These matters are discussed in greater detail in chapter 4.) Moreover, health providers who believe that a prescribed course of treatment is on the whole beneficial may conclude that anyone who would refuse such treatment is therefore irrational or incompetent. In other words, assessments of incompetence may be used to mask paternalism.

## The Beneficiary of Beneficence

In the health care traditions, the principal beneficiary of beneficence has generally been the *individual* patient. This focus on the individual is deeply rooted in the one-on-one therapeutic relationship. In contemporary society this approach gains even greater importance given our current emphasis on the rights of the individual.

Although traditionally beneficence in health care has been understood mainly in relation to the individual patient, there is no reason in principle to thus restrict its scope. Indeed, the codes of ethics of the various health professions typically express some broader commitment to do good. In nursing, this broader understanding of beneficence is also evidenced by the profession's very strong public health orientation, and its more holistic concern with health in the context of family and community.

However, when we extend the scope of benefit beyond the well-being of the individual, beneficence becomes even more complex. How should the benefit owed to one individual be weighed against possible benefits (and perhaps harms) to others? This question might arise in any number of contexts. For example, the nurse might need to balance the patient's good against the good of the patient's family, to whom he or she might also have some obligation. How much weight should be given to the possible burdens on the family in a difficult neonatal situation? Such questioning can be further complicated by ambiguity about who precisely is the patient on whose behalf the nurse is committed to acting beneficently. On at least some occasions, there is a possibility of conflict between the good of a pregnant woman and the good of her unborn child. In such a situation, are there two patients? Nurses working in the community may speak about the "nursing of families" or of the "family as patient." What does this mean when there is conflict between individuals within the family, or individual family members with competing goods?

Increasingly, considerations of justice are coming to the fore in the health care system. How should the nurse proceed when the good of an individual patient or group of patients is in competition with that of others? In a busy hospital ward, too much time spent with one patient might mean not enough time spent with another. How ought benefits to be distributed in such a situation? How should nurses respond under circumstances in which, as a consequence of institutional restructuring, they lack the time or the resources to provide the level or kind of care their patients require?

Doing good and benefiting others is much more than a matter of having good intentions. Upon careful examination, the apparent simplicity of the concept of beneficence proves to be somewhat deceptive. Each case that follows illuminates a different feature of beneficence and accentuates different issues.

## Case 1: Pediatric Ethics and Vulnerable Persons

Nurses who care for children and adolescents with serious illnesses know that the burden on parents is immeasurable. When parents are deciding on treatment plans for a child with a life-threatening illness, in asking about what is best for their child they want certainty. Yet sometimes the best available answers lack precision. Given that one of the worse possible things a parent can face — something almost unimaginable — is the possible death of a child, parents may respond by grasping for hope and miracles. Struggling to decide what is best for the child can be an ethical and emotional roller coaster. Parents search for the best outcome and the least suffering. Yet all the choices may well be tragic.

In the past decade consent legislation and nursing responsibilities regarding obtaining informed consent have changed. In many jurisdictions, there is no longer a legal age of consent. The test is whether the person understands and appreciates relevant information, options, and consequences of decisions, and makes the decision freely. This legal change demands that nurses in pediatric care settings must ensure that adolescents and even younger children who are able to make an informed decision — referred to as "mature minors" — have the opportunity to direct their care. In the following case, parents and the adolescent's treatment team disagreed on treatment plans. No doubt this case raises ethical tensions for nurses as parents, siblings, and caregivers.

*In November 1998, in Saskatchewan, a thirteen-year-old adolescent, Tyrell Dueck, was diagnosed with osteosarcoma (osteogenic sarcoma). Tyrell's cancer team at the Saskatoon cancer clinic recommended to his parents that their son have chemotherapy and that one leg be amputated. The parents' decision, based on their Christian fundamentalist beliefs, was to refuse the conventional treatment recommended. They wanted Tyrell to have the alternative therapies offered by a U.S. biologics clinic in Tijuana, Mexico. Tyrell's father asked the pediatric oncology clinic staff not to speak to Tyrell without his family present.*

*Dr. Christopher Mpofu, Tyrell's oncologist, said there was a 65 per cent chance of children diagnosed with osteosarcoma surviving if they received conventional cancer therapy. The parents' preferred alternative treatment plan had not been studied, and the response rates were unknown. Tyrell's parents refused a second opinion. The health care providers did not believe that his parents had given a coherent reason for refusal of the recommended treatment. Tyrell's cancer team thought his parents were not acting in their son's best interests. They challenged the parents' right to continue to be his decision-makers for treatment, and the issue went before the court. The Saskatchewan children's protective agency was granted guardianship of Tyrell with respect to health care decisions. Tyrell subsequently underwent two courses of chemotherapy. Then, in February 1999, Tyrell told his health care providers that he did not want further treatment. Once again the case returned to court. This time the question was whether or not Tyrell was a mature minor able to make his own health care decisions, and the court found him not to be a mature minor. In March 1999 Justice Allison Rothery ordered that Tyrell continue conventional cancer treatment.*

*By the time the legal issues were resolved, the cancer care team decided that it was too late for the conventional cancer treatment to help Tyrell. At this stage the best option for him was palliative care. Cancer had spread from his leg to his lungs. The prognosis was that he had only a few months to live. His parents resumed decision-making authority and took Tyrell to the Mexico clinic. The clinic and his family said the treatment was effective. Tyrell returned to his home, where he died in July 1999.*

## Commentary

The case was a lightning rod for those who think the family should always decide what is best for their child or children. This case can be compared to the well-known situations of Jehovah Witnesses who refuse blood transfusions for their children and young adolescents. The other way of looking at the case is that chemotherapy was imposed on the adolescent against the wishes of Tyrell and his parents.

The case can be reduced to one of the government overruling parents' beliefs and rights, or of health care providers denying hope to parents. But nurses need to be critical thinkers and probe beyond headlines and sound bites. The main conflict in this case is between the oncology team's desire and duty to do what they think is best for the patient, and the parents' duty and legal right to make decisions in the best interests of their son. The values in conflict are beneficence and respect for autonomy.

This case presents several important lessons to be learned about beneficence. First, nurses have a duty to respect patients' wishes that are based on their faith, ethnicity, and spiritual values. This duty requires them to respect patients' choices even when they think patients are not making the best choices. Still, certain conditions must be met in this regard. The person must understand and appreciate the relevant information and be allowed to decide freely. In short, the patient or parent has to be seen as capable of making valid decisions. However, when the transfer of parental values to children will clearly harm the children, nurses must advocate for the best interests of the child. Dependent children and young adolescents do not have the opportunity to decide if they want to accept, revise, or reject their parents' values. In short, children are not chattel (property) of the parents.

When treatment is refused or futile care requested for a child, the first question should be why. Nurses must explore the reasoning of parents and substitute decision-makers. Several questions must be answered. Did the parents receive adequate information? Did they understand the information, and were they allowed to decide freely? In Tyrell's case the clinical team did provide pertinent information, but it was unclear whether his parents appreciated the low probability of their son surviving without the recommended treatment. Their understanding of the proposed alternative treatment led to a different decision that they thought was justified and valid.

For many nurses the other way of looking at the case — that the chemotherapy and possibly an amputation be imposed against the wishes of the parents and the adolescent — raises questions about the extent of the government's authority to overrule parents' decisions. Nurses should ask whether paternalism was justified. Nurses know that beneficence is the foundation of the protection of vulnerable persons, a long-held tenet of our society. From the clinical staff's perspective, their motivation was to improve Tyrell's chance of survival. Given the gravity of the situation, challenges to the parents' decision-making were justified. The assessment of the nurses' ability to decide must be based on what is best for the child and not on an evaluation of the parents' religious and family values. The legal and ethical concept of *parens patria* requires that the government should act as a parent when vulnerable persons lack a guardian acting in their best interests. This concept is the basis of child protection laws. Given that Tyrell was not found to be a mature minor, the government agency was obligated to act paternalistically.

Tyrell was assessed to determine whether he could make his own decisions (a mature minor). The answer was no. He was found to have the capacity to decide on his treatment, but lacked an adequate understanding of his situation. The court's reasoning was that it removed the decision-making authority for treatment away from his parents and to a child protection agency as an attempt to reduce the serious risk of the boy dying if he did not swiftly receive conventional treatment.

This case received intense media attention. However, nurses working in pediatrics know that questions about capacity and consent and what is best for the child are not rare questions. There are several layers to this ethical reality. First of all, nurses practise in a diverse society — and in doing so they also represent the diversity of Canada. It is predictable that there will be disagreements based on values and ethnicity about following the Western, evidence-based approach to health care. Second, patient and family-focused care is fundamental to caring for children. Nurses and their peers must establish a collaborative, respectful alliance with families. Also, the understanding of just what a family is has evolved. In our diverse society, many people, including nurses, rely on alternative therapies that fall outside the mainstream, Western, evidence-based health care. It can only be expected that many people will place great hope on alternative and complementary therapies, and nurses have a duty to respect the wishes of these people. Still, when a hybrid approach poses harm to the patient, patients must be informed of the risks. Through education and dialogue nurses may find a compromise.

Nurses must adapt to the new environment for pediatric nursing. Furthermore, nurses must know and understand families' values and be aware of their own values. Nurses must reflect on their approaches to patients and parents who disagree with their recommendations. When nurses and patients agree, it is easier to make ethical decisions and act on these decisions. Conflicts are inevitable. The test is how conflicts are managed. At the system and unit level, ways of resolving ethical disagreements must be put in place and used. Self-reflection and tolerance are needed if nurses are to establish and maintain therapeutic relationships in the face of tensions and disagreements. Nurses, with their knowledge of the child and parents' worldviews, can play a vital role in conflict resolution.

The overriding focus must be on the well-being of the child. To fulfill this ethical obligation, nurses must help to ensure that parents and guardians have an understanding of their child's health problems and have all the necessary information.

### Case 2: "Don't Treat Me Like a Baby, Leave Me with Some Dignity!"

Nurses are committed to holistic caring and to a respect for how patients experience their health and illness. This ethical duty may be tested when patients make decisions that nurses believe are regrettable or imprudent, and that may lead to harming, not helping, the patient.

These kinds of problems are arising more frequently because nurses are exercising professional and ethical autonomy. Nurses are now entering the profession with an undergraduate degree. Many are studying in post-diploma courses. Experienced nurses want their expertise to be recognized. Thanks to their education and professional experience, nurses have the knowledge, judgement, and skill to assess patients and propose treatment. Many ethical problems arise because while nurses, patients, and families want the same end — the best interests of patients — they may disagree about the preferred treatment goals and treatment plan.

The promotion of patient choice has gained momentum in recent years. To assist nurses to use evidence-based practice and promote patients' well-being, the Registered Nurses Association of Ontario (RNAO) has developed guidelines for achieving "best practice" in patient-centred care and in establishing therapeutic relationships (RNAO, 2002, 2006). The documents include clinical recommendations about how to help patients to be informed and respected decision-makers. Yet there are times when nurses must stop and think, can I accept this decision? Can I provide the requested care? Can I agree to this refusal of treatment? These questions faced the nurses involved with one patient, Julia, who had a serious swallowing problem and had nevertheless decided on her own to continue to enjoy her favourite meals and drinks.

*Julia, aged forty, is a patient on a stroke unit. A massive stroke that she experienced a month ago was a major blow. She is known to be resilient and strong. For ten years she had been living independently, in her own home, with multiple sclerosis (MS). Now she needs help with all her daily activities, including eating meals. Her suffering, she says, has gone "off the Richter scale" because she has lost all independence. She remains mentally alert and communicates clearly. An assessment by a speech pathologist concludes that Julia cannot* swallow safely. An aphasic (soft food) diet is ordered. When the meal arrives, Julia is furious and says she will not eat the soft foods. She makes it clear that she understands that if she eats solid foods and drinks clear liquids she will have a higher chance of aspirating food. One risk is that she would develop aspiration pneumonia (the result of food travelling to her lungs). Another risk is that she may choke and die when eating regular food and drinks. Julia speaks to her nurses and makes it clear that she understands her situation and the possible choices and consequences of her decisions. She does not want to be treated if she develops pneumonia. If she aspirates, she does not want anyone to try to save her life. She refuses the soft diet.

Julia's rationale is that food, coffee, and the occasional glass of wine are among the few pleasures she has left in life. Furthermore, she feels that the soft diet reduces her to feeling like a baby. When being fed "baby food" she loses her dignity. She tried the soft diet and thickened fluids, and found them unpalatable. She rejects the advice that the diet is "not that bad" and that eventually patients get used to it.

Julia's partner, Michael, says that she has become unbalanced and is now a different person. Consequently, he believes that her wishes cannot be respected. Nurses ask for a mental health assessment of Julia's capacity to decide about nutrition and hydration. These analysts find that she is able to make her own decisions. Michael rejects their assessment. During this controversy, nurses are worried about whether they should help her with her meals. They are concerned that if Julia aspirates when they are helping her with a regular diet, they will be held responsible for her death. Her nurses believe that the best outcome would be for her to change her mind and adapt to the soft diet. They will only feed her soft foods.

Julia goes on a hunger strike. Michael insists that she be force-fed through a feeding tube.

## Commentary

The major ethical issue in this case is the conflict between the desires and opinions of Julia on one side and of Michael and her nurses on the other. Another layer to the case is the importance of food and beverages in our society. In this case, nutrition and hydration are a life-saving intervention. If Julia's hunger strike persists, she will die.

This case demonstrates that patients, families, and nurses are influenced by long-held values about what is a life worth living. Accepting and refusing food and water may have different emotional and ethical significance, depending on our ethnicity and traditions. Julia's nurses and Michael share the same values and wishes. They want to promote her well-being by reducing her risk of aspirating. They know that honouring Julia's request to have a regular diet will certainly increase her risk of dying from aspiration.

A first step is to decide whether Julia is capable of making this decision. She has demonstrated that she understands and appreciates her situation, her choices, and the consequences of her choices. She knows the moral significance of her decision and that she risks dying sooner rather than later. She knows that aspiration remains a risk with an aphasia diet, but that the risk is significantly reduced. The decision is also authentic. Julia has always enjoyed good meals, excellent coffee, and wines. Certainly no one is putting pressure on Julia to make this decision. Significantly, her ability to make decisions about nutrition and hydration was confirmed by a mental health team. Also, her wish is persistent.

Michael's position that his partner is not reasoning soundly and is irrational deserves consideration. "Rational" is a plastic term that can be code language for a patient who agrees with the clinical recommendations (see chapter 4). It is preferable to talk in terms of logical or understandable, as opposed to rational and reasonable. Julia can explain why she has made this decision. The act of disagreeing with nurses and their colleagues can carry the risk of being labelled irrational — but that is an unfair assessment. It is necessary to understand the reasons and values behind a decision. If asked, Julia would present her reasoning based on her non-negotiable principles in life: the minimum conditions for believing that her life is worth living.

Also to be considered is the position that Julia may be logical, informed, authentic, and not coerced, but that the decision itself demonstrates that she is not deliberating effectively. The case can be made that anyone who chooses danger over safety — or in this situation a high-risk option over a lower risk way of being fed — is being un-reasonable and irrational. However, in terms of respect for autonomy, there is a strong case to be made that Julia has deliberated effectively and that the decision is logical in terms of her experience of living with MS and now a stroke. The Best Practice Guidelines (BPG) regard-ing patient-centred care and establishing a therapeutic relationship (RNAO, 2002, 2006) recommends that nurses listen to patients, ac-knowledge that patients are experts on their own experience of living with illness, and that they control the management of their condition. Julia does understand and appreciate her condition, her options, and the result of her choice. She has explained that her life would not be worth living if she had to give up the few pleasures left to her — food, coffee, and wine. The decision is thus sound and logical for Julia, if not for her partner and nurses.

Philosophers Drane (1988) and also Culver and Gert (1990) studied the question of when and why capable people's wishes can be over-ruled. Their answer is that this can be done when the decision is un-reasonable and irrational: in other words, when people are making a choice that will bring serious harm to themselves, their decisions can be overruled. Obviously, libertarians would object to this stance and argue that decisions that will harm only the particular person in ques-tion should be permitted. But if the decision will harm another person, libertarians would agree on the need for paternalism. Some would say that Julia's decision will only harm herself. Others may argue that her decision will result in harm to Michael.

Times have changed. Nurses are sensitive to the possibility that uncooperative patients will be labelled incapable. The response to a nurse-patient conflict about treatment options is no longer to auto-matically find the patient incapable. Nurses no longer consider com-petency to be global, but instead, decision-specific and time-specific. In this case the question is whether or not Julia has the capacity to de-cide about nutrition and hydration and not other treatment decisions. Nurses have learned that case by case, patients must be assessed to find out if they have an understanding of their situation and their choices. Among nurses and colleagues, decisions about capacity and consent may generate heated debates about what patients understand and appreciate. This approach is preferable to rubber-stamping difficult or uncooperative patients as being incapable of making a decision. One criticism is that this approach is time-consuming and that rapid decisions are needed. While, indeed, it might be time-consuming, making a decision of this importance should be allowed to take whatever time is necessary; and an appeal process should be available. When life and limb are immediately at risk, staff must act more swiftly. But when prior wishes are known, those values must be respected.

This case opens the door to thinking about what would happen if Julia was found to lack the capacity to make treatment decisions. The assessment is a process. Nurses, who need to know their patients, can contribute to the assessment. Reasons for doubting her capacity would include a lack of understanding of her situation over a period of time. For example, Julia thinks the risks of eating solid foods are exaggerated. This belief may reflect a need for further education. When patients lose the capacity to decide, they have a legal option to appeal. If Julia's appeal is lost, Michael would become the substitute decision-maker. This is an unenviable and onerous responsibility.

His first duty is to respect Julia's wishes and values as expressed when capable. This advance directive can be a statement, but a legal document is preferable. Her prior wishes were known. Michael could reason that her wishes were made when she was not capable. The next step for Michael would be to decide what is in his partner's best interests. A number of questions can guide his decision-making in this regard — keeping in mind that using these four questions to decide what will benefit a patient is a complex matter.

First, will Julia's situation be improved by the treatment? The answer is unclear. If the treatment proceeds, Julia will doubtless want to remove the feeding tube. She will require chemical and physical restraints to stop her from doing so. She remains at risk for aspiration when force-fed by a feeding tube. There are also other risks that come with the use of physical and chemical restraints. She is at risk of developing bed sores, and being in restraints is humiliating. Will Julia's situation improve, or is it likely to improve without the treatment? The question can be reworded. If she is force-fed, will she do better than if she was allowed to remain on a hunger strike? When put in these terms, the answer is yes: yes, she will stop starving and in this sense her condition will improve. But health is more than physical well-being and sustenance. In terms of her mental and spiritual health, it is debatable whether her situation will improve when force-fed.

Second, will the expected benefits of having a feeding tube outweigh the expected risks of harm to Julia? To answer this question we need to compare benefits and risks. The moral math is difficult. On the plus side, Michael could argue that she will stop starving, receive nutrition, and reduce her risk of dying. He will be buying time. Julia may change her mind and accept a soft diet. Michael may add that he benefits because he will still have his partner. Julia can become stronger and will have the chance to become more independent. On the negative side, she may aspirate, need restraints, develop bed sores, feel humiliated, and find ways of sabotaging the intervention. Her relations with Michael and her nurses will deteriorate. For Michael, the benefits outweigh the possible harms, and these harms are real. For Julia, her life may not be worth living, from her perspective. The psychological harm would outweigh any benefit.

Third, is the proposed treatment of a feeding tube the least harmful, invasive, and restrictive treatment that meets the requirements? Julia has refused the less harmful, invasive, and restrictive intervention of accepting an aphasic diet. Before taking the drastic measure of force-feeding her, the medical staff itself could devote more time to understanding Julia's needs, values, and suffering. There is a conflict, and education, negotiations, and diplomacy at the bedside may lead to a compromise and resolution of the conflict.

Finally, following through with the decisions raises other ethical problems. It will be nurses who have to force-feed Julia. The nurses have already experienced moral distress when they fed her soft food and she pursed her lips and pleaded for them to stop. Force-feeding would increase their moral distress. If, when assisting her to eat regular food, Julia aspirated, the nurses would not be responsible for the outcome because they would be respecting her informed and freely made decision about how she wanted to live. Then too, they would require support to help them deal with the aftermath of witnessing the death of a patient — someone they might otherwise have helped.

### Case 3: The Good of One and the Good of Many

Traditionally nurses followed the ancient dictum, "First do no harm." Contrary to popular belief, the famous dictum is not in the Hippocratic Oath. It is often described as a Latin paraphrase, by Galen, of a Hippocratic saying. But no specific mention in Galen's writings has been found. The closest approximation to the phrase that can be found in the Hippocratic Corpus is "to help, or at least to do no harm," taken from Epidemics, Book. I, Section V.

For modern nursing, the ethical priority is respect for autonomy and patient choice. Nurses have come to reject paternalism and to work collaboratively with patients. Respecting values and wishes and supporting what is best for patients and society can create ethical problems for nurses. By respecting patients' choices, nurses may not be supporting what they think is best for patients. Changes to consent and capacity legislation have put respect for informed consent above acting in what nurses consider to be their patient's best interest. This shift in ethical priorities is seen in nursing standards and best practice guidelines about how to help patients direct their own care. The ethical duty remains to advance the well-being of patients and reduce their exposure to harm.

Also, traditionally nurses thought about doing good in terms of the patients under their care. Ethical guidelines focused on the one-to-one relationship with patients. But in this regard a major shift has occurred in nursing education and practice. Nursing students are learning that patients cannot be separated from their support network and community. Given the reorganization of patient care and increased focus on health promotion, more nurses are employed in the community. In this new environment nurses find that promoting health and reducing harm require different interpretations of what it means to act in the best interests of patients. Consequently, nurses must practise at the individual and system levels. For example, nurses who provide care to homeless persons living on the streets and in hostels also advocate for affordable housing and safe shelters. Community and public health nurses who help vulnerable and marginalized persons base their practice on a philosophy of harm reduction. Their peers, community members, and politicians may receive these programs warmly; but it is also possible that nurses may meet fierce opposition when assisting stigmatized individuals and communities.

Vancouver's Downtown Eastside, with a population of 16,000, has become well-known for its economic, social, and health problems. The grim area is known for illegal drug use, poverty, homelessness, and unsafe streets. In 2000 the number of injection drug users (IDUs) living in Downtown Eastside was estimated at 4,700. Intravenous drug use is a very high-risk activity. In British Columbia illicit drug use is the leading cause of death for adults aged thirty to forty-nine years. In new cases of HIV, IDUs account for 26 per cent of the cases. Users who meet on the streets to inject drugs are at increased risk of exposure to blood-borne infections because they share equipment (Kerr & Palepu, 2001). Another group at risk, Aboriginal IDUs, are becoming HIV-positive at twice the rate of non-Aboriginal IDUs (Craib et al., 2003).

The INSITE Clinic in Vancouver's Eastside opened as a pilot project to respond to the needs of injection drug users. The Vancouver Coastal Health Authority (VCH) established the clinic under section 56 of the Controlled Drugs and Substances Act. Health Canada provided the VCH with funds to evaluate the service, and VCH contracted with the BC Centre for Excellence on HIV/AIDS to undertake the evaluation. INSITE has been subject to rigorous, independent third-party research and evaluation by the BC Centre for Excellence, which is recognized as one of the world's leading research organizations. The Centre's research has been published in peer-reviewed journals, including the New England Journal of Medicine, British Medical Journal, Canadian Medical Association Journal, and The Lancet.

Results include:
- INSITE's work has led to an increased uptake into detoxification programs and addiction treatment.
- INSITE has not led to an increase in drug-related crime: rates of arrest for drug trafficking, assaults, and robbery remained roughly on the same level after the facility's opening, and rates of vehicle break-ins/theft declined significantly.

- *INSITE has reduced the number of people injecting in public and the amount of injection-related litter in the Downtown Eastside.*
- *INSITE is attracting the highest-risk users — those more likely to be vulnerable to HIV infection and overdose, and who were contributing to problems of public drug use and unsafe syringe disposal.*
- *INSITE has reduced the overall rates of needle-sharing in the community; and among those who used the supervised injection site for some, most, or all of their injections, 70 per cent were less likely to report syringe sharing.*
- *Nearly one-third of INSITE users received information relating to safer injecting practices. Those who received help injecting from fellow injection drug users on the streets were more than twice as likely to have received safer injecting education at INSITE.*
- *INSITE is not increasing rates of relapse among former drug users, nor is it a negative influence on those seeking to stop drug use.*

*Significant increased rates of HIV are attributed to IDUs (from 9.1 per cent prior to 1995 to 29.2 per cent in 1998) (Health Canada, 2001). In Canada 46.8 per cent of all new HIV cases involve addicts and IDUs (Health Canada, 2001), and 70 per cent of all new Hepatitis C virus (HCV) infections are related to the sharing of drug paraphernalia.*

*The nurses and other health care professionals employed at INSITE are providing a safe, health-focused clinic in which patients can inject drugs safely and under supervision. Users on the street can enter the storefront clinic and find cubicles where they can take drugs using clean equipment. They find nurses who offer help with their complex health and social problems. Patients can get access to the Vancouver network of social and health services at the clinic. The clinic operates at full capacity, with over 8,000 people using the facility to inject drugs. Since its doors opened the clinic has provided more than 220,000 clean injections, at an average of more than six hundred visits a day. About 80 per cent of those daily visits are for injecting drugs. The remaining 20 per cent are for support* services. Nurses encourage users to seek counselling and treatment. The result has been an increased use of treatment programs, including detoxification services.

Many local and provincial residents and politicians clearly see the benefits of the INSITE Clinic, but it also faces strong opposition. Critics argue that the clinic staff condone and promote drug use and illegal behaviours. Opponents instead endorse policies that criminalize drug sellers and users, promote abstinence, and offer rehabilitation to intravenous drug users. According to this approach, clinicians employed at the clinic violate their ethical duties to do no harm. The federal Ministry of Health made plans to close the clinic, but after public appeals it extended the pilot project. How should health care workers respond to these concerns?

## Commentary

The philosophy of harm reduction provides a starting point for this case. The program is based on a Four Pillars Approach of Prevention, Treatment, Enforcement, and Harm Reduction (City of Vancouver, 2004). Harm reduction strategies are in IDUs' best interests when cessation and abstinence are not realistic or immediate goals. The patients live in poverty, are often homeless, have chronic health problems, and typically cannot find appropriate health care. Some patients have entered the sex trade to support their addiction. Others may turn to stealing and violence to obtain drugs. IDUs avoid encounters with health care providers, for good reasons (Griffiths, 2002). They may encounter judgmental attitudes, receive inadequate services, and risk arrest.

INSITE does not permit the sharing of drugs and needles. It supplies condoms to promote safe sexual practices. Also, nurses reduce risk and promote well-being when they respond to the serious health issues that are common to IDUs, such as abscesses, infection, vascular damage, poor nutrition, endocarditis, perinatal infection, mental health problems, and death. The clinic has reduced the risks and harms associated with IV drug use, including needle sharing, improper syringe disposal, and unprotected sex (Wood et al., 2006).

IDUs need treatment, but typically find it extremely difficult to obtain. The barriers include risk of arrest, further stigmatization, and lack of access to rehabilitation programs. At INSITE, nurses can link IDUs with the network of health services offered by the Greater Vancouver Health Authority. Users are offered education, employment training and jobs, supportive and transitional housing, and accessible health care. At the clinic patients find outpatient and peer-based counselling, methadone programs, daytime and residential treatment, housing support, and ongoing clinical care (MacPherson, 2001). The prevention of drug use requires long-term planning, integrated with outreach, education, and political action directed at the root causes of this problem. At-risk communities need to make prevention a priority.

Enforcement, the third pillar, is about responding to the community's and city's need for peace and quiet, public order, and safety. Legal reform is needed to create a regulatory system for illegal drugs to increase control of harmful substances and limit activities that organized criminals have over their distribution and sale. Police may direct resources toward fighting organized crime, drug-dealing, drug houses, and businesses involved in the drug trade. Law enforcement officers have partnerships with health services and agencies that offer harm reduction and treatment programs. Safe injection sites are not only effective in decreasing the spread of HIV and HCV, but also increase the safety of the community by decreasing crime. In turn there is a reduced burden on the criminal justice system and a decrease in the ineffective use of correctional services. Arrest and sentencing do not address the health problems of persons with substance abuse problems. The prison experience limits the availability of and access to rehabilitation programs, and incarceration increases the exposure to high-risk behaviours. Ironically, people who think IDUs are socially unacceptable persons who should be punished have reason to support the clinic. Enlightened self-interest can lead them to the logical conclusion that, compared to the criminalization of IDUs, harm reduction has a greater benefit for them and society.

Harm reduction benefits the one and the many and is grounded in the ethical principle of beneficence. Outcomes for individuals include a decrease in overdose deaths, HIV, and other infections (Fischer et al., 2006). INSITE users rate the services as highly satisfactory. The staff is perceived to be helpful, trustworthy, and respectful. Nurses have successfully helped over three hundred persons with overdose events, and no overdose deaths have occurred at the clinic. At the community, city, and provincial levels, there are also benefits: a reduced public use of drugs and decrease in community complaints about public drug use; reduced costs to health care and to the criminal justice system (Wood et al., 2006); and savings for emergency services because managing overdoses at the clinic proves to be less costly. In that event the emergency medical services are not called, the overdosed person is not rushed to a busy emergency room, and an admission may be averted.

Advocates can also appeal to reasons of justice to support the clinic. If the clinic is closed, drug users will be denied access to needed health care. In 2008 Mr. Justice Ian Pitfield released his ruling permitting Vancouver's Supervised Injection Site to remain open for another year (*PHS Community Services v. Attorney General of Canada*, 2008). Judge Pitfield asked that key sections of the Controlled Drugs and Substance Act be repealed on the grounds that they are unconstitutional. He reasoned that addicts' rights under section 7 of the Charter of Rights and Freedoms to life, liberty, and security of person are violated when needed health services are not provided. Given that only 5 per cent of the local addicts come to INSITE and the clinic is at full capacity, the lack of access is already an ethical problem. Removing legal barriers and opening more harm reduction clinics ought to be the ethical imperative.

Arguments that harm reduction programs are unethical because the staff support unhealthy and illegal behaviours do not, then, stand on solid ground. Indeed, the lessons of this case can be applied to many areas of nursing. Often remission and cure of illness are not possible. When nurses help patients cope with chronic conditions, this is a form of harm reduction. For example, when cancer patients cannot benefit from aggressive treatment, nurses offer palliative care — the goal of which is to reduce suffering and harm and promote comfort. The philosophy of harm reduction is the foundation of many well-received public health programs. Notable examples that have been easier for the public and politicians to accept are reduction of childhood obesity, smoking cessation, and safer-sex education programs. Programs such as these support the ethical imperative of beneficence while providing for the good of one and the good of many.

## Conclusion

The health good of patients is rightly regarded as a matter of primary concern for those who are trusted with the duty to promote health and provide health care. In this chapter, we have seen that caring for others in a manner befitting their profession poses considerable challenges for nurses. In some cases there may be uncertainty about how much giving and caring beneficence requires of the nurse. In other cases there may be uncertainty or disagreement about which course of action will be the most beneficial. In yet other cases, the commitment to the good of an individual may be in conflict with the commitment to the good of others.

Even when the requirements of beneficence are relatively clear to the nurse, other ethical issues may arise when other values are also at stake in the situation. The patient's values and wishes may be incompatible with the nurse's values, or with the plan of care the nurse believes to be most beneficial. In such situations, the nurse must weigh concern for the patient's health good against respect for the patient's autonomy or right to choose. Unchecked, the nurse's commendable desire to do good can easily slide into paternalism. Ethics may not forbid paternalism, but at the very least it requires that one be prepared to give justifications if one puts the patient's autonomy second to the patient's good.

## Notes

1   The word "benevolence" is closely related in meaning to beneficence, but whereas beneficence has to do with *good deeds or acts,* benevolence has to do with *good wishes or intentions.* Reeder (1982) distinguishes the two as follows: "Benevolence, as I use it, names a disposition to desire and act so as to increase good and decrease evil for human beings; beneficence signifies a principle or ideal of conduct" (p. 83).

2   The rhetoric of caring, particularly as "caring" is set against "curing," has been called into question. For example, see Diers (1988) and Levine (1989).

3   A more complete discussion of various means by which duty can be grounded or derived is given in Abrams (1982).

4   Jameton (1984, pp. 214-216) analyzes this issue with reference to the concept of justice.

5    In answering this question, one must also consider the possibility of "burn-out," for if this happens the nurse will not be much good to anyone.

6    Jameton (1984, p. 216) suggests that the nurse consider several points before undertaking personal risk, such as the degree and urgency of patient need as weighed against the gravity of the risk as *assessed realistically*. This is good advice, especially when one considers issues that have arisen in connection with Acquired Immunodeficiency Syndrome (AIDS) and often exaggerated concerns about personal risks in caring for people with AIDS. For a discussion of the rights and responsibilities of nurses caring for persons with HIV, see Yeo (1995).

7    Debra Shogan (1988) expresses the same distinction in terms of "caring about" and "caring for." She points out:

> One can care for (tend to) someone or something and not care about the person or thing and one can care about someone or something and not care for (tend to) it. Those in the 'helping professions,' for example, tend to (care for) others as part of their work responsibilities; they may not care about these people, although often they do. (pp. 7-8)

Buchanan (1982, pp. 35-36) also has an insightful discussion of these two aspects of beneficence.

8    This definition has since been updated (see Spasoff et al., 1987, p. 1).

9    For a discussion of a definition of health that has been very influential in Canadian nursing, see Kravitz and Frey (1989).

10   Shogan (1988, p. 17), for example, restricts beneficence to include only concern for the welfare of others, and uses the term "caring" to encompass concern for the other in a broader and more inclusive sense.

## References

Abrams, N. (1982). Scope of beneficence in health care. In E.E. Shelp (Ed.), *Beneficence and health care* (pp. 183-198). Dordrecht, Holland: D. Reidel.

American Nurses' Association. (2008). *Code for nurses with interpretive statements*. Kansas City.

Beauchamp, T.L., & Childress, J.F. (2001). *Principles of biomedical ethics* (5th. ed.). New York: Oxford University Press.

Benner, P. (Ed.). (1994). *Interpretive phenomenology: Embodiment, caring and ethics in health and illness*. Thousand Oaks, CA: Sage.

Benner, P. (2001). *From novice to expert: Excellence and power in clinical nursing practice* (Commemorative Edition). Englewood Cliffs, NJ: Prentice Hall.

Benner, P., & Phillips, S. (Eds.). (1994). *The crisis in care: Affirming and restoring caring practices in the helping professions*. Washington, D.C.: Georgetown University Press.

Benner, P., Tanner, C., & Chesla, C. (1996). *Expertise in nursing: Caring, clinical judgment and ethics*. New York: Springer.

Benner, P., Hooper-Kyriakides, P., & Stannard, D. (1998). *Clinical wisdom and interventions in critical care: A thinking-in-action approach*. Philadelphia: Saunders.

Benner, P., & Wruebel, J. (1989). *The primacy of caring: Stress and coping in health and illness*. Menlo Park, CA: Addison-Wesley.

British Columbia Court. (2008). Judge I. Pitfield. *Community Services v. Attorney General of Canada*. BCSC661.

Buchanan, A.E. (1982). Philosophical foundations of beneficence. In E.E. Shelp (Ed.), *Beneficence and health care* (pp. 33-62). Dordrecht, Holland: D. Reidel.

Callahan, D. (1973). The WHO definition of "health." *Hastings Center Studies* 1 (3), 77-87.

Canadian Community Epidemiology Report on Drug Use. (2003). *National Report, 2002*.

Canadian Medical Association. (2004). *Code of ethics for Registered Nurses*. Ottawa.

Canadian Nurses Association. (2005). Fact sheet. Legislation and Regulation: An introduction to *the Nursing Act, 1991*. Ottawa.

Canadian Nurses Association. (2008). *Code of ethics for nursing*. Ottawa.

City of Vancouver. Four Pillars Drug Strategy. (2004). <http://city.vancouver.bc.ca/fourpillars/fs_fourpillars.htm>.

College of Nurses of Ontario (CNO). (2002). *Professional standards*. Toronto.

College of Nurses of Ontario. (2005). *Practice standard: Infection prevention and control*. Toronto.

College of Nurses of Ontario. (2006). *Practice standard: Therapeutic nurse-client relationship*. Toronto.

College of Nurses of Ontario. (2009). *Practise standard: Ethics*. Originally published March 1999 as "Ethical framework." Toronto.

Craib, K.J.P., Spittal, P.M., Wood, E., Laliberte, N., Hogg, R.S., Li, K., Heath, K., Tyndall, M.W., O'Shaughnessy, M.V., & Schechter, M.T. (2003). Risk factors for elevated HIV incidence among Aboriginal injection drug users in Vancouver. *Canadian Medical Association Journal*, 168 (1), 19-24.

Culver, C., & Gert. B. (1990). *Philosophy in medicine: Conceptual and ethical issues in medicine and psychiatry*. New York: Oxford University Press.

Diers, D. (1988). On clinical scholarship — again. *Image: Journal of Nursing Scholarship* 20 (1), 2.

Doig, C., & Burgess, E. (2000). Withholding life-sustaining treatment: Are adolescents competent to make these decisions? *Canadian Medical Association Journal*, May 30, 162 (11).

Drane, J.F. (1988). The many faces of competency. In R.B. Edwards & G.C. Graber (Eds.), *Bioethics* (pp. 169-177). San Diego: Harcourt Brace Jovanovich.

Dworkin, G. (1971). Paternalism. In R.A. Wasserstrom (Ed.), *Morality and the law* (pp. 107-126). Belmont, CA: Wadsworth.

Edwards, S. (2002). Defining new boundaries. *Nursing Standard* 17 (2).

Faden, R., Beauchamp, T., & King, N. Foundations in moral theory. In F. Baylis, J. Downie, B. Hoffmaster, & S. Sherwin (Eds.), *Health care ethics in Canada* (2nd ed.). Toronto: Thomson-Nelson.

Fischer, B., Popova, S., Rehm, J., & Ivsins, A. (2006). Drug-related overdose deaths in British Columbia and Ontario, 1992-2004. *Canadian Journal of Public Health* 97 (5), 384-387.

Gadow, S.A. (1985). Nurses and patient: The caring relationship. In A.H. Bishop & J.R. Scudder Jr. (Eds.), *Caring, curing, coping: Nurse, physician, patient relationships* (pp. 31-43). Birmingham: University of Alabama Press.

Gadow, S. (2003). Restorative nursing: toward a philosophy of postmodern punishment. *Nursing Philosophy*, July 4 (2), 161-167.

Gordon, S., Benner, P., & Noddings, N. (Eds). (1996). *Caregiving: Readings in knowledge, practice, ethics, and politics*. Philadelphia: University of Pennsylvania Press.

Griffiths, H. (2002). Dr. Peter Centre: removing barriers to health care services. *Canadian Nursing* 34, 5-10.

Health Canada. (2001). *Harm reduction and injection drug use: an international comparative study of contextual factors influencing the development and implementation of relevant policies and programs*. Toronto.

Jameton, A.L. (1984). *Nursing practice: The ethical issues*. Englewood Cliffs, NJ: Prentice-Hall.

Jamiesan, E.M., Sewall, M.E., & Suhrie, E.B. (1966). *Trends in nursing history: Their social, international and ethical relationships*. Philadelphia: W.B. Saunders.

Kerr, T., & Palepu, A. (2001). Safe injection facilities in Canada: Is it time? *Canadian Medical Association Journal* 165 (4), 436-437.

Kondro, W. (2007). Conservative government scuttles needle exchange. *Canadian Medical Association Journal* 176 (3), 308.

Kravitz, M., & Frey, M.A. (1989). The Allen nursing model. In J.J. Fitzpatrick & A.L. Whall (Eds.), *Conceptual models of nursing: Analysis and applications* (2nd ed., pp. 313-329). East Norwalk, CT: Appleton & Lange.

Levine, M. (1989). The ethics of nursing research. *Image: Journal of Nursing Scholarship* 21 (1), 4-6.

MacPherson, D. (2001). A framework for action: A four pillars approach to drug problems in Vancouver. <http://vancouver.ca/fourpillars/>.

Mangham, C. (2001). Harm reduction and illegal drugs: The real debate. *Canadian Journal of Public Health* 92 (3), 204-205.

Mitika, M. (2003). Office-based primary care physicians called on to treat the "new" addict. *Journal of the American Medical Association* 290 (6), 735-736.

Pauly, B., Goldstone, I., McCall, J., Gold, F., & Payne, S. (2007). The ethical, legal and social context of harm reduction. *The Canadian Nurse* 103 (8), 19-23.

Pellegrino, E.D., & Thomasma, D.C. (1988). *For the patient's good: The restoration of beneficence in health care*. New York: Oxford University Press.

Reeder, J.P. Jr. (1982). Beneficence, supererogation, and role duty. In E.E. Shelp (Ed.), *Beneficence and health care* (pp. 83-108). Dordrecht, Holland: D. Reidel.

Registered Nurses Association of Ontario (RNAO). (2002). *Best practice guidelines: Client centred care*. Toronto.

Registered Nurses Association of Ontario. (2006). *Best practice guidelines: Establishing therapeutic relationships*. Toronto.

Shelp, E.E. (1982). To benefit and respect persons: A challenge for beneficence in health care. In E.E. Shelp (Ed.), *Beneficence and health care* (pp. 199-222). Dordrecht, Holland: D. Reidel.

Shogan, D.A. (1988). *Care and moral motivation*. Toronto: OISE Press.

Spasoff, R.A., Cole, P., Dale, F., Korn, D., Manga, P., Marshall, V., Picherack, F., Shosenberg, N., & Zon, L. (1987). *Health for all Ontario: Report of the panel on health goals for Ontario*. Toronto.

Stoltz, J., Wood, E., Small, W., Li, K., Tyndall, M., Montaner, J., & Kerr, T. (2007). Changes in injecting practices associated with the use of a medically supervised safer injection facility. *Journal of Public Health* 29 (1), 35-39.

University of Toronto, Joint Centre for Bioethics. (2005). *Stand on guard for thee: Ethical considerations in preparedness planning for pandemic influenza*. Toronto.

Veatch, R. (2000). *The basics of bioethics*. Upper Saddle River, NJ: Prentice Hall.

Wainberg, M.A. (2006). The need to promote public health in the field of illicit drug use. *Canadian Medical Association Journal* 175 (11), 1395.

Watson, J. (1979). *Nursing: The philosophy and science of caring*. Boston: Little, Brown, and Company.

Watson, J. (Ed.). (1994). *Applying the art and science of human caring*. New York: NLN.

Watson, J. (1999). *Postmodern nursing and beyond*. New York: Churchill Livingstone.

Watson, J. (2002). *Instruments for assessing and measuring caring in nursing and health sciences*. New York: Springer.

Watson, J. (2005). *Caring science as sacred science.* Philadelphia: F.A. Davis.

Wood, E. (2008). Bevel up for nursing and medical students. Review. *Canadian Medical Association Journal* 179 (4), 348-349.

Wood, E., Tyndall, M., Spittal, P., Li, K., et al. (2001). Unsafe injection practices in a cohort of injection drug users in Vancouver: Could safer injecting rooms help? *Canadian Medical Association Journal* 165 (4), 405-410.

Wood, E., Tyndall, M., Montaner, J., & Kerr, T. (2006). Summary of findings from the evaluation of a pilot medically supervised safer injecting facility. *Canadian Medical Association Journal* 175, 1399-1404.

Yeo, M. (1995). Emergency Department's personnel's safety vs. a duty to treat. In K.V. Iserson, A.B. Sanders, & D. Mathieu (Eds.), *Ethics in emergency medicine* (2nd ed., pp. 406-412). Tucson, AZ: Galen Press.

# Study Questions: Beneficence

## Case 1: Pediatric Ethics and Vulnerable Persons

1. Define the term "mature minor." Why was Tyrell found not to be a mature minor?

2. Nurses play a major role in helping children and their parents understand complex health information. They must be careful to educate and inform and not persuade or coerce. In this case, how would you educate Tyrell's parents and manage the conflict about what is best for their son?

3. If the case was changed to a situation of Jehovah's Witness parents refusing a life-sustaining blood product to their child, explain how you would feel toward the parents and why. Then decide on the decisions you think are justified in such a case.

4. If you had the opportunity to talk to parents refusing proposed care on the basis of what you consider to be weak reasons, how would you approach the topic with them? Bear in mind that your obligation is to advance the best interests of the child.

5. Consider how you would respond if you agreed with Tyrell's parents. What would you say to your peers and to his parents?

## Case 2: "Don't Treat Me Like a Baby, Leave Me with Some Dignity!"

1. *The Best Practice Guideline: Establishing Therapeutic Relationships* recommends that nurses have self-awareness of their values and self-knowledge about the origin of their values. Eating and food are associated with family, cultural, and religious values. What are your values about food, hydration, and what makes your life worth living? How did you come to have these values?

2. Ethical reasoning requires sound descriptive analysis. Julia needs to compare the probability of aspiration if she has a regular diet versus the risk of aspiration when being fed through a tube. Julia needs this information to make an informed decision. Find recent research on this question and, based on that research, discuss the benefits and risks of both options.

3. Decide whether or not you think Julia's wish should be respected, and why. Discuss this, considering under what circumstances Julia's wishes should be overruled.

4. Julia and the stroke team believed that they should consider what would benefit Julia and her partner, not only Julia. Do you think that Julia's best interests should be their sole concern?

5. When deciding if a decision should be respected, do you agree with these approaches or not? Why?

   a) The patient has to demonstrate that she or he had reached a decision based on an understanding and appreciation of the relevant information. No matter what the decision, it must be respected.

   b) The litmus test is the final decision. A decision that will result in serious harm to the patient cannot have been based on a sound understanding of the relevant information.

6. Imagine that you are caring for Julia and she is being nourished by a feeding tube every four hours. When you go to start the infusion, she tries to stop you. You know you have an order to restrain her. How would you feel in this situation? What would you say and do?

**Case 3: The Good of One and the Good of Many**

**Class activities.** You may want to have a debate with representatives of different groups presenting their case.

1. You are an intravenous drug user who uses the INSITE Clinic. Explain why the harm reduction program benefits you.

2. You are a nurse employed at INSITE. Explain why your practice is based on the ethical values of nurses.

3. You are the mayor of Vancouver. Explain why you support the continuation of the INSITE Clinic in terms of the benefit for the city and province.

4. You are a politician who thinks the INSITE clinic should be closed. The clinic promotes and condones illegal and harmful behaviours. The staff members are enablers of drug users.

5. You live in the Lower Eastside neighbourhood. You want the clinic closed. You want the IDUs arrested. Years ago the neighbourhood was a good place to live in. Now property values are very low. The streets are often unsafe. The war on drugs policy should be put in place so you can have a safe community again.

# 4 AUTONOMY

*The only freedom which deserves the name is that of pursuing our own good, in our own way, so long as we do not attempt to deprive others of theirs, or impede their efforts to obtain it.*

—J.S. MILL, *ON LIBERTY*

---

*Autonomy means self-determination — the right to make independent decisions concerning your own life and well-being. When a patient's exercise of autonomy is at odds with health goals, health professionals — educated and oriented primarily toward restoring, maintaining, and preserving health — may be tempted to resist that autonomy in one way or another. Under what conditions is it justifiable to impede or restrict a patient's autonomy? Issues of autonomy can be complicated when uncertainty exists as to whether or not the patient is mentally competent to assess various treatments or procedures and to give a properly informed consent.*

*The cases in this chapter discuss caring for vulnerable patients, consent in the research context, and end of life decision-making.*

---

## The Nature of Autonomy

In the past, health care professionals, and physicians in particular, were entrusted with broader authority for decision-making in health care than they are today. Often the wishes of the patient were not solicited, and even if known were sometimes ignored. Frequently information was withheld or presented in a misleading way to avoid causing the patient worry or harm. The early development of nursing as an adjunct to medical care made nurses partners in these practices. Nurses educated a generation or more ago will recall that as students they were instructed not to give patients such basic information as temperature, blood pressure, or even the name of a medication. Such practices — which today are quite shocking — were supported and rationalized through the paternalistic notion that "the doctor knows best." The nurse was expected to passively follow physicians' orders.

However understandable the motivation behind this paternalism, it is no longer acceptable today. Patients have come to expect greater autonomy, and respect for autonomy has become prominently enshrined in the codes of ethics of the various health professions.

Autonomy means self-rule or self-determination. In its original construction, the term had a predominantly political meaning. A political state would be autonomous only if it determined its own laws. A state would not be autonomous if, like a colony, it was ruled by another state and governed by laws that came from the outside. At the level of the individual, people are autonomous to the extent that they act on the basis of laws or rules that they set for themselves, recognize as reasonable, or at least voluntarily submit to. Children are not autonomous to the extent that they lack the maturity of reason to govern themselves; until they reach the age of maturity they are subject to rules unilaterally laid down by parental authorities.[1]

Over time, and especially in health care settings, the term "autonomy" has come to be used in several different senses or meanings, which are often confused. Indeed, arguments about issues rooted in autonomy will be at cross-purposes if different people have in mind different meanings of the concept. To help clarify things, we can distinguish four main meanings of autonomy in health care contexts: (1) autonomy as free action; (2) autonomy as effective deliberation; (3) autonomy as authenticity; and (4) autonomy as moral reflection.[2]

## 1. Autonomy as Free Action

A common meaning of autonomy, both in health care situations and more generally throughout society, rests in the sense of "free action" — a meaning similar to the concept of liberty. It means being able to do what you want to do or, conversely, not being forced to do what you do not want to do. Your autonomy in this sense is diminished when something or someone forms an obstacle to your liberty.

Health problems can present an obstacle or impediment insofar as they reduce or compromise your abilities or powers. Someone who has had a stroke may no longer have the freedom to complete mental and physical activities that were once taken for granted. An elderly person living with chronic arthritis of the hip may become considerably less independent despite working with health professionals to maintain and regain diminished abilities in the activities of daily living. The limitation of freedom is different in cases in which choice is limited or restricted by someone in a position of authority. Healthy elderly persons who want to go for a walk can put on their coat and walk outside. A young child who wants to go outside for a walk has to ask for permission from a parent or guardian, who, for one reason or other, may say no or otherwise curtail the child's freedom.

In a health care setting, administrators and health care professionals can deprive patients of freedom in a number of circumstances. Schedules, policies, and practices can interfere with patients making meaningful choices. Residents of long-term care facilities who try to maintain lifelong habits and preferences run the risk of being labelled "difficult" and of having uneasy relationships with nurses and care aides — people they rely on to meet their basic needs. When patients are heavily dependent, nurses need to be especially sensitive to finding ways of supporting their autonomy, respecting their choices. Nurses sometimes also need to work for changes in institutional practices and policies that thwart patients' desire to maintain or gain more control over their lives.

A controversial way in which liberty is constrained in health care settings is through the practice of using physical restraints on patients' arms and legs, and around their waists. The use of physical restraints is widespread, although the majority of health facilities today have a policy of using the least restrictive kind of restraint needed to provide a safe environment for the patient.[3] Mental health hospitals and many long-term care facilities use a secure unit to prevent involuntarily detained patients or patients with dementia from freely leaving. Medications, such as sedatives, provide another form of restraint, which is referred to as chemical restraint.

The use of restraints or limitations of autonomy in the basic sense of liberty or free action are often justified by the argument that the patient is not sufficiently autonomous (in another sense of the term, discussed in the next section) to live safely without supervision and containment in a secure area. In too many instances, staff employ physical and chemical restraints as alternatives to dealing with patients at risk of falling or wandering; they do this rather than addressing the reasons for restlessness and risk of falling. When individual patients pose a serious risk of harm to themselves or others, and interventions to avoid restraints have been tried and found wanting, restraint can be justified even if the patients are considered to be competent.

Whenever restraints are used, there must be frequent review of the situation with the aim of discontinuing their use as soon as possible (College of Nurses of Ontario, 2009). Staff must use seclusion only to reduce the risk of harm to the patient and others. Seclusion must never be used to "teach" patients or punish undesirable behaviours.

## 2. Autonomy as Effective Deliberation

Autonomy in the simple sense of "freedom to act" leaves open to question the quality of the decision to act. A quite different sense of autonomy — autonomy as effective deliberation — concerns the quality of the reasoning process by which a person makes decisions. If the reasoning is seriously flawed or compromised, the resulting decision is not autonomous in this sense.

Effective deliberation presupposes two main requirements: knowledge and reasoning ability. To deliberate effectively, the person must be able to understand and appreciate:

- his or her situation;

- relevant information;

- the risks, detriments, and benefits of various options; and

- the logical relationship between the options under consideration and the end or outcome that he or she wants to attain.

When they evaluate any deliberation, nurses should consider whether the means of action chosen are consistent with the end or outcome desired. The evaluation includes deciding whether the person has erred in the process of deliberation. It is crucial to decide if the person arrived at the decision through a process of reasoning that is at least minimally rational. The question of what counts as "rational" is key to this sense of autonomy. For sure, the litmus test of rationality is not being "co-operative" and agreeing with the clinical team. Such labelling of patients should be avoided, yet unfortunately the habit persists. Patients labelled as difficult, troublemakers, and different should not be assumed to be irrational. What is critical is the integrity of the thought process, which can be compromised by several factors.

Lack of relevant information or incorrect information about one's condition or about treatment options is one factor that can compromise or impede effective deliberation. Increasingly, people are using the Internet to obtain information about their health conditions and treatment options. Nurses play a major role in helping patients obtain and understand information pertinent to their treatment decisions and their health-related choices, thus promoting effective deliberation. For example, in the case of someone suffering from terminal brain cancer who has expressed the goal of dying peacefully and with as much dignity as possible, it is crucial to provide correct, clearly stated information about the palliative care options. Otherwise the patient might refuse a certain palliative treatment, believing that it will only prolong life and work counter to his or her desired goals.

Even when a person has reliable and adequate information, the reasoning process itself can be impaired by other factors. Cognitive functioning can be diminished by dementia, mental illness, and acquired brain injury. Someone who has had a major head injury could lose the capacity to problem-solve simple mental tasks and may not be able to make decisions on complicated surgical options. Capacity to decide may be temporarily compromised by intoxication, medications, or strong emotions.

Still, a person with a mental illness such as clinical depression or schizophrenia does not necessarily lack the capacity to deliberate effectively. Each patient must be carefully assessed. For example, a mature minor is an adolescent who can reason effectively at a young age. However, the capacity to reason develops over time; children and adolescents differ in the pace at which this capacity develops. Moreover, young children may have the capacity to decide whether or not to have orange juice or milk, but a decision about whether or not to have an immunization may be beyond their reasoning capacity.

Autonomy as effective deliberation is probably the most important sense of autonomy in health care settings and underpins the doctrine of informed consent. Assessing effective deliberation requires assessing capacity or competency to make decisions. We discuss the process of capacity assessment in detail in a later section.

## 3. Autonomy as Authenticity

Autonomy as authenticity involves the relationship between a given choice of action and a person's total being or character. Is the choice expressed consistent with the settled dispositions, values, and character of the person? Does it express who the person really is in some deep and abiding sense? Or is the choice something of an anomaly, perhaps less an expression of the person's true self than of some momentary influence?

Pain, sickness, and suffering may constitute a major assault and cause someone to behave "out of character." In such circumstances, the person's expressed wish may be less an expression of character than a response to experiencing pain or sickness. Such experiences can compromise autonomy to the point that the person is no longer being his or her self. For example, a normally outgoing person may become quiet and withdrawn, which family and friends may see as being out of character.

Character is not static. We all change over time in response to life experience. We may reject values that we have held for a long period of time, and go on to embrace new values. For example, we may change long-held political views, or move toward or away from a religious affiliation. The experience of losing health and independence can reinforce a person's values, or change them radically. Facing death can be a life-changing experience. Hence, nurses should make inquiries and not jump to conclusions when patients make decisions that appear to be out of character. For example, imagine a middle-aged woman who has led a quiet and uneventful life and is known to her family to be passive, selfless, and conservative in her life choices. After learning that she has cancer, she decides to go on a safari before beginning treatment. Her family is worried that her response to the bad news could be dangerous and might jeopardize her recovery. They want her to begin treatment immediately. They see her as acting out of character, and are concerned that she is not thinking clearly — which is possible, of course. But it is also possible that she has been shaken to the core by learning that she has cancer and as a result has reassessed and changed her values. The change in values may reflect a change in character, and her decision may very well be authentic from that new standpoint. In short: just because a decision appears to be out of character does not establish that it is inauthentic. The key is to know the person and understand the reasoning behind decisions made.

### 4. Autonomy as Moral Reflection

Choices express values, and people may be more or less self-conscious about the values they express in their choices. Moral reflection involves becoming aware of the values expressed in making choices and choosing consistently in view of values and principles that have been subjected to thoughtful examination. Have the values informing the choice been freely and deliberately chosen, or have they been adopted unconsciously and uncritically?

Autonomy as moral reflection is similar in meaning to autonomy as authenticity, but in addition to consistency it requires a certain measure of self-examination. People who fail to consider the impact of their decisions on others may be acting authentically, provided this is in character. Yet if they have not reflected on the values guiding their decision, they have not achieved autonomy in the sense of moral reflection. Do they know that they are acting in a selfish or arrogant manner? Have they made an explicit choice to be that sort of person?

In health care situations, autonomy can be used in one or several of the four main meanings: as free action, effective deliberation, authenticity, and moral reflection. While the first three typically apply to patients, autonomy as moral reflection (otherwise known as moral autonomy) tends to be applied more to health professionals. To be autonomous in this sense, nurses need to examine themselves: they should try to become aware of and examine their own values and reflect on the influence of their values on their decisions. Likewise, they ought to know the values of the profession and be guided by these values in their decision-making. By becoming more aware and explicit about their own values, nurses will place themselves in a better position to help patients become reflective about their own values as those values bear on necessary treatment decisions.

## Autonomy, Advocacy, and Empowerment

Nurses' involvement in promoting autonomy can be more or less active. There are different ways of promoting autonomy, and different views about those ways, depending on how autonomy is construed. The consumer model of health care, for example, tends to see autonomy in relatively narrow terms, as free action. This sense reduces the nurse to little more than an instrument of the patient's wishes. Respect for autonomy means little more than non-interference; the nurse's essential role is to provide information or technical assistance and to ensure that the information provided is accurate and complete. The patient is viewed as a bearer of rights and is left alone to make decisions. Consumerism says to the individual, "You have been informed about your options, now do what you like."

More active roles for the nurse in promoting patients' autonomy tend to build on deeper conceptions according to which the goal is construed in terms of empowerment, control, and authenticity. "Respect for patients' autonomy," Storch (1988, p. 215) writes, "essentially means that patients be kept as much in command of themselves, their symptoms, and their situation as possible." Viewed along these lines, the nurse's role is to assist patients to assume command in situations in which, for any number of reasons, they may feel very much out of control. Implicit here is a graduated conception incorporating the possibility that the patient, at least initially, may not be in a position to exercise full autonomy. Perhaps disoriented by sickness or the loss of control that sometimes comes with being in an alien environment, a patient may need help to regain autonomy. The nurse needs to look beyond the surface to identify barriers to understanding and comprehension, and help the patient to critically reflect on the information. Under these circumstances, the nurse is an enabler and supporter of patients making informed decisions.

Gadow's (1980) notion of existential advocacy is a good example of how respect for autonomy can be construed in more active terms. "The ideal which existential advocacy expresses," she writes, is "that individuals be assisted by nursing to authentically exercise their freedom of self-determination" (p. 85). Existential advocacy views nurses as co-experiencing situations with patients in order to assist the patients to make authentic decisions.[4] Gadow emphasizes "the effort to help persons become clear about what they want to do, by helping them discern and clarify their values in the situation, and on the basis of that self-examination, to reach decisions which express their reaffirmed, perhaps recreated, complex of values" (p. 85).

In this view, advocacy goes beyond merely ensuring that the patients' wishes are considered and respected (for example, as with consumerism) and includes helping patients to clarify relevant values and to decide what they really want to do in light of these values.

The kind of in-depth interaction that Gadow proposes cannot be equally attained with all patients, and in some cases is not possible at all. This is especially obvious with so-called "silent patients" who are unable to express their preferences. Gadow (1989, p. 535) notes that in our dealings with silent patients the concept of autonomy may seem inappropriate, and "other moral approaches such as utilitarianism and beneficence are tempting alternatives" to autonomy-oriented advocacy. If autonomy is represented in the image of the fully alert and mentally competent adult processing information and weighing alternatives, it is clear that silent patients are not autonomous, and that advocating on behalf of their autonomy would make no sense. However, autonomy can also be interpreted in terms of authenticity and consistency with personal values. Although silent patients cannot assess treatment options in light of preferred values, those who make choices on behalf of silent patients can. Respect for autonomy, in such cases, requires that decisions now taken on behalf of the individual be consistent with what is known about the values of that person.

This consideration of advocacy and empowerment in connection with autonomy calls for a few caveats. For one thing, autonomy is not the only value that matters in health care or in society at large. For example, beneficence (promoting the good of others) and justice (ensuring fairness) also matter, and one or the other of these values can come into conflict with autonomy. When such conflict exists, nurses must choose among competing values.

A second and related caveat is that in some measure autonomy is viewed and valued differently from one cultural or ethnic group to another, and even from one individual to another. This is a particularly important consideration in a richly multicultural society such as Canada. Some ethnic groups have an expectation that spouses, family members, or other members of the community will play a significant role in the decision-making process. This expectation is at odds with the prevailing value of autonomy in the health professions and is therefore a potential source of conflict. To point this out is not to say that nurses should submit to the moral norms of the culture or ethnic group of the patient; but nurses should at least be sensitive to such norms and take them into consideration in their practice and decision-making. Moreover, patients from some traditions may have an understanding of health and illness that is quite different from that of the perspective of Western health care (Coward & Ratanakul, 1999). Their different values may have a bearing on "how patients interpret their illnesses and comprehend the diagnostic, prognostic and treatment-related information provided by members of the health care team" (Hunter, 2005, p. 308).

A third caveat is the belief, on the part of some commentators, that autonomy has been given too much prominence in contemporary health care and society, and that this prominence distorts our understanding of the individual person and the complex of relationships in which individuals exist and maintain their identities. In this regard some thinkers argue for a reconceptualization of autonomy. The Canadian philosopher Susan Sherwin (1998) argues that autonomy is only ever enacted in a complex network of relationships between individuals and organizations, and that such relationships are themselves embedded in broader sociopolitical contexts.[5] She has therefore coined the term *relational autonomy*. According to this perspective, patients are not isolated individuals acting alone, but are deeply affected by the people, social institutions, and sociopolitical discourses around them. If we are to help them to realize their autonomy in an authentic way we must try to understand, and connect across, the differences that these relationships create (Doane & Varcoe, 2005). For example, when we encounter a person in an emergency department who has been living on the street and has drug addictions, we ought to consider how that person has been affected by experiences in her or his family of origin, by schooling, or by illnesses or injury. In particular we ought to consider how they will be damaged by the negative stereotyping that they too often meet as they enter the emergency department ("just a drug addict," "medication-seeking," "frequent flyer," for example).

## Autonomy and the Process of Informed Consent

Most accounts of autonomy specify that to act autonomously a person must have the rational capacity or maturity of reason to deliberate effectively; the liberty or freedom to decide and act unimpeded by others; and a certain minimum of knowledge or information relevant to the action. These three elements — capacity, voluntariness, and knowledge — are key in the theory of informed consent.[6]

To begin with the issue of voluntariness, we first have to ask: what constitutes a truly *voluntary* decision? For one thing, the decision-making process sometimes has to do with whether or not other people are exerting a coercive influence. No one is completely free from influences, and influence is not necessarily a bad thing. Questions arise, therefore, about how to distinguish coercion and manipulation — both of which seriously compromise the voluntariness of a choice — from persuasion, influence, and advice, which do not. The degree of coercion and the ability to deal with coercion are factors in the process. One way in which nurses can promote patient autonomy is by helping patients to become aware of and manage coercive pressures.

The knowledge aspect of informed consent has to do with understanding and appreciating information related to the situation and the decision at hand. What constitutes a truly informed decision? Here questions arise concerning how much information is necessary for informed choice — and of what sort, and how well understood. The scope of information necessary for an informed decision — the amount of detail about proposed treatments and alternatives, for example — varies depending on the type of decision being made. One helpful way of determining what information is necessary for a decision is the *reasonable person test*: asking yourself what a reasonable person in the particular circumstances of the patient would want to know. Still, this test is by no means straightforward; patients can differ a great deal in their decision-making styles. Health professionals must therefore take care to develop a relationship with and come to know their patients.

For health professionals, responsibilities in connection with informed consent include involving patients in planning and deciding about their own health care (enabling or at least permitting them to make their own decisions) and providing and explaining information pertinent to the choice (informing the patient).[7]

Nurses play an important role in the informed consent process. They are often in a position to observe the dynamics of a patient's situation, including the possible coercive influence of family members or even other health professionals. Nurses are also well positioned to provide patients with information that is key to decision-making. They can explain this information and help patients reason through their decisions.

To clarify the nurse's responsibilities Davis (1988, pp. 91-92) described five main roles that nurses play in the informed consent process: watchdog, advocate, resource person, co-ordinator, and facilitator. Many years later her findings remain relevant. The nurses she interviewed worked at deepening the patients' understanding of options and at responding to specific questions. Often they talked with patients about the meanings of words that appeared on consent forms or words used by physicians. Davis found that nurses tend to view informed consent as a process that occurs over time rather than as a one-time, all or nothing event. Tellingly, many of the examples she gives of nursing involvement with particular patients occurred only after informed consent, in an official or institutional sense, had already been solicited and obtained. This finding suggests that nurses may view informed consent somewhat differently than it is institutionally understood and practised. Indeed, many nurses interviewed acknowledged that the "assessment of patient comprehension was usually superficial and perfunctory" (Davis, 1988, p. 90).

In some clinical areas nurses are responsible for obtaining informed choice (whether this turns out to be consent or a refusal). Nurses cannot, for instance, insist that patients receive nursing care: patients must consent to a treatment plan. Usually patients make an initial agreement, which is then assumed to represent their consent for the duration of the therapeutic relationship. But a health care professional can only obtain consent for care that he or she will give. It is inappropriate for a nurse to seek consent for a procedure that another health care professional intends to conduct. Most health care agencies and provincial associations have guidelines for nurses' responsibilities in relation to such consent processes.[8]

Traditionally health care professions displayed resistance to the practice of informed consent and to respect for autonomy more generally. One reason for this was the prevalence of the view that the clinical information needed to make treatment decisions is too complex for patients to understand. A fundamental concern was that patients might make what the health professionals would consider to be wrong choices, or that the provision of information might be harmful to patients (Loftus & Fries, 1979).

The past forty years or so have seen a change in attitudes and beliefs and in legal and professional norms and expectations concerning informed consent. Nonetheless, in some measure attitudes and beliefs contemptuous of informed consent persist. Although legal and professional duties mandating informed consent are now well established, these norms are not always followed. Moreover, the process of obtaining informed consent often amounts to little more than an empty ritual enacted to satisfy the letter of the law. Along these lines, Beauchamp (1989, pp. 181-182) distinguishes what he calls "legal" or "institutional consent," which may have little to do with promoting autonomy, from consent for which the patient has given "autonomous authorization," and which truly does promote autonomy.

In contemporary multicultural society cultural factors have a bearing on informed consent. Members of some ethnic groups have an expectation that spouses, family members, or other members of the community will play a significant role in the decision-making process — an expectation that can be at odds with the prevailing Western conception of autonomy. Moreover, patients from different traditions may have unique perspectives on health and illness. Their distinct values may influence "how patients interpret their illnesses and comprehend the diagnostic, prognostic and treatment-related information provided by members of the health care team" (Hunter, 2005, p. 308). Clearly, when cultural values conflict with the requirements of informed consent, nurses need to appreciate the values of patients. The guiding principle should be to support the patients' ability to become informed and make sound decisions about their own lives.

## Competence and Capacity to Decide

Assisting patients to make informed choices presupposes that they have the competence or capacity to make an informed choice in the first place — something that in many cases can be in question. Given that treatment often turns upon issues of competence or capacity, the standards used to assess capacity are bound to be controversial.

Wong, Clare, Gunn, and Holland (1999) distinguish three main ways of assessing capacity. One way is to look at the outcome — the decision made. The test of capacity is the quality of decisions made. If the decision is "reasonable," the person has the capacity to decide. This approach may seem attractive for its simplicity, but it turns on the answer to a crucially important question: who decides what is "reasonable"? Many of us make decisions that others deem to be "unreasonable." It is unacceptable that a health professional or team deems a decision made by a patient to be unreasonable and concludes that the person is therefore incapable of deciding, for the sole reason that the caregiver or team wants to make a different decision. Regrettably, providers sometimes do form opinions about a patient's capacity based not on any explicit standard of competence but, rather, on whether the patient's views about treatment converge with their own. They therefore deem the patient who is "non-compliant," or who elects for an option contrary to what is recommended, to be incapable. In such instances, the patient's apparently irrational or unreasonable decision becomes evidence of incapacity based on the doubtful presumption that no one in his or her "right mind" would make such a decision.

This line of thinking is not defensible. That someone makes a decision that appears foolish or uninformed to others, or that a patient disagrees or refuses to comply with the plan of care favoured by the health team, does not by itself prove incapacity. For example, it could be that the decision, although irrational or unreasonable from the point of view of others, is consistent with the patient's values, goals, or religious or cultural beliefs. Granted, some caregivers might argue that these cultural or religious beliefs are themselves irrational or unreasonable. But in a multicultural, pluralistic society, people working within the health care system are not in a position to decide which beliefs are rational and which are not. To be sure, a patient's decision to choose something apparently "irrational" from the standpoint of the health professional may well provide a good reason for pursuing an assessment of capacity. Capacity assessments are often initiated on such grounds. When an otherwise stable person makes an out of character decision that will potentially lead to significant personal harm, caregivers may find that reason enough to conduct an assessment. However, indications that signal the need for a capacity assessment ought not to be confused with legitimate tests of competence to be used in such assessments.

A second way of looking at capacity assessment is the status approach: based on membership in a specific group, the patient is deemed not to have the capacity to make decisions. The designated groups may include children, adolescents, persons with mental illness or cognitive impairment, and persons incarcerated in correctional institutions. The problem with this approach is that it is based on a generalization or statistical norm. All members of a group are denied the opportunity to exercise autonomy; but it is conceivable, perhaps likely, that some of them will have the capacity to make decisions for themselves. Being institutionalized, for example in a prison, psychiatric hospital, or group home for persons with severe physical challenges, does not automatically mean that these vulnerable persons cannot deliberate effectively and process information with enough understanding and appreciation to make treatment decisions. Many people with chronic health problems, such as schizophrenia, multiple sclerosis, and end-stage renal disease physical disabilities, live independently in the community. Although they have serious mental and physical health problems, they still have the capacity to manage their treatment and financial affairs in much the same way as everyone else does.

A third method of assessing capacity, and the one most consistent with best practices, is the functional approach: assessing capacity based on an understanding of the person's decision-making skills and abilities as applied to the particular decision to be made at a particular time. In the past capacity was thought to be a general condition, an all or nothing affair: people were thought able to make decisions about either all aspects of their lives or no parts of their lives. Today, consistent with the functional approach, nurses and their colleagues recognize that our lives involve many different types of decisions, with different levels of complexity. A doubt about capacity represents a doubt about specific tasks or decisions, and not necessarily about all decisions. A person with depression could have the capacity to decide what medications to take, but when faced with decisions about entering a research study the same person might lack the capacity to assess the risks and benefits of participation.

Competence or capacity can also fluctuate over time. For example, a person taking pain medications may develop a delirium, become acutely confused, and within a matter of hours lose the capacity to make decisions. A person with Alzheimer's disease may exhibit the "sundowning effect" — that is, the ability to reason and deliberate is relatively intact in the morning but diminishes considerably toward the end of the day.

Appelbaum, Lidz, and Meisel (1987, p. 88) analyze competence or capacity in terms of the patient's ability to meet one or more of four tests:

i. evidencing a choice, which (depending on the circumstances) can be a simple nod of the head or demonstration of agreement by co-operating with a request. The choice thus evidenced may or may not be based on an understanding of the request;

ii. actually understanding the information about the treatment under consideration. This means understanding the relevant facts of the situation;

iii. engaging in decision-making in a rational way, with an appreciation of potential outcomes. This means that the person has been able to apply the information to his or her situation. The costs and benefits for the person in light of their situation are considered;

iv. reaching a decision about the treatment that is reasonable. The crucial issue with this test concerns who determines whether the decision itself is reasonable. There is a clear danger with this test that health professionals may deem a decision unreasonable simply because it is not the decision that they believe should be taken.

Some commentators propose a sliding scale for assessing competence, with the standard to vary according to the consequences of the decision at hand. Thus a high standard of competence would be used for a decision with grave consequences; a lower standard would be used for a decision upon which little hangs in the balance (Drane, 1988). Moreover, consistent with the functional approach, different standards of competence or capacity may be appropriate in different contexts. Again, a patient may have the capacity to make certain decisions, but not others (for example, compare the decision to take an analgesic for a headache as opposed to considering treatment for schizophrenia).

The term "capacity" — as opposed to "competence" — is the legal term of choice in some jurisdictions, for example, in Ontario. According to Ontario's mental health and consent legislation (Ontario, 1996, 2000), a person is assessed as having the capacity (or competence) for informed choice if he or she:

- understands information relevant to making a decision about the specific treatment; and

- appreciates the reasonably foreseeable consequences of the decision or of failing to make a decision.

Both conditions and criteria must be met for a positive assessment. These general criteria can be further elaborated. With respect to information, the caregivers need to determine whether the patient understands:

- his or her condition for which treatment is recommended;

- the nature of the recommended treatment;

- the risks and benefits of the recommended treatment;

- the alternative treatments, including no treatment.

In addition, caregivers need to establish that:

- the person acknowledges that treatment is recommended;

- the person understands that, and how, the proposed treatment or lack of treatment can affect his or her quality of life; and

- the person's decision is not substantially based on a delusional belief.

It is important to keep in mind that these criteria are intended to establish whether the patient is capable of making a reasoned choice and not whether the choice the patient makes is in itself "reasonable." As a rule, caregivers should assume that the patient is capable of making an autonomous decision unless they have good reason to believe otherwise. Evidence of confused or delusional thinking, severe pain or anxiety, severe depression, and impairment by drugs or alcohol does not in itself indicate a lack of capacity. Still, the existence of those signs may be reason enough to question whether the patient has the capacity for informed choice and can be taken as an indication of the need for an assessment of capacity.

Most jurisdictions fall under the purview of mental health legislation that provides strict guidelines to protect the rights of people found to lack the capacity to make decisions. Those people can appeal decisions within a specific time period and seek the assistance of a rights advisor or patient ombudsman. During the period when an appeal is pending, the person is assumed to be capable.

The care of adolescents can pose special ethical challenges for nurses. As with a person of any age, the capacity to consent of an adolescent is determined based on the ability to understand and appreciate pertinent information and make informed decisions. Typically, in their early teen years adolescents have acquired the cognitive ability to understand the information necessary to make significant treatment decisions. However, in many jurisdictions there is no age requirement for giving consent. Each case must be decided on the capacity of the individual patient to make a treatment decision that is informed and not coerced. An adolescent who is identified as a "mature minor" can make treatment decisions. A mature minor is someone between the ages of twelve and eighteen who is considered to be capable of understanding the scope of his or her illness and the consequences of accepting or rejecting treatment for that illness.

It is generally agreed that nurses should involve adolescents in the consent process (Schacter, Kleinman, & Harvey, 2005, p. 534). Challenges can arise, though, when adolescents thought to be quite capable of making treatment decisions by accepted standards are not seen as such by their parents; and when adolescents confer with nurses and physicians without their parents' knowledge and request that their confidentiality be respected.

In the well-known Canadian case of Tyrell Dueck, the thirteen-year-old Saskatchewan boy diagnosed with bone cancer, the parents were found to be not acting in their son's best interests (see Case 1 in chapter 3). The boy was not permitted to make his treatment decisions because upon assessment it was decided that he was not a mature minor. In this case the provincial child protection agency was granted the responsibility for making treatment decisions.

## Substitute Decision-Making

Except under specific circumstances, such as an emergency, all care given must be authorized by consent. When a patient clearly lacks the capacity to make specific treatment decisions, the responsibility to decide on that patient's behalf falls to others. The substitute decision-maker can be a family member, friend, partner, or even court-appointed guardian. A health care professional providing care to the patient cannot assume this responsibility.

Substitute decision-making can be guided by two standards: the patient's expressed wishes, and the patient's best interests.

### 1. The Patient's Wishes and Advance Directives

Autonomy has primarily to do with being in control of one's life and as far as possible being able to shape one's life in accordance with one's own desires, hopes, beliefs, and values. When someone loses the capacity to make informed choices, that does not mean that autonomy is no longer a consideration in decision-making about that person. In such instances, and indeed perhaps especially in such instances, respect for autonomy remains a central value. This is so not because the patient who is now incapacitated may at some later point be restored to autonomy; in some cases this may be extremely unlikely or even impossible. Rather, respect for autonomy continues to be of importance insofar as the patient once was autonomous, and any desires, hopes, beliefs, and values that the patient affirmed at that time continue to be relevant.

The substitute decision-maker exhibits respect for autonomy to the extent that he or she is guided by the patient's wishes. Faced with a decision about treatment for an incapacitated person, the substitute decision-maker's ideal is to make a choice based on what the patient would decide if the patient had the capacity to do so. The more the substitute decision-maker knows about the patient and the patient's wishes, the better the position to meet this ideal.

Living wills or advance directives can be useful in this regard. In some jurisdictions advance directives have legal weight, and health care professionals are legally obliged to follow them. Such directives usually have two components: a proxy component, which designates the person who is to act as substitute decision-maker; and a directive component, which provides instructions to the substitute decision-maker about the person's wishes. This instruction may in a general way indicate the patient's wishes or values regarding treatment decisions — such as how he or she feels about risk-taking or quality of life issues — or may be specific about particular conditions that could arise and preferences regarding treatment options for those conditions.

## 2. Patient's Best Interests

When prior wishes are unknown, the substitute decision-maker must make a decision based on the patient's best interests. Acting in a person's best interests is an onerous responsibility, and to clarify matters decision-makers can consider a number of questions.

- Will the person's situation be improved by the treatment?

- Is the person's situation likely to improve without the treatment?

- Will the expected benefits outweigh the expected risk of harm to the person?

- Is the proposed treatment the least harmful, invasive, and restrictive way of improving the person's situation?

In Canada, based on child protection legislation, the common law, and the *Charter of Rights and Freedoms* (1982), parents must act in the best interests of their children. Nurses in pediatric settings may encounter difficult situations in which they believe that parents or guardians are not acting in the best interests of the child or adolescent. When nurses think that a refused treatment would be in the best interests of the child, the clinical team must contact the child protection authorities and ask them to assess the situation. They may decide to seek guardianship and decide on treatment options.

Obviously, all of these considerations contain an element of subjectivity — which is unavoidable and indeed an essential aspect of ethical decision-making. The decision-maker must consider the effect of the decision on specific patients, who are unable at a particular moment to direct their own lives. To be sure, the decision-makers' own values enter into this, and they should try to be aware of those values. The key is to avoid putting the best interests and values of others, including those of the substitute decision-makers, before those of the patients.

### Limiting Autonomy: Paternalism, Protection of Third Parties, and Justice

One important sense of autonomy has to do with the freedom and ability to make decisions for ourselves according to our own wishes, preferences, and values. Autonomy in this sense is highly valued by individuals and protected by society in various laws and statements of rights; and it is highly valued in the health professions, which deal with people whose autonomy may already be compromised by illness.

Health professionals can promote autonomy by respecting the wishes of patients and assisting them to make informed choices. However, in the context of health care — as in society more generally — there are circumstances in which it may be justifiable not to comply with someone's autonomous wishes or even to limit someone's autonomy. What these circumstances are is a matter of considerable debate.

Autonomy — in the sense of liberty or freedom of action — is limited in a variety of ways as a matter of circumstance. If I am poor, I lack the freedom to do all of the many activities that require money. If I have a broken leg, I lack the freedom to walk to the store or to the park. If I don't have the required education, I lack the freedom to pursue certain careers. Here, though, we are concerned with the *deliberate* limitation of someone's freedom.

Health professionals deliberately or without intention limit patient autonomy in several ways: by information control (for example, withholding information, equivocation, and deception); by limiting options (not offering or providing certain options); and by impeding the patients' ability to act upon their wishes (refusal to assist, constraint, and compulsory treatment). Nurses must reflect on their practice and determine whether they are limiting patients' freedom by means of their standard practices and procedures.

To justify a given limitation, caregivers can apply three main considerations.

- *The capacity of the person.* The ability to understand and appreciate relevant information can vary significantly, for many reasons. To the extent that a patient lacks the capacity to make a free and informed decision, caregivers may be justified in limiting the person's ability to choose.

- *Potential harm to others.* In some cases the patient may pose a significant risk to others, and it may be justifiable to limit the patient's ability to choose, or to act in order to protect third parties from harm. For example, quarantining patients severely limits their freedom, but can be justified if it is necessary to prevent an infection from spreading to other people.

- *Potential harm to the patient.* In some cases patients can pose a considerable risk to themselves. For example, a patient may prefer a treatment option that in the view of the health team will expose that patient to significant risk. In such instances, caregivers may be justified in not providing that option to the patient.

The third consideration — potential harm to the patient — is the most controversial of the three. Restricting or limiting people's autonomy for their own good is referred to as "paternalism," which comes in different varieties, some of them more acceptable than others.[9]

## 1. Paternalism and the Limitation of Autonomy

One widely accepted variety of paternalism — what Feinberg (1971, p. 113) calls "weak paternalism" — justifies limiting autonomy "to prevent self-regarding harmful conduct only when it is substantially non-voluntary, or when intervention is necessary to establish whether it is voluntary or not." If a patient lacks capacity, or if there is good reason to believe this is the case, it may be justifiable to limit freedom *for his or her own good*, at least until such time as an assessment can be done.

Closely related to weak paternalism is what Komrad (1988) calls "limited paternalism," which takes into account the possibility that the autonomy of the sick person may be greatly diminished because of sickness and justifies paternalistic intervention insofar as its ultimate end is the restoration of autonomy. "The restitution of diminished autonomy," Komrad (1988, p. 147) writes, "is the only rationalization of medical paternalism that does not profane autonomy."

What these two forms of paternalism share in common is a belief that the capacity of the person being treated is in question, at least temporarily. Under such conditions, paternalism is widely accepted in principle throughout our society, and no one takes issue with it as such.

The strongest form of paternalism, and the one most difficult to justify if plainly put, involves limiting liberty when the person's capacity to make the decision is not in question. It is mainly this kind of "strong paternalism" in health care that has been the object of criticism in recent years: limiting the autonomy of a competent person for his or her own good.

The classic critique of strong paternalism dates back to the nineteenth-century philosopher John Stuart Mill. In *On Liberty*, Mill ([1859] 1975, pp. 10-11) asserted a simple principle as a means of making a decision on whether or not the restriction of someone's liberty is justifiable:

> That principle is that the sole end for which mankind are warranted, individually or collectively, in interfering with the liberty of action of any of their number, is self-protection. That the only purpose for which power can be rightfully exercised over any member of a civilized community, against his will, is to prevent harm to others. His own good, either physical or moral, is not a sufficient warrant. He cannot rightfully be compelled to do or forbear because it will be better for him to do so, because it will make him happier, because in the opinions of others, to do so would be wise, or even right.

Mill was a major exponent of the liberal philosophy that has shaped modern society and politics. His principle of liberty established autonomy as a higher value than beneficence. Concern for the good of the other is limited and held in check by respect for the other's autonomy.[10] Respect for autonomy trumps beneficence.

Mill's views, although widely held, remain controversial, especially in the context of health care. Beneficence has traditionally been the supreme value for health professionals. Several commentators, concerned that respect for autonomy has been given too much value in health care, have sought to restore beneficence to a position of higher value (for example, Zembaty, 1986; Clements & Sider, 1988; Pellegrino & Thomasma, 1988). Is there something special about the health care context — for example, the vulnerability of the sick — that justifies the subordination of respect for autonomy to beneficence? Alternatively, to what extent can we interpret beneficence more broadly (and more favourably) to incorporate respect for autonomy? In considering whether strong paternalism is justified, caregivers will find it useful to consider the questions of duration and severity of the harm anticipated. An irreversible harm is weightier than a harm that endures only briefly; a life-threatening harm is weightier than a harm that has little impact on overall health.

Health care involving people with mental illness is probably the field in which paternalism is most prevalent. Nurses need to know the legal grounds for involuntary admission and treatment in their jurisdiction. For example, in Ontario in 2000 Brian's Law (Mental Health Legislative Reform), amended the *Mental Health Act* and *Heath Care Consent Act* to enable community treatment orders (CTOs) for persons with serious mental illness. The amendments expand the current assessment and committal criteria to include chronically mentally ill persons and to allow their families and health professionals to intervene at an earlier stage in the committal process. The amendments provide for consent to a community treatment plan by the person or his or her substitute decision-maker. They specify community support prerequisites, the terms, conditions, responsibilities, and other formal details of a CTO, and the responsibilities of the issuing physician, or other services. Critics argue that patients are coerced to accept CTOs because the alternative is to remain in hospital. If patients under a CTO do not meet the conditions of the CTO, involuntary admission may result. Also, critics suggest that capable patients refusing admission may be admitted and treated involuntarily if in the past they have been shown to respond well to treatment.

Perhaps the relational approach to autonomy that Sherwin (1998) and others promote can help nurses to navigate difficult issues concerning patient choice. For example, if we adopt a relational approach with a patient who is refusing what we think is beneficial (or even essential) treatment, we would listen to the patient's (and family's) stories, examine our own assumptions and biases, and negotiate a plan of care *with* the patient/family instead of *for* them (Doane & Varcoe, 2005).

### 2. Protection of Third Parties and the Limitation of Autonomy

Although Mill's principle ranks respect for autonomy as a higher value than beneficence, it also places a limit on autonomy. According to Mill, it is not justifiable to limit someone's autonomy for his or her own good. However, it is justifiable to limit someone's autonomy to prevent him or her from harming someone else.

Despite widespread agreement on this aspect of Mill's harm principle, difficult questions arise about its application.[11] When the harm to others that will follow from action is great, as when someone is violent, a clear case can be made for limiting autonomy to prevent the person from harming other people. The matter is less clear when the harm foreseen is less severe, or when uncertainty exists as to whether the harm will materialize. What degree of harm to others, and what probability that the harm will occur, is sufficient to warrant limiting someone's autonomy?

### 3. Justice and the Limitation of Autonomy

Paternalism and a concern to protect others from immediate harm are not the only bases upon which autonomy may be limited in health care. Health care can be expensive. Resources are not infinite. When resources are provided to one patient, the pool of resources available to others is diminished. To meet the *wishes* of one patient may mean not being able to meet the *needs* of another. Accordingly, there is an increased emphasis on maximizing efficiency and effectiveness in the use of resources. Meeting needs comes before meeting wishes.

Considerations along these lines have to do with the concept of justice. Rationing resources is in a tension with patient autonomy. When resources are rationed with a view to maximizing efficiency and effectiveness for the general good, patients may not be able to gain access to what they want, or even what they need — for example, access to expensive treatments and drugs. Similar principles also apply to low-tech and high-touch care, such as home care. Fractured hips are a common health problem for elderly women. Community-based geriatric rehabilitation programs cannot meet the demand. Therefore, some patients will be transferred from surgical units to long-term care facilities (or sent home, with no professional support) for convalescence, even though they would prefer to go to a rehabilitation centre. Such constraints on choice are different in kind from those sanctioned by paternalism or based on a concern to protect third parties from harm.

Whatever the reason for limiting patient autonomy in all senses, the limitation must be the least invasive or restrictive of liberty under the circumstances, and no more than is necessary to accomplish the desired purpose.

## End of Life Decisions

Issues of autonomy can arise for virtually any treatment decision, but not all decisions are equally serious. The greater our stake in the decision at hand, and the more serious the consequences, the greater will be the issues of autonomy. There is a vast difference in significance between deciding whether to have surgical or chemical treatment for breast cancer and deciding whether to have a minor procedure to remove a wart. End of life decisions are therefore especially problematic from the standpoint of autonomy because they concern not just quality of life but life itself. Respecting autonomy can be challenging enough even when relatively minor things are at stake; when the quality of life and when and how to die hang in the balance, the challenges are that much greater.

Dying can be a terrifying, lonely, and painful experience, particularly for those who fear losing control of how they will die. Caring for the dying and trying to make their last days comfortable in physical, psychological, and spiritual terms is noble work. When caring for the terminally ill, nurses can face difficult ethical challenges concerning autonomy. Together with other health care providers, nurses need to decide whether or not and why they should comply with a patient's wishes in a given case. For some nurses, there may be a tension or even conflict between their professional and legal obligations and their individual moral consciences.

Nurses generally find it less morally distressing to accept and comply with a patient's wishes or the decision of a substitute decision-maker if they agree that the wish or decision is informed, freely made, and for the patient's good — or at least less harmful than other options. However, often these situations are not clear-cut. There may be issues concerning the patient's capacity to decide, or about a substitute decision-maker's interpretation of the patient's previously expressed wishes or best interests. There could also be issues about complying or co-operating with the wishes or decisions even of the competent patient.

The concepts we use to reflect on and discuss end of life issues are complex, and they can be confusing. Often the issues fall under the rubric of *euthanasia*, in some instances inappropriately. The literal meaning of the word "euthanasia" is "good death," but in contemporary parlance the term evokes considerably more than that. Euthanasia tends to mean knowingly and intentionally performing an act that is explicitly intended to end another person's life.

Euthanasia issues are difficult not just because so much is at stake — and the issues are understandably deeply felt — but also because the terminology in which they are couched is so slippery. In common parlance, euthanasia is the intentional act of ending the life of a person. This so-called "good death" is based on compassion. When the act is carried out in accordance with the person's wishes, it is called *voluntary* euthanasia. *Involuntary* or *non-voluntary* euthanasia, by contrast, is sanctioned not by the person's own wishes but rather by what someone else believes to be in the best interests of that person.

The distinction between voluntary and involuntary euthanasia is clear enough, and virtually everyone would agree that this distinction has at least some moral relevance. The situation is more complex with regards to another common distinction used in debates about euthanasia, namely, that between *passive* and *active* euthanasia. Passive euthanasia involves omission, the withholding or withdrawing of certain treatments, such as withholding food and fluids or otherwise deciding not to take steps that would keep the patient alive. This could be construed as "letting die." It is not a case of direct action. Active euthanasia consists of taking specific, deliberate steps to hasten the person's death, such as administering a lethal injection. This can be called assisted suicide, assisting in death, or homicide. Passive euthanasia is not illegal in Canada; active euthanasia is a criminal act.

Some commentators argue that, if the desired outcome is the same — ending a life, ending suffering, facilitating the person's death — passive and active euthanasia are morally equivalent, or even that active euthanasia is preferable to passive euthanasia. Such analysis questions the moral difference between, on the one hand, removing a patient from a ventilator when that patient or decision-maker has requested that act, and, on the other, the action of administering a lethal dose to end a life when that action has likewise been requested.

The conceptualization of active and passive euthanasia has shifted over time. Schafer (2009) writes:

> When I began teaching ethics to undergraduate medical students in 1970, the hot-button issues were passive and indirect euthanasia. "Passive euthanasia" referred to the withholding or withdrawal of life support, from the motive of mercy, usually at the request of a dying patient. Doctors used to worry about both the ethics and the legality of hastening a patient's death by "pulling the plug."
>
> "Indirect euthanasia" was the term then in use to describe the administration of large, sometimes very large, doses of analgesia with the direct aim of relieving pain but in the knowledge that, indirectly, this pain relief was likely to depress the patient's respiratory system and thereby bring on death more quickly.

"Passive euthanasia" is now called "appropriate care." Today, it is universally practised in Canadian hospitals, and no physician has been charged with a criminal offence for withholding or withdrawing life support, whether at the request of a dying patient, in compliance with a living will or at the request of the patient's family when the patient was no longer competent.

Given that terms such as active and passive euthanasia are open to different interpretations, it may be best to use the language of euthanasia judiciously, or even to avoid using it. The key thing to recognize is that at least four main factors bear on the moral evaluation of end of life decision-making: the wishes of the person whose life is in question; the intention of those assisting the person; the action to be taken (or inaction); and the effect of the action (or inaction). These factors can come into play in five distinct types of scenarios concerning end of life decisions: palliative care; the right to refuse life-saving treatment; life-saving interventions deemed to be futile; assisted suicide; and involuntary active euthanasia.

### 1. Palliative Care

The Canadian Nurses Association (CNA, 2000) defines palliative care as the "active, compassionate care of dying persons and their families when neither the prolongation of life nor curative treatment is any longer an appropriate goal." The goal of palliative care is to support a patient to have a comfortable death by providing holistic care. The priorities are relieving suffering through pain management and attending to complications that can arise in the dying process.

In some instances the most effective available measures to reduce suffering can have the effect of hastening death. For instance, a patient might be given a dose of analgesics sufficient to relieve pain to the point that the dose is no longer effective. Increasing the dose could have the effect of hastening death. Notwithstanding this possible effect, a higher dose is ordered for breakthrough pain. Shortly after that treatment, the patient dies. Based on the assumption that the higher dose was intended to manage pain and not to kill the patient, the act of administering the drug should not be construed as euthanasia, but as proper palliative care. The goal was to manage the pain; the intended effect was adequate pain management. To be sure, death was hastened in consequence of the increased dose; this effect was anticipated, but it was not intended as the goal.

Hurst and Mauron (2006, p. 108) compare palliative care with voluntary euthanasia and assisted suicide. They find that proponents of palliative care and proponents of euthanasia or assisted suicide share the common goals of reducing suffering, avoiding the medicalization of death, and giving dying patients control of their lives. Where these two sides differ is in how to respond to human suffering. Palliative care providers tend to reject the idea of deliberate killing, emphasizing instead the "sanctity of life," and they tend to be suspicious of the ideas, such as a "good death" and "natural life span," employed by euthanasia advocates. Additionally, they worry that if assisted death is permitted even under very strict conditions, our society will begin a slide down a slippery slope in which assisted suicide or euthanasia will "cease to be viewed with appropriate gravity."

Another worry is that programs of palliative care might be cut back, or at least eroded, if active euthanasia were to become legalized in Canada (Ericksen, Rodney, & Starzomski, 1995) — and palliative case is already limited. There is some reason for this concern. In examining access to palliative care services, a Senate Committee found that only 5 per cent to 15 per cent of Canadians had access to palliative care services (Special Senate Committee on Euthanasia and Assisted Suicide, 1995). Yet another worry is that persons lacking access to appropriate palliative care could turn to euthanasia as an alternative. Then too, when health care costs become a consideration, some terminally ill patients may want to relieve the financial burden on their families.

## 2. The Right to Refuse Treatment: The Case of Nancy B.

Life-sustaining treatment or care is any intervention, no matter how simple or complex, that is essential for the maintenance of life. Depending on the circumstances, this treatment may include food, water, a ventilator, a feeding tube, or any combination of other high-tech or low-tech interventions. Patients sometimes refuse an intervention by requesting that it not be started, or request that an intervention already started be discontinued. Sometimes patients may ask for an intravenous or a feeding tube to be removed. If an intravenous tube falls out or needs replacing, patients might request that it not be put back in or replaced.

The 1991 case of Nancy B. brought issues concerning life-sustaining treatment to the fore in Canada. Nancy B., a twenty-five-year-old woman with Guillain-Barré syndrome, suffered from extensive muscular atrophy. She was paralyzed and ventilator-dependent. After having been confined to bed for two years, she asked to have her respirator disconnected. The request created uncertainty among those caring for her about whether to comply with her wishes. At the time Nancy B. was a patient at the Hôtel-Dieu Hôpital in Quebec City, and the hospital administration sought guidance from the courts about how to proceed. They wanted to know whether compliance with her wishes would violate legal sanctions against homicide and assisted suicide. The case made its way to the Superior Court of Quebec, which ruled that compliance with her wishes should be construed in terms of her right to refuse treatment, and not in terms of homicide or assisted suicide or euthanasia. Essentially, the court determined that Nancy B. was a competent adult who was refusing treatment. To give treatment without consent is the legal offence of battery. Nancy B. had a right to refuse the continuation of life-sustaining care, and those responsible for her care were duty bound to honour her refusal. Following the decision, her wishes were respected. She died shortly after she was removed from a ventilator.

The case of Nancy B. clarified the legal issues surrounding refusal of life-sustaining treatment and helped shape a professional consensus. It confirmed that Canadians have a legal right to refuse even life-sustaining treatment, including feeding tubes, surgical interventions, blood transfusions, and cardio-pulmonary resuscitation (CPR).

If patient autonomy means anything at all, it means the right to accept or refuse treatment or care. This right is recognized and enshrined in law and in various codes of ethics in nursing. Provided that the patient is capable, and the decision is informed and voluntary, the patient's decision must be respected. To be sure, other values beside respect for autonomy may come into play, including respect for life itself, but the right to refuse treatment is a weighty element indeed.

### 3. Life-Saving Interventions Deemed to Be Futile

The *right to refuse treatment* should not be confused with a *right to receive treatment* deemed to be futile or ineffective. When the practice is always to perform cardio-pulmonary resuscitation when requested (whether by the patient or by his or her surrogate), nurses can find themselves calling a code for a person who they know will not survive the resuscitation efforts. This can contribute to moral distress. Nurses may feel that they have done harm or caused an indignity to the person by providing futile care at the time of death.

The Joint Statement on Resuscitative Interventions (1995), of which the CNA is a co-author, sought to address these problems. It pronounced that CPR should not be given on demand and allowed that under certain conditions nurses and colleagues may refuse to honour requests for this intervention when it is deemed futile.

Requests for excessive treatment can arise out of miscommunication, fear of dying, and fear of abandonment by the health care team — and nurses should take care to recognize these tendencies. Good and open communication is essential. A relational approach to autonomy means opening up, rather than closing, conversations with patients and their families at the end of life (Storch, 2004).

### 4. Request for Assisted Suicide: The Case of Sue Rodriguez

In the first three scenarios concerning end of life decision-making, the intent of the health professionals is not to cause or even hasten the death of the patient but to carry out actions that may have death as an unintended effect. Our last two scenarios are markedly different in this respect.

Sue Rodriguez suffered from amyotrophic lateral sclerosis (known as ALS or Lou Gehrig's disease). She clearly stated her desire to have a health professional assist her to die at the point at which her terminal condition became intolerable to her. However, the *Criminal Code*, in section 241(b), prohibits intentional killing or assisting someone to die. Therefore, she applied to the Supreme Court of British Columbia for an order that section 241(b) be declared invalid on the grounds of the *Charter of Rights and Freedoms*. She argued that the section infringed her rights both with respect to not being subjected to "cruel and unusual punishment" and to equality. Due to her physical disabilities, she needed help to commit suicide. She argued that forbidding others from helping her do what able-bodied people would have been able to do for themselves constituted discrimination. The B.C. Supreme Court dismissed her application, and the judgment was upheld on appeal to the B.C. Court of Appeal. Her subsequent appeal to the Supreme Court of Canada was dismissed in 1993 by a five to four majority decision. In February 1994 she died with the assistance of an anonymous physician, who administered a lethal injection.

Autonomy is central in both the Nancy B. and Sue Rodriguez cases, but in different ways. In both cases the patient was expressing a wish to die and seeking co-operation from health professionals in realizing that wish, but the similarities end there. Nancy B. was not requesting an intervention but rather refusing a treatment or intervention. Notwithstanding that complying with her wish would have the effect of hastening her death, the intent of the professional can be construed as respecting her right to refuse treatment, and not as assisting her to die. By contrast, Sue Rodriguez was seeking an intervention, and there was no doubt that she was requesting help to die. She was not refusing treatment — not asking someone to remove life-sustaining care — but claiming a right to have a physician actively assist her to die. Hers is a clear example of physician-assisted suicide and active euthanasia.

Polls indicate that Canadians favour the legalization of assisted suicide under strict conditions — although given the confusion about the meaning of different terms used to discuss euthanasia, the meaning and significance of such polls are open to interpretation and debate. Regardless, public opinion polls do not constitute an appropriate basis for changing clinical practice and laws. Sound ethical reasoning should be the basis of any changes in the law.

In 1995 a Senate commission reviewed the issues concerning assisted suicide with an eye to whether the law about these matters should be changed. In keeping with the line of argument developed in the case of Nancy B., the commission distinguished between respecting a person's wish to refuse life-sustaining treatment and assisting someone who wishes to die. The commission recommended that assisted suicide should not be legalized. The issue continues to be debated in Canadian coffee shops and classrooms.

## 5. Involuntary Active Euthanasia: The Case of Tracy Latimer

Another case that garnered great attention and put the issue of euthanasia on the front pages of newspapers was the case of Tracy Latimer, a twelve-year-old girl suffering from cerebral palsy caused by brain damage at birth. She was a quadriplegic. She was unable to speak or recognize her own name, and had vision problems. She suffered seizures and extreme pain from muscles tensing, and had gone through several operations related to the condition. It was uncertain whether or to what extent further surgery would alleviate her pain, and whether her family would be able to continue looking after her at home. Resources to support families with children with special needs are limited. By all accounts the Latimer family was attentive and devoted to Tracy.

Tracy's father confessed to ending Tracy's life by carbon monoxide poisoning. He argued that he did so because he was certain that his daughter's condition would not improve and he wanted to end her pain and suffering. Latimer viewed his actions as mercy killing. In 1995 he was found guilty of second-degree murder.

A crucial difference between this case and the cases of Nancy B. and Sue Rodriguez is that Tracy Latimer was not able to express any wishes in the matter. Her case is thus a clear-cut example of involuntary euthanasia. Regardless of Latimer's motives — and even if his intentions were entirely beneficent and centred on what he believed best for his daughter — his action counts as murder in Canadian law.

In 2002 the Netherlands legalized voluntary, active euthanasia. Euthanasia is still a criminal offence, but the *Dutch Euthanasia Act* states that euthanasia and physician-assisted suicide are not punishable provided that an agreed-upon process is followed. It includes a requirement that euthanasia arise from the patient's request, that the patient's suffering is unbearable and hopeless, that the patient is provided with information and reasonable alternatives, and that another physician is consulted. Similar legislation was passed in Belgium. In North America the only jurisdiction to allow legally assisted death is Oregon, which passed a right-to-die law in 1999. Oregon voters have twice upheld a law that permits the terminally ill to take an overdose of drugs if two doctors agree with the diagnosis and conclude that the patient is of sound mind. Still, involuntary active euthanasia — as in the Latimer case — is not accepted in any of these jurisdictions. However, voluntary active euthanasia — as in the Rodriguez case — is legal.

In Canada both voluntary active euthanasia and involuntary active euthanasia are legally forbidden. Whether the law should be changed is an ethical, social, and political question that remains much debated. In 2009 the Quebec College of Physicians cautiously expressed support for limited euthanasia, calling for an open debate on the topic (Quebec College of Physicians and Surgeons, 2009). The College reported its belief that the legislation in place does not reflect the clinical reality of patients or their doctors and has restricted the development of appropriate end of life care. The College concluded that when death is both inevitable and imminent, hastening death could be considered appropriate medical care.

Canadian nurses undoubtedly hold a range of views about euthanasia, and it is important for them to participate in public debate on the issue — keeping in mind the various distinctions related to the concepts.

## The Challenges of Autonomy

Respect for autonomy represents a formidable commitment for nurses, especially given the different meanings of the concept. There may well be doubt as to whether a particular patient is autonomous, or about what course of action will best promote autonomy. When emphasis is placed on the patient's right to make decisions, difficulties can arise if the option selected is incompatible with the nurse's professional judgement, with the agency or institution's policy or practices, or with the plan of care. In some cases, advocacy on behalf of the patient's autonomy can lead to moral distress. Nurses should discuss these difficult cases with colleagues, mentors, and perhaps their professional organization. In some institutions a clinical ethics committee may be available for consultation.

Acknowledgement of the patient's right to participate in decisions affecting personal health and welfare carries a corresponding obligation for the nurse to assist the patient to have access to and understand relevant information. Nurses need to be sensitive to Canada's multicultural composition. In Western countries, personal freedom is highly valued — and not infrequently placed above the welfare of others or of the community. Many ethical problems are framed as conflicts between the rights of one person or group and the rights of another person or group. However, for some ethnic groups and some individuals, respect for individual autonomy is not an ethical priority. Consideration of the well-being of family and community may be immensely important to these patients. In such situations nurses can find themselves conflicted in their commitment to respect patient autonomy.

Difficult issues, then, can arise in connection with autonomy — and as the following cases illustrate, a respect for autonomy can quite easily come into conflict with other cherished values in nursing.

### Case 1: Advocating on Behalf of Vulnerable or Voiceless Patients

Respect for autonomy goes well beyond honouring the wishes of a clearly competent patient, as important as that may be. It also comes into play with respect to patients whose autonomy is in question, or who for one reason or another cannot make their preferences known. This first case, then, focuses on instances of treatment refusal or disagreement involving patients who are incapable of engaging in discussions with their health practitioners.

Individuals, such as young children or persons with dementia unable to identify or articulate their needs and preferences, may be at risk of being ignored or deprived of adequate care. With such patients, the nurse's advocacy role is appropriate and may complement the role of substitute decision-maker taken on by a family member or legal guardian. Likewise, nurses may spend long hours with patients and know better than anyone else what care the person wants or does not want. In this decision-making process the team should give consideration to the known preferences or wishes of the patient. These wishes should be shared with colleagues immediately and clearly documented.

In the case of patients whose autonomy is diminished or otherwise impaired, but who may still be capable of some measure of autonomy, respect for autonomy may require a special effort. Nurses will need to determine what the patients really want, perhaps by empowering them to become more assertive and helping them to achieve greater control over their situations. The task may be increased when institutional arrangements are not conducive to the flourishing of patient autonomy. In some institutions, patients may be treated in ways that effectively infantilize or manipulate them and suppress autonomy.

*Marianne, thirty-five, is a registered nurse who normally works in intensive care. She now happens to be a patient in the same hospital that employs her. Marianne is well-liked and respected by her colleagues there. An accomplished amateur hockey player, she fell on the ice during a game and sustained a concussion. Examinations revealed a brain tumour. Her clinical team thinks her prognosis is good. The doctors recommend surgery.*

Marianne is accompanied to the hospital by her same-sex partner, Joanne. As an experienced nurse, Marianne knows that before the surgery she will be asked about resuscitation. She wants to say no to the resuscitation, but is worried that her colleagues will resent that decision — she well remembers hearing comments made when patients with a good prognosis ask for no CPR: "Why are we bothering if they don't want to live?" She now fears that her colleagues will be thinking, "Why are we working so hard, if she doesn't want CPR?" But Joanne supports her decision, and together they approach her nurses, ask for a DNR order, and complete an advance directive saying that if she has a cardiac arrest during the procedures, she does not want CPR. Marianne takes the time to explain her point of view: if she arrests, the probability of her recovering from the surgery will be significantly diminished. But she also makes clear that she does want other life-support interventions of intubation, oxygen, and antibiotics. The neurosurgery team expresses surprise at her decision. The team argues that if she does have a cardiac arrest she could come through it and do well. Marianne says she is not willing to take that chance.

Marianne starts to put her affairs in order. She calls her parents. She has had little contact with them for the past five years; when she "came out," they did not approve of her lifestyle, largely because it conflicted with their religious beliefs. She left her hometown and moved to a large urban community. She has kept in touch through cards on annual holidays, phone calls, and emails with her parents. They take the "don't ask, don't know" approach. When they hear she has brain cancer, they take an airplane trip from the East Coast to be with her. They plan to stay in the city until after the surgery. They take turns with Joanne at her bedside.

The day before her surgery Marianne has pre-operative medication that will sedate her. Joanne is exhausted and goes home for some rest. The parents stay at their daughter's bedside. Joanne plans to return to be with Marianne during the evening before surgery. Marianne, in an induced coma, arrests. Her parents are with her. They tell her nurse, Suzanne, to call a code. Suzanne hesitates. She says that Marianne stated that she would not want *to be resuscitated. The parents insist, and Suzanne calls a code. The team works for twenty minutes before the code is cancelled and Marianne is declared dead.*

## Commentary

In this case the patient had clearly planned ahead, making her wishes known and taking the time to do so especially in the event that she arrested. Given that she was in a same-sex relationship but not married, she took the precaution of appointing her partner, Joanne, as her power of attorney for personal and financial care, making sure that Joanne's status was established and her own wishes would be respected. Her parents were unaware of her wishes and would not have approved because of their religious beliefs. They were not her substitute decision-makers. Her nurse, Suzanne, was aware that same-sex partners rank higher than parents on the list of substitute decision-makers, and she knew what Marianne wanted. Still, in the face of the insistence from Marianne's parents, Suzanne followed their wishes.

Despite the intense pressure she was under, Suzanne had a moral obligation to advocate for her vulnerable patient and explain to the parents that they should respect their daughter's stated wishes. If they objected, she would have to explain that Joanne has been assigned the role of substitute decision-maker. The prior wishes should not be overruled. Their duty as parents, like the duty of the nurse, is to respect Marianne's advance wishes.

Unfortunately, when Marianne was conscious her nurses did not help her discuss her wishes with her parents; and Marianne's team could not inform her parents of these wishes because the information was confidential. Still, the team members could have explained to Marianne how important it was for her parents to understand her wishes, even if they could not agree.

Given that this conversation did not happen, the parents were shocked and insisted on cardio-pulmonary resuscitation. Suzanne and the team complied with the parents' frantic demand that Marianne's life be saved. In the urgency of the moment Suzanne was influenced by the emotional pleas of Marianne's parents. Instead the nurse ought to have been Marianne's advocate during a time when the patient could not speak for herself.

To prevent this situation from happening again, the unit team reviewed the hospital policy regarding advance directives, changes regarding same-sex partners as decision-makers, and cases in which hospital staff can refuse requests from a family that are contrary to the patient's prior wishes. Certainly it is difficult to advocate for a voiceless person at such a time. Yet Suzanne and members of the arrest team ought to have respected the patient's wishes. One consequence of their decision was that Marianne experienced a less peaceful death than should have been the case. Suzanne, along with all the clinical team at the arrest, had a duty to advocate for the good of the patient.

This issue can also be approached through the principle of autonomy. Nurses should be aware of any impediments to the realization of patient autonomy and act in ways that increase the opportunities for patients to become more autonomous. Nurses need to think about whether patients are intimidated or silenced by the culture of the unit. Patients may be hesitant to ask for cessation of life support, oxygen, antibiotics, DNR, or a transfer to palliative care. As an intervention that can be refused, CPR is only one of many that are available to sustain life. No CPR does not mean no to all other interventions. Each option must be discussed. Marianne did not want CPR, but she did want surgery, oxygen, antibiotics, and intubations, for example. It is possible that the unit's expectations that patients fight their illnesses have the effect of silencing or making it stressful for patients to ask questions, challenge their clinical team, ask for a second opinion, and refuse recommended care.

The diminished autonomy of patients may be in part a result of how the unit staff relates to them. Explicitly stated and implied expectations can convey equally strong messages. For example, when clinical staff members use the language of war — that is, we will beat or defeat this disease — a patient who says "Enough" may fear being considered weak and a coward. The patient may think she or he is letting the team down. A vicious circle might be at work here: the patients, feeling vulnerable, put themselves in the hands of the oncology staff; in turn the staff responds by putting forward a brave manner, offering everything in their arsenal to beat the illness or disease. It is difficult to challenge the culture under such circumstances.

It takes empathy and time to respect autonomy by allowing patients to voice fears and ask questions, and in waiting for them to make complex decisions. Patients need to know that they can disagree with recommendations without being penalized. Sad to say, treating patients like objects may be more economical than treating them as human beings. Keeping them at a distance can also prevent engagement, which can in turn lead to morally distressing situations, such as the one in which Marianne's nurse found herself.

The value and benefits of respect for autonomy and dignity are hard to measure qualitatively. In contrast, the outcome of treatments and physical care is measurable. Nurses also suffer when the prerequisites for respecting patients' wishes are missing, when they lack professional autonomy and feel that they have no voice. When they have insufficient time and resources, they will find it difficult to respect patient autonomy, advocate for patients, and provide high-quality, compassionate care. In this case nurses need to consider how they can advocate for themselves, so they too can be autonomous. Unless nurses themselves have autonomy, they cannot carry on their own practice effectively, and cannot in turn respect patients' wishes.

After this incident Suzanne and her colleagues recognized that they had to work to change the culture of the unit. They wanted patients to feel free to ask questions and change their treatment plans without running the risk of rejection or angering the team. The entire unit's staff became aware of their influence over patients. They reminded themselves that patient-focused care meant that they had "to walk the talk." They admitted that some of them were not up to date on the rights of same-sex couples. Looking at their practice, nurses realized that they needed to find ways of exercising their moral authority and of being supported by their team. They recognized that they had to respect a patient's informed and freely decided wishes. The discussion with colleagues and the administration confirmed that the nurses' decision in such a case would be supported. They talked about the thorny issue of not providing CPR when the clinical facts make it clear that the person will not survive the resuscitation. Previously nurses had been calling slow codes to avoid these problems. Because of their frank discussions, they now know that slow codes should not have to be called.

The nurses, with support from the professional development staff, took and implemented a program about learning how to communicate empathetically with cancer patients and to support them to make informed, freely made decisions. Staff learned that when a patient accepts some interventions but not others — for example, oxygen, antibiotics, and surgery but not resuscitation and intubations — it is not a question of patients being weak and of staff being let down.

In choosing how to respond to this issue, nurses are making a decision about what kind of practitioners they want to be. If they conform to the tradition of the unit, they might well be sacrificing their moral integrity. Suzanne had the support of her colleagues when she asked that they all learn from the situation.

Sometimes nurses who advocate for the profession and for patients are at risk of being labelled as troublemakers. The work environment may be soured; the nurse may feel isolated and want to leave the profession. Professional practice standards should include welcoming calls to examine practice to make certain that caregivers are both hearing and respecting the autonomy of patients.

### Case 2: Autonomy in the Research Context

Research is essential to the goal of furthering knowledge, and such knowledge in turn is important to promote health and help people who are sick; but research projects can give rise to slightly different kinds of autonomy issues. The good to be gained from research must be balanced against concern for the subjects of the research. That concern is directed not only to the good of the research subjects, conceived in terms of possible harms and benefits, but also more broadly to their autonomy.

Over the years — and against the background of publicized abuses — ethical guidelines for research involving human subjects have been drafted by many institutions and a number of different professions. The Canadian Nurses Association (CNA, 2002) and the Tri-Council (1998) guidelines emphasize the importance of respect for autonomy in the research context. One of the main ethical concerns in research ethics has to do with protocols for informed consent. The CNA and Tri-Council guidelines require that the person being invited to participate must understand and appreciate relevant information, including the purpose of the research, how they, as subjects, will be involved, the risks to themselves, any benefits they may enjoy, and how their identity and information will be kept confidential. They must be told that they can refuse to participate, or that they can leave the study without penalty. All of these conditions for informed consent need to be interpreted with reference to particular cases. Such an interpretation is not like the application of a mechanical formula. There are grey areas.

Research involving human subjects can be divided into two main kinds: therapeutic and non-therapeutic.[12] Non-therapeutic research holds out no benefit for the research subjects, who, therefore, have no self-interest in participating. Therapeutic research does offer research subjects a possibility of benefit, and this prospect may be decisive in motivating them to participate in the research.

The ethics of therapeutic research are especially complex. As Thomas (1983) points out, such research introduces the possibility of a serious role conflict. In the context of therapeutic research, the research subject is also a patient; the researcher may also be a caregiver. The caregiver-patient relationship is different from the researcher–research subject relationship. The foremost concern of the caregiver is the good of the patient; the foremost concern of the researcher is the success of the research.

Problems can arise if roles become blurred and relationships overlap. The trust conferred upon someone by virtue of being in a caregiver role might carry over if the same person happens also to relate to the patient as a researcher. The patient may fear that a refusal to participate in research will jeopardize the quality of care or subsequent therapeutic relationships. Elements of coercion, intended or not, can come into play and compromise the integrity of the informed consent process. Students, residents of institutions, and members of vulnerable populations can be more attracted to incentives and reimbursements for research participation than financially stable persons will be. For this reason, an ethical design includes an informed consent, and a consent that is not pressured or coerced (Grant & Sugarman, 2004).

Capacity or competence to consent is a focal point of concern in the research context. The assessment of capacity can be especially difficult when, as is often the case, the patient's cognitive status varies from time to time, or when the patient is deemed capable of making some but not all decisions. Elderly patients present special problems because they often have diminished autonomy and may be more vulnerable than other patients. The following case concerns a double-blind study in which neither the Registered Nurse giving the medication nor the research subject/patient knows what is being administered: an experimental drug or a placebo.

*Mohammed Mansour, a senior nurse researcher, is participating in a national study to examine the coping strategies of families that have a child or adolescent diagnosed with juvenile diabetes. He received approval to run the study in the diabetes clinic of the local children's hospital. In preparing the study for ethics approval he was guided by research codes and guidelines (CNA, 2002). According to the study plan, the diabetes clinic staff will ask families to take home information packages about the study; and information about the study will be posted in the clinic. Mohammed, the principal investigator, asks the nurse manager and the staff to encourage families to take part in the study. Routinely, the families who participate will meet with Mohammed and his staff to discuss the management of the patients' diabetes. The clinic staff members themselves will not know which of their patients are taking part in the study.*

*Shirley Walsh, the nursing manager, is uneasy with this request. Her staff has close relationships with the families, and she is worried that the families will feel pressured to join the study. She asks her staff what they think, and they respond that they feel uncomfortable with asking families to consider joining the study. They all agree that families will feel pressured to consent. They think that the request will interfere with their therapeutic relationship with the families.*

*Shirley has a meeting with her staff to discuss their concerns. They look at the questionnaire and consent form. They can see that the questionnaire raises sensitive issues about the short-term and long-term effects of living with juvenile diabetes. They decide that these issues should be discussed in a face to face interview. The nurses also notice that the identified risks for families do not include the emotional distress that a family may experience during or following the interview with the researcher. In the case of adolescents, they think that, rather than asking the parents, the researcher should ask the teenagers themselves if they want to participate. Some families and individual children and adolescents have been waiting for counselling for several weeks. The clinic staff is a great source of support for the parents, children, and teenagers. Given what individuals and families have told them, they fear that the design of the study does not adequately protect the autonomy of individuals or protect them from a reasonable harm that can arise after they are asked questions about the mortality and morbidity of juvenile diabetes. The unit staff agrees. They cannot ask families and individuals to participate in the study.*

*The unit staff members also feel that the design, in its present format, is lacking in some specifics. They ask the principal investigator to revise the study to take into account their valid concerns based on their day to day knowledge of the patients and how they live with this difficult condition. They meet and have a productive meeting. The requested changes are made, and Mohammed can complete his important research. He appreciates that Shirley and the other front-line nurses have a responsibility to act as patients' advocates. The patients' good is their priority. He also learns about the importance of working more closely with the nursing staff when developing a research proposal. Mohammed contacts other pediatric agencies where the study is being conducted and suggests that they make the same changes.*

## Commentary

This case raises several issues. First, the nurses correctly ascertained that in asking patients and their family members to join the study they would be putting pressure on those families to participate. The nurses would be in a conflict of interest. Their first priority is to act in the patient's best interest, not to advance nursing research. They recognize that they have an obligation to support nursing and health sciences research, but not at the cost of coercing someone to join a study. The nurses have a relationship based on therapeutic goals, on working for the best interest of the patients. They know that they can preface their invitation to join the study with a statement that participants can refuse to join and leave the study whenever they wish. Yet they know that this statement, along with a declaration that they will not know who enters the study, will not remove the pressure placed on patients; the very fact that the request came from them in itself would constitute pressure.

The second issue is who to ask for consent. When the patient is young, the parent, parents, or guardian would be approached. Yet some patients are mature enough to be making treatment decisions for themselves. They are what are termed, legally, a mature minor. Although young in years, they have met the standard of understanding and appreciating relevant information and can make decisions freely. Some adolescents in their early teens may be found to be mature minors, depending on their individual attributes.

Thus the nurses are wise to be reluctant to approach the parent or parents of a patient who is a mature minor and ask if their family unit is interested in joining the study. The first person to ask is the mature minor. The consent does not mention that the interviews may touch on sensitive topics, and that family members may feel distressed. Also, the research project makes no offer of help for families who find they need to talk about any feelings or difficulties that come to the surface during the research interview. Thus the project neither identifies a potential harm to the participants nor provides a way of responding to potential harm.

Thirdly, the front-line nurses who know the patients best were not consulted when the study was designed. If they had been, they could have helped the researchers understand the lived experience of patients and their families in coping with juvenile diabetes. They could have helped the researchers create a study that would be sensitive to the vulnerabilities of patients and their families.

Shirley calls the ethicist who is the head of the Clinical Ethics Committee, which approved the study. The hospital ethicist, the principal investigator, and Shirley meet to review the study. The investigator listens and realizes that valid points have been raised and must be addressed. The Clinical Ethics Committee is contacted.

First, Mohammed agrees to changes in the design and consent form. He will employ a research assistant to contact potential participants. No one involved with patient care will talk to the patients about the research. The research assistant must tell those contacted that they are under no obligation to join, and the clinic will never know their response.

Second, Mohammed goes ahead to change the project design. He recognizes that the questions about coping and anxiety are best broached in an interview. All participants will be asked to meet with Mohammed to discuss how they are coping with living with the illness. The questionnaire is changed to gather demographic and clinical management issues. The consent form is changed to explain that there will be an interview and questionnaire. Also, Mohammed makes himself available for follow-up with any patients who find the research process stressful. Mohammed agrees to include, in the explanation of the study and the consent form, examples of the types of questions that will be asked, and to warn that some people may find the questions and interview distressing. The researchers will provide a phone number for a counselling service to assist any individuals involved in the study.

Mohammed thanks Shirley for pointing out that adolescents should be asked to participate as individuals. The researchers also agree that they will not give the names of adolescents who agree or refuse to participate to their parent or parents. Thus, the research assistant who contacts teenagers will ask their consent before they approach their parents to invite participation.

Without these changes, the consent would not be informed or voluntary. Informed consent requires that the subject be informed about the nature, risks, and possible benefits of the research or therapy, and of reasonable alternatives where this is applicable. Given the involvement of the clinic staff in their patients' care, the staff members themselves are not the appropriate persons to obtain consent.

Research involving children, students, prisoners, residents of health care organizations, and persons with diminishing or diminished mental capabilities raises serious ethical concerns about respect for autonomy. The recruitment of subjects should be planned to overcome this problem of coercion.

### Case 3: End of Life Decisions

The ethical issues surrounding dying and death are a topic of great interest to nurses. These issues make the front pages of newspapers and draw intense medical attention. The Terri Schiavo case was widely discussed, from all-news cable stations to coffee shops across North America. This case reveals the complexity of the issues regarding assisted suicide and passive euthanasia (Annas, 2005).

Schiavo was a young Florida woman living in a persistent vegetative state (PVS). Her situation in 2005 attracted the attention of State Governor Jeb Bush and his brother, President George W. Bush. The case became a cause célèbre for those who oppose any form of assisted suicide and promote the sanctity of all life, and the clinical facts are crucial.

*Terri Schiavo suffered a cardiac arrest in 1990 at the age of twenty-seven. After that she lived in a persistent vegetative state and required a feeding tube for nourishment and hydration. Persistent vegetative state is a subgroup of comatose states of patients who have suffered anoxic brain injury and progress to a state of wakefulness without awareness. People in a persistent vegetative state do not feel pain, because pain requires consciousness. Furthermore, because she had brain-stem damage, with this severe neurological condition she would not experience thirst, hunger, pain, or suffering and could not respond to any external stimuli. Video clips on television presenting her as responding to her mother and her eyes following directions were tragic to watch. They also gave the false impression that she could respond to stimuli. Schiavo's condition was irreversible. Her autopsy showed that she was severely and irreversibly brain-damaged and totally blind.*

*Dehydration, brought about by a prolonged lack of food and water, causes kidney failure, which leads to elevated toxins and chemicals in the blood that in turn cause the person to slip into a coma. The severe biochemical changes in the blood impair the electrical system that controls the heart. Elevated potassium causes the heart to go into an arrhythmia and to stop beating.*

*Although Schiavo did not issue a formal advance directive, she had stated her wishes for treatment before she went into a coma, and her husband, Michael, wanted her statements in that regard to be respected. In 1998 he petitioned the court to get permission to discontinue the feeding tube. Food and water have special moral significance for many because they are associated with nurturing and caring. Hence the withdrawal of a ventilator may be more acceptable than removal of a feeding tube because of the meaning associated with food and feeding. Schiavo's parents did not agree with her husband's request, and the case went before the courts to decide the patient's fate. In 2005 her husband's petition was granted.*

*The parents, Robert and Mary Schindler, objected. First, they denied that the statements made should be taken as prior wishes. Second, they stated that removal of the feeding tube was active involuntary euthanasia and assisted suicide. With the removal of the feeding tube, Schiavo would be starved to death. Her parents, believing that this step represented the intentional end of her life, ironically said that it would be kinder to give her a lethal dose than it would be to prolong the dying process. They appealed the court decision, asserting that, given their daughter was being helped to die, she should receive palliative care. They argued that the court should overlook any statements made about never wanting to be dependent on life support.*

*The case presented many legal hurdles and challenges. Her parents were supported from many areas, including their faith group and "right to life" organizations. When the courts decided that Schiavo's wishes should be respected and gave her substitute decision-maker, her husband, permission to discontinue the feeding, the parents again objected. They argued that the husband was not acting in his wife's best interests and had undermined his integrity as her substitute decision-maker because he had, in the meantime, started a new family. These charges were not upheld. His motives and devotion to respecting his wife's wishes were affirmed by the courts and all who knew him. Judges found clear and convincing evidence that Terri Schiavo was in a permanent or persistent vegetative state and that, if she could make her own decision, she would choose to discontinue life-prolonging procedures (Annas, 2005). Terri Schiavo died on March 31, 2005, thirteen days after the feeding tube was removed.*

*During the thirteen days between removal of the feeding tube and her death, marches and demonstrations protesting the decision took place. The protesters charged that the hospital staff and her husband were engaged in active euthanasia. The supporters responded that the issue at hand was a case of respecting a person's prior wishes and of passive euthanasia.*

## Commentary

Although the media reports often reduced this to a case about active euthanasia and the "starving" of Terri Schiavo, the ethical issues are not so black and white. The principle of autonomy is central to the case. Autonomy entails self-determination and the right to make independent decisions concerning one's own life and well-being. Although Schiavo had lost the capacity to make informed choices, her autonomy was respected. Several judges accepted that her statements were sufficient to guide decision-making when she could not direct her own care. In this case there was not a living will or an advance directive prepared by the patient and witnessed. But her wishes and values were deemed to be known; her husband, as her substitute decision-maker, was acting on what he believed she would have wanted.

Her parents questioned whether her husband was properly fulfilling the responsibilities of a substitute decision-maker. They reasoned that the prior statements were not valid and that her husband should not be making decisions about what was in their daughter's best interests. For them, the answer was clear. It was in their daughter's best interests to continue being fed through the tube and to be allowed to live as long as possible. For them it was a case of others intending to end their daughter's life. They argued that if the clinical staff thought death was near and she was in distress, they could give her analgesia or sedation. This intervention would be palliative care. The intent would be to relieve suffering and not to hasten death. If death did occur, it would be an unintended end. The theory of double-effect is relevant. The primary intention was to relieve discomfort, and the secondary and unintended result would be her death, which was imminent.

It is fair to assume that her husband would have reached a different conclusion about what was in his wife's best interests based on the quality of her life. Yet he said he was not using the best-interest criteria. For him and the judicial system, it was a case of respect for expressed wishes. Once those concerned decide that a feeding tube will be removed, the question arises: what is happening here, clinically and ethically? Clinically, with the disconnection of the tube, neurologists explained, given her severe brain-stem injury she would not experience distress. It would take several days for her to die.

The ethical significance of what happened is not so easy to discern. Her parents argued that the removal of the nutrition and hydration was the cessation of a life-support system, and the obvious outcome would be death. To argue that proposed actions were based only on respect for her wishes is to deny what everyone knew would happen. Terri Schiavo would die because the feeding tube was removed. Her husband and other supporters of the tube removal saw this firstly as a case of respect for autonomy and, secondly, a case of passive euthanasia.

The conceptual base for the actions in this case depends on a belief in whether or not there is a moral difference between active and passive euthanasia. In a well-known paper James Rachels (1975) made the case that there is not a moral difference, reasoning that in both cases the expected outcome is the same. If you push a man who cannot swim into a river, the result will be his death. If you watch a man struggling in a river and do not act to save his life, you are just as responsible for his death.

Based on the argument made by Rachels, caregivers could argue that when letting someone die by removing life-saving care would prolong suffering, it would be more merciful to end the person's life quickly. But many commentators insist that there is a morally significant difference between deliberate killing and letting someone die, and that health providers should stand by the age-old code against deliberate killing. Clinicians are educated to save lives and to do no harm. Allowing prolonged suffering is psychologically troubling, but for many clinicians it is less so than deliberately killing a person or assisting him or her to die. Moreover, when requested by the patient, the removal of treatment can be conceptualized in terms of respect for that patient's autonomy rather than as letting him or her die.

Nurses who reject the distinction between killing and letting die place themselves in a difficult position. Thus far, efforts to legalize assisted suicide under strict conditions have been unsuccessful in Canada. Nurses will have to decide for themselves whether a death like that of Terri Schiavo was passive or active euthanasia. Depending on their conclusions they may want the professional and legal expectations revised to make it clear when caregivers can respond to patients' expressed wishes for assisted suicide.

As well as a case of passive euthanasia, this situation could also be considered a case of palliative care. Very often palliative care patients with end-stage terminal conditions are not given nourishment or fluids and are given only comfort measures to help relieve any suffering in the end. Terri Schiavo's condition prior to the removal of the feeding tube was not considered end-stage terminal, but there was no cure for her condition; and the prolongation of her life was not an appropriate goal given her stated wishes. After the feeding tube was removed she would have been given comfort measures, and the family would have been given emotional support.

Her quality of life was nil, and not the way she would have wanted to live. She was unable to get any pleasure or enjoyment out of her life; and to work at keeping her alive in such an existence was unethical. There was no reasonable hope for recovery or improvement, and she was unable to experience any benefit from treatment. The autopsy proved that she was severely and irreversibly brain-damaged. There was no hope of recovery.

## Conclusion

Being committed to promoting and respecting autonomy is one thing; knowing how and being able to put this commitment into practice is another. Sometimes it may not be clear exactly what respect for autonomy entails. Often the situation of patients with respect to autonomy is ambiguous. Autonomy may come into conflict with other values such as beneficence and justice. When respect for autonomy can be realized only at the expense of some other value, it may be difficult to decide which value should take precedence.

These challenges are even more difficult given that most nurses are employees in health care facilities and have an obligation of fidelity to their employers, not to mention a prudential interest in getting along well with the powers that be.

The traditional idea of the physician as leader of the health care team may persist, and operate as a constraint. This culture comes with the expectation that nurses will promote compliance with the medical plan of care. In some instances, such compliance may conflict with the moral autonomy of nurses and their duty to advocate on behalf of patient autonomy.

Nurses are accountable and responsible for their practice. They must use their knowledge, judgement, and skills to decide what care to provide, why, and when. If respect for patient autonomy is not to be a mere slogan, nurses will have to think carefully about these matters. They will need to weigh respect for autonomy as a value together with other possibly conflicting values and to develop sound judgement in determining how best to advocate for their patients.

## Notes

1    A number of contemporary theorists point out that we ought to pay more attention to children's capacities for autonomous participation in health care decision-making. See Carnevale (2004).

2    This analysis is based on Miller (1981, pp. 24-25) but slightly diverges from it. For a more detailed analysis of the concept of autonomy, and of the various meanings the concept has taken on, see Dworkin (1988).

3    Note that health care agencies in some jurisdictions, such as Ontario, are required to have "least restraint" policies. The restraint standard of the

College of Nurses of Ontario (2009) presents the professional responsibility of nurses in respect to restraint use. The Registered Nurses of Ontario (2002), *Prevention of falls and falls injuries in the older adult: Best Practice Guidelines*, provides evidence to support least restraint policies.

4    Gadow (1980) uses the concept of authenticity somewhat differently than does Miller (1981). What Gadow means by autonomy is closer in meaning to what Miller calls "moral reflection."

5    Mackenzie and Stoljar (2000, p. 21) explain: "An analysis of the characteristics and capacities of the self cannot be adequately undertaken without attention to the rich and complex social and historical contexts in which agents are embedded; they point to the need to think of autonomy as a characteristic of agents who are emotional, embodied, desiring, creative and feeling, as well as rational, creatures; and they highlight the ways in which agents are both psychically internally differentiated and socially differentiated from others." Agents are seen as relational "because their identities or self-conceptions are constituted by elements of the social context in which they are embedded" and "because their natures are produced by certain historical and social conditions" (p. 22). (See also Bergum, 2004; Rodney, Brown, & Liaschenko, 2004.)

6    The term "consent" suggests a certain passivity in relation to the decision to be taken. For this reason, some people prefer to speak instead of "informed choice." There is some difference of opinion in the literature as to whether informed consent should be thought of and justified primarily in terms of autonomy or in terms of beneficence. Proponents of the latter view (e.g., Appelbaum, Lidz, & Meisel, 1987) emphasize the therapeutic value of informed consent, presenting clinical evidence that participation in decision-making serves clinical goals and is in fact good for the patient. Informed consent is to be valued in health care insofar as it serves the goals of beneficence. Proponents of the former view (e.g., Faden & Beauchamp, 1986) tend not to put as great an emphasis on the therapeutic value of informed consent, arguing that it promotes autonomy and is valuable for that reason alone — even if it should turn out to be contra therapeutic.

7    For a detailed account of informed consent geared to practitioners, see Appelbaum, Lidz, & Meisel (1987). For a more philosophical account, see Fadden & Beauchamp (1986). See also Mogg and Bartlett (2005); Schacter, Kleinman, & Harvey (2005).

8    See, for example, the CRNBC (2005) policy on informed consent.

9    More precisely, acting on behalf of people's own good can be broken down into acting to prevent harm to them and acting to provide benefit for them.

As a justification for limiting autonomy, the latter is obviously much more contentious. Similarly, limiting someone's autonomy on behalf of the good of others may be done either to prevent harm to others, or to provide benefit to others. Here too the latter is much more contentious.

10   Mill makes it clear that he does not intend this principle to apply to people who are not autonomous (e.g., people not of legal age, people with serious mental problems, and so forth). Frequently, issues of paternalism hinge on whether the person really is autonomous; that is, on whether the principle applies at all.

11   Mill's principle is further complicated by the distinction between actions that would harm only one and actions that would harm other people. This distinction between so-called "self-regarding" and "other-regarding" actions may be blurred. For example, a person's decision to refuse treatment may indirectly risk harm to others in his or her family.

12   The distinction between therapeutic and non-therapeutic research has been challenged on several grounds and no longer enjoys the vogue it once had. To be sure, we agree that the distinction is problematic but nonetheless believe it is useful for getting at an important point about role conflict.

## References

Annas, G.J. (2005). "Culture of life" politics at the bedside — The case of Terri Schiavo. *New England Journal of Medicine*, April 2, 1352, 1710.

Appelbaum, P.S., Lidz, C.W., & Meisel, A. (1987). *Informed consent: Legal theory and clinical practice.* New York: Oxford University Press.

Beauchamp, T.L. (1989). Informed consent. In R. Veatch (Ed.), *Medical ethics* (pp. 173-200).

Bergum, V. (2004). Relational ethics in nursing. In J. Storch, P. Rodney, & R. Starzomski (Eds.), *Toward a moral horizon: Nursing ethics for leadership and practice* (pp. 485-503). Toronto: Pearson-Prentice Hall.

Canadian Medical Association. (2005). *Joint statement on resuscitative interventions.* Ottawa.

Canadian Nurses Association. (1998). *Nursing ethics, ethics in practice. Advance directives: The nurse's role.* Ottawa.

Canadian Nurses Association. (2000). *End of life decisions.* Ottawa.

Canadian Nurses Association. (2002). *Ethical research guidelines for registered nurses.* Ottawa.

Canadian Nurses Association (2008). *Code of ethics for registered nurses.* Ottawa.

Carnevale, F.A. (2004). Listening authentically to youthful voices: A conception of the moral agency of children. In J.L. Storch, P. Rodney, & R. Starzomski

(Eds.), *Toward a moral horizon: Nursing ethics for leadership and practice* (pp. 396-413). Toronto: Pearson Education.

Carstairs, S. (2005) *Still not there: Quality end-of-life care: A progress report.* Ottawa.

Clements, C.D., & Sider, R.C. (1988). Medical ethics' assault upon medical values. In R.B. Edwards & G.C. Graber (Eds.), *Bioethics* (pp. 150-158). San Diego: Harcourt Brace Jovanovich.

College of Nurses of Ontario. (2009). *Restraints.* Toronto.

College of Registered Nurses of British Columbia (2005). *Practice standard for registered nurses and nurse practitioners: Consent.* Vancouver.

Coward, H. & Ratanakul, P. (Eds.) (1999). *A cross-cultural dialogue on health care ethics.* Waterloo, ON: Wilfrid Laurier University Press.

Culver, C., & Gert, B. (1990). The Inadequacy of incompetence. *The Millbank Quarterly* 68(4), 619-643.

Davis, A.J. (1988). The clinical nurse's role in informed consent. *Journal of Professional Nursing* 4 (2), 88-91.

Doane, G.H., & Varcoe, C. (2005). *Family nursing as relational inquiry: Developing health promoting practice.* Philadelphia, PA: Lippincott, Williams, & Wilkins.

Drane, J.F. (1988). The many faces of competency. In R.B. Edwards & G.C. Graber (Eds.), *Bioethics* (pp. 169-177). San Diego: Harcourt Brace Jovanovich.

Dworkin, G. (1988). *The theory and practice of autonomy.* Cambridge: Cambridge University Press.

Edwards, R.B., & Graber, G.C. (Eds.). (1988). *Bioethics.* San Diego: Harcourt Brace Jovanovich.

Ericksen, J., Rodney, P., & Starzomski, R. (1995). When is it right to die? *Canadian Nurse* 91 (8), 29–34.

Faden, R.R., & Beauchamp, T.L. (1986). *A history and theory of informed consent.* New York: Oxford University Press.

Feinberg, J. (1971). Legal paternalism. *Canadian Journal of Philosophy* 1 (1), 105-124.

*Fleming v. Reid.* (1990). 82 D.L.R. (4th) 289 (Ont. C.A.) at 316.

Gadow, S.A. (1980). Existential advocacy: Philosophical foundations of nursing. In S.F. Spicker & S.A. Gadow (Eds.), *Nursing: Images and ideals* (pp. 79-101). New York: Springer.

Gadow, S.A. (1989). Clinical subjectivity: Advocacy with silent patients. *Nursing Clinics of North America* 24 (2), 535-541.

Gordon, R.M. (2000). The emergence of assisted (supported) decision-making in the Canadian law of adult guardianship and substitute decision-making. *International Journal of Law and Psychiatry* 23 (1), 61-77.

Grant, R., & Sugarman, J. (2004). Ethics in human subjects research: Do incentives matter? *Journal of Medicine & Philosophy* 29 (6)(December 2004), 717-738.

Hunter, L. (2005). From the local to the global: Bioethics and the concept of culture. *Journal of Medical Philosophy* 30 (3) (June), 305-320.

Hurst, S., & Mauron, A. (2006). The ethics of palliative care and euthanasia: exploring common values. *Palliative Medicine* 20, 107-112.

Komrad, M.S. (1988). A defence of medical paternalism: Maximizing patient autonomy. In R.B. Edwards & G.C. Graber (Eds.), *Bioethics* (pp. 141-150). San Diego: Harcourt Brace Jovanovich.

Kuhl, D. (2002). *What dying people want: Practical wisdom for the end of life*. Toronto: Doubleday Canada.

Loftus, E.F., & Fries, J.F. (1979). Informed consent may be hazardous to health. *Science* 204 (4388), 11.

Mackenzie, C., and Stoljar, N. (2000). Autonomy refigured. In C. Mackenzie and N. Stoljar (Eds.), *Relational autonomy: Feminist perspectives on autonomy, agency and the social self* (pp. 3–31). New York: Oxford University Press.

Mill, J.S. ([1859] 1975). On liberty. In D. Spitz (Ed.), *On liberty: A Norton critical edition* (pp. 1-106). New York: W.W. Norton.

Miller, B.L. (1981). Autonomy and the refusal of lifesaving treatment. *Hastings Center Report* 11 (4), 22-28.

Mogg, A., & Bartlett, A. (2005). Refusal of treatment in a patient with fluctuating capacity — theory and practice. *Journal of Forensic Psychiatry and Psychology* 16 (1), 60-69.

Ontario Ministry of Health and Long Term Care. (1996). *Health Care Consent Act, 1996* (amended 1998, 2000, 2002, 2004, 2006). <www.e-laws.gov.on.ca>.

Ontario Ministry of Health and Long Term Care *Mental Health Act*, Bill 68. (2000). <www.e-laws.gov.on.ca>.

Pauly, B.M. (2004). Shifting the balance in the funding and delivery of health care in Canada. In J. Storch, P. Rodney, & R. Starzomski (Eds.), *Toward a moral horizon: Nursing ethics for leadership and practice* (pp. 181-208). Toronto: Pearson-Prentice Hall.

Pellegrino, E.D., & Thomasma, D.C. (1988). *For the patient's good: The restoration of beneficence in health care*. New York: Oxford University Press.

Peternelj-Taylor, C. (2004). An exploration of othering in forensic psychiatric and correctional nursing. *Canadian Journal of Nursing Research* 36 (4), 131-146.

Quebec College of Physicans and Surgeons. (2009). *Physicians, appropriate care and the debate on euthanasia*. Quebec.

Rachels, James. (1975). Active and passive euthanasia. *The New England Journal of Medicine* 292, January, 78-80.

Registered Nurses of Ontario. (2002). *Prevention of falls and falls injuries in the older adult: Best practice guidelines*. Toronto.

Rodney, P., Brown, H., & Liaschenko, J. (2004). Moral agency: Relational connections and trust. In J. Storch, P. Rodney, & R. Starzomski (Eds.), *Toward a moral horizon: Nursing ethics for leadership and practice* (pp. 154-177). Toronto: Pearson-Prentice Hall.

Schacter, D., Kleinman, I., & Harvey, W. (2005). Informed consent and adolescents. *Canadian Journal of Psychiatry* 50 (9), 534-540.

Senate Standing Committee on Social Affairs, Science and Technology. (2000). *Quality end-of-life care: The right of every Canadian*. Subcommittee to update "Of Life and Death." Ottawa.

Shafer, A. (2009). The great Canadian euthanasia debate. *The Globe and Mail*, Nov. 5.

Sherwin, S. (1998). A relational approach to autonomy in health care. In S. Sherwin and the Feminist Health Care Ethics Research Network (Eds.), *The politics of women's health* (pp. 19–47). Philadelphia: Temple University Press.

Special Senate Committee on Euthanasia and Assisted Suicide. (1995). *Of life and death: Report of the Special Senate Committee on euthanasia and assisted suicide*. Ottawa.

Storch, J.L. (1988). Ethics in nursing practice. In A.J. Baumgart & J. Larsen (Eds.), *Canadian nursing faces the future: Development and change* (pp. 211-221). St. Louis: C.V. Mosby.

Storch, J.L. (2004). End of life decision making. In J. Storch, P. Rodney, & R. Starzomski (Eds.), *Toward a moral horizon: Nursing ethics for leadership and practice* (pp. 262-284). Toronto: Pearson-Prentice Hall.

Thomas, J.E. (1983). The physician as therapist and investigator. In J.E. Thomas (Ed.), *Medical ethics and human life* (pp. 213-221). Sanibel, FL: Samuel Stevens.

Tri-Council (Medical Research Council of Canada, Natural Sciences and Engineering Research Council of Canada, and Social Sciences and Humanities Research Council of Canada). (1998). *Tri-Council policy statement: Ethical conduct for research involving humans*. Ottawa.

Williams, J.R. (2008). Consent. In P.A. Singer & A.M. Viens (Eds.), *The Cambridge textbook of bioethics* (pp. 11-16). Cambridge: Cambridge University Press.

Wong, J.G., Clare, I.C.H., Gunn, M.J., & Holland, A.J. (1999). Capacity to make health care decisions: its importance in clinical practice. *Psychological Medicine* 29, 437-446.

Zembaty, J.S. (1986). A limited defence of paternalism in medicine. In T.A. Mappes & J.S. Zembaty (Eds.), *Biomedical ethics* (2nd ed., pp. 60-66). New York: McGraw-Hill.

# STUDY QUESTIONS: AUTONOMY

## Case 1: Advocating on Behalf of Vulnerable or Voiceless Patients

1. For the nurses, when the parents insisted that their daughter have CPR, what would be the justification in ethical and legal terms for not following their request?

2. In health care, tensions often arise between nurse and nurse, nurse and patient, and nurse and clinical team. Analyze this case in terms of these three tensions. How can nurses respond and manage these tensions?

3. Nurses need to be aware of their biases and values. In this case, did the nurses make assumptions about Suzanne because she was a nurse, and, if so, what did they assume? Identify biases you may have because of a patient's education and life experiences.

4. Discuss whether and why you agree or disagree with the statement: "Respect for autonomy in theory and in books is noble. But in practice it is different. By respecting autonomy we may be helping someone to die." In these cases should nurses refuse to respect wishes?

5. Discuss this statement: "Respect for autonomy is the right thing to do in theory. But sometimes if wishes are respected, scarce resources are used for futile care. We should be able to say no."

6. Discuss how nurses, their colleagues, and institutions and institutional factors such as structures, policies, or rules can either promote or suppress autonomy. What can be done to change this situation?

7. Consider this statement. "There are some times when you have to say no to requests made by patients." Discuss it with reference to health care, explaining under what conditions you agree and you

disagree. Give an example of when refusing a request is justifiable and not justifiable.

8. Pain management is an ethical issue. Patients' requests for more pain relief are sometimes not respected out of fear of them becoming drug-dependent. Identify the ethical issues associated with pain management and the response that nurses ought to give to this question.

## Case 2: Autonomy in the Research Context

1. Researchers and health care professionals (caregivers) have different responsibilities and wear different hats, so to speak. Describe issues that can arise if the same person wears both hats at the same time.

2. In the event that potential participants are not mentally capable of giving consent, under what conditions, if any, would it be morally permissible for their substitute decision-makers to consent to research participation?

3. The case provides no information about the possible harms and benefits of the study outcomes. What moral relevance might such information have? Would informed consent be less important if the risk of harm was minor or the promise of benefit great? How would this case be different if the effects of a medication were being studied that had no promise of benefit for the participant?

4. Do you agree with the statement that children, students, and persons in prisons and institutions are vulnerable and may find it difficult if not impossible to say no to researchers? What ways, if any, can be used to support these persons regarding informed and freely given consent?

5. Do you think research participants should receive payment for participation? What are the benefits and risks of paying participants? Grant and Sugarman (2004) examine these questions.

6. Aboriginal communities have been the subjects of considerable research. Why do you think a community may refuse to participate in a study about their social and economic challenges?

## Case 3: End of Life Care

1. The terms active and voluntary euthanasia vary greatly. Define these terms. Decide if you think there is or is not a valid moral distinction.

2. Do you think Terri Schiavo's parents were ethically justified when they asserted that the removal of their daughter's feeding tube was assisted suicide?

3. Terri Schiavo's husband argued that the removal of the feeding tube was a case of respect for her wishes. Do you think he was consenting to her dying by means of active or passive euthanasia?

4. What is required for a person's prior wishes to be respected?

5. Under what conditions do you think a person's requests to have care withdrawn should be respected?

6. Compare the Susan Rodriguez, Nancy B., and Terri Schiavo cases. When the nurses followed the patients' wishes, were they engaged in assisted suicide, passive euthanasia, and/or palliative care?

7. Judge Sopinka, when discussing the Sue Rodriguez case, said that passive suicide is a legal fiction. By this he meant that passive suicide is helping someone to die. However, to protect the person from legal problems, it is called passive euthanasia. Do you agree or not? Do you think the present legislation and professional codes give nurses sufficient protection from legal challenges if they respect patients' wishes regarding end of life sustaining care?

# 5 TRUTHFULNESS

*The truth is rarely pure, and never simple.*

-OSCAR WILDE

---

*The paternalism that has for so long been entrenched in the health professions has been especially pronounced in matters of truthfulness and truth-telling. New attitudes toward death and dying, increased emphasis on personal autonomy, and the recognition of a right to informed consent have all called such paternalism into question. The general presumption today is in favour of openness and the disclosure of information to patients. How to tell the truth is as important as what to tell. Obfuscation, talking in jargon, ambiguity, and communicating in mixed signals may be impediments to the honest communication of the truth. Cultural and religious differences may also be barriers. Issues of disclosure and truth-telling are especially complicated in nursing because in many settings a "no-new-information" policy inhibits nurses from disclosing information to patients that has not already been communicated by physicians. The limited autonomy of the profession in this area poses ethical and political challenges.*

*Case studies in this chapter explore deciding whether to disclose a diagnosis, withholding information from a patient at her family's request, and how best and when to give a trauma patient the bad news that her partner died in the accident.*

---

## Truthfulness and Truth-Telling in Health Care

Health professionals possess much general knowledge about the functioning of the body and the symptoms of and treatments for various conditions, as well as salient information and opinions about the health status of patients. The imbalance of knowledge and expertise between health professionals and their patients gives rise to a number of difficult ethical issues, especially with respect to information related to diagnosis and prognosis or that otherwise bears on a patient's ability to make informed choices. Given that the practitioner possesses knowledge of concern to the patient, what are the ethics of concealing and revealing this information? Under what circumstances, if any, is it justifiable to withhold information from or lie to a patient? How important is being truthful as weighed against other values?

Historically, the health professions expressed little concern for truthfulness in their ethical codes (Bok, 1978, pp. 223-224) and are indeed somewhat unique with respect to norms of truth-telling. While it would be unacceptable for lawyers or accountants to deceive their patients, in medicine deception has been widely practised, if not prescribed. To understand why this has been so, one must look at the value system that informs and has shaped the health professions.

Until recently, the good of the patient was the overriding concern. In the hierarchy of values, truthfulness was assigned a subordinate place in relation to benefiting the patient and preventing harm. Decisions about what, when, and whether to tell patients the truth about their medical condition were based on what would be best for the patient's own good. Health professionals subscribed to what Veatch (1976, pp. 206-209) refers to as a special sort of "utilitarianism," in which the anticipated harms and benefits of being either truthful or untruthful are compared to determine which will result in the greatest net benefit. Since in so many instances the disclosure of the truth has been associated with harmful consequences such as anxiety and distress, truth-telling often lost out to the primary concern to do good for the patient (beneficence), or at least to do no harm (nonmaleficence).

Attitudes toward truth-telling among health professionals have undergone much change in the last several decades, as is apparent when one compares surveys conducted on the topic over the years.[1] For example, in a 1961 study, 88 per cent of 219 physicians surveyed said that they did not as a rule inform their patients of a cancer diagnosis (Oken, 1961). By comparison, a 1977 study based on an almost identical questionnaire reported that 98 per cent of 278 physicians surveyed said that it was their general policy to disclose this information (Novack et al., 1979).[2] This data is dramatic evidence of a profound attitudinal shift that is by no means limited to communications about cancer.[3]

Several factors may account for this change in attitude. In the first place, being truthful with patients is less associated with harm than it used to be. In the case of people who are gravely ill, this is partly because there is greater openness about the once taboo topic of death and dying (Goldberg, 1984, p. 949). Today, there is a greater recognition of the therapeutic *benefits* of information disclosure in general. Even from the perspective of the patient's good as the primary concern, there is reason to be more truthful.

Even more important is that the perspective of beneficence is no longer accorded the primacy it once had in the health professions. In the last few decades, the traditional paternalistic style of practice has been superseded by a more co-operative approach that places greater emphasis on patient autonomy, patient education, and informed participation in health care decision-making. Beneficence — especially as associated with paternalism — has been devalued in proportion to the ascent of patient autonomy as a value. A study of communication by specialists in four diverse regions found that Canadian oncologists were more likely to support autonomy over beneficence in discussions about patients' diagnosis and prognosis (Bruera et al., 2000, p. 295).

The ethical consensus today, although by no means unanimous, is that patients have a right to know the truth, even if disclosure is likely to be harmful. There may be rare occasions when less than full and frank disclosure is morally defensible, but as a rule "erring on the side of telling the truth is the safest — and most ethical — policy that caregivers can follow" (Wagner, 1991, p. 68).

## Arguments For and Against Truthfulness in Health Care

Sociological and historical considerations aside, it is important to consider the arguments that can be cited both for and against openness and truth disclosure in the health care context. These will be considered below. The main arguments on either side of the issue depend on how one situates truthfulness in relation to two other values; namely, beneficence and respect for autonomy. Two lesser considerations, one based on the nature of the practitioner-patient relationship and the other on the knowledge gap between health professionals and patients, will also be considered.

### 1. Truthfulness and Beneficence

The main argument given in defence of limited disclosure and even deception is that health professionals have a duty to prevent harm to patients, and telling the truth may very well cause harm. This argument is usually made with reference to information that may cause the patient distress.

One response to this argument is to point out that, although the duty to do no harm is important, health professionals have other duties as well, such as being truthful with patients and respecting their autonomy. If a disclosure will have harmful consequences, truth-telling is indeed at odds with beneficence (or nonmaleficence). The greater the harm foreseen, the more serious the conflict between the obligations. Argued in these terms, the issue depends on how one weighs these duties relative to each other.

Another way of responding to this argument would be to challenge the association of disclosure with harm. There is reason to doubt the factual basis of the worry that disclosure will result in harm, or in balance will result in greater harm than benefit. As it happens, both evasion and frank dishonesty can cause the patient considerable distress and may even prolong the adjustment process (Fallowfield et al., 2002, p. 301), but to what extent is the practitioner able to *predict* this in advance with any accuracy? A blanket assumption that disclosure will prove harmful is dubious at best.[4] In its review of the subject, the

President's Commission for the Study of Ethical Problems in Medicine and Biomedical and Behavioral Research (1982) found that the fears of health professionals about the negative consequences of disclosure tend to be exaggerated:

> Despite all the anecdotes about patients who committed suicide, suffered heart attacks, or plunged into prolonged depression upon being told "bad news," little documentation exists for claims that informing patients is more dangerous to their health than not informing them, particularly when the informing is done in a sensitive and tactful fashion. (p. 96)

The Commission's point about informing patients in a "sensitive and tactful fashion" is an important one. To the extent that disclosure *may* have harmful consequences, the harm can be minimized, if not avoided altogether, by the development of a thoughtful and sensitive bedside manner (Rassin et al., 2006; Matzo et al., 2003). Much attention has been paid to preparing health professionals to deliver "bad news," and algorithms have been developed to facilitate that process (Schoefl, 2008, p. 57).

Indeed, much can be said in support of the claim that the consequences of disclosure, rather than being harmful, or in addition to being harmful, may be beneficial. Bok (1978) writes:

> The damages associated with the disclosure of sad news or risks are rarer than physicians believe; and the *benefits* which result from being informed are more substantial, even measurably so. Pain is tolerated more easily, recovery from surgery is quicker, and cooperation with therapy is greatly improved. The attitude that "what you don't know won't hurt you" is proving unrealistic; it is what patients do not know but vaguely suspect that causes them corrosive worry. (p. 234)

Other benefits could be added to Bok's list. Disclosure makes it possible for patients to express their feelings, and this alone may have therapeutic value. Knowing what is wrong and what to expect can remove needless fears and anxiety, and may enhance the patient's ability to cope (Pratt & Wilkinson, 2003).

## 2. Truthfulness and Autonomy

Although the main arguments supporting limited disclosure and deception tend to centre on beneficence (or nonmaleficence), those supporting greater openness and disclosure tend to focus on respect for autonomy. For example, grounding the duty to tell the truth in human dignity, the American Nurses' Association (ANA, [1976] 1985) states that "truth telling and the process of reaching informed choice underlie the exercise of self-determination, which is basic to respect for persons" (Statement 1.1). The Canadian Nurses Association *Code of Ethics* (2008) asserts that many health care professionals believe that "clients have the right to and will benefit from full disclosure" (p. 13). Clients need relevant information in order to fully exercise their autonomy. In this regard, arguments for openness and disclosure parallel those in support of informed consent. Thus the ANA claims that "clients have the moral right to determine what will be done with their own person; to be given accurate information, and all the information necessary for making informed judgments" (Statement 1.1). To promote informed decision-making, nurses "work to ensure that health information is given to individuals, families, groups, populations and communities in their care in an open, accurate and transparent manner" (CNA, 2008, p. 11). In order to be self-determining in matters of their own health care, patients require adequate and reliable information. The health professional is often in a position to present information that is relevant to a patient's choice, and may do so more or less truthfully. In being truthful, health professionals enable patients to make informed choices on the basis of the truth presented. Conversely, lack of information, or false information, impedes the patient's capacity to make rational choices.

A closely related point is that truthfulness also promotes autonomy by helping patients to maintain a sense of control over their lives. The dying, in particular, have an obvious interest in planning whatever time remains to them, and knowing the truth about their situation affords them the opportunity to do so (Fallowfield et al., 2002).

On the other side of the issue, it is sometimes given as a justification for deceiving or withholding information that some patients, particularly when the medical problem is severe or fatal, do not want to know about their condition (Rassin et al., 2006). In such cases, telling patients the truth may be not only harmful, but would also fail to respect their autonomy. The crucial question raised by this argument concerns what counts as evidence that the patient does not wish to be told the truth. A clear statement to this effect from the patient is one thing; an inference based on a generalization is another. It would not be sufficient simply to assume or project that the patient does not wish to know, especially as there is evidence that in general people do want to know the truth.[5]

## 3. Truthfulness, Trust, and the Practitioner-Patient Relationship

Arguments based on beneficence and autonomy aside, another approach to the issue of disclosure is to ground the practitioner's obligations in the practitioner-patient relationship.[6] This approach tends to conclude in favour of openness and disclosure.[7] The concept of trust plays a pivotal role in analysis along these lines. It is emphasized that the practitioner-patient relationship is a fiduciary one based on mutual trust. Such trust requires that the partners in the relationship relate to each other in a truthful manner. Patients are expected to disclose all relevant information fully and frankly, and practitioners are expected to be truthful in return (Weir, 1980, p. 111). Deception or the withholding of information would endanger this trust and jeopardize the relationship.[8]

## 4. Truthfulness and the Practitioner-Patient Knowledge Gap

The difference between health professionals and patients with respect to their ability to assess, understand, and interpret information is often used as a basis for arguments in support of deception or limited disclosure. One argument, which is sometimes raised in connection with informed consent, takes as its major premise that the information in which health professionals trade is too difficult for lay people to understand. A related argument has it that health professionals are sometimes unable to tell patients the truth with regard to their exact condition or prognoses because they themselves do not know this. Practitioners may be uncertain about the meaning and implications of the information available to them, and reluctant to communicate information that may be misinterpreted or lead the patient to jump to unwarranted conclusions. The field of genetic counselling, which is fraught with uncertainty, is a special case in point (Tercyak et al., 2001).

Although the knowledge gap between practitioners and patients is undeniable, the fact that such a gap exists is not a sufficient reason for being untruthful. Because patients are unable to understand things as deeply or in as great detail as practitioners does not mean that they are unable to understand anything at all. Being truthful with patients does not require that practitioners communicate in five minutes everything that they know, but only what is relevant to the patient's wishes, needs, and interests. It is important to distinguish between *complete information* and *accurate information* (Curtin, 1982, p. 328). The fact that our knowledge may be incomplete or uncertain does not exempt us from the duty to be open and accurate about what we do know. To be sure, the communication of this knowledge will sometimes pose a challenge, but this is part of the professional role. To the extent that the practitioner feels incapable of communicating relevant information to the patient in an understandable way, he or she is deficient in a very important clinical skill and should seek to become more competent in communicating with lay people.

## Truth, Truthfulness, and Untruthfulness

In the previous section we considered arguments bearing on whether or why one should as a rule tell patients the truth. On balance, these arguments tend to support a general presumption in favour of openness and disclosure. Such a presumption, however, does not dispense with the need for judgement. What is morally appropriate in matters of disclosure will depend very much on the particular situation in which the communication of information is at issue. A presumption in favour of openness and disclosure does not mean that there are no exceptions, but it does mean that exceptions must be justified.

A different issue arises with respect to what it means to tell the truth in the first place. What is truth? Weir (1980, p. 98) points out that in the medical literature the nature of the truth is often taken to be "self-evident" or unproblematic. The truth is equated with "the facts," and telling or not telling the truth is reduced to being "accurate" or "inaccurate" in presenting patients with information about their medical condition.

Such a framework is much too narrow. A *factually true statement* is not necessarily a *truthful statement*. A statement may be accurate as judged against the facts, but deceptive, as when a practitioner speaks in jargon knowing that the patient will not understand what is being said. Similarly, we can be truthful although stating something that is factually untrue, as when we are unknowingly in error. Considerations such as these demonstrate the need to distinguish between truth in an empirical or *factual sense* and truth in a *moral sense*, to which Bok (1978, p. 6) applies the term *"truthfulness."*[9] Truthfulness is not so much a matter of accuracy as it is of honesty. Thus Bok insists that the "moral question of whether you are lying is not *settled* by establishing the truth or falsity of what you say. In order to settle this question, we must know whether you *intend your statement to mislead*" (p. 6).

The moral status of practices such as withholding information, equivocating, being ambiguous, communicating mixed signals, misleading, and outright lying can be ascertained only if we go beyond the factual accuracy of what is said to consider the communicative context in which it is said. This context encompasses not only the intentions of the speaker, but also the wishes, interests, expectations, and cognitive competence of the listener. What are the listener's interests in the matter? What or how much does the listener want to know? Under the circumstances, how is the listener likely to interpret what is said? What does the speaker intend the listener to understand or infer from what is said?

Along these lines, Jameton (1984, p. 172) distinguishes the verbal act from its effects on others. What is literally said may be one thing; how it is likely or predictably to be interpreted in the context may be something altogether different. This difference between what is said and what will be understood or inferred can be exploited for the purpose of deception.

Even without saying anything inaccurate, our statements (and silences) can have the deliberate effect of creating or confirming a false belief, allowing a false belief to go uncorrected, or otherwise keeping the truth concealed. We can deceive just as surely by telling the literal truth as by telling a literal lie. In what Veatch calls the "truthful lie," health professionals superficially fulfill the duty to tell the truth by using medical jargon, knowing that the patient will be unable to decipher from what is said the truth the practitioner knows (Veatch, 1976, p. 222). The language may be factually accurate, but the communication is untruthful to the extent that its intended effect is not to reveal the truth but to conceal it from the patient.

To be truthful — as opposed to merely uttering something that is true — is to communicate with the intent that, on the basis of our communication, the listener will understand what we ourselves know or believe to be true about some matter of concern. To be untruthful, on the other hand, is to intend as the effect of our communication that what we know or believe to be true is and remains concealed from the other. Lying, in which we say something we know to be untrue for the purpose of deceiving another, is but an extreme instance of a phenomenon that includes gestures, false clues, understatement, exaggeration, manipulation, the use of jargon, withholding information, evasion, and silence. For example, by withholding or omitting information we are untruthful to the extent that by remaining silent we are *deliberately* concealing something from the other. In many cases nurses struggle with the idea of deceiving and lying to their patients (Tuckett, 2004, 1999, 1998). Disclosure is influenced by their intention, the nature of their role, the relationship with their patients, and the institutional culture (Tuckett, 1998).

### Dialogue and Beneficent Truth-Telling

Presuming that one intends as a rule to be as truthful with patients as possible, other questions arise about how best to achieve this. Untruthfulness is not the only barrier to the communication of truth. A practitioner may say something false believing it to be true, and in so doing will be speaking truthfully or honestly. Nevertheless, the *effect* of the communication will be that the patient will not learn the truth. Certainly the intention to speak the truth is important, and patients are generally owed this much at least, but patients are entitled not just to honesty but also to reliable information. The practitioner's commitment to the patient requires that efforts be made to ensure accuracy as well as honesty.

Even if the truth is presented honestly and accurately, communication may still fall short of an important goal insofar as information is presented in a manner that is not *understandable* or relevant to the patient. The truth at issue in clinical situations may be very difficult for patients to understand, especially if their mental competence is diminished or they are in the grip of powerful emotions. The truth is more than an impersonal body of facts and statistics, and must be tailored to the specific context or circumstances of the patient.

In order to ensure that the patient understands, practitioners need not only good intentions and a reliable knowledge base but also good clinical skills in understanding and communicating with patients as the unique individuals that they are. Although some patients will be limited in their ability to understand by intelligence and education, and will be overwhelmed by too much detail, others will be very keen to understand and will appreciate being given as much information as possible. Especially if the truth amounts to "bad news," various psychological factors such as denial or intellectualization may impede the patient's ability to understand what is being said.

Tobin and Begley (2008) argue that truth-telling is not a single event but a process, or part of an ongoing dialogue. The objective of such dialogue is not simply to impart information to patients but to help them to understand over time what the truth means to them in their particular circumstances. An honest communication of the facts may not be enough, since the patient will be concerned to know what the facts mean.[10] In a sense, the practitioner and patient could be viewed as "co-interpreters" of the truth. Ongoing dialogue makes it possible for practitioners to base their decisions about what, when, and how to communicate information on the specific wishes, interests, and capacities of the individual patient.

The truth that is at issue in many clinical situations is of a sort that may be very painful and hard to bear. This may not be a good enough reason to be untruthful with the patient, but it is nonetheless important.

The resolve to communicate the truth does not mean that one must do so in a blunt or insensitive manner. As far as possible, one ought to communicate the truth in such a way as to preserve one's duty to benefit and prevent harm to the patient.

To this end, matters such as word choice and the timing and manner of disclosure may be critical. Nurses are expected to "provide persons in their care with the information they need to make informed decisions related to their health and well-being. They also work to ensure that information is given … in an open, accurate and transparent manner" (CNA, 2008). Ongoing dialogue with patients provides practitioners with an understanding of their wants, needs, and capabilities in light of which information can be communicated not only truthfully, accurately, and understandably, but also in accordance with concern for the patient's good.

A further point to be raised in discussing the clinical-ethical interface concerns the cultural variability of norms and expectations about truthfulness and truth-telling. In some cultures and faiths, the provision of information to people who are seriously ill or dying is in many cases forbidden. Some elements of the Jewish faith, for example, remain primarily oriented around beneficence (Kinzbrunner, 2004).[11] As defensible as the norms that have evolved in North American society may be, they are not universally embraced. In a multicultural society such as ours, it is important to be sensitive to the wishes and expectations of people who do not share our values, and to avoid imposing these values on others.

### Truthfulness and the Predicament of Nursing

Thus far truth-telling has been discussed generically as an issue for all or any health professionals. In nursing, truth-telling presents particular challenges because the role of nurses in the health care system often places them between the physician and the patient. In hospital settings, the *client* is also a *patient* of one or more physicians. Ideally, the roles of physicians and nurses will be complementary, but in some instances they may conflict.

Information disclosure is one issue around which conflict often arises. While the nurse and the physician alike may possess or have access to information of concern to the patient, the disclosure of much of this information is primarily the prerogative of the physician. Jameton (1984, p. 167) points out that many nurses are institutionally bound by a "no-new-information" policy, according to which they are not permitted to provide medical information that has not already been given to the patients by physicians, and that practice continues today.

To the extent that nurses are bound by such a policy, they can become caught in difficult predicaments. The nurse may feel obliged to communicate certain information to the patient, yet be forbidden to do so, or able to do so only at the price of conflict with the physician. The fact that in many situations nursing work is performed in continuous proximity with patients makes the predicament more acute. Patients and their loved ones often direct their questions to nurses. How should nurses respond when they possess the information necessary to answer questions accurately and appropriately but are bound not to because such disclosures are deemed to be the exclusive prerogative of the physician? Tuckett (1998) describes nurses' experience of not revealing the whole truth to patients for whom they are providing care.

When the roles of nurse and physician are differentiated according to a "no-new-information" policy, the nurse's ability to act in accordance with the duty to be truthful is limited. Although it is understood that role differentiation is necessary, in the area of psychosocial care there is room for debate about exactly how these roles should be differentiated, especially with regard to truth-telling. Granted, one should not speak beyond one's competence, and whoever imparts information should understand what is being imparted so as not to misinform. However, these conditions are not enough to disqualify nurses from having greater authority with respect to information disclosure than they currently have in many settings.

Indeed, Jameton (1984) argues that in many ways nurses are ideally suited for communicating information to patients since they possess special training in patient and family education. Because of differences in education, he claims, "nurses are likely to be better at communicating with patients than physicians are" (p. 174). Moreover, the closeness of their contact with patients makes it possible for them to establish the kind of "ongoing dialogue" that Goldberg (1984) rightly emphasizes is so important for communicating the truth.

Issues of truth-telling for nurses, as Freel (1985) points out, "are embedded in broader practice issues," such as "the scope of nursing practice and professional dominance" (p. 1023). Yarling (1978) makes a cogent argument that the decision to inform the patient is "a moral decision rooted in the recognition of the patient's moral right to such information" (p. 49). The medical expertise of physicians, therefore, does not entitle them to a monopoly over these decisions. As far as morality is concerned, nurses and physicians stand as equals.

As compelling as arguments may be that nurses are entitled to greater decision-making authority with respect to the communication of information, at the present time, and in many circumstances, rules that may be less than ideal are in effect. Curtin (1982) cautions that even if the nurse has ethics on his or her side, "the physician through means of position power and coercive power generally will secure compliance in moral as well as medical decisions or assure disciplinary actions" (p. 333). The reality in many practice settings is that disagreement with the physician concerning disclosure may be costly to nurses, both personally and professionally.[12]

In deciding what is appropriate in a given situation, it is prudent for nurses to consider the professional and legal implications of communication that may be perceived as being beyond their scope of practice. "Until the entire profession of nursing adopts a mutually supportive stance and institutionalizes it through enabling legislation and agency policies," Curtin (1982) notes, "individual nurses will be placed in uncomfortable if not untenable positions when conflicts arise regarding professional prerogatives, moral and ethical duties and patients' rights" (p. 333).

## Case 1: Deciding When to Disclose a Diagnosis

Nurses who practice in mental health settings know that the populations they serve are especially vulnerable. The health situation of these patients, and medications they are taking for their condition, may make it difficult for them to understand relevant information. Their ability to communicate may be reduced, and they may feel too intimidated to say no. These problems can be challenging for patients, their families, and the professionals who work with them. The following case illustrates such a challenge experienced by nurses and their colleagues concerning the disclosure of a diagnosis of mental illness.

> *Barry Taggart, who is seventeen years old, presents himself at the emergency department. He is with a friend who says they have just come from a party. The friend reports that some people at the party had drugs and he knows that Barry has had both cocaine and marijuana. It turns out that Barry also had these drugs the day before with another friend and has used marijuana almost daily in the last few months. Barry presents with disorganized speech and some disorientation, and says that two groups of people he just passed on the street know who he is and are "out to get" him. He says if they come near him he will kill them before they kill him.*
>
> *Barry's parents are away on vacation and are expected to return home in two days. The emergency team agrees that Barry should be admitted because of the imminent risk of harm to others, and to determine whether he is experiencing a drug-induced psychosis or symptoms of a psychotic disorder. His parents, reached by telephone, agree to the treatment.*
>
> *On their return from vacation Barry's parents visit him in hospital and meet with the treatment team. Barry is now more organized in his thoughts and fully oriented, but his paranoia persists and he is not attending to his self-care. He also spends most of his time in his room. Barry's parents provide collateral information. His grades at school have recently deteriorated and he tends to spend more time in his room. His parents were surprised that he*

actually went to a party with his friend. They report that Barry has an older sister who was diagnosed with schizophrenia five years earlier; for reasons of not following her medication regimen, among others, she now lives in a shelter and has sporadic contact with her family. He has an aunt who has had multiple hospitalizations for treatment of refractory schizoaffective disorder. The aunt has recently spent nine months in a unit of the local mental health facility, showing little improvement during that time. The team tells Barry's parents that they believe Barry may have paranoid schizophrenia.

As the week progresses it becomes increasingly clear to the team that Barry has a psychotic disorder. The parents' early suspicions that he has paranoid schizophrenia are confirmed. What do they tell Barry? Granted that Barry has the right to know his diagnosis, is it safe to provide him with this information at this time? Barry has already begun to ask the nurses whether he is "crazy like everyone else in here." He asks, "Will I be in and out of hospital, like my aunt and sister? If I will be like them, I do not want to live. My aunt's life is a tragedy. She looks like she is drugged, lives in a bad rooming house, and is poor." He adds that his sister lives in a shelter and he has heard that she is often back in hospital. Barry says that if they tell him he has the same illness as either his aunt or sister, he will kill himself. His plan is to jump off a bridge near his house. Barry says he believes that this illness robs you of any life worth living.

The nurses have told him that they know things are difficult for him right now, but that it will take a little time to be certain about what is going on. They know from their experience that it is better to wait until younger patients are in a stable condition before giving them the diagnosis. As well it takes time to confirm a psychiatric diagnosis. They take Barry's talk about suicide seriously. So much more is involved than telling him that he has a chronic mental illness, and they think these discussions can only happen when he is more stable. They know that timing is important. When Barry is more settled, he will be able to understand his diagnosis, treatment options, and prognosis and appreciate *that he can make choices about how he will live his life with a persistent mental illness. His parents visit him and can see that he has the same problems as Barry's aunt. They are well educated about schizophrenia and think that his threat of suicide should be taken seriously. His aunt made a serious suicide attempt when she had her first "break." That is when she had her first hospitalization with the same illness. Barry is made an involuntary patient because of the serious threat to his safety.*

## Commentary

Barry is a young adult who has just been diagnosed by his clinical team with a severe, persistent mental illness. They have not told him his diagnosis. Yet he is aware of the possible repercussions of this illness and is terrified that he has the same illness as his sister and aunt. In claiming that if he has this diagnosis, the only possible recourse for him is to end his life, Barry demonstrates that he could be in serious danger when he is given his diagnosis. The staff need to decide how much information to disclose, and in considering this question recognize that they are caught between truthfulness and beneficence, How can they best address the conflict between these two ethical principles?

Let us consider the options. First of all, the nurses could be vague and disclose very little in response to Barry's queries. This decision, however, presents a number of problems. All members of the team will need to be sure to give the same response, which amounts essentially to an omission of relevant information or, to be direct, deception. In the information age of today patients are sophisticated consumers and can readily locate considerable information electronically. Barry could easily search out and put together information that would indicate he has schizophrenia. The team knows that this way of learning his diagnosis would provide him with little immediate support, and it could put him at even greater risk of killing himself than if he were told directly. Also, if he learns that information is being withheld, his trust in his nurses would be undermined. It would be understandable if he became angry and did not want to communicate with the team. They would lose the opportunity to help him understand his situation and learn about treatment options and available resources. Continuing care is based on trusting those who provide that care, and this eventuality would be a very poor start for Barry's relationship with his mental health team.

A second option is to talk to Barry hypothetically about having the diagnosis he fears. They could tell him that there seems to be a problem, but not provide a name. This "what-if" approach also carries a risk. He probably would ask them directly whether he has schizophrenia. His nurses may try to buy time and tell him that it is too early to know for sure, and in some respects this may be true. Yet it is doubtful that this so-called white lie would quell his fears, build his trust in his nurses, and dampen his wish to end his life. In short, it is unlikely that a vague answer would help him. Even if they softened the truth by saying he has a psychosis or a psychotic illness that is acute and may not be chronic, they would have no guarantees that Barry will not see through their efforts to sidestep the truth.

A third option is to explain his diagnosis, answer his questions honestly, and then respond to his reactions. The nurses can be empathetic and supportive, and provide a safe environment. They know that suicide is a risk, but they will work to reduce the risk as much as possible. The team can provide education and discuss treatment options and resources, providing the kind of support that Barry and his parents need.

The first two options are based on paternalism and beneficence, approaches that have been prominent in health care over the years. Deception or lying for the best interests of the patient is one form of paternalism. A study of nurses who used deception or lying in their practice (Tuckett, 1998) reported that some participants distinguish between the two. They see lying or bending the truth as different from what they describe as stepping back from the truth. Lying is spoken, while not disclosing or not fully disclosing is not lying. The reasons that nurses gave for lying or deceiving were to benefit or improve the patient's well-being, or to avoid harm. Their commitment to care in some circumstances involved not telling the whole truth. One example was not telling a patient with Alzheimer's disease the truth when the person asked about a partner who had died many years earlier. The justification was that the patient would not recall the answer a few minutes later, whereas at the moment in time, when asked, telling the truth would cause the person extreme grief. Nurses in this example argued that in this case the moral good would be to avoid causing grief, and not to tell the truth. They felt that it was preferable to deceive the patient, which would do no harm, instead of causing harm by telling the truth.

On the whole, the staff favours option three, that is, explain to Barry gently but honestly his health problem and treatment options, and, hoping, with the information and support offered, to reduce the risk of suicide. While the team is concerned that he will try to follow through with his plan to kill himself after he learns that he has schizophrenia, they know they can make him an involuntary patient and put him on continuous observation, if necessary. Yet it would be better if the approach to disclosure could be based on the therapeutic relationships developed with Barry, which are based on "active listening, trust, respect, genuineness, empathy and responding to patient concerns" (RNAO, 2006, p. 15). Many team members are concerned that if they do not tell Barry the truth they will lose the trust that he has in them. The CNA *Code of Ethics* (2008) says that nurses should recognize the potential vulnerability of their patients and not exploit their trust and dependency in a way that could threaten the quality of the therapeutic relationship (p. 8). Then again, if a relationship begins by being laced with deception or outright lies, that is not a good dynamic for working with someone over time.

When the team tells Barry that he has schizophrenia, an appropriate approach to providing continuing support is to work through the relationships that the team members have established with Barry and his parents. A meeting between the various professionals and the family provides a forum for discussions of this kind. The RNAO *Best Practice Guideline: Supporting and Strengthening Families* (2006) points out that "partnerships with families are built on mutual trust, honesty and collaboration" (p. 21) and that it is essential to recognize families' perspectives. It is understandable that Barry's parents are concerned for their son's well-being, especially because they are aware of his experience with his sister's and aunt's efforts to live with a persistent mental illness.

In a literature review, authors concluded that most patients want to hear the truth about their situations (Tuckett, 2004). Truth-telling supports autonomy, and it also conveys respect to the patient, both of which are important to the therapeutic relationship and to care. The question in this situation is, what is the truth? Further, what knowledge is necessary and sufficient for Barry to have so that he might continue with his treatment and recovery? Barry already knows that he has a condition that was made worse by street drugs and was then made better by time, medication, and learning how to deal with some of his thoughts and fears. Barry knows that to proceed with his recovery and his plans to continue his education he should avoid drugs, take medication, manage stress, and continue to find ways of coping with thoughts that he finds disturbing.

Is it important for Barry to know his diagnosis? In this society truth-telling is valued highly, but the question is, what is the truth? Interestingly in the mental health population, not all patients who have been told their diagnosis actually agree with or accept it. Some indicate that they refuse to accept such a label, and others simply refuse to acknowledge that their condition has anything to do with themselves. Yet many in this group continue to take medication and see a professional care provider on a regular basis. The health professional should not be the one to decide what to tell a patient (Gold, 2004). The meaning of the diagnosis varies from person to person. Barry may see the diagnosis as a sentence to a life of institutionalization, or respond by wanting to make the most of his life despite his challenges. His nurses need to know what the information means to him and how it will influence how he lives day to day. As Gold (2004, p. 579) puts it, "The needs of each person must be evaluated individually because illness is, in the first instance, a subjective experience, influenced by cultural, personal and religious beliefs and traditions."

Barry's health care team has the ethical responsibility of explaining to him and his parents as much as possible about his condition — explaining, for example, that each person experiences an illness in a different way and that the trajectories of illnesses are as varied as those who have them. The health care information — such as his diagnosis, possible treatments, and resources to support recovery — belongs to Barry; and the nurses, along with other members of the health team, are custodians of that information. The team needs to determine for each patient the best environment, time, and manner for disclosure. The team needs to decide how best to address Barry's needs in this regard.

## Case 2: Withholding Information at the Family's Request

Many nurses practise in areas in which patients and their families hold a variety of values regarding the disclosure of information about health status. Not every family believes that an ill member should be the first to know the diagnosis and prognosis. Some believe that disclosure will pose a risk to the patient's health, either physical or psychological. Some are concerned that if a patient is informed of a less than favourable prognosis, the news might reduce that person's chances of fighting the illness. Nurses are aware that individuals are part of a family and a community, and sometimes the health team provides care to all of these people. Attending to families' values along with specific requests made to the team constitutes part of the work of health care providers. The work requires careful and thoughtful responses to these requests.

*Mrs. Ito, aged seventy-five, lives with her husband and three grown children. She came to Canada ten years ago. She knows a little English. Her family describes her as a traditional Japanese elderly lady. For the last number of months she has been excitedly helping to arrange her son's wedding. But lately Mrs. Ito has been feeling extremely weak and tired. Her family takes her for a medical assessment. When a doctor tells her family privately that she has a metastasized cancer, and possibly has only a short length of time to live, her family insists that she not be told about the diagnosis. They do not want her to be upset, especially with the wedding date drawing near. Also, they explain that traditionally in their culture it is an accepted practice for a person not to be told that he or she has a terminal illness. They believe that given this knowledge the person's situation will deteriorate and there will be increased suffering for no purpose.*

*Some of the nurses who have provided care for Mrs. Ito believe that she should be told about both her diagnosis and prognosis. Their reasoning is that they have a duty to tell her about her health condition. Second, they think that now is the right time for telling her. At her son's wedding she will come into contact with many family members and friends whom she has not seen for a long time and who live some distance away. Given that the wedding will probably be the last time she sees these friends and relatives, she may want to find the opportunity to have conversations or connect with them in some way that would be especially meaningful to her. Other nurses argue that the family's wishes should be respected based on the accepted pattern of decision-making about health matters in this and other cultures. They also believe that the bad news should not be allowed to interfere with Mrs. Ito's and the family's enjoyment of this very special day.*

## Commentary

To be in a position to decide whether to adhere to or respect a request made by a patient or family members suggests that a nurse holds considerable power over those making the request. To work with patients in a way that is respectful and reflects fidelity in the therapeutic relationship involves giving care that keeps patients at the centre in terms of their needs and wishes, as they see them. The nurse-patient relationship is one of unequal power, with the nurse having more power. The patient, no matter the age, education, or communication skills, is vulnerable because of an altered health state and dependency on nurses and their clinical team for information. Nurses and their colleagues must be aware of and sensitive to the power imbalance. Patients expect that they can trust their nurses to work for the patients' best interests, which includes telling them what they need to know to make informed decisions.

Cultures differ in their preferences for receiving health information and in thought patterns related to decision-making. Some ethnic groups value patient independence and autonomy, while others value interdependence and a network of obligations (Candib, 2002). Surveys of cultures regarding preferences for being informed about a diagnosis found that in Western populations 83 to 99 per cent of respondents would like to be informed, compared with 24 to 74 per cent of non-Western populations (Gold, 2004). While these figures vary widely from culture to culture, it cannot be assumed that even the preferences of people of the same culture will be identical (Gold, 2004). In cases involving truthfulness and culture, a clash of cultures can easily arise.

Western society normally assumes a practice of full disclosure. Ethical codes, standards, and consent legislation support or require telling patients the truth to enable them to make informed decisions about their care. In this situation, the truth refers to the health information known by the clinical team, such as diagnosis, options, and prognosis. Privacy legislation reinforces the protection of confidential information, and health care professionals are custodians of that information. Ultimately, the patient should control who knows what and when. In Western society the focus of decision-making is usually on the individual, not the family or the community.

Mrs. Ito's culture is one that is commonly identified as family-oriented (Woo, 1999), and family members are normally involved in decisions about health information and decision-making. Elderly persons are revered and cared for with great respect. Mrs. Ito's family provided direction to the health team about their preferences for handling information about her prognosis, which suggests that they expect their wishes to be respected.

The RNAO *Best Practice Guideline, Embracing Cultural Diversity in Healthcare* (2007), recommends ways in which individual nurses can reflect about their own sensitivity to patient and family needs as related to the particular culture, conflicts they might have with colleagues regarding these matters, and their capacity to deal with these issues. This guideline recommends that nurses "acquire knowledge of the range of cultural norms, beliefs and values, relevant to patients and colleagues as a starting point to foster understanding — and further inquiry" (p. 31). Some nurses work at acquiring cultural competence to assist them in providing care. Others, influenced by critiques of the Eurocentric medical model that permeates Western health care, frame their approaches to caring for patients by being mindful of the impact of white privilege, which is aligned with elements of power and control (Puzan, 2003).

The nurses who care for Mrs. Ito are divided. Some think that she should be made aware of her condition so that she can plan the last stage of her life, which includes making a point of connecting with friends and family whom she might never see again. Here the Western norm of truthfulness takes priority. Nurses believe in being truthful in relations with their patients. They consider deception in the nurse-patient relationship to be unethical, and as moral agents nurses want the basis of their care of individuals and families to be accurate and honest. For many, deception is not morally defensible in any situation. For them it is a question of integrity. Their values must be put into action. This moral steadfastness, when compromised, leads to moral distress and even burnout.

Yet, if family-centred care has merit, the option of disclosing information to Mrs. Ito does not reflect a respect for the wishes of everyone concerned. For example, Mrs. Ito may follow the practice of her culture — that it is traditional for parents to rely on their children for decision-making regarding health care. Mrs. Ito may have assented to her family providing direction in her care — an approach that does not follow the usual Western practice of obtaining explicit, informed consent. Some nurses may disagree with the family's request. The patients' culture and the nurses' culture, or values about communication with patients, may clash. In some instances, given the diversity of Canadian society and the nursing profession, the nurse's culture and values may be in accord with those of Mrs. Ito's family.

Some nurses, then, will support the view that Mrs. Ito's family should decide what health information is to be disclosed. Others will consider this to be a matter of deception, which can take several forms. While it can involve telling a lie, something completely contrary to the facts, it can also involve an avoidance of the truth. In other words, a person can deceive both by avoiding disclosure, essentially avoiding or leaving out the facts, or by disclosing only certain pieces of information. In common parlance, this is called putting a "spin" on information. This is what Mrs. Ito's family is asking the team to do. They do not want her to be aware that she has metastasized cancer and possibly only a short while to live. They want her last days to be as happy as possible.

One problem with deception resides in the tension that it can create within the therapeutic relationship, along with moral dissonance for the professionals involved. Kant tells us that it can have a negative impact on the one who is doing the deceiving (Infield, 1963). At times nurses are left in the position of "keeping secrets" because they serve as confidantes of both patients and family members (Wros, Doutrich, and Izumi, 2004, p. 137). For this reason they also often assume a role as facilitator of communication between the family and physician (Wros et al., 2004, p. 137).

Mrs. Ito's nurses have a duty to learn about her culture. They can learn from her family and other resources about Japanese traditions. They can keep in mind too that for something to be known, it does not necessarily need to be explicitly stated. In a study of American and Japanese nurses, Wros et al. (2004) found that Japanese nurses noted that even though patients may not have been given information about their diagnosis and prognosis, they are often aware of what is truly happening or perhaps have a sense that their condition is terminal. Still, even with this awareness patients might not want to hear the information put explicitly into words. Often health professionals communicate to patients about their condition and situation without being explicit. Expert clinicians often give information to patients indirectly, "using metaphors or non-verbal messages, without breaking cultural rules of communication" (Wros et al., 2004, p. 137). Clearly this is not a black and white situation.

To respond to Mrs. Ito's family's request and to continue to provide care, the nurses will need to employ excellent skills of communication and assessment. There is no "one size fits all" rule that guides every approach to truth-telling. Instead, what might work best is a "case-by-case clinical judgment based on a relationship and thoughtful understanding of the context" (Wros et al., 2004).

The nursing staff should respect the preferences of Mrs. Ito and her family regarding the disclosure of health information and in making decisions about care. They should be available to the patient and family, and vigilant regarding cues to their preferences. The staff could start by respecting their cultural values. Yet if Mrs. Ito makes it clear that she wants to know more — perhaps to confirm what she thinks is her situation — then her nurses need to reassess their response. They will need to meet with the family and explain that in their view Mrs. Ito now wants and needs to know. The process for informing her must be planned with her family.

Nurses, then, need to understand the cultural norms of their patients. They also need to be aware of their own personal and professional values and ensure that they do not work in opposition to the wishes and needs of the patients and their families.

### Case 3: Emergency and Trauma Nurses: When to Give Bad News

Nurses in trauma centres face distinct ethical challenges. Decisions need to be made quickly with the best information available — and that information is often insufficient. Family and friends may not be available to give consent. Police officers may want to conduct an investigation. Patients are critically ill, often fighting for their lives. Urgent surgery is often required. Decisions have to be made in minutes, sometimes seconds.

Under these urgent conditions, nurses and their colleagues may find it difficult to honour their duty to discuss with patients their condition and options, which is an expected practice in other areas of nursing. In emergency and trauma centres, when patients are fighting for their lives, what to say to the patients becomes an ethical issue. Some nurses may consider the consequences of the information they give when life is in the balance. Other nurses may think that they have an absolute duty to tell patients all the known information.

This case explores the question of when to tell the truth in situations when, given the patient's physical and psychological condition, delivering devastating news might potentially jeopardize a patient's health, and possibly life.

*Amira Mullins is out on a highway driving in a car with her partner, Casey, and their three-year-old daughter, Samantha. They are hit by a drunk driver in a multi-vehicle accident. Ambulances quickly arrive on the scene, and Amira and Casey, both seriously injured, are rushed to a nearby hospital in separate ambulances. Samantha, with minor injuries, is taken in another ambulance to a children's hospital ten kilometres distant.*

*In the hospital emergency room Casey's vital signs are absent. The trauma team tries to resuscitate her, but their efforts fail. Amira, awake in the same hospital's trauma room, is not aware of her partner's death. She asks about her family. At the same time her vital signs deteriorate because she has lost a lot of blood. Her colour is pale and her lips are cyanotic. One lung has collapsed and her breathing is laboured. She has had kidney damage on one side, sustained as a result of the impact from another vehicle. She urgently needs to have surgery. Whether she will survive the surgery is uncertain. If she does survive, she will be in an induced coma for a week to allow her body to heal. Her physical status is unstable, and the nurses and their colleagues fear that any further stress might seriously impair her capacity to survive the surgery and post-operative care in a coma. She loses consciousness briefly and then suddenly awakes and asks, "How is Casey?" and "Where is Samantha?"*

*The nurses tell her that Samantha is well and at another hospital. No one on the team wants to answer Amira's question about Casey. They are aware of the risks of telling her now. But they are also afraid that she might die in the operating room without knowing the truth about Casey.*

*The police officers ask to speak to Amira before she goes to surgery. They want a statement from her before she loses consciousness.*

## Commentary

If Amira survives her surgery, she will then learn the truth about her partner. The question is when she should be told. To deceive a patient is not a normal part of nursing practice, especially when we consider the nature of the therapeutic relationship. Kant would support this position, adding that the practice of lying can also destroy credibility (Kant, 1955, p. 43). How do nurses decide when and how Amira should be told the bad news about her family?

Nurses know that nonmaleficence is of primary importance in their work with patients. Harm of any kind interferes with the patient's well-being and overall health status. At times, however, the question arises as to which kind of harm should be avoided over another. No matter when or what Amira is told, she will undoubtedly be harmed. If she is told the tragic news about her partner's fate in the emergency room, her response may have a serious effect on her chances of survival. Her condition may deteriorate, and her condition could become even more unstable.

While giving patient-centred care involves consulting patients about their goals or preferences for the care process (RNAO, 2002), nurses are obliged to consider how to rank those goals against the potential benefits for and risks to the patient. In this case, Amira is requesting information that clearly has a high personal priority. There is other information that she may not have and also needs to know — that is, that she is critically ill and has an urgent need for surgery. Under the circumstances, learning about her partner's death might seriously threaten her own fragile status. Her level of consciousness fluctuates as her physical condition plummets. The emergency room nurses have extensive experience with trauma cases and understand the potential risk to her health status from the physiological, psychological, and emotional reaction that she could experience given her precarious state. They also have a dilemma as to when to disclose the information being requested by their patient.

Some nurses caring for Amira argue that they have an implicit obligation to keep her safe and protect her physical health status — that is, to promote actions that will increase her probability of surviving. If providing certain information will do her grave harm in the short term, the nurses will support the decision to withhold that information until Amira is able to survive the shock of hearing the truth. These nurses argue that they will invoke the therapeutic privilege to withhold information because disclosure will pose serious and imminent harm to their patient.

Truth-telling and the use of therapeutic privilege (that is, deception and lying) are central concepts in deliberations about morally defensible actions. Participants in a study of nurses practising in different settings (Tuckett, 1998) indicated that in their view a lie can only be that which is actually spoken, whereas deception involves leaving out information. As well, "not telling or not answering or avoiding the question is not lying — but it could be conceived as dishonesty." From Kant's perspective, equivocation can be justified to reduce questioning and to silence a patient or family member who wants to "exhort the truth when we cannot tell him" (Infield, 1963, p. 229). One nurse in Tuckett's (1998) study said, "In order not to hurt others sometimes you step back from being blatantly truthful ... bending the truth is lying — telling only as much as is necessary to answer the question is not" ( p. 299). Tuckett summarizes this point by saying: "These nurses give precedence to a notion of caring as indicative of the virtues of benevolence and nonmaleficence. Situations and relationships exist when to care deeply about another may mean not revealing the whole truth" (p. 300).

Planned deception may well apply to the case of Amira, if all members of the team agree to a plan to communicate partial or erroneous information to the patient and family (Erlen, 1995). This is a form of paternalism, but it can be argued that Amira's physical well-being takes precedence over the quality of the therapeutic relationship or support for her autonomy at this point in time. Beneficence in this case trumps autonomy.

A plan for Amira may involve avoiding questions about her family or providing answers that do not disclose the whole truth until Amira's physical status is more stable. Ideally Amira should be told as soon as possible; most likely, when she regains her strength she will not be put off for long. The team should formulate a plan in that event: decide how to give Amira the news, and designate someone to tell her. The nurses should take into account any family members who might be able to be at her side at the time when the information is given out. It may well be that all of the practitioners cannot, with integrity, participate in this plan. In that case, they may ask not to be involved in that patient's care, if this is feasible. This request should be respected.

Other nurses and team members who care for Amira might agree that she should be given the information she requests. They will base their position on a mandate to be honest. The CNA *Code of Ethics for Registered Nurses* (2008) states that nurses must build trustworthy relationships. The College of Nurses of Ontario has identified truthfulness as one of the important values for nurses in providing care (CNO, 2008). The Code also directs nurses to maintain commitments, which includes keeping promises and meeting implicit or explicit obligations toward their patients (CNO, 2008).

If a health care team agrees that deception in this case is not, and in their opinion is never, morally defensible, their position is supported in a summary of a literature review by Tuckett (2004), who found that most patients (though not all) want to know the truth about their situations. Accordingly, practices among doctors and nurses now lean more toward truth-telling and honest disclosure. To tell the truth is considered to be in the patient's best interests. The truth may be devastating, but the team can respond by giving the patient support and providing hope to fight for her or his life. In this case, they can remind Amira about the importance of her role as caregiver to their daughter.

When considering the police request to interview Amira, the team's priority is Amira as a patient. Any delay in her care that could harm her is unacceptable. The staff needs to consider that even sensitive police questioning can lead to added distress. Also, she may glean from the questions that her partner has died. Emergency room nurses need to be familiar with the hospital policy regarding police access to the trauma area, where the officers can observe the patient receiving care and get access to confidential information. These policies favour respect for privacy and confidentiality. In this case Amira should not be interviewed by the police.

Case conferences and ethics consultations (Erlen, 1995) can be helpful in such situations to support the team in determining and providing the best approach to care. Establishing a standard way of responding to these cases, which are not uncommon in trauma units, is recommended. After responding to this case, the team should consider a critical incident debriefing.

Whatever their decision, the team must be extremely sensitive to the physical condition of the patient when they make a disclosure about the status of the patient's family, and if deception is used they must consider the potential damage to the therapeutic relationship. Therapeutic communication (Tuckett, 2004) and patient-centred care are central to these approaches. As this case demonstrates, any decision-making has to include both the context for nurses and the condition of patients. Nurses in crisis and trauma situations need to make decisions quickly. Being clear about their values and how to rank truth-telling over beneficence and nonmaleficence will help nurses prepare for these difficult cases.

## Conclusion

Issues of truthfulness and disclosure are among the most difficult and delicate ethical issues for health professionals. Because of changing values, health professionals are expected and obliged to be more open and truthful in communicating with patients than they were in the past.

The cases we have examined illustrate some of the challenges that the commitment to truth and truthfulness presents for health professionals, and especially for nurses. In assessing and evaluating one's options in light of this commitment, contextual factors are crucial. In matters of truthfulness and truth-telling, it is especially important that ethical sensitivity be backed up by good clinical and interpersonal skills.

## Notes

1    Useful summary reviews of the empirical data can be found in Novack et al. (1979) and in Moutsopoulos (1988).

2    This attitudinal shift does not appear to be anywhere near as dramatic as concerns prognosis. Annas (1994) reports on a 1982 study in which fewer than half the physicians surveyed would offer a frank prognosis to patients "with fully confirmed diagnosis of lung cancer in an advanced stage" (p. 223). By contrast, 85 per cent of Americans surveyed wanted a "realistic estimate" of how long they had to live if they had a type of cancer that usually led to death in less than a year.

3    Recent studies about oncologists in North and South American and European countries indicate that these trends continue in varying degrees, with Canadian doctors especially tending to disclose (Bruera et al., 2000). Less research has been done on the attitudes of nurses with regard to truthfulness with patients. Jameton (1984, p. 169) has an insightful discussion of two studies (Popoff, 1975, and Sandroff, 1981) that are frequently cited, and the comparison of which suggests a trend toward greater truthfulness in nursing.

4    Moutsopoulos (1988) reports that, after an exhaustive review of the medical literature on disclosure, he was able to find only "one instance where a patient suffered acute physical or psychological reaction to the truth that led to harm, namely one case of suicide" (p. 99). He goes on to point out

that the same study mentions the suicide of two patients "who had not been informed of their diagnosis."

5    Bok (1978) cites studies that "show that there is generally a dramatic divergence between physicians and patients on the factual question of whether patients want to know what ails them in cases of serious illness such as cancer" (p. 229). Patients tend to want to know more than their physicians think they do.

6    For examples of arguments along these lines, see Veatch (1976, pp. 218-222), Fromer (1981, pp. 333-335), and Moutsopoulos (1988, pp. 103-104).

7    Ellin (1981), who argues that the fiduciary relationship *does not* preclude deception, is something of an exception.

8    The consequences of deceptive practices may extend beyond the particular relationship to jeopardize the practitioner-patient relationship more generally. If, as a result of the publicization of deceptive practices, it came to be believed that such practices were common, people entering therapeutic relationships would become more uncertain that they were being told the truth and hence more distrustful.

9    Weir (1980) gives a very helpful gloss on Bok's distinction:

> For a person to be able to "speak the truth" depends upon that person's knowledge of a certain sphere of information and ability to give an accurate representation of that knowledge .... to "speak truthfully" depends, in contrast, not on that person's knowledge or professional competence in some field, but on the person's moral choice to be honest and straightforward in speech. (p. 100)

10   Truth is never entirely objective, as is evident if one considers that facts are always embedded in some context. A study by Tobin and Begley (2008) explores the information and psychosocial needs of oncology patients and chronicles the changes in meaning and knowing that they experienced throughout the "bad news trajectory."

11   Hattori et al. (1991) present research on the attitudes of Japanese physicians and their patients toward information disclosure. Several cultural differences stand out in this study, such as the fact that in Japanese society the family plays a much more important role in information disclosure than it does in North American society. Wros, Doutrich, and Izumi (2004) compare the values and ethical concerns of nurses from Japan and the United States, noting differences related to truth-telling. For example, Japanese nurses tend to use a more indirect style along with metaphors in their communications.

12    Jameton (1984, pp. 166-170) describes a publicized case that underscores some of the personal and professional hazards of communicating more or different information to patients than has been communicated already by their physicians.

## References

American Nurses' Association. ([1976] 1985). *Code for nurses with interpretive statements.* Kansas City.

Annas, G.J. (1994). Informed consent, cancer, and truth in prognosis. *The New England Journal of Medicine* 330 (3), 223-225.

Begley, A. (2008). Truth-telling, honesty and compassion: A virtue-based exploration of a dilemma in practice. *International Journal of Nursing Practice* 14, 336-341.

Bok, S. (1978). *Lying: Moral choice in public and private life.* New York: Pantheon Books.

Bruera, E., Neumann, C. M., Mazzocato, C., Stiefel, F., & Sala, R. (2000). Attitudes and beliefs of palliative care physicians regarding communication with terminally ill cancer patients. *Palliative Medicine* 14, 287-298.

Canadian Nurses Association. (2008). *Code of ethics for registered nursing.* Ottawa.

Candib, L. (2002). Truth telling and advance planning at the end of life: Problems with autonomy in a multicultural world. *Families, Systems & Health* 20 (3), 213-228.

College of Nurses of Ontario. (2005). *Ethics.* No. 41034. Toronto.

College of Nurses of Ontario. (2006). *Therapeutic nurse-patient relationship.* No. 41033. Toronto.

College of Nurses of Ontario. (2008). *Ethics practice standard.* No. 41006. Toronto.

Curtin, L.L. (1982). Case study XIV: A patient's right to know, a nurse's right to tell. In L.L. Curtin & M.J. Flaherty (Eds.), *Nursing ethics: Theories and pragmatics* (pp. 321-335). Bowie, MD: Robert J. Brady.

Ebbinghaus, H. (1913 [1885]). *Memory.* H.A. Rueger & C.E. Bussenius, Trans. New York: Teachers College.

Ellin, J.S. (1981). The solution to a dilemma in medical ethics. *Westminster Institute Review,* 1 (2), 3-6.

Erlen, J. (1995). Should the nurse participate in planned deception? *Orthopedic Nursing* 14 (2), 62-66.

Fallowfield, L.J., Jenkins, V.A., & Beveridge, H.A. (2002). Truth may hurt but deceit hurts more: Communication in palliative care. *Palliative Medicine* 16, 297-303.

Freel, M.I. (1985). Truth telling. In J.C. McCloskey & H.K. Grace (Eds.), *Current issues in nursing* (2nd ed., pp. 1008-1024). Boston: Blackwell Scientific Publications.

Fromer, M.J. (1981). *Ethical issues in health care.* St. Louis: C.V. Mosby.

Gold, M. (2004). Is honesty always the best policy? Ethical aspects of truthtelling. *Internal Medicine Journal* 34, 578-580.

Goldberg, R.J. (1984). Disclosure of information to adult cancer patients: Issues and update. *Journal of Clinical Oncology* 2 (8), 948-955.

Hallenbeck, J., & Arnold, R. (2007). The art of oncology: When the tumor is not the target. A Request for nondisclosure: Don't tell mother. *American Society of Clinical Oncology* 25 (31), 5030-5034.

Herring, B.F. (1984). *Jewish ethics and halakhah for our time: Sources and commentary.* New York: Ktav Publishing.

Hodkinson, K. (2008). How should a nurse approach truth-telling? A virtue ethics perspective. *Nursing Philosophy* 9, 248-256.

Infield, L. (1963). *Immanuel Kant Lectures on Ethics.* New York: Harper & Row.

Jameton, A.L. (1984). *Nursing practice: The ethical issues.* Englewood Cliffs, NJ: Prentice-Hall.

Kant, I. (1955 [1785]). Fundamental principles of the metaphysics of ethics. Thomas Kingsmill, Trans. London: Abbott Longman's, Green and Co.

Kinzbrunner, B. (2004). Jewish medical ethics and end of life care. *Journal of Palliative Medicine* 7 (4), 558-573.

Laporte Matzo, M., Witt Sherman, D., Sheehan, D.C., Rolling Ferrell, B., & Penn, B. (2003). Teaching strategies from the ELNEC curriculum. *Nursing Education Perspectives.* July/August.

Liaschenko, J. (1998). The shift from the closed to the open body: Ramifications for nursing testimony. In S.D. Edwards (Ed.), *Philosophical issues in nursing* (pp. 11–30). Houndmills, Eng.: Macmillan.

Lokich, J.J. (1978). *Primer of cancer management.* Boston: G.K. Hall.

Matzo, M., Sherman, D., Sheehan, D., Ferrell, B. & Penn, B. (2003). *Nursing Education Perspectives* 24 (4), 176-183.

McNeil, B.J., Pauker, S.G., Sox, H.C., & Tversky, A. (1982). On the elicitation of preferences for alternative therapies. *The New England Journal of Medicine* 306 (21), 1259-1262.

Moutsopoulos, L. (1988). Truth telling to patients. In R.B. Edwards & G.C. Graber (Eds.), *Bioethics* (pp. 93-105). San Diego: Harcourt Brace Jovanovich.

Novack, D.H., Plumer, R., Smith, R.L., Ochitill, H., Morrow, G.R., & Bennett, J.M. (1979). Changes in physicians' attitudes toward telling the cancer patient. *Journal of the American Medical Association* 241 (9), 897-900.

Oken, D. (1961). What to tell cancer patients: A study of medical attitudes. *The Journal of the American Medical Association* 175 (13), 86-94.

Pratt, R., & Wilkinson, H. (2003). A psychosocial model of understanding the experience of receiving a diagnosis of dementia. *Dementia* 2 (2), 181-199.

President's Commission for the Study of Ethical Problems in Medicine and Biomedical and Behavioral Research. (1982). *Making health care decisions: A report on the ethical and legal implications of informed consent on the patient-practitioner relationship* (Vol. 1). Washington, DC: Government Printing Office.

Puzan, E. (2003). The unbearable whiteness of being (in nursing). *Nursing Inquiry* 10 (3), 193-200.

Rassin, M., Levy, O., Schwartz, T., & Silner, D. (2006). Caregivers' role in breaking bad news. *Cancer Nursing* 29 (4), 302.

Registered Nurses Association of Ontario (RNAO). (2002). Client centred care.

Registered Nurses Association of Ontario (RNAO). (2006). Establishing therapeutic relationships.

Registered Nurses Association of Ontario (RNAO). (2007). Embracing cultural diversity in health care: Developing cultural competence.

Ruddick, W. (1999). Hope and deception. *Bioethics* 13 (3/4), 343-357.

Rycroft-Malone, J., Seers, K., Titchen, A., Harvey, G., Kitson, A., & McCormack, B. (2004). What counts as evidence in evidence-based practice? *Journal of Advanced* 47 (1), 81-90.

Schindler, R. (1982). Truth telling and terminal illness: A Jewish view. *Journal of Religion and Health* 21 (1), 42-48.

Schoefl, R. (2008). Breaking bad news. *Digestive Diseases* 26, 56-58.

Tercyak, K.P., Hughes, C., Main, D., Snyder, C., Lynch, J., Lynch, H., & Lerman, C. (2001). Parental communication of BRCA1/2 genetic test results to children. *Patient Education and Counseling* 42, 213-224.

Tobin, G., & Begley, C. (2008). Receiving bad news: A phenomenological exploration of the lived experience of receiving a cancer diagnosis. *Cancer Nursing* 31 (5), 31-39.

Tuckett, A. (1998). "Bending the truth": Professionals' narratives about lying and deception in nursing practice. *International Journal of Nursing Studies* 35, 292-302.

Tuckett, A. (1999). Nursing practice: Compassionate deception and the good Samaritan. *Nursing Ethics* 6 (5), 383-389.

Tuckett, A. (2004). Truth-telling in clinical practice and the arguments for and against: A review of the literature. *Nursing Ethics* 11 (5), 513.

Veatch, R.M. (1976). *Death, dying and the biological revolution.* New Haven, CT: Yale University Press.

Wagner, M. (1991). A question of informed consent. *Nursing* 91, 21 (4), 66, 68.

Weir, R. (1980). Truthtelling in medicine. *Perspectives in Biology and Medicine* 24 (1), 95-112.

Woo, K. (1999). Care for Chinese palliative patients. *Journal of Palliative Care* 15 (4), 70-74.

Wros, P., Doutrich, D., & Izumi, S. (2004). Ethical concerns: Comparison of values from two cultures. *Nursing and Health Sciences* 6, 131-140.

Yarling, R.R. (1978). Ethical analysis of a nursing problem: The scope of nursing practice in disclosing the truth to terminal patients (Part II). *Supervisor Nurse* 9 (6), 40-50.

# Study Questions: Truthfulness

## Case 1: Deciding When to Disclose a Diagnosis

1. If you were caring for Barry, what would your position be on telling Barry his diagnosis, and what ethical principles would support your position?

2. Discuss the risk to the therapeutic relationship between Barry and his health care providers if deception were used. Why would this be a concern?

3. Do you think there is support or no support for the use of deception in a situation like Barry's? What ethical principles underlie your position?

4. If one of your colleagues believed that Barry should be told the truth "no matter what," what would your response to her/him be? What moral defence would support your position?

5. This case illustrates that telling the truth is far more than giving a diagnosis. How can his nurses support truth-telling and Barry's understanding and appreciation of his health problem?

## Case 2: Withholding Information at the Family's Request

1. Present your recommendations to Mrs. Ito's health care team about respecting her family's request to withhold information. Provide a rationale for your position, including reference to cultural values.

2. If Mrs. Ito makes it clear that she wants to know what is happening, how would you approach the family? What process would you recommend for giving Mrs. Ito the information she wants? To come to an understanding of how difficult these discussions about truth-telling can be for nurses and families, you might try to role-play these scenes in class.

3. Nurses come from many cultures and backgrounds Consider your cultural and personal values about truth-telling. Would you want to withhold news of terminal illness from a family member? Why or why not?

4. Discuss how moral distress can develop for a nurse who cares for people who are in a position like that of Mrs. Ito and her family. How would you support a colleague who experiences moral distress in a similar situation? What could the organization offer to help?

5. Based on cultural considerations, discuss situations in which caregivers might dispute the family's request for the person to be protected from bad news.

## Case 3: Emergency and Trauma Nurses: When to Give Bad News

1. Does planned deception have a role in providing health care today? Support your answer with reference to ethical principles and values.

2. What would your position be with respect to telling Amira the truth about her partner's condition? How is this approach morally defensible?

3. What would your position be with respect to not telling Amira in the emergency room about her partner's condition? How is this approach morally defensible? What would you do if you disagreed with the approach that the team decided to use?

4. Imagine a situation in which Amira is told — but only after she starts to recover — the news that her partner has died. She responds that she was deceived and will never again be able to trust nurses and other clinicians. How would you in turn respond to this?

5. Have you been in a situation similar to that of the team caring for Amira? Describe the situation. What is your position about your decision now and why? Compare your decisions. Has your thinking been influenced by considering these concepts related to truth-telling?

# 6 CONFIDENTIALITY

*I ... will hold in confidence all personal matters committed to my knowledge in the practice of my calling.*

— FLORENCE NIGHTINGALE PLEDGE

*What I may see or hear in the course of the treatment or even outside of the treatment in regard to the life of human beings which on no account one must spread abroad; I will keep to myself, holding such things shameful to be spoken about.*

— HIPPOCRATIC OATH

In the health professions confidentiality has long been a central, even foundational, value, as evidenced by the physicians' Hippocratic Oath, an ancient source dating back to the fifth century BC. Its importance springs in large part from the need for trust in the professional relationship. Patients must be able to trust health professionals to preserve confidentiality. Otherwise they will not have the openness necessary for the appropriate and effective delivery of care. Breaches of confidentiality, even when apparently harmless, can undermine the patient's trust in health professionals.

Historically, confidentiality has been based on the assumption that the patient provides the ultimate reference point for the authorization of disclosure of personal information. Nevertheless, the law does require health professionals to disclose confidential information when the health or safety of another person is seriously at stake. Indeed, non-consensual disclosure is increasingly being permitted or even mandated in a variety of areas in which the information is deemed crucial to the proper delivery of health care.

*In the case studies in this chapter we discuss four different issues of confidentiality: a nurse working in an occupational health unit whose superior demands the health record of an employee asking for sick leave; a fertility-clinic team working with a patient who tests positive for the HIV virus and wants this information concealed from his spouse; a nurse working in a small town who is asked to share information about patients; and a nurse working in an emergency department.*

---

## Health Professionals, Persons, and the Personal

Every day we all live our lives through different relationships and in different roles: employee, employer, colleague, friend, lover, spouse, parent, child, and so on. In whatever role we play we selectively reveal and conceal different parts of ourselves. In a relationship with a spouse we might reveal things that we conceal, or at least remain silent about, with colleagues; our children know things about us that we would never share with acquaintances. If our lives are like stories, we are not open books; different pages and chapters are open, and closed, to different people.

That we open and close ourselves selectively does not necessarily mean that we are deceitful, although that is always a possibility. Rather, this condition attests to the multidimensional character of life. The ability in some measure to choose which dimensions will be open to which people is part of what it is to be a human being.

The personal dimension is especially important in the context of health care. Health care professionals will inquire about parts of their patients' lives that are off limits to most other persons. In the interest of promoting, preserving, and restoring health, people allow health professionals access to knowledge about themselves that is otherwise guarded as being private or personal. Patients allow their bodies to be examined. They sometimes open pages of their lives that are closed even to others in their most intimate relationships. In doing so, they become vulnerable. Their personal dignity, well-being, and even security can be threatened. The information revealed or otherwise gleaned in this work, if publicly revealed to others outside the therapeutic context, has the potential of causing harm.

That health care reaches deeply into personal lives and makes people vulnerable adds gravity to the imperative for health care professionals to be respectful of privacy and hold in confidence knowledge disclosed in the therapeutic relationship. Patients open personal dimensions of their lives to health professionals, trusting their promise to hold in confidence what is disclosed to them. A sense of control over personal information can be vital to a patient's integrity and well-being. This control alone can have therapeutic value.

## Privacy and Confidentiality

The issues of confidentiality and privacy are closely linked, but they are by no means the same thing. Winslade (1978, p. 195) emphasizes the connection between the two in defining *confidentiality* in terms of the protection of, and control over, information privy to persons in special relationships. But if privacy and confidentiality overlap, they are also distinct. For example, privacy can relate to the issue of personal modesty or dignity. A nurse who averts her eyes from a patient who is undressing is demonstrating respect for the patient's privacy; confidentiality comes into play when the nurse does not disclose to anyone else what he or she observed.

Privacy, however, is a surprisingly complex concept.[1] Some writers believe that privacy has a core, essential, unitary meaning; others believe that the concept gathers meanings related not so much by essence as by overlapping family resemblances. Warren and Brandeis (2001, p. 278) offer perhaps the most famous and influential definition: they define privacy as a species of the "right to be let alone." Their account is noteworthy not only for the assertion of privacy as a right but also because they specifically ground privacy in "inviolate personality" (p. 278), which resonates with terms such as "self-determination" and "autonomy." Alan Westin (1984, p. 7), the "father" of contemporary privacy studies, carries this line of thinking forward in defining privacy as "the claim of individuals, groups, or institutions to determine for themselves when, how and to what extent information about them is communicated to others." Fried (1984, p. 206) defines privacy along similar lines, as "the control we have over information about ourselves."

Although grounding privacy in self-determination or control is common in the scholarly literature, that approach is not unchallenged. For example, Gavison (1984) contests the incorporation of norms such as "self-determination" or "control" in the definition of privacy. She defines privacy in normatively neutral terms, as a matter of non-accessibility to others, and breaks this formulation down into three dimensions: "the extent to which we are known to others, the extent to which others have physical access to us and the extent to which we are the subject of others' attention" (p. 347). These three dimensions, Gavison tells us, correspond approximately to "secrecy," "solitude," and "anonymity." These dimensions raise questions to be settled independently of the definition of privacy itself: that is, why non-access (i.e., privacy) in any of these three dimensions should be valued, and whether the ability to exercise control over access is a good thing.

Other commentators distinguish different aspects of privacy. McLean (1995) sees four forms of privacy: access-control privacy, room to grow privacy, safety valve privacy, and respect privacy. Allen (1997) also distinguishes four, albeit different, forms: physical privacy, informational privacy, proprietary privacy, and decisional privacy.

Adding to this mix is the concept of *group and community privacy*. The disclosure of information about me, and my genetic information in particular, may also reveal (or even be taken falsely to reveal) information about others. It may well contribute to a composite picture of some group to which I belong (or even falsely am inferred to belong to), and that picture thus formed may harm the interests of others in that group, whether I am harmed or not. For example, research about Aboriginal peoples' health problems can lead to the stereotyping of all Aboriginal people. For this reason some groups of people — and particularly groups prone to stereotyping — insist that the community as a whole consents to research studies that may reflect negatively on the community.

In health care the issues of privacy and confidentiality can be distinguished as follows: moral claims in connection with privacy concern the right of individual patients to limit access of other persons to their person or personal information. Confidentiality, by contrast, pertains to the duty or obligation of those who have become privy to personal information not to disclose it. Privacy pertains broadly to individual people, in their personhood and dignity; confidentiality pertains to information about a person held in a special relationship of trust. Privacy is a *right* or moral claim of the patient; confidentiality is a *duty* of a health professional.[2]

We could say, then, that a nurse who receives confidential information from a patient is under a duty of confidentiality; and that duty corresponds to a right of privacy on the part of the patient with respect to this information.

## Breaches of Confidentiality

The duty of confidentiality is enshrined in the various promissory statements — ethical guidelines, codes of ethics, legislation — that govern the profession. However, professional promise and official statements notwithstanding, in practice the observance of confidentiality has often fallen short of the ideal. In a landmark study of the issue in Ontario, Justice Krever (1980) chronicled many disturbing breaches of confidentiality in the health care system. Partly as a result of the kind of scrutiny that Krever brought to bear on these matters, jurisdictions in Ontario and elsewhere tightened checks and controls to preserve confidentiality and introduced specific legislation. However, problems persist, and, moreover, changing information technologies have led to new problems and challenges.

Breaches of confidentiality can be either deliberate and intentional or inadvertent and unintentional. Deliberate and intentional breaches of confidentiality occur when health professionals, quite aware that confidentiality is in question, knowingly and deliberately decide to subordinate confidentiality to some other good or value. In some such cases, a breach of confidentiality may be justified as an exception to the general rule that confidences should be preserved. Inadvertent or unintentional breaches of confidentiality, by contrast, occur when health professionals do not realize that they are breaching confidentiality or engaging in practices that can result in improper disclosures. A conversation among nurses overheard in a cafeteria, an unguarded answer to a seemingly innocuous question about a patient, a chart or record left momentarily unattended, a computer screen that does not close automatically after the user leaves the terminal: these are but a few examples.[3]

Inadvertent and unintentional disclosures, then, need to be considered in context, and health care providers are not necessarily to blame for them. To be sure, breaches are sometimes the result of carelessness or thoughtlessness, and the nurse in question should be held to account. However, in the past decade a major reversal has occurred in how we think about errors, not just with respect to breaches of confidentiality but more generally in the provision of care.[4] Increasingly practitioners recognize that factors beyond the nurses' control can also cause, or at least contribute to, error.

Systemic evaluations can reduce the risk of the errors of inadvertent disclosure. Making sure that proper security systems are in place will help. Protocols can clarify and remind nurses about what information can be disclosed to whom under what circumstances. Private areas can be provided for counselling and discussion out of earshot of those who have no particular need or right to hear what is being said. Charts can be securely stored away from prying eyes. Computer terminals can be programmed to close after the computer is left idle for a short time. Patient boards can be placed out of public view.

An emphasis on system changes should not, however, be construed as absolving nurses from individual responsibility. For example, individual nurses need to be sensitive to potential breaches. Nurses need to exercise care and be vigilant about not identifying patients when they mention or discuss cases away from their unit — which sometimes happens, quite properly, for instance, in a cafeteria when a nurse meets up with a colleague and takes the opportunity to have an important discussion about patient care. The norms and attitudes that nurses hold are critical. One study found a positive and significant correlation between nurses' attitude of promoting and protecting privacy and their planned behaviours to follow through on their attitudes and norms (Tabak & Ozon, 2004). Ways of influencing attitudes and behaviours include education and workplace policies that support nurses in carrying out their responsibilities in connection with confidentiality.

Inadvertent breaches of confidentiality are sometimes due to a lack of clarity or confusion about confidentiality and what constitutes a breach of confidentiality. *A breach of confidentiality occurs when information about someone is shared with or made available to others without patient authorization, and when that information is a matter of confidence between nurse and patient.* In a given case, it may be difficult to determine whether one or the other of these conditions obtains or applies.

## 1. Information-Sharing and Patient Authorization

It has long been recognized that the ultimate authority over confidential information is the patient, and the health professions' overriding goal is to safeguard information for the patient in trust. The sharing of confidential information is thus authorized or not depending on whether the patient agrees or consents to passing on that information. If confidential information is released to an outside party without the patient's consent, that act represents a breach of confidentiality; if the patient consents to the release, it is not a breach.

Yet patients do not specifically have to agree to and authorize every instance of information-sharing in the health care setting. Historically, the nursing profession has understood confidentiality as a matter of permitting information-sharing on a "need to know" basis with other health professionals who have a part in the care of the patient. The patient's consent for "need to know" sharing may reasonably be implied based on two provisions: that the sharing is indeed necessary for the purpose for which the care is being sought; and that the patient has not indicated any wishes to the contrary.[5] Increasingly, too, it is not the patient's authorization that matters but someone else's (for example, hospital policy or legislation may authorize disclosure without consent) — and this practice, though certainly debatable, is gaining more and more prominence.

The trend toward a team-based approach to health care (which requires greater information-sharing) presents new difficulties and challenges on this front.[6] Interdisciplinary health care teams in hospitals and the community collaborate on many aspects of care. Integrated health care systems extend the team to include health care professionals along a continuum of care. The team can include nurses, physicians, and chaplains; home-care workers, nutritionists, speech therapists, physiotherapists, laboratory technicians, management, and clerical staff and volunteers. Those involved may have to use judgement to determine not only just who is in the "circle of care" but also how the "need-to-know" sharing can proceed on the basis of implied consent.

*Judgement may be needed not only to determine who should know, but also what others should know.* Not all persons in the circle of care need to know all the details entered in the patient's health record. It is enough for most of them to know only what they need to know in order to contribute effectively to the patient's care. For example, on a "need to know" basis, the nursing staff in a nursing unit would have access to patient laboratory reports, but clerical staff would not. In some cases decisions about what information is needed for care purposes and by which caregivers are in a grey zone.

## 2. Determining Whether Information Is Confidential

Related to the issue of authorization to disclose confidential information is the question of determining whether a given item of information is confidential to begin with. Suppose that in an occupational setting a senior manager asks the occupational health nurse to provide a log indicating whether a certain employee has been to the health unit in the past six months. Is this information confidential? The answer here is clear-cut. The employee and the health unit have an implicit agreement that information collected under the auspices of the unit is confidential and will be treated as such. In this case, even the very fact of visiting the health unit is confidential, and therefore cannot be shared without authorization.

Suppose, though, that in a birthing centre one mother asks a nurse if another mother admitted at the same time has delivered her baby yet, or whether she had a boy or a girl, or whether the baby is healthy. Should that kind of information be considered confidential? It might be hard to imagine why the patient would care, and a nurse might understandably assume that the patient wouldn't mind this information being passed along. The information in question, after all, is normally considered to be "happy news" and even somewhat non-consequential. On the face of it, the news that the new mother had a healthy boy, for instance, would appear to be no more confidential a matter than that she chose cauliflower for her dinner instead of carrots. It might be hard to imagine why the patient would care.

The patient would, however, have reasonable grounds for objection if this information were shared without her consent. Some information is more personal or sensitive than other information, and there may very well be reasons as to why a patient would consider information about a birth — or even what she had for dinner — to be a sensitive matter.

In any case — regardless of whether the patient or the nurse considers the information to be sensitive — the information is confidential because of the context. You can't rely upon your own estimation of the information's intrinsic sensitivity to determine whether it is confidential or not. What makes information confidential is not its specific detail. Confidentiality is also not just a matter of the possibility of the nurse being wrong about what the patient holds to be personal or sensitive. The decisive thing, rather, is the context in which the nurse becomes privy to the information: it happens in a heath care setting, in his or her professional capacity, and in view of a strong expectation of confidentiality.

As a general rule, therefore, the answer to the question as to whether information is confidential and needs to be treated as such is simple: if nurses become privy to information in the course of their professional duties, the information is confidential. It is not appropriate for nurses to share confidential information — however innocuous that information may seem — without the permission of the patient.

In some cases the patient's consent to share confidential information, although not expressly given, may reasonably be implied; but the nurse's assumption that consent is implied can be subject to error. The more that is assumed or left implicit between nurse and patient, the greater the risk of misunderstandings. "But I assumed that you would treat that as being confidential between us!" a patient might say. Nurses can guard against such misunderstandings and potential complications by being as explicit as possible with patients about what sorts of things will or should be protected under the umbrella of confidentiality. This approach is especially important in cross-cultural exchanges — in situations in which significant differences exist in the cultural backgrounds of providers and patients and their families, where sensibilities about privacy and confidentiality vary even more greatly between individuals. The cultural backgrounds of all individuals (providers, patients, and their families) will influence their perceptions and the meanings that they attribute to health care encounters (Coward & Ratanakul, 1999).

### Exceptions to the Rule of Confidentiality

The duty of confidentiality is not absolute: exceptions to the rule of confidentiality and conditions under which it is justifiable to breach it do exist. When it comes into conflict with other duties, confidentiality must sometimes yield. Indeed, under certain circumstances nurses are required by law to breach confidentiality.

Considerable controversy exists concerning what constitutes a legitimate or justifiable exception to the rule of confidentiality.[7] The legal exceptions typically have to do with preventing a serious harm from occurring. A landmark legal case in this regard is *Tarasoff v. Regents of the University of California*.[8] The case involved a man who had killed his girlfriend — and had previously confided his intention to do so to his psychologist, who was employed by a hospital at the university. Although the psychologist took steps to protect against this danger, even at one point having the patient detained by the university police, he did not communicate the threat to the woman. Obviously, he did not do enough to prevent harm from coming to her. After the young woman was murdered her family took the matter to court, arguing that she should have been warned or otherwise protected from the danger. The court ruled that if in the course of a therapeutic relationship a therapist is given reason to believe that a patient may present a danger to others, that therapist has a "duty to warn" of the danger.

Both the magnitude (how bad would it be if it happened?) and the probability of the harm foreseen (how likely is it to happen?) are morally relevant and have to be weighed together in decisions to disclose without consent. As concerns magnitude, harms can be distinguished along a continuum ranging from the very minor, such as a pinprick, to the most serious, death. The more serious the harm foreseen, the more compelling is the case for a breach of confidentiality. As concerns probability, the risk of the harm may range from being very low to very high. The psychologist whose patient confided an intention to kill a former girlfriend apparently believed — mistakenly — that this act had a low probability of actually occurring.

The ethical codes of the various health professions agree that under certain conditions it is justifiable, and sometimes obligatory, to disclose confidential information in the interests of averting harm.[9] For example, the Canadian Nurses Association (2002a) provides a limitation to the duty of confidentiality: "Nurses must disclose a person's health information only as authorized by that person, unless there is a substantial risk of serious harm to the person or to other persons, or a legal obligation to disclose" (p. 14).[10] The nurse is not morally obligated to maintain confidentiality when the failure to disclose information will place the patient or third parties in significant danger. Generally, legal requirements or privileges to disclose are morally justified by the same criterion. For example, nurses in Ontario and many other jurisdictions are bound by law to report suspected abuse to the Children's Aid Society or a child protection agency.

In exceptional cases in which it is justifiable or even mandatory to breach confidentiality, this act should be carried out in as respectful and minimally invasive a way as possible. The CNA Code (2002a) notes that in circumstances in which the law requires disclosure without consent, nurses "should attempt to inform individuals about what information will be disclosed, to whom, and for what reason(s)" (Confidentiality, principle 6). In Ontario, practice standards for ethics advise that before information is disclosed without consent nurses should consult with the health team and, if appropriate, report the information to the person or persons affected. The patient or substitute decision-maker should be informed that the nurse has a duty to report, and in light of this knowledge the person should be given the opportunity to disclose him/herself (CNO, 2009, p. 8). One exception to this rule would be when giving patients a chance to disclose could place others at significant risk. For example, in cases of abuse there may be a concern that with disclosure the suspected abuser will remove or contaminate evidence or that the abused person could be at increased risk.

Patients are entitled to know, at least in a general way, the conditions under which confidential information about them might be released to others without their consent. In this regard, nurses should be aware — and as appropriate make their patients aware — of any laws or policies that might permit or require nurses or other health professionals to disclose confidential information.

## Confidentiality in the Age of Information Technology

The health system has undergone vast changes due to computerization and the movement from paper to electronic health records. Confidentiality has been, and remains, very much at issue in these changes.[11]

In its computerized form, health information is easier and less costly to reproduce, process, and share. The information is thus more useful and valuable for a variety of purposes, many of them not directly related to the provision of care to the patient whose information has been collected. Emerging policy goals such as population health and the prevention of harm to others have also contributed to increased access demands for health information. Efforts to improve the health system and to manage it more effectively are information-intensive. More information is sought in order to promote accountability.

A number of initiatives and developments indicate the magnitude of recent changes that are access-intensive and arouse what has been called "data lust":

- the creation of health information systems and networks and of a Health Infoway across the country to facilitate greater access to, and sharing of, information scattered in various repositories or "silos";

- the movement toward comprehensive electronic health records;

- the proliferation of databases linking information from a variety of sources, including registries for various diseases and conditions;

- a trend to public/private partnerships in connection with health information systems and, related to this, the increasing commercialization of health information;

- the emergence of the Internet, with its potential for the extensive collection of health-related information, sometimes quite surreptitiously;

- the reliance of health reform initiatives (e.g., primary health care) on access to information and the prominence of information technology in these initiatives;

- developments in the field of genetics and genomics and increased interest in access to genetic samples and information for a variety of purposes.

All of these changes involve a trend toward information linkages: piecing information together from diverse data sources or silos to form composite, revealing pictures of individuals and populations. Research in population health, including population genetics and research on broad determinants of health, exemplifies this trend. Often that research relies upon the extensive collection of information pertaining to lifestyle, financial situation, and personal relationships. Alpert (1998, 2003) safely predicts that interconnections and linkages between databases will inevitably grow as the volume and scope of data tracked and manipulated increase.[12]

Health information collection is also increasingly indirect. Before computerization, there was much less value in information gathered for purposes secondary to the provision of care. With information scattered in filing cabinets, the human and financial costs of gaining access to or assembling it were prohibitive. With computerization, the costs of access and collection become greatly reduced. Information collected for clinical care is now increasingly sought for secondary purposes, such as research, and demanded by those with no direct clinical relationship to the patient (Naser and Alpert, 2000).[13]

The use of smart cards and computer information systems raises apprehensions that Big Brother (or Big Sister) will monitor every detail of patient interactions with the health system. Developments in genetic testing raise still other concerns. The information gleaned from such testing may be revealing, and sensitive. There are a variety of reasons as to why such information might be of interest or even of importance to third parties, including employers, insurance companies, the police, and family members.

Although the information technology age we live in increases the urgency of concerns about privacy and confidentiality, the key moral questions and issues arising are far from new. Traditionally, disclosure without consent has been justified under very tightly limited, specific conditions; but these traditional norms have become increasingly strained, largely in consequence of increased demands from secondary users of health information — for instance, health planners, health care professionals, and researchers.

Questions about who should have authorized access to confidential information, and under what conditions, go to the heart of confidentiality. These questions are vigorously debated today. It is important to distinguish these sorts of questions from others having to do with implementing measures to protect information so that those who do not have a right to it are unable to access it — in other words, to distinguish these questions from issues of security.

Given the sensitivity of health information, patients are rightly worried about failures of security. The danger of hackers breaking into computer systems, or of people inside an organization gaining access beyond what they are rightfully entitled to, is serious. Health care professionals, managers, and designers of health records systems should be held responsible and accountable for the use of these systems. Patients cannot be expected to be experts on the design of system security, just as most nurses are not experts. They rely on information technology experts, many of whom are nurses with expertise in informatics. They trust organizations to have security measures in place to prevent unauthorized access to, and modification or deletion of, confidential information, such as entry codes, audit trails, and encryption.[14]

In view of information technology changes, many provinces have enacted legislation specifically addressing access to confidential information in the health system. At the federal level, the *Personal Information and Protection of Electronic Documents Act* (Government of Canada, 2002) elaborates principles of fair information practice that address issues of privacy, confidentiality, and the security of computerized information. Typically, such legislation has extensive provisions allowing the disclosure of confidential information without consent, for a variety of purposes. It also contains provisions allowing patients to gain access to and, according to certain procedures to correct, their health information, as well as measures to ensure accountability in connection with the custody of health information.

The trend appears to be that health professionals have less and less control over the information that they have been entrusted with by their patients, and at the same time patients have less control over the information that they give to health professionals. There are good reasons, based on professional norms, for resisting this trend. Beyond this resistance, however, when nurses do find themselves lacking the ability to control information flow on behalf of their patients, they should at the very least make this situation known to their patients, and qualify their promises of confidentiality accordingly.

### Case 1: Confidentiality in the Workplace

Many employers have occupational health departments that employees can visit to seek help for work-related health problems. An occupational health nurse working in such a department may work alone, and often without the support of other health professionals on site. Occupational health settings are also unique because the patient and the nurse are both employees of the same company or institution. Occupational health nurses may find themselves in a conflict because they are expected to represent the interests of both the management and the patient/employee.

Employers of nurses know that providing a healthy workplace is a priority, but managers in the organization may have different priorities than the nurses. For one thing, they may attach much less weight to confidentiality.

The setting for our case study here is an occupational health unit in a large urban hospital — a setting that adds complexity because most of the patients are also nurses. Nurses have the highest number of sick days of any profession in Canada (Aiken et al., 2002; Health Canada Office of Nursing Policy, 2001). The reasons for this are complex, but the physical and emotional stresses of the work are most likely contributing factors.

*John Le Blanc is the nursing manager of the occupational health unit in the hospital. He reports to the vice-president of Human Resources, Rose Christie, who is also a nurse. In their work history John and Rose have clearly differed in the value they attach to matters of confidentiality: John believes that Rose should pay more attention to the principle.*

*One day this difference, never really tested before, comes into focus when Rose asks John for the health record of Evelyn Green, a registered nurse who has been employed by the hospital for some twenty years. Evelyn has an excellent employment and attendance record, but after her husband's death a year earlier she developed a serious alcohol problem. Last week Evelyn came to the occupational health unit and asked John to help get her into a recovery program as soon as possible.*

*John immediately arranged for her to be assessed by an alcohol and drug addiction program contracted with the hospital. Plans were made for her to enter a recovery program the following week. On Evelyn's behalf John also filled out a form certifying that she had an illness and would need to be granted sick leave. In keeping with accepted procedure, the form did not indicate the nature of the sickness. This omission was important to Evelyn, who feared that she might lose her job if her employer learned about her drinking problem.*

*John knows that Rose is concerned about the high costs of replacing Evelyn temporarily, but he is also aware of his duty to preserve confidential information. He explains to Rose that the information she has requested is confidential and cannot be provided. Rose responds that she needs to have the information to ensure the continuous provision of safe patient care on the unit. If Evelyn is going to be away for an extended period of time, Rose will have to arrange either to employ a permanent employee or to rely on a nursing agency that charges considerably more per hour.*

*After listening to the pressures Rose is under, John reaffirms his initial stand. Rose responds sternly, "I know this is hard for you. But I have to be guided by what is best for patients and staff. I need the information on my desk by tomorrow morning!"*

## Commentary

The issue raised in this case involves a conflict between the employer's need to know and the nurse's duty of confidentiality. A key factor in analyzing the issue is why the employer needs to have the requested information. For example, if the information were urgently needed in order to prevent some serious harm, that reason would hold weight. In this case, though, there appears to be no urgency. Although Rose has a legitimate concern about ensuring continuous care, and her concerns about replacement costs are also legitimate, accomplishing her purpose does not depend on seeing the health record of the patient.

On the other hand, the information at issue could potentially be harmful to the patient; and the patient, when initially making the information available to health professionals, would have had reason to expect confidentiality. The disclosure of the information to the employer might also undermine general employee trust in the health service. If other employees learned that personal information from the health service would be disclosed to the employer on demand, they would be discouraged from using the service.[15]

In this case there does not appear to be legitimate grounds for breaching confidentiality. Doing so would be inconsistent with the nursing profession's code of ethics and standards of practice, as well as with the requirements of the law.

A further complication, though, is that John could put his own job in jeopardy if he fails to co-operate with his superior. Even if preserving confidentiality is the right thing to do, failing to comply with Rose's demands could be perilous. Then again, if he follows Rose's instructions and violates his duty to preserve confidentiality by handing over confidential records, he may be protecting his job at the cost of sacrificing or compromising his integrity. This course of action would also entail serious professional risk. The disclosure without the patient's consent of information given in confidence would be in contravention of professional norms and could make him vulnerable to charges of professional misconduct.

What options does John have? He could discuss the issue with Evelyn Green and ask her to release the information voluntarily. Under the circumstances, such a request might be somewhat coercive. Evelyn might well feel a sense of guilt or responsibility if she finds out that John's job is at stake.

A better alternative for John would be to discuss the matter further with his superior. Although Rose is a nurse-manager, her priorities appear to be administrative. She is under immense pressure to provide staffing economically. John could support his position by providing Rose with information about the professional norms and constraints under which nurses and other health professionals practise. For example, guidelines published by the Ontario Occupational Health Nurses Association (1993) recommend that access to confidential information "be confined to the occupational health physicians and nurses and the occupational health nurse," and also explicitly advise that "employee health records should be located separately from general personnel files" (p. 2). As a nurse, Rose should be sensitive to these professional duties and norms.

A compromise of sorts could be worked out. Although it would be improper for John to give Rose the health record, or even to mention the diagnosis, to carry out her planning and take action Rose does not need to know these details. She needs to know, in essence, approximately how long Evelyn might be off work. Without breaking confidentiality John could indicate that he expects Evelyn to be off work for a certain length of time and he will keep tabs on the patient's progress; he will update management and provide proper notice of her return, thus allowing effective planning. If John has any doubts about whether providing this general information to Rose represents a breach of confidentiality, he could talk to Evelyn and explain to her the employer's need to plan for continuous care in her absence.

If this approach fails, John could appeal to a senior nursing administrator, possibly someone with a broader perspective on the issue. The administrator might be able to intervene and convince Rose that the policy of preserving confidentiality is in the best interests of employees and, in the long run, of the hospital. If these steps prove to be dead ends, John and/or management could try other options, such as contacting an outside person to mediate. Resources for John include nursing professional organizations and the provincial self-regulatory body.

Another less positive possibility is that in the end John will find himself faced with no attractive options and be required to make a tragic choice that will make his position untenable, or perhaps cost him his job. Although John has good arguments on his side, and in an enlightened workplace his position regarding confidentiality would prevail, the unfortunate reality is that some workplaces prove to be less than ideal.

### Case 2: Confidentiality in a Family Context

In the case of the hospital occupational health unit, the third party who wanted confidential information was not an intimate of the patient and had interests clearly at odds with those of the patient. Often, though, requests for confidential information come from family members or significant others who share the nurse's concern for the well-being of the patient. This intimacy and concern may seem to give these other parties a greater claim to confidential information. Indeed, usually a patient is quite willing to share information with intimates, whose desire to know often arises out of concern. Perhaps they are worried or anxious and knowing more will help them to cope with the situation. Perhaps knowing more will put them in a better position to help or support the patient.

Sometimes, however, the patient may not want family members or intimates to have access to health-related information; or the patient may want family to know some things, but not others; or perhaps may want only certain family members to be informed. Patients may be estranged from their families, or certain members of their families. They may want to protect family members from bad news, or feel guilty or ashamed. A variety of reasons can come into play.

Acquired immune deficiency syndrome (AIDS) has presented many challenges to confidentiality. AIDS is mainly transmitted through sexual behaviour, and sexuality is a deeply personal and private part of most people's lives. Moreover, partners, friends, family, and health care professionals may judge lifestyle choices harshly and negatively. Consequently, patients may choose to keep this dimension of their lives secret. Indeed, some people conceal aspects of their sexual lives even from those with whom they are sexually and emotionally intimate.

Because AIDS is infectious, and its consequences are severe, screening protocols to detect the human immunodeficiency virus (HIV) have been established in a number of areas in the health care system. People agree to the testing, for instance, because they want to be considered for employment or receive certain services. Persons may be required to be tested when seeking health insurance or assistance with fertility problems. The screening can turn up information about patients' sexual history and behaviour that they would rather keep to themselves. Valid concerns about coercion can arise in these instances.

In our case study the issue of confidentiality is further complicated because the testing has been carried out in the context of a treatment involving a married couple.

*After four years of trying unsuccessfully to have a baby, and numerous medical consultations, Valerie and Alan Joblonski have been referred to a fertility clinic. The consultations have raised the suspicion that their inability to conceive is due to Alan having a low sperm count. If that is the case, they have been told, their chances of conceiving would be greatly enhanced if Alan underwent a procedure wherein his sperm is collected and concentrated and then later artificially inseminated in Valerie during the optimal period in her ovulation cycle.*

*The clinic screens couples for a number of health problems, including HIV. The couple are provided with counselling about the purpose of the testing and told that the results will be given to them alone. According to clinic policy, if a patient tests positive, treatment will be interrupted until after a counselling team, including a social worker and psychologist, meets with the couple. The team discusses options with the couple. They can continue with fertility treatments on the condition that they are also seen by an HIV team that advises them on ways of reducing the risk of transmission. They must agree to the risk-reduction program to receive assistance with conception.[16] The clinic staff explains that couples who test positive for HIV must seek counselling from an HIV clinic before they can return to the fertility clinic.*

*Valerie's test for HIV is negative, but Alan's is positive. In a private post-test meeting that he alone attends with the clinic nurse, Ethel Kapanga, Alan reveals that he had an extramarital sexual encounter when he was out of town at a conference, and that Valerie does not know about it. Alan is afraid that Valerie will leave him if she learns of his affair, and does not want her to know. The nurse tries to impress upon him the importance of telling his wife.*

*He refuses and says he will not continue with the treatment. He will simply tell his wife that he changed his mind about undergoing the treatment.*

## Commentary

A key question raised by this case is whether the clinic is morally required to disclose to Valerie that Alan is HIV-positive. Ownership of, and rights with respect to, the information about Alan's HIV status is relevant to this question. The health professional-patient relationship is complex because more than one person is involved in the treatment for which Alan presented. There is even some ambiguity about whether Valerie and Alan constitute two discrete patients or are in some sense a single patient. Although the information at issue is clearly confidential, some uncertainty exists as to whether Alan alone owns and has the exclusive right to control it. After all, Alan and Valerie presented at the clinic as a couple and not as two strangers. It is as a couple that they would be the subjects of the treatment. Seeing them together as a patient rather than as two discrete patients means that each of them is privy to whatever information is generated or otherwise brought to light in the course of the therapy.[17]

Certainly this line of argument stretches the concept of confidentiality as it is traditionally understood. In the paradigm case for confidentiality, the patient is normally (and unambiguously) a discrete individual. But the case of Valerie and Alan is clearly different. In any event, the argument that Valerie is entitled to this information insofar as she is a sort of co-owner depends in part on the nature of the understanding and promise in light of which the couple began the program in the first place. If, for example, the clinic staff had made it clear from the beginning that any information made available to one would also be made available to the other, the argument for disclosure would be stronger. In this instance, it appears that the clinic's policy in this regard is ambiguous. It is not clear precisely what the couple was promised with respect to individual confidentiality. This issue is a critical point that the clinic should address by making the policy unambiguous and ensuring that patients understand exactly what policy is in place.

Even if sharing the information about Alan's HIV status with Valerie could be construed as a breach of confidentiality, the question would remain as to whether such a breach is justified in this case. Confidentiality, after all, is not an absolute value, and the duty to preserve confidentiality is not absolute. Other values also come into play: in this case, beneficence and truthfulness.

One of the factors that sets this case apart from the previous case is that the patient is putting someone else at immediate and significant risk. Although Valerie has not yet acquired HIV, there is a chance that she may well do so. Perhaps she already has, but is in the "window period" in which HIV does not show up in testing. Certainly the risk is serious, both in terms of its probability (if they continue to have unprotected sex) and its magnitude if she becomes infected. If they manage to conceive without the treatment, they also face the risk that the child conceived could have HIV. Valerie could take steps to reduce these risks if she knows about Alan's HIV status.

The clinic therefore has good reason for insisting that Valerie be informed about her risk, even if the only way this can happen means breaching confidentiality with Alan. The first thing Nurse Kopanga should do is discuss options with the team. One option is for the team to meet with Alan and ensure that he fully understands the nature of his condition and the risk of infecting others. Learning about being HIV-positive can be devastating. Understandably, Alan may be in shock and not know how to deal with the news. He should, of course, be offered counselling. The team could offer him further support if he elects to inform his wife; they could arrange to meet with them as a couple to discuss the issue. If he still refuses to inform her, they should make it clear that they intend to inform his wife, and why, and that they will advise her of steps to take for her own protection.

### Case 3: Confidentiality and Seemingly Innocuous Information

Frequently, confidential information concerns matters that a patient obviously wants to keep from certain others — information, for instance, that could rebound in harm to the patient. Our first two cases concerned information of this sort. However, a good deal of the personal information gained about someone in a health care setting is not like that at all. Much of it seems innocuous because there is no obvious reason why the patient would have an interest in keeping the details from others. For example, there is no apparent reason why disclosing that Mrs. Smith in the next hospital room is a schoolteacher, or that Mr. Jones down the hall has three children, would matter to them.

With regard to such seemingly innocuous information, nurses may find it tempting to relax the normal constraints concerning confidentiality. Indeed, such information may not be perceived as coming under the protective umbrella of confidentiality at all.

Our next case raises issues that can arise in connection with information of this kind. The context in which this information is being shared with others — among friends of the patients in a small rural community — adds another dimension to these issues.

*Sandy Young grew up in a small town in Canada and went to a nearby city to study nursing. After graduating, and being unable to find employment, she went to the United States and worked in a busy teaching hospital there for three years. She jumped at the opportunity to return to her hometown when a nursing home there offered a job. She found herself caring for the parents and grandparents of her own friends. Some patients were mentally alert and others had varying degrees of cognitive impairment. Although her workload was heavy, she found time to talk to the patients and their families. She received many cards of appreciation.*

*Sandy became active in the social life of the community. At parties and community events, and in her volunteer work, relatives and friends of her patients would often approach her seeking "news" from the nursing home. The questions they posed ranged from the health and mobility of a patient to who came to visit, and how often.*

*Although Sandy believed that the people asking these questions were well-meaning and genuinely concerned, and moreover thought that her patients would probably approve, she nevertheless felt uncomfortable sharing this "news." She mentioned her feelings to her colleagues at the nursing home, but they did not think it was a problem. Most of them had worked at the home for a long time and could not recall any concern expressed by the residents. "Sandy, you're not in the big city anymore — things here are a lot more friendly and informal," one of the older nurses told her. Despite these assurances, Sandy continued to be troubled about the matter.*

## Commentary

Sandy is uncertain as to whether the information in question ought to be subjected to the normal constraints of confidentiality. In this case three related considerations might bear on her deliberations. In the first place, the information seems innocuous: no harm, it seems, is likely to come to her patients from its disclosure. Second, the people to whom she is disclosing the information are friends and relatives of her patients. In a small community such as this one, it might even be tempting to think of them as a kind of extended family. They care about her patients, and their desire to know what is happening seems to be motivated by genuine concern. Third, Sandy believes that her patients would probably want these people to have the information or news that she is able to share.

To help us analyze the question that troubles Sandy, we can express each of these considerations in the form of a possible rule. The first consideration might be expressed by a rule to the effect that disclosure of personal information is morally permissible if the information is harmless, or if the patient has no interest in keeping it confidential. The most obvious problem with this rule is that the judgement that a given item of information is harmless, or that a patient has no interest in keeping it confidential, is fallible. The nurse may very well be mistaken.

For causes or reasons that the nurse could hardly imagine, seemingly innocuous information may well turn out to be harmful. This is especially true given that what counts as harm can be subjective. Moreover, if such a judgement is to be made, the patient and not the nurse should make it.

A different objection is that even if you can be certain that no harm will come from passing on the information, there may still be another reason for guarding it as being confidential. Even if you can know for certain that a secret entrusted in confidence will not come back to harm the person who entrusted it, you would nevertheless be breaking your promise of confidentiality by revealing it.

The second consideration can be expressed as the rule that disclosure of personal information about a patient is permissible provided it is disclosed only to family or friends of the patient, who presumably have a genuine concern. One problem with this rule is that a nurse can be mistaken in distinguishing those who are genuinely concerned from those who are not. Even the fact that someone is a family member is not sufficient evidence that they are genuinely concerned about the patient.

Moreover, even if they are genuinely concerned, knowing confidential information could still put them in a position to cause harm to or violate the interests of the patient — even if unintentionally. Furthermore, even if the nurse can be certain that the person's concern is genuine, and that no harm could come from their knowing, the patient simply may not want that person to know.

The third consideration can be expressed as the rule that the disclosure of personal information about a patient is permissible only if the patient wishes it to be disclosed, and even then only to a person approved by the patient. This rule puts the emphasis not on the nature of the information, or even on the context in which it might be shared, but rather on the autonomy of the patient, on the right of the patient to control the disclosure of personal information.[18] Given the importance of autonomy in contemporary health care, this rule has much to recommend it. However, it does not obviate the need for sound judgement on the part of nursing staff. Patient consent or authorization may be more or less explicit. The less explicit the authorization (for example, based on what I know about the patient, I think he would want me to tell his good friend Charlie that he may not recover from his bout of pneumonia), the greater the possibility of error.

The surest way of determining what the patient wants is to ask. Sandy might be able to resolve her problem simply by talking to her patients and soliciting their opinions on the matter. However, some of them are cognitively impaired. What about those unable to express their wishes? If she is unable to get explicit consent (or refusal), should Sandy play it safe and disclose nothing at all? Alternatively, might there be someone else who could speak for these patients?

It may be that her patients do want news about them to be communicated in the social settings in which Sandy finds herself. People in small communities often pride themselves on their neighbourliness and caring attitudes and feel distinct from people in large cities in which "nobody knows anybody else." Some customs and rules that are appropriate in a big-city climate of anonymity and indifference may not be as appropriate in a smaller community. Informality and openness tend to be more highly valued in small towns than in large cities.

Some of Sandy's patients may not want personal news to be shared even with concerned friends and neighbours. Some patients might look on such exchanges of information as a kind of gossip that they would rather avoid. Some may value their privacy more than others, and might regard a lack of privacy as being a negative feature of life in small towns. Indeed, the lack of privacy is why some residents of small towns go elsewhere for health services or treatments that they would like to keep to themselves.

In analyzing the issue that troubles her, Sandy could reflect on the factors that combine to generate the issue in the first place. One such factor concerns a certain ambiguity about the status of the information in question. The people who approach Sandy for information, and perhaps Sandy herself, appear to view this information as being news. Viewed in this way, disclosure seems appropriate. But Sandy only becomes privy to this news in the context of a professional-patient relationship. As such, the information is confidential. Viewing the information as "news" may obscure this important point.

Another key has to do with the relationship between Sandy's professional role, on the one hand, and her personal or social life on the other. The issue arises, after all, because Sandy appears in the same circumstance wearing two hats. At a social function, she is both a member of the community and a nurse privy to confidential information of interest or concern to those she encounters socially. Those who ask her for information, and perhaps Sandy herself, may blur or fail to differentiate these two roles. In her professional nursing role, Sandy assumes certain obligations to her patients. These obligations are binding even when she takes off her uniform and participates in the community. Clarifying and communicating this point to those who approach her for news will help Sandy deal with the situation.

Clarifying the issue will also help Sandy deal with her co-workers, who, it appears, are quite open about such informal disclosures. Having translated her initially vague feeling of discomfort into an analysis, Sandy will be in a better position to convince others that there is an issue that needs to be addressed. Sitting down with other nursing staff and exploring their views and beliefs on confidentiality could prove to be productive. All of them might learn from each other, and develop guidelines or criteria for responding to issues of confidentiality arising from within the community.

## Case 4: Privacy Issues in the Emergency Department

In an emergency department, issues about privacy and confidentiality are frequent and often complex. The nature of clinical practice in the emergency department requires nurses to complete assessments quickly. To permit appropriate and timely decision-making about their treatment options, patients may need to reveal health information that they have preferred to keep hidden for years.

This practice environment presents its own set of challenges in connection with privacy and confidentiality. There are physical barriers to providing privacy. Stretchers may be lined along hallways; patients may be separated only by curtains. When no private interview area is available, or staff has no time to take the person to a quiet area, assessments and interviews may have to be completed within earshot of other patient and families. Relatives, friends, health care professionals in other departments and organizations, the press, and police officers may ask nurses and their colleagues for confidential health information.

Health organizations have complex communication and organizational systems. Nurses in the emergency department collaborate with interdisciplinary teams, including physicians, social workers, chaplains, and volunteers. They must establish who is included in the circle of care and also when and why they can disclose requested information. They need to be aware of ethical responsibilities and organizational policies regarding disclosure with and without patients' consent. Nurses should know what is legally required regarding mandatory disclosure in their jurisdiction.

Domestic or family violence is an underdetected and underreported serious health problem. A minority of cases are reported to health care professionals and the police. This silence is understandable, and often when it is broken there are major social, financial, and emotional consequences, especially when children are involved. The victims, mainly women, differ in age, ethnicity, and socioeconomic status. Physical, sexual, emotional, and financial abuse is increasing in Canada and worldwide (CNA, 2002c). Nurses may be the first health care professional called upon to meet people — of all ages — who are victims or witnesses of violence. Nurses in the emergency department can play a critical role in identifying, assessing, responding to, and reducing the continuation of a pattern of living with violence.

Issues of suspected abuse or illegal activity can pose especially difficult privacy and confidentiality issues for nurses. The kind of holistic assessment that nurses do includes being on the alert for abuse, neglect, and domestic violence across the lifespan. Disclosure of information may be essential to protect vulnerable persons at risk of serious and imminent harm. Many emergency department nurses can consult with specialists in domestic abuse involving children, adults, and older persons when they suspect neglect and abuse. Administrators and quality-risk management staff may need to become involved in complex cases.

*Inderjeet is the team leader in the emergency department in a downtown urban hospital. The surrounding community is ethnically diverse, with thousands of young families and older adults living in the area's many apartment buildings. Frequently these residents come to emergency for help because they do not have a family physician available on weekends. The emergency department employs two primary care nurse practitioners. Other resources available to the emergency staff are a domestic violence team and a geriatric nurse clinician specializing in emergency care. In the past year all of the staff have had specialized training in the assessment of abuse and neglect and cultural sensitivity.*

*On the Sunday of a long weekend, several patients had arrived by noon. First came Jason, aged twenty, a university student living in residence. Jason had a serious but not life-threatening gunshot wound. He was shot when leaving an ATM machine on campus. Shortly after he was rushed into the trauma room, police officers arrived and told staff that they believed he was a victim of a gang shooting. They wanted to know his name, age, and the nature of his injuries. They also wanted to interview him.*

*A short while after Jason came out of surgery, Inderjeet and the trauma physician asked him if he wanted to speak to the police. He indicated quite definitely that he did not want to talk to them. When Inderjeet passed this response on to the police, she added* that given his present condition she did not think that the patient was well enough to be interviewed. She also refused to tell the officers how he was injured and what his prognosis was. She told them that this information was confidential and that the emergency personnel were not permitted to divulge confidential information when there was no serious and imminent threat to another known person. The police officers responded by threatening to lay charges of obstruction of justice against her and the physician. In response, Inderjeet conferred with the emergency department management and trauma team physician and went back to the police, repeating her reason for not providing them with the information they sought. She added that mandatory reporting of gunshot wounds is not the law in their province.

A second case involved Karen Park, a thirty-five-year-old woman with a bruised eye and broken arm. She came with her twin sons, aged three years old. The boys had bruises on their arms and backs. Karen initially explained that her children had fallen when they were playing on playground equipment. Inderjeet noted that the wounds were not consistent with playground equipment injuries and asked the domestic violence team to assess the family. The team established a trusting relationship with Karen, who disclosed to them that her husband had hit her because he was frustrated with her. She blamed herself because she had been giving all her time and attention to the twins. Karen refused to notify the police. The team informed her that they had a legal obligation to report suspected abuse, and to involve the Children's Aid Society in connection with the children's injuries.

When Karen asked to call her husband, to tell him what was happening, Inderjeet explained that if he was alerted about the Children's Aid Society involvement their investigation could be compromised. Karen understood; moreover, after considering all her options she agreed with the plan recommended by the domestic violence team that she and her boys move to a safe home and not return to their residence. Inderjeet was relieved that Karen chose this option. Domestic violence is the leading cause of female homicides in Canada.[19] At the safe home, Karen would be protected *from involvement with her husband during the investigations and would receive counselling and legal advice.*

*Mrs. McDonald, age seventy-five, came to the emergency department with her only son, James. She had a fractured hip. Her son had called 911 (emergency response services) saying that his mother had fallen in the bedroom and he couldn't lift her. Inderjeet noticed that Mrs. McDonald was nervous and evasive when asked about her fall. In addition, the patient had bruises on her arms and back, which she said came from falls in the bathroom. It was obvious to Inderjeet that the bruises could not have been caused by falls, and abuse seemed a more likely explanation. Inderjeet's suspicion of abuse was heightened when one of the nurses remembered that James himself had recently been brought by the police to emergency in connection with substance abuse. The police had found him inebriated and causing a disturbance in a shopping mall. They had considered charging him but decided it would be more helpful to bring him to the emergency department, where, they hoped, he might be able to get help for his drinking problem. James had refused the offer of admission to a rehabilitation program.*

*Considering all this information, Inderjeet decided to ask Keith, the hospital's geriatric nurse clinician, to assist with the assessment of suspected physical abuse. They met with Mrs. McDonald in a private area without her son present. After an initial evasion, Mrs. McDonald opened up and revealed that her son was rough with her and had pushed her when he was helping her walk to the bathroom during the night. She admitted that it was not the first time he had pushed her and she had fallen. Even so, Mrs. McDonald excused her son, saying that he had his own problems and couldn't cope with her. She noted that James sometimes lost his temper when he drank, but that afterwards he always apologized and treated her very well. Inderjeet and Keith also learned that Mrs. McDonald had made James her power of attorney for financial matters. Since she could not get out to the bank, he was cashing her pension cheques. He paid the rent and household bills; because he had been unemployed, he was also taking some of the money for himself. There was little money left for her.*

*After much discussion, and even though she admitted she was afraid to go home, Mrs. McDonald still refused to report what was happening to the police. She believed the situation would bring shame on her and her son and figured that she had an alternative way of resolving the situation: after she recovered, she would move to a retirement home. She would also cancel her appointment of James as her power of attorney for finances and regain control of her income. James would be allowed to remain in her home at no cost to him.*

*Inderjeet and Keith both had doubts that this plan would work; nonetheless, they respected Mrs. McDonald's decision not to involve the police and her refusal to permit discussions with her son about the situation. Inderjeet did explain that if she decided to return home and subject herself to the risk of further serious harm, she and Keith would have an obligation to inform the police of suspected abuse. Mrs. McDonald agreed with them. Inderjeet and the emergency nurses who assessed her documented the extent of her serious injuries. Keith agreed to follow Mrs. McDonald during her hospital stay and to intervene if she decided to return to the high-risk environment of her own home.*

## Commentary

Inderjeet and her colleagues had to deal quickly with all of these challenging issues in a hectic and demanding environment. Such situations clearly benefit from advance knowledge of the Canadian Nurses Association *Code of Ethics* statement about confidentiality and other relevant regulatory standards (CNA, 2001, 2002a, 2002d; CRNBC, 2006). Inderjeet appears to have been well-versed in these ethics and policy standards. According to the *Code*, and enshrined in regulatory standards, nurses can reveal confidential information outside the patient's circle of care without consent only when failure to disclose would cause significant harm. In some jurisdictions — Ontario, for example — it is mandatory for nurses and other emergency department health care professionals to report all gunshot wounds to the police; Inderjeet knew that this was not a requirement in her jurisdiction (Ovens,

2004). In the case of Jason, she demonstrated integrity and respect for confidentiality when she refused to divulge confidential information to the police officers.

The approach taken in Karen's case was likewise well-informed and considered. Across the country, the reporting of suspected child abuse is mandatory for child protection agencies. To be silent is to be complicit and to be equally responsible for the abuse or neglect. The domestic violence team demonstrated respect for Karen and did not coerce her to report the injuries. They gave her time to think through the options available to protect her children and herself. Because of their respectful approach, she was persuaded to accept that they had an ethical and legal duty to report her children's injuries; she did not feel betrayed or controlled by the emergency department staff. The emergency staff members were on solid moral ground in not complying with her wish to let her husband know what was happening. They had a serious obligation to reduce the possibility of future risk to the children. If the husband had been informed of the Children's Aid Society involvement, he might have changed his story before being interviewed. Advance warning gives suspected offenders time to tailor their evidence and may put children or spouses in even greater danger.

Sadly, Mrs. McDonald's case is not uncommon.[20] With older persons, financial abuse is the most common form of mistreatment, and this case also included emotional and physical abuse. Like Mrs. McDonald, many older persons who are neglected or abused by family members are deeply embarrassed. They also know that they are extremely vulnerable. Many fear revictimization if they tell anyone about their situation and especially if they get health care professionals, lawyers, or the police involved.

Inderjeet and Keith respected Mrs. McDonald's privacy by taking her to a private room and by talking with her alone. They demonstrated respect for her autonomy in accepting her choice to remove herself from her home and thus avoid further conflict, even if they did not think it was the right or the best choice. After carefully explaining the options and consequences of each option to her, they properly left the choice to her to make. At the same time they clarified their obligations to her and explained that if she decided to return to her home, they would be prepared to alert the police.

## Conclusion

Until the late 1980s nurses working with a patient typically documented the case in a chart that was available to a restricted number of colleagues — specifically, only those who needed to have that information in order to provide care to the patient. With extensive computerization and developments in health informatics, the realities of practice have changed dramatically. In addition, with the restructuring of health care and other social changes, nurses are no longer primarily employed in hospitals but are found in a widening variety of settings and contexts — clinics, industry, the community, schools, remote outposts — and they are often members of health care teams that serve large organizations and large populations.

In the name of health and caring, nurses are afforded privileged access to what is otherwise private information about patients. With this knowledge, nurses also acquire power — a double-edged power that can bring ill as well as good upon patients. In turn, patients, already made vulnerable by illness, become even more so. In such a relationship, trust is vitally important. In assuming this trust, nurses should be as clear as possible about what they can and cannot promise by way of information disclosure, and about what patients can and cannot expect. Granted, all human interaction takes place against a background of understandings and assumptions that can never be rendered fully explicit. But when the consequences of misunderstanding will be serious, nurses and patients together should endeavour to make their shared understanding as explicit as possible.

The strains and stresses on confidentiality are changing. As nurses try to keep abreast of these changes they need to remember the fundamentals of confidentiality and clarify to their patients as precisely as possible what they and their workplaces are promising in the area of confidentiality.

## Notes

Some of the material in this chapter has been adapted from Yeo (2004).

1    Alpert (2000) has a succinct, useful overview of the literature attempting to define privacy (see esp. pp. A6–12). For an encyclopedic account of privacy,

see Greenawalt (1978). See also Winslade (1978) for an overview of the concept of confidentiality. Rachels (1975) has a good philosophical account of privacy.

2   Privacy is a broader concept than is confidentiality. In its own right, it raises many important concerns in health care. The right to privacy, for example, has been invoked in the context of the abortion debate. Arguments against mandatory screening (e.g., for genetic defects, for illicit drugs) and testing (e.g., AIDS, hepatitis B) are frequently couched in terms of "invasion of privacy." For an extended discussion of the relationship between privacy and confidentiality, see Yeo and Brooks (2003).

3   Many inadvertent breaches of confidentiality occur in the context of what Glinsky (1987) calls "shop talk." Glinsky uses an interesting example to show how such "shop talk," although seemingly innocuous, can in fact result in harm. Quallich (2002) presents several cases involving breaches of confidentiality common in nurses' everyday practice. For example, a fifty-year-old male patient comes to a urology clinic for treatment of erectile dysfunction. The patient volunteers that he wants treatment because of a new relationship outside his marriage. He requests that his wife not know. The staff should note that his request for privacy be respected.

4   For a comprehensive discussion of this new approach to error, see Rubin and Zoloth (2000).

5   The Canadian Nurses Association *Code of Ethics for Registered Nurses* (2002a) acknowledges that private health information can be shared with the patient's health care team. In many institutions, as a matter of policy patients will be informed about need to know sharing of information (e.g., as part of the process of admission to hospital). When nurses meet with patients for the first time, clarifying up front who is in the circle of care reduces the likelihood of issues arising down the line. CNA provides more guidance in *Privacy of Personal Health Information* (2001) and *Privacy and Health Information: Challenges for the Nursing Profession: Ethics in Practice for Registered Nurses* (2002d).

6   Siegler (1982) argues that confidentiality as traditionally conceived in terms of one-to-one relationships has become outmoded in contemporary health care, which requires that patient information be widely shared with and made available to many different health professionals.

7   Veatch and Fry (1987, pp. 141-154) distinguish three main justifications for breaching confidentiality: because required to do so by law; to protect the patient from harm; to protect some third party from harm. These conditions can be found in the CNA *Code of Ethics* (2002a).

8   For the text of the 1976 court decision (majority opinion), see Tobriner (1986). For an important dissent, see Clark (1986).

9   In addition, many professional associations have issued policy statements or guidelines in connection with privacy. In particular, see Canadian Medical Association (1998) and Canadian Nurses Association (2001). The Canadian Nurses Association (2002d) also has a useful discussion paper on privacy and challenges to the nursing profession (the paper overlaps with the discussion here; Michael Yeo was involved in the drafting of the document). Regarding the protection of the rights of research participants or subjects, a seminal work is the World Psychiatric Association's *Declaration of Hawaii* (1977). The CNA *Ethical Research Guidelines for Registered Nurses* (2002b) is another important resource.

10  Going beyond a concern for the safety of third parties, the CNA statement also includes a concern for the safety of the patient as a justifiable reason for disclosing confidential information without consent. (See also Singer, 2003, for a similar position.) Some would object to this inclusion on the grounds that it is paternalistic. The difference between harm to the patient and harm to third parties, it can be argued, is morally relevant. If the patient is willing to assume the risk of personal harm rather than disclose certain information, that is the patient's decision to make. Unsuspecting third parties, however, have no choice in the matter, and thus the argument that there is an obligation to intervene on their behalf is more cogent.

11  Johnson (2000) identifies (albeit generically and not with reference to health care) a number of ways in which computer and information technology has changed record-keeping: "(1) It has made a new scale of information gathering possible; (2) It has made new kinds of information possible, especially transaction generated information; (3) It has made a new scale of information distribution and exchange possible; (4) The effect of erroneous information can be magnified; (5) Information about events in one's life may endure much longer than ever before. These five changes make the case for the claim that the world we live in is more like a panopticon than ever before" (p. 117). We would add that, because of the sorts of things that Johnson lists, computerization has enhanced the value of the information, and thus increased demand. It has also increased the potential for the secondary use of information to occur without the knowledge or consent of those involved in the care.

12  See Iezzoni (2002) for a related policy analysis.

13  Research has become increasingly invasive in consequence of developments in information technology. Research in Canada is governed by

the Tri-Council Policy Statement: *Ethical Conduct for Research Involving Humans* (Medical Research Council of Canada, 1998). The Canadian Institutes of Health Research (2005) has issued specific guidelines for health information research. For information about the implications for nurses in Canada, see Canadian Nurses Association (2002c) and Oberle and Storch (2004).

14     For an insightful description of patients' concerns here related to disclosure of HIV status, see Whetten-Golstein, Hguyen, & Sugarman (2001).

15     Reducing the rate of sick days and injuries of nurses is an important issue. Recruitment and retention of nurses are essential. For more information about strategies to provide a healthy workplace, see Health Canada, Office of Nursing Policy (2001). The College of Registered Nurses of British Columbia has a *Duty to Report* (2006) document that raises pertinent issues. The document states that agencies are required to report to the College if a nurse has been hospitalized for a substance use problem: "If a health professional is hospitalized for psychiatric care or treatment for drug or alcohol addiction and is therefore unable to practise, the chief administrative officer of the hospital and the attending physician must report to the registrar of the appropriate regulatory body" (p. 1). The implications of this new requirement remain unclear.

16     For a fuller discussion of confidentiality in the context of family situations, see Brody (1988) and Quallich (2002).

17     For a critical discussion of the idea of the family as patient, see Christie and Hoffmaster (1986), especially pp. 68-84. See also Nelson and Nelson (1995).

18     Most accounts link confidentiality both with autonomy and the duty to do no harm (nonmaleficence). Accounts differ depending on the degree to which confidentiality is linked with these values. Fleck (1986) makes a good case for emphasizing the link with autonomy. Brody (1989) is even stronger in rejecting nonmaleficence as the basis for confidentiality in health care.

19     In Ontario, between 1974 and 1990 an average of thirty-two women were killed by their partners each year. This constituted 61 to 78 per cent of all women killed in the province. The rate of spousal homicide is similar throughout Canada. More women are killed or injured by abuse than in automobile accidents. It is difficult to determine exactly the proportion of abused women who seek health care, but the figure has been estimated to be between 8 per cent and 39 per cent of women. Incidents of assault typically increase in frequency and become more severe, despite promises to the contrary by the abuser (Health Canada, Family Violence Prevention Unit, 1991). In June 2006 the Chief Coroner of Ontario released the third

annual report of the provincial Domestic Violence Death Review Committee (Ontario Ministry of Community Safety and Correctional Services, 2006). It was reported that forty-one people — twenty-four women, fourteen men, and three children — died in domestic or murder-suicide incidents in 2005. The number of deaths in 2004 was thirty-eight and in 2003, forty. The rate of homicides has not been reduced despite improved training for police officers and prosecutors and also special domestic violence courts. The province's chief coroner analyzed 100 of 111 incidents over the previous four years and found that women were victims in 93 per cent of cases; men committed the murders in 94 per cent of the cases. Although many deaths occurred in large urban centres, 25 per cent took place in communities of less than 25,000. The coroner recommended a greater understanding of the warning signs of domestic violence, emphasizing the importance of nurses identifying persons at risk, whether in small or larger communities.

About sixty-five spousal homicides take place in Canada annually. For statistics on family violence (all incidents including homicides), see Canadian Centre for Justice Statistics (2009). This report is published on a regular basis.

For in-depth consideration of ethical issues that arise with caring for women suspected of being abused, see Varcoe (2004).

20    The Canadian Nurses Association's Position Statement on Violence (2002c) includes a strong statement against violence in families, the workplace, and society. It presents ways of identifying and eliminating violence. Abuse of partners or spouses, older adults, and children is regarded as being underreported. The Canadian Centre for Justice Statistics, *A Statistical Profile* (2009), presents a detailed report of the incidence and responses by the justice system.

Domestic or family violence is an underdetected and underreported serious health problem. Physical, sexual, emotional, and financial abuse is increasing in Canada and worldwide (CNA, 2002c). Nurses may be the first health care professional to meet persons of all ages who are victims or witnesses of violence. Nurses in the emergency department can play a critical role in identifying, assessing, responding to, and reducing the continuation of a pattern of living with violence. For in-depth consideration of ethical issues that arise with caring for women suspected of being abused, see Varcoe (2004). See Gallagher et al. (2002), Kaufman (2001), and Lachs (2003) for analyses of some of the ethical issues involved in health care for older persons.

# References

Aiken, L.H., Clarke, S.P., Sloane, D.M., Sochalski, J., & Silber, J.H. (2002). Hospital nurse staffing and patient mortality, nurse burnout, and job dissatisfaction. *Journal of the American Medical Association* 288 (16), 1987-1993.

Allen, A. (1997). Genetic privacy: Emerging concepts and values. In Mark Rothstein (Ed.), *Genetic secrets: Protecting privacy and confidentiality in the genetic era.* New Haven, CT: Yale University Press.

Alpert, S. (1998). Health care information: Confidentiality, access and good practice. In K.W. Goodman (Ed.), *Ethics, computing and medicine: Information and the transformation of health care* (pp. 75-101). New York: Cambridge University Press.

Alpert, S. (2000). Privacy and the analysis of stored tissues. *Research Involving Human Biological Materials: Ethical Issues and Policy Guidance.* Vol. 2. *Commissioned Papers.* Rockville, MD: National Advisory Commission.

Alpert, S. (2003). Protecting medical privacy: Challenges in the age of genetic information. *Society for the Psychological Study of Social Issues* 59 (2), 301-322.

Baer, O.J. (1985). Protecting your patient's privacy. *Nursing Life* 5 (3), 51-53.

Brody, H. (1988). Confidentiality and family members. In R.B. Edwards & G.C. Graber (Eds.), *Bioethics* (pp. 81-85). San Diego: Harcourt Brace Jovanovich.

Brody, H. (1989). The physician-patient relationship. In R.M. Veatch (Ed.), *Medical ethics* (pp. 65-91). Boston: Jones & Bartlett.

Canadian Centre for Justice Statistics, Statistics Canada. (2009). *Family violence in Canada: A statistical profile.* Ottawa. <http://www.statcan.gc.ca/pub/85-224-x/85-224-x2009000-eng.pdf >.

Canadian Institutes of Health Research. (2005). *Best practices for protecting privacy in health research.* <http://www.cihr-irsc.gc.ca/e/29072.html>.

Canadian Institutes of Health Research. (2000). A compendium of Canadian legislation respecting the protection of personal information in health research. Kosseim P. (Ed.). Toronto <http://www.cihr-irsc.gc.ca/e/6824.html>.

Canadian Medical Association. (1998). Health information privacy code [policy summary]. *Canadian Medical Association Journal* 159 (8), 997-1006.

Canadian Nurses Association. (1991). Position statement: Human rights.

Canadian Nurses Association. (2001). Position statement: Privacy of personal health information.

Canadian Nurses Association. (2002a). *Code of ethics for Registered Nurses.* Ottawa.

Canadian Nurses Association. (2002b). *Ethical research guidelines for Registered Nurses.* Ottawa.

Canadian Nurses Association. (2002c). Position statement: Violence. Ottawa.

Canadian Nurses Association. (2002d). Privacy and health information: Challenges for the nursing profession. Ethics in Practice for Registered Nurses Series.

Christie, R.J., & Hoffmaster, C.B. (1986). *Ethical issues in family medicine.* New York: Oxford University Press.

Clark, W.P. (1986). Minority opinion in Tarasoff v. Regents of the University of California. In T.A. Mappes & J.S. Zembaty (Eds.), *Biomedical ethics* (2nd ed., pp. 155-158). New York: McGraw-Hill.

College of Nurses of Ontario. (2004). Practice standard: Ethics.

College of Nurses of Ontario. (2009). *Practice standard: Confidentiality and privacy — Personal health information.* Toronto. <http://www.cno.org/docs/prac/41069_privacy.pdf>.

College of Registered Nurses of British Columbia. (2006). *Practice standards for Registered Nurses and Nurse Practitioners: Duty to report.* <www.crnbc.ca>.

Coward, H. & Ratanakul, P. (Eds.). (1999). *A cross-cultural dialogue on health care ethics.* Waterloo, ON: Wilfrid Laurier University Press.

Dickens, B. (1988). Legal rights and duties in the AIDS epidemic. *Science* 239 (4835), 580-586.

Flaherty, M.J. (1982). Case study XIII: Confidentiality of patients' records. In L.L. Curtin & M.J. Flaherty (Eds.), *Nursing ethics: Theories and pragmatics* (pp. 315-320). Bowie, MD: Robert J. Brady.

Fleck, L.M. (1986). Confidentiality: moral obligation or outmoded concept? *Health Progress* 67 (4), 17-20.

Fried, C. (1984). Privacy: A moral analysis. In F.D. Shoeman (Ed.), *Philosophical dimensions of privacy: An anthology.* Cambridge: Cambridge University Press.

Gallagher, E., Alcock, D., Diem, E., Angus, D., & Medves, J. (2002). Ethical dilemmas in home care case management. *Journal of Healthcare Management* 47 (2), 85–96.

Gavison, R. (1984). Privacy and the limits of the law. In F.D. Schoeman (Ed.), *Philosophical dimensions of privacy: An anthology.* Cambridge: Cambridge University Press.

Glinsky, J. (1987). The perils of "shop talk." *Nursing Life* 7 (6), 24.

Government of Canada. (2002). *Personal Information and Protection of Electronic Documents Act.* S.C. 2000, c.5.

Greenawalt, K. (1978). Privacy. In W.T. Reich (Ed.), *Encyclopedia of bioethics* (Vol. 3, pp. 1356-1363). New York: The Free Press.

Health Canada, Family Violence Prevention Unit. (1991). A handbook dealing with woman abuse and the Canadian criminal justice system: Guidelines for physicians. Prepared by L.E. Ferris, A. Nurani, and L. Silver. Ottawa.

Health Canada Office of Nursing Policy (2001). *Healthy nurses, healthy workplaces*. Ottawa.

Hodge, J.G., Jr. (2003). Health information and privacy. *Journal of Law, Medicine and Ethics* 31, 663-671.

Iezzoni, L.I. (2002). Ethical considerations in conducting health-care research: Protecting privacy. In M. Danis, C. Clancy, & L.R. Churchill (Eds.), *Ethical dimensions of health policy* (pp. 355-378). New York: Oxford University Press.

International Council of Nurses. (2000). *Code for nurses: Ethical concepts applied to nursing*. Geneva.

Johnson, D. (2000). *Computer ethics* (3rd ed.). Englewood Cliffs, NJ: Prentice-Hall.

Kaufman, S.R. (2001). Clinical narratives and ethical dilemmas in geriatrics. In B. Hoffmaster (Ed.), *Bioethics in social context* (pp. 12–38). Philadelphia: Temple University Press.

Krever, H. (1980). *Report of the commission of inquiry into the confidentiality of health information* (3 vols). Ottawa: Queen's Printer; J.C. Thatcher.

Lachs, J. (2003). Dying old as a social problem. In G. McGee (Ed.), *Pragmatic bioethics* (2nd ed.; pp. 207-217). Cambridge: Bradford Book.

McLean, D. 1995. *Privacy and its invasion*. Westport, CT: Praeger.

Medical Research Council of Canada, Natural Sciences and Engineering Research Council of Canada, and Social Sciences and Humanities Research Council of Canada. (1998). Tri-Council policy statement: Ethical conduct for research involving humans. <http://www.pre.ethics.gc.ca/english/policystatement/policystatement.cfm>.

Merril, A., & Downie, J. (2004). Mandatory reporting of gunshot wounds: Rebuttal. *Canadian Medical Association Journal* 170 (April), 1255-1256.

Mitchell, C., & Smith, L. (1987). If it's AIDS, please don't tell. *American Journal of Nursing* 87 (7), 911-914.

Naser, C., & Alpert, S. (1999). *Protecting the privacy of medical records: An ethical analysis* (White Paper). Lexington, MA: National Coalition for Patients Rights.

Naser, C., & Alpert, S. (2000). *Protecting the privacy of medical records: An ethical analysis*. Portland, ME: National Coalition for Patient Rights <http://www.nationalcpr.org.>

Nelson, H.L., & Nelson, J.L. (1995). *The patient in the family: An ethics of medicine and families*. New York: Routledge.

Oberle, K., & Storch, J.L. (2004). Nursing ethics and research. In J. Storch, P. Rodney, & R. Starzomski (Eds.), *Toward a moral horizon: Nursing ethics for leadership and practice* (pp. 357-377). Toronto: Pearson-Prentice Hall

Ontario Hospital Association. (1990). *Guidelines on confidentiality of occupational health information in health care facilities*. Toronto.

Ontario Ministry of Community Safety and Correctional Services. (2006). *Domestic Violence Death Review Committee Annual Report*. Toronto.

Ontario Occupational Health Nurses Association. (1993). *Code of Ethics. Guidelines to the occupational health nurse: Confidentiality of health records*. Toronto.

Ovens, H. (2004). "Why mandatory reporting of gunshot wounds is necessary": A response from the OMA's executive of the section on emergency medicine. *Canadian Medical Association Journal* 170 (8) (April 13), 1256-1257.

Pauls, M., & Downie, J. (2004). Shooting ourselves in the foot: why mandatory reporting of gunshot wounds is a bad idea. *Canadian Medical Association Journal* 170 (8) (April 13), 1255-1256.

Quallich, S. (2002). Issues of Confidentiality. *Urologic Nursing* 22 (5), 340-342.

Rachels, J. (1975). Why privacy is important. *Philosophy and Public Affairs* 4 (4), 323-333.

Rubin, S.B., & Zoloth, L. (Eds.) (2000). *Margin of error: The ethics of mistakes in the practice of medicine*. Hagerstown, MD: University Publishing Group.

Siegler, M. (1982). Confidentiality in medicine — A decrepit concept. *The New England Journal of Medicine* 307 (24), 1518-1521.

Singer, B.J. (2003). Mental illness: Rights, competence, and communication. In G. McGee (Ed.), *Pragmatic bioethics* (pp. 151-162). Cambridge: MIT Press.

Stephenson, P. (1999). Expanding notions of culture for cross-cultural ethics in health and medicine. In H. Coward & P. Ratanakul (Eds.), *A cross-cultural dialogue on health care ethics* (pp. 68–91). Waterloo, ON: Wilfrid Laurier University Press.

Tabak, N., & Ozon, M. (2004). The Influences of nurses' attitudes, subjective norms and perceived behavioural control on maintaining patients' privacy in a hospital setting. *Nursing Ethics* 11 (4), 366-377.

Tobriner, M.O. (1986). Majority opinion in Tarasoff v. Regents of the University of California. In T.A. Mappes & J.S. Zembaty (Eds.), *Biomedical ethics* (2nd ed., pp. 151-155). New York: McGraw-Hill.

Varcoe, C. (2004). Widening the scope of ethical theory, practice, and policy: Violence against women as an illustration. In J. Storch, P. Rodney, & R. Starzomski (Eds.), *Toward a moral horizon: Nursing ethics for leadership and practice* (pp. 414-432). Toronto: Pearson-Prentice Hall.

Veatch, R.M., & Fry, S.T. (1987). *Case studies in nursing ethics*. Philadelphia: J.B. Lippincott.

Warren, S.D., & Brandeis, L.D. (2001). The right to privacy. In Daniel Bonevac (Ed.), *Today's Moral Issues* (4th ed., pp. 274–283). Boston, MA: McGraw-Hill. Originally published 1890, 4 Harvard Law Review 193.

Westin, A. 1984. The origin of modern claims to privacy. In F. Schoeman (Ed.), *Philosophical dimensions of privacy: An anthology*. Cambridge: Cambridge University Press.

Whetten-Golstein, K., Hguyen, T.Q., & Sugarman, J. (2001). So much for keeping secrets: The importance of considering patients' perspectives on maintaining confidentiality. *AIDS Care* 13 (4), 457-466.

Winslade, H.J. (1978). Confidentiality. In W.T. Reich (Ed.), *Encyclopedia of bioethics* (Vol. 1, pp. 194-200). New York: The Free Press.

World Psychiatric Association. (1977). Declaration of Hawaii. *British Medical Journal* 2, 1204-1205.

Yeo, M. (2004). Biobank research: The conflict between privacy and access made explicit. Ottawa: Canadian Biotechnology Advisory Committee <http://cbac-ccb.ca/epic/internet/incbac-cccb.nsf/en/ah00514e.html>.

Yeo, M., & Brooks, A. (2003). The moral framework of confidentiality and the electronic panopticon. In C. Koggel, A. Furlong, & C. Levin, *Confidential relationships: Psychoanalytic, ethical and legal contexts* (pp. 85-112). Amsterdam, Netherlands: Rodopi Press.

# Study Questions: Confidentiality

## Case 1: Confidentiality in the Workplace

1. Would it make any difference if this scenario took place not in a hospital but in a manufacturing plant?

2. In recent years health reform has come to be associated with a more business-like approach to health care management. To what extent might it be true that health professionals and business people have different mindsets — with health professionals oriented around patient well-being and business people around the bottom line of profit? How is "the health care business" different from other businesses?

3. Suppose that, having learned about John's predicament, Evelyn approached him and volunteered to release her health record to management. What ethical issues would this raise for John and the occupational health unit? Should he approve of her offer? What could be the consequences for Evelyn?

4. Some employers have attendance management programs. One approach is that staff must report to the occupational health department when they are away. The days away are tallied, and staff members who are away more days than agreed upon for sick leave annually must agree to see a health care professional and manager to develop a plan to reduce their sick days. Do you approve or disapprove of this type of approach to reduce the number of days that staff take for sick leave? Why do you approve or disapprove?

5. Some employers require mandatory screening for communicable diseases and the use of drugs and other substances. Under what circumstances, if any, would you approve of this policy?

## Case 2: Confidentiality in a Family Context

1. Nursing places a great deal of emphasis on the family as one unit. What arguments can you think of for conceiving of the family as a whole as one patient — as opposed to seeing individual members of the family as separate patients? Or what arguments could be made against viewing the family in this way?

2. Imagine that a public health nurse is working in a community health centre with a family, and she begins to suspect that child abuse is occurring in that family's home. In what ways, if any, would the issues of confidentiality be similar to, and in what ways different from, the issues that arise in our case no. 2?

3. If Alan agreed to share information about his HIV status with his wife, and after counselling he and his wife still wanted to try to have a baby, would you support or not support their decision, and why?

4. Suppose that Alan agreed to having his wife told that he was HIV-positive, but wanted her to be told that he had acquired the virus when he had a blood transfusion following a car accident, which took place sometime before they met. Would clinic staff have an obligation to disclose the truth to Valerie?

5. Research participants typically are promised that information given and obtained in the study will be kept confidential and their identities will be protected. A nurse researcher is studying how families cope with the death of a child from cancer and considering ways of helping families deal with this tragedy. The researcher learns through interviews with parents that some parents have anger management problems and they admit to emotionally and physically harming their partners and children. What are the obligations of the researcher in this situation? The Canadian Nurses Association's *Ethical Research Guidelines for Registered Nurses* (2002b) provides guidance.

## Case 3: Confidentiality and Seemingly Innocuous Information

1. Should moral principles be universally applied regardless of setting and context (for example, a small rural community as opposed to a large urban centre)?

2. Does a nurse who discusses patients and events of the workday with her or his spouse or partner breach confidentiality in doing so?

3. Describe a scenario in which seemingly innocuous information about a patient turns out to be harmful.

4. Discuss the statement: "Nurses shouldn't be too lax about confidentiality, but on the other hand they shouldn't be too legalistic or bureaucratic either."

5. When you are presenting a clinical case to colleagues — for example, to a small group in your clinical setting or to a larger group at a conference — what steps would you take to protect the identity of the patient?

## Case 4: Privacy Issues in the Emergency Department

1. What is the law regarding mandatory reporting of gunshot wounds in your jurisdiction? What are the arguments for and against mandatory disclosure of gunshot wounds to the police? Which side of the argument do you agree with, and why?

2. Abuse and neglect have different meanings. Define these terms and give examples. Why would it be ethically justifiable to disclose suspected abuse and neglect? Under what circumstances, if any, is it ethically justifiable to disclose the suspected abuse and neglect of a child and adult who refuses to have anyone, any social agency, or the police informed of a dangerous situation?

3. Culture is a complex composite of personal meanings, shared values, and group traditions. Culture is *not* the same thing as ethnicity. Compare culture and ethnicity. Each person's culture is influenced by such factors as gender, sexual orientation, income level, education, rural or urban location, community values, religion, country of origin, and language fluency. For example, in some groups, hitting children is a traditional form of discipline. What do you think about this form of discipline, and why? Do you support allowing physical discipline in a specific group when it is seen as part of their cultural tradition? Should there be a total ban on corporal punishment, or exceptions permitted to allow some people the freedom to bring up their children in the way they think is right?

4. When women have been abused, putting pressure on them to report the abuse to the police can lead to them feeling more disempowered, and can even escalate the danger they are in. Women need support in identifying possible choices and in coming up with a plan, or plans, that they can implement when they are ready. Why would women refuse to report abuse and neglect of themselves? What are the ethical arguments for and against allowing women to refuse to report abuse?

# 7 JUSTICE

*If social factors play a large role in determining our health, then efforts to ensure greater justice in health outcomes should not focus simply on the traditional health sector. Health is produced not merely by having access to medical prevention and treatment, but also — to a measurably greater extent — by the cumulative experience of social conditions over the course of one's life.*

— NORMAN DANIELS, "JUSTICE, HEALTH AND HEALTHCARE"

---

*Issues related to the concept of justice are at the heart of the discussion of the strengths in, and challenges to, our Canadian health care system. They are key to how nurses can respond to strengthen both their practice and the health care system as a whole. Indeed, an informed and effective participation in health care delivery and health policy planning requires a basic knowledge of the theoretical foundation of issues of justice.*

---

## Justice in the Distribution of Health Resources

The concept of justice has a variety of meanings and applications. In the broadest sense it has to do with fairness in determining what someone or some group is owed, merits, or is otherwise entitled to. Does the student really deserve an A+ on the assignment? Does the drug dealer merit a long sentence of imprisonment? Are people with physical disabilities entitled to special consideration in the hiring process?

Issues of justice in the context of health and health care are most often matters of *distributive justice*: they involve the allocation of resources for health and health care. These issues are most urgent whenever the supply of resources fails to meet the need or demand for them. Choices must then be made between competing resource claims.

In recent years resource allocation issues have become more prominent, as evidenced by the increased attention paid to them in the ethics literature and popular press. For example, the news media report widespread indignation about long waiting lists for surgical procedures. They have paid increasing attention to the shortage of long-term care facilities for the elderly. Some commentators have suggested that alcoholics should be denied liver transplants in favour of those whose livers fail through no "fault" of their own.[1]

Several factors account for the high profile of health-related justice issues. A heightened consciousness about personal health and advances in health care have fuelled public expectations. Much more can be done to help people. Improved health care makes it possible for the elderly to become more elderly, for at-risk babies to become children (and later elderly), and for disabled persons to become more fully integrated members of our society. With these added benefits come added costs.

On the supply side, reports indicate a growing concern about health care expenditure and a growing consensus about setting limits. The cost of health care, measured on a number of scales, has been rising steadily, although less so in Canada than in the United States, and less than much of the rhetoric would suggest (Armstrong & Armstrong, 2003; Commission on the Future of Health Care in Canada, 2002). In an effort to control costs, business and government and other institutions give greater scrutiny to how resources are allocated: "efficiency," "cutbacks," "reallocation," "cost containment," and "rationing" are watchwords of the day. An understanding of the application, and misapplication, of watchwords like these is an essential tool in informed and responsible decision-making about justice issues — which in turn calls for a full understanding of the main theoretical perspectives on justice.

**Theories of Justice**

Our views on particular issues of justice in health care are informed or influenced by our intuitions about the nature of justice. Disagreements about these issues arise because different people have different intuitions and emphasize different values in thinking about them. Theorists try to probe existing intuitions and values pertaining to justice, and to systematize them. In doing this they have articulated different theories about justice, and foremost among those theories are libertarianism, utilitarianism, and egalitarianism (Beauchamp & Childress, 1994, pp. 326-394).

## 1. Libertarianism

Above all else, libertarians value individual freedom or liberty. For them, issues such as which services should be made available, and made accessible under what terms and conditions, are to be decided mainly with reference to this value. Libertarians favour a free-market approach to resource allocation as being most compatible with the ideal of individual freedom (and additionally, most likely to yield an efficient distribution of resources). A free-market system distributes health care resources in accordance with what consumers are willing and able to pay for those items. Libertarians tend to view allocation systems in which some people are required to subsidize expenditure for the health needs of others as unjustifiable intrusions on freedom.

## 2. Utilitarianism

The main value that guides utilitarian decision-making in matters of resource allocation is beneficence or producing good. For the utilitarian it is not so much the good of the individual that is the focus of concern (as was the paradigm case in chapter 3, on beneficence) as it is the aggregate good of society as a whole. What allocations or distributions will produce the greatest amount of good or benefit for the greatest number of people? The answer to this question requires a comparative cost-benefit analysis of the various options. The resource allocation likely to produce the most overall benefit would be favoured.

## 3. Egalitarianism

In matters of justice people with an egalitarian orientation are guided by the main value of equality with respect to meeting needs. This equality can be interpreted in a number of different ways. For example, equality of opportunity is different from equality of outcome. Gorovitz (1988, p. 570) distinguishes four main senses of equality: equality in the amount of money spent on each individual; equality in individual health status; equality in the maximum to which each person is benefited; and equality in the treatment of similar cases. Each sense of equality furnishes a different standard for making resource allocation decisions.

Most egalitarians put special emphasis on how people have unequal needs. They believe that we ought to give according to our means and receive according to our needs. They would be willing to give more than an equal share of resources to those in our society who are sickest because generally those people have greater needs.

### Tensions among Theoretical Orientations

These three theoretical approaches to justice may be complementary with respect to a given allocation decision, but they will often be in conflict. For example, allocating resources on the basis of the ability to pay (libertarianism) is bound to result in an unequal distribution of resources; yet an allocation that best realizes equality (egalitarianism) may not produce the most overall benefit (utilitarianism). Furthermore, each theory of justice is closely tied to a related political theory (Rodney et al., 2004). Rawls's comprehensive and very influential *Theory of Justice*, which overall is egalitarian, mediates the tension between liberty, utility, and equality.

These theoretical orientations have their tensions in public policy debates about health care. For example, the U.S. health system is primarily oriented along libertarian lines: it is based on the belief that the market is the most efficient means of allocating resources. The reform initiatives of President Barack Obama challenge this orientation from an egalitarian point of view; the objective is to ensure that adequate health insurance is extended to the entire population, a large percentage of which has long been underinsured or without coverage. The utilitarian approach also challenges the libertarian status quo, positing that the money spent by the United States on health care could be deployed more efficiently to produce greater benefit if government played a greater role. Libertarians tend to dispute this claim, arguing that greater government intervention will not only infringe on liberty but also increase inefficiency.

In Canada the dynamics of current policy debates are almost the opposite. The philosophical foundations of the Canadian health care system are primarily egalitarian (Williams, 1989).[2] The movement to increased privatization of the Canadian system challenges its egalitarian premises primarily from a libertarian point of view, as evident in the recent debates surrounding a decision about private health insurance at the Supreme Court of Canada (see Yeo & Lucock, 2006; Yeo, Emery, & Kary, 2009). Additionally, proponents of increased privatization argue that privatization will increase efficiency in the health system and produce more benefit. Egalitarians dispute this claim, arguing that privatization is likely to have the opposite effect.

## Substantive Principles of Justice

As people analyze and argue about particular justice issues, they may well find themselves divided along the lines of these three theories about justice. Certainly, all of us could find it immensely helpful to be familiar with these approaches and to probe our own intuitions and values in relation to them.

Delving further into these theories, we can differentiate between a number of more specific principles or value orientations that are relevant to a consideration of justice: liberty, utility, equality, need, and restitution.

These principles are *substantive* in that they specify *a distributive criterion for resource allocation decisions and indicate what a just outcome would be*. A substantive principle of justice helps complete the sentence "A fair distribution of resources would be one in which ..." Think of a pie to be divided among a determined number of persons. Will everyone get a slice of the same size? Will the person who is most hungry get the largest slice? Will the person who made the pie get a larger serving? Will the obese person get any at all?

### 1. Liberty

Liberty, the fundamental value or principle underlying the theory of libertarianism, pertains to the right or liberty of individuals to make choices in matters of their own good and with respect to their own business, without interference from others. One such right — which is claimed especially by libertarians — is the right to dispose of your personal resources as you see fit. A just distribution of health care resources is one that is based on respect for this right. Protection of free choice is paramount.

Some people value the idea of liberty so much that they object to the exercise of government or state power that collects money from people in the form of taxes to pay for services such as health care used by everyone. Health resources, they believe, ought rather to be allocated in accordance with what people are willing and able to pay for them. Less strict libertarians will agree to limited taxation and provision of health services, if only because of enlightened self-interest. The poor health of the population is linked with poor economic development and serious social problems. It benefits everyone when all members of society have access to health care and other public services.

For those who hold liberty as the most fundamental principle, the ideal system for allocating health care resources is a free market in which supply is adjusted to consumer demand. These people believe that the market approach is the most efficient and compatible with liberty.[3] Access to health care is not regarded as a right, nor is it regarded as a duty of government to provide for everyone's health care needs. A just society protects property and liberty. Health insurance should be private, and purchase must be voluntary. Private insurance companies have liberty rights, and society is not obligated to dip into public funds gathered through taxation to pay for insurance.

Some commentators seek to combine liberty with equality, arguing that everyone should have "equal" access to a specific allocation of health care through health care credits. Under this plan, each person gets the same allocation of resources, usually calculated in health care dollars spent. When this quota is expended, the person must find ways to pay for health care. Those who have not used their health care account can sell shares, and presumably make a profit. In this market system, health care is a commodity to be traded. Libertarians think this approach gives individuals more freedom and encourages accountability. The counterargument is that persons with illnesses are penalized for health problems that they did not bring upon themselves.[4] They will eventually run out of credits and will not have access to health care unless they have the funds to purchase health care or buy credits. The end result will be unequal access for persons with health problems.

A benefit of the approach based on the principle of liberty is that those who can purchase health care or health care insurance will go to the head of the line, and generally (but not necessarily) get excellent care. But this approach has its problems with respect to other substantive principles of justice. Basing allocation decisions on liberty places certain individuals or groups at a disadvantage. Some people will simply not have the means of purchasing health care. Insurers will deem others with poor health status or conditions ineligible for health care. Some people might be eligible but will be expected to pay prohibitive rates. Insurers can pick and choose the people they want to accept. In the United States not only low-income persons but many middle-class families are unable to obtain health care insurance. Those insured must deal with a complex bureaucracy to have services approved and paid. When millions of people are uninsured, mortality and morbidity rates for the uninsured rise, with resulting economic and social costs.

Canada in the past decade has seen a movement toward greater privatization. The reasons for this are complex and several, but appeals to liberty do figure in this movement, as expressed in catch phrases such as "consumer choice." A number of health care services have been privatized (Pauly, 2004), and some publicly available services have become less accessible. Private, for-profit providers fill the gap.

From the beginning of medicare some health services, such as dentistry and pharmaceuticals, were not covered. The public needs to purchase these services unless they have benefits that cover these expenses in full or in part. Across the country there has always been a patchwork approach to home care, rehabilitation, and payment of medications needed for catastrophic illnesses (Commission on the Future of Health Care in Canada, 2002; Storch, 2010). Egalitarians argue not only that privatization should be resisted, but also that the public system should be expanded to cover additional private services. When the costs are not covered in part or in full, individuals rely on their benefits, insurance, and savings. Family members, especially women, sometimes have to give up gainful employment to look after their ill relatives (Peter, 2004). Some individuals and families have to do without care due to the cost.

The principle of liberty has other applications in health care beyond issues of distributive justice. For example, the principle of liberty also relates to the notion of autonomy and encompasses the freedom of individuals to make treatment choices based on adequate information and to select the caregivers who will administer to their health needs.

## 2. Utility

The principle of utility is expressed in the imperative "Do what will yield the greatest good for the greatest number." The basic premise is simple: among available options, choose the one that will produce the most good or benefit overall. Measure and compare the benefits and costs: options that yield the most benefit for the least cost are favoured. Decision-making thus becomes reduced to measurement and calculation.

Cost-benefit comparisons — and some more so than others — are bound to be controversial when human lives and health are at stake. How can health and health benefit be measured? Health care economics and epidemiological research play a major role in such measuring. Objective measures of morbidity and mortality get at something essential, but they cannot capture important dimensions of health and benefit. More and more they are complemented by subjective evaluations of quality of life, including physical, social, and psychological well-being. Nurses and other health care professionals have used several measures of subjective health status in attempts to make more comprehensive cost-benefit analyses (see, for example, Howlett et al., 2001; Staniszweska, 1998).

Utility calculations and comparisons of various sorts are pervasive in health care resource allocation in Canada and elsewhere. The principle of utility underlies many public health interventions, such as health promotion and disease prevention programs. Consider, for example, a child immunization program. Utilitarian reasoning would have us first calculate both the likely cost and the benefit of such a program, both short-term and long-term, and compare the results to the costs and benefits of other options. When these sorts of calculations are done, public health interventions often appear in a favourable light and indeed may save costs in general.

Information from utility measurements and calculations is no doubt useful, and even necessary, in allocation decision-making, including decisions about what treatments should be funded. But using the principle of utility as the sole basis for decision-making can be problematic. This is so not just because other issues can arise about how the measurements and calculations are done, but because other things matter besides aggregate utility. For example, in applying only the principle of utility, and depending on the calculations, researchers might logically conclude that programs to promote smoking — as opposed to preventing or ending it — make sense because with the push to continued smoking fewer people would live to old age, and thus the associated health care costs would decrease. Even if you accept this approach as maximizing utility, other objections to it would arise. It would mean, for instance, that you are willing to sacrifice the health and well-being of some people — those whom the program influences to smoke — for the supposedly greater good that would come about through cost-saving. The problem here is that the principle of utility considers only the aggregate good, and does not consider the distribution of benefits and costs among individuals and groups.

## 3. Equality

Equality is the main principle that informs an egalitarian approach to justice. Intuitions about equality in health care are rooted in a sense of solidarity, of being together in the same boat with everyone else and sharing a common humanity. The Canadians who banded together in Saskatchewan in the 1930s to start what would evolve into our publicly funded national health care system realized that they had to form a co-operative to cover health care expenses that were beyond the reach of many of them (see Storch, 2006, 2010).

Equality can be applied in different ways, including equality of access, equality of shares, and equality of health status. Distributing health care equally means that it can be equally distributed according to need or restitution.

A key consideration is that individuals differ in their circumstances and their needs. In this regard we can distinguish horizontal equality (equal resources for equal needs) and vertical equality (unequal resources for unequal needs). It can be justifiable to allocate resources unequally because people have unequal needs, and some will therefore require more than an equal share of resources to reach a condition of health that approaches equality with that of others in society. The injunction "treat like cases alike" permits differential treatment based on need while forbidding discrimination based on factors such as sexual orientation, gender, race, and religion.

### 4. Need

The principle of need is based on the belief that the condition of being in need imposes an obligation on the part of others to help meet this need. At the level of politics, a just society is one that is compassionate and humane. A critical measure of this objective is how well it meets "basic" or "essential" needs, which include health needs. Sickness and disability are significant impediments to well-being and prosperity in society (Daniels, 1985), and we are not all equal in our health needs. Due to the social and "genetic lottery," each of us is born with different opportunities to achieve health and happiness. Some people require more resources than others to meet their health needs and to have more or less equal opportunities in society. As Daniels (2001) observes, "By keeping people close to normal functioning, healthcare preserves for people the ability to participate in the political, social and economic life of their society" (p. 3).

Egalitarian theory combines the principles of need and equality. According to the theory, government should provide for the basic needs of people, making available the services necessary to meet those needs and ensuring equal terms and conditions to meet that goal. In general, nursing practice in Canada is based on this egalitarian approach. Just as at the level of patient care nurses should allocate their time to those they serve based on the assessment of the patients' *needs,* so too at the level of public policy resources government should allocate resources proportionate to needs among the population. The *Code of Ethics for Registered Nurses* in Canada (CNA, 2008) is at least implicitly egalitarian in the sense of the "fairness" it invokes in this passage: "Nurses make fair decisions about the allocation of resources under their control based on the needs of persons, groups or communities to whom they are providing care. They advocate for fair treatment and for fair distribution of resources for those in their care" (CNA, 2008, p. 17).

*5. Restitution*

According to the principle of restitution, individuals or groups disadvantaged as a consequence of injustice done them in the past deserve preferential consideration. On these grounds, for example, Aboriginal people are entitled to a proportionately greater share of health resources based on their historic victimization by unjust practices that have contributed to their present state of need (Commission on the Future of Health Care in Canada, 2002; Royal Commission on Aboriginal Peoples, 1996; Stephenson, 1999). Another important example is the so-called "healing packages" given to First Nations people who were abused as children in residential schools. It was also on the grounds of restitution that the Canadian government offered compensation packages to persons who unknowingly received blood products carrying the HIV virus.

Restitution, then, is about compensating people who have been in some sense "victimized." But not all questions of past injustice are equally obvious. For instance, one stream of thought would hold people responsible for personal decisions that have hurt their own health and consequently created health needs. Along these lines, health services directed to needs resulting from supposedly voluntary behaviour (e.g., tobacco smoking) would be granted a lower priority, and individuals or groups presenting with health needs related to such behaviour would have reduced access to available services, or be denied access altogether. This is an approach that could amount to "blaming the victim." One problem with its logic is that people who engage in tobacco smoking or excessive alcohol consumption or intravenous drug use or other such activities are profoundly influenced by social factors such as the support they received in their family of origin, their level of income, their access to safe housing, or the availability of detoxification and rehabilitation services (MacDonald, 2002; Pauly, 2008).

## Procedural Principles of Justice

Procedural justice concerns the process followed in making decisions. If substantive principles answer questions related to the criteria that determine the outcome of resource allocation and the public funding of services, procedural principles answer questions such as, "Who has the rightful authority to make or influence these decisions?" and "Which individuals or groups need to be consulted or considered in decision-making?" and "What is a fair process for making decisions?" They help complete the sentence "A fair process for making resource allocation decisions in health care is one in which ...". These questions fall under the rubric of three main procedural principles: explicitness or publicity; accountability; and autonomy.

According to the principle of *explicitness or publicity*, the criteria for allocation decisions and the processes by which they are reached must be explicit and open (transparent) to public scrutiny. The public has a right to know how decision-makers reach their decisions and on what grounds.

The principle of *accountability* signifies that those entrusted to make allocation decisions must be accountable — and capable of being held accountable — for the decisions that they make. Decisions should be supported by reasonable explanations. In furnishing these reasons and making them available as appropriate, decision-makers can be held accountable for their decisions. Procedures should be in place to ensure that their decisions are consistent with whatever mandate they have been given that authorizes their decisions. Furthermore, the principle of accountability requires a process to be in place for appealing a decision that harms an individual or group.

According to the principle of *autonomy*, people are entitled to input or representation in decision-making that has a direct impact on them or in which they have a stake, and the greater their stake, the more input or representation they should have. In a publicly funded system the public is the ultimate source of authority, and therefore decisions ought to express the will of the public, however that will be determined. At the level of macro allocation, considerations of autonomy inform trends toward "devolution" or "decentralization" in resource allocation decision-making (although such initiatives may have less to do with promoting autonomy than with reducing costs or shifting responsibility). At the micro level, the doctrine of informed consent is rooted in the principle of autonomy.

### 1. Integrating Substance and Process

In the context of substantive justice, fairness has to do with outcomes. To say that a given allocation is fair means that it is consistent with or follows from a preferred substantive principle of justice. From the standpoint of substantive norms, the evaluative question takes the form of "Is the outcome of this decision — i.e., the distribution of resources that will follow from it — fair with respect to substantive values such as equality, need, and benefit?" In other words, does it distribute benefits more or less equally? Is it superior to other options with respect to meeting needs? Will it yield more benefit for the cost than other alternatives? The main challenge here is that sometimes several competing values need to be considered, interpreted, and balanced by decision-makers.

In the context of procedural justice, fairness has to do with process. To say that a given allocation is fair in this sense means that it has been decided by a process consistent with procedural principles of justice. From the standpoint of procedural norms, the evaluative question becomes: "Has the decision been reached through a process that is fair?" That is, was the decision-making open to public scrutiny? Can the decision-makers articulate the reasons for deciding as they did? Were they sufficiently representative of the stakeholders of the decision, and were stakeholders given appropriate influence over the decision? The main challenge posed by these procedural values concerns how best to translate principle into practice.

In general, procedural principles are more complementary than are substantive principles. Indeed, they are rooted in a common value — the quintessential democratic value — namely, the right of stakeholders to have a voice or representation in decision-making that concerns them.

The commitment to values of process poses considerable difficulties. Some of these concern the practicalities of realizing these values. How do we determine which stakeholders should be involved in decision-making? Exactly what form should this involvement take? Does having one or two designated public representatives on a decision-making body mean that the process is participatory? How should they be selected? Given that the people and organizations that tend to be most effective in consultative processes are articulate and financially well supported, decision-makers have a duty to ensure that the voices of vulnerable and disadvantaged persons and groups are heard. Outreach to community organizations is needed, and innovative ways of obtaining input should be pursued. Where public input is sought, decision-makers ought to make the role of the public clear.

Other difficulties and questions penetrate deeper. What is the value of the procedural principles? Decision-makers need to think about the point of greater public involvement in choices around the allocation of resources. Is decision-making valued for its own sake, or because it is expected that such involvement will lead to better decisions? If the latter, is this a reasonable expectation? Experts may worry that the public is not sufficiently informed and qualified to work through the clinical, economic, and scientific issues on which many allocation issues turn. Supporters of public involvement argue that the public cannot be stereotyped. Some people may want to learn more than others do. Some may join a well-informed advocacy group. Patients and their families may contend that they are the real experts because they live with the health problems and have to work with the health care system.

The realization of substantive and process principles for health care decision-making can involve various mechanisms. Efforts have been made to "decentralize" or "devolve" decision-making away from provincial planners and move it closer to the ultimate users of health care.[5] Different ways of ensuring greater stakeholder participation include public opinion polling, referenda, focus groups, town hall meetings, toll-free phone lines, and the appointment of community representatives on health care boards. Nurses are represented by their professional bodies on many local, provincial, and federal health care committees and ought to be proactive in their commitments to substantive and procedural principles of justice.

## Resource Allocation and Decision-Making

Resource allocation issues are prominent in society, as evidenced by ongoing attention paid to these matters in the ethics literature and media. Recent stories that have attracted the public's attention include patients going to the United States for specialized treatment, lack of services in rural and remote areas, and the lack of health care professionals across the country. Such media reports have served to inform the public about problems with the health care system, and have foregrounded Canadians' concerns about the sustainability of health care. Nurses must therefore be able to understand — and influence — justice in the allocation of health care resources.

### 1. Levels of Decision-Making

Resource allocation decisions can be grouped into *two main kinds*: decisions related to the allocation of already available resources to or among individuals; and decisions related to which services and programs, and of what quality, will be available. The former is the level of *micro-allocation*. At this level, what is mainly at issue is the question of access. Which individuals will receive the limited resource (e.g., treatment, organ, prenatal class)?

Access to resources depends on prior decisions that have determined availability or supply. How much funding or support is allocated to which services and programs? If a given resource (e.g., a liver transplant, home care) is available in a supply that is less than the need or demand for it, individuals will be in competition for the resource — thus leading to the issue of which of these individuals should have access to it. The more limited the availability or supply, the more acute are issues of access or micro-allocation. These issues do not arise if the resource in question is available in a supply adequate to the demand for it, or indeed if the resource is not available at all.

Decisions about resource availability can occur on the level of *meso-allocation* and *macro*-allocation.[6] The meso-allocation of resources occurs *within* an institution or community. Macro decisions are broader public policy issues and include the allocation of resources *to* an institution or community — for example, decisions made by federal, provincial, and territorial governments about funding and priorities.

Micro-, meso-, and macro-allocation decisions, respectively, take place at progressively higher levels of generality. Decisions at a higher level of generality constrain decision-making at a lower level of generality. For example, government macro-allocation decisions about how much money will go to health as against other sectors establish limits that constrain allocation decisions *within* health spending. In turn, decisions at this level, such as how much money will go to hospitals as against community health, health promotion, and other programs, set limits on and constrain decision-making at a lower level, such as *within* a hospital or a neighbourhood health centre. Eventually, we reach the micro level, at which decision-makers allocate to or among individuals a resource that is limited in supply as a consequence of meso- and macro-allocations made at higher levels of generality.

The notion of *opportunity costs* is crucial for understanding the dynamics of the decision-making. The opportunity cost of deciding for a given option is the lost opportunity of meeting some other demand or realizing some other option. For example, funds allocated to health care may reduce what is available for other useful services or programs such as education, preserving the environment, and a national daycare program.[7] Within health care, dollars spent on acute care are dollars not available for health promotion. At the front line of health care, providing resources for one patient may come at the cost of not being able to provide resources for another patient. These lost opportunities are opportunity costs, and can involve difficult "trade-offs." With the choices at each level of allocation come opportunity costs to be considered. The goal is to make fair and transparent decisions about how to distribute the limited resources.

Understanding how decisions to allocate available resources at each level are made in the first place is important — for example, how decisions are made about the nursing staff to be available on a particular unit, and how the resultant staffing ratios will influence the amount of nursing care time available for allocation to individual patients on a particular unit. Such decisions are not necessarily based on a fixed "reality," but reflect values-based choices linked to beliefs about what our society and health care agencies owe to the public (Stein, 2001; Varcoe and Rodney, 2009). Short-term decisions to cut costs can create significant long-term financial (and human) costs. For example, discharging a frail patient too early from an acute care unit to make room for a patient in the emergency room may lead to the frail older person experiencing serious complications — and having to return to the emergency room in a few days, requiring a readmission and subsequent long-term care. In our health care system's resource allocation, such long-term implications are often invisible (Varcoe & Rodney, 2009).

## 2. Micro-Allocation and Access

Micro-allocation concerns "the distribution of resources such as a treatment, a piece of equipment, a drug or procedure, to an individual in need" (O'Brien, 1983, p. 218). At this most face-to-face level of allocation, health care professionals are supposed to have control over the allocation of certain resources to individuals. They are to decide who gets access to the resource, and to how much of it. With an unlimited supply of resources, justice issues would probably not arise at the micro level. However, the allocation of a resource to a given individual may come at the expense or cost of foregoing some other opportunity to which the resource might otherwise have been directed. The resources used (money, labour) for a costly diagnostic test or a surgical procedure, for example, might otherwise be used to produce some other benefit (for some other individual or group of individuals).

Health professionals understandably find it difficult to weigh opportunity costs, especially when the opportunities foregone by a resource allocation decision are abstract, unlike the concreteness of an individual patient in a face-to-face encounter. Traditionally, the professional-patient relationship has relied on the understanding that the professional's paramount duty is to the good of the individual patient rather than acting as a "gatekeeper" for resources (CNA, 2008; Curtin, 1980; Pellegrino, 1986). There is reason to be concerned that the patient's trust in the health care professional will be eroded if this duty is moderated by a consideration for the good of others outside the relationship. Nurses whose roles involve a significant amount of gatekeeping (e.g., triage nurses in emergency departments and community care case managers) must therefore constantly balance the resources of their agencies with the needs of the individual patients and family members for whom they are responsible. Such balancing, particularly in an era of cost constraint, requires a great deal of professional skill. The health care professionals in such gatekeeping roles must be provided with personal as well as logistical support (Rodney et al., 2006).

The gatekeeping role is particularly challenging in cases in which both the opportunity costs and the allocation option for a given individual are concrete. For example, when the supply of a given resource — a transplant, a therapy, or even the professional's time — falls short of the needs of different individuals seeking access to it, nurses have to make a choice between identifiable individuals. In this case the opportunity costs are readily apparent: a decision granting access to one individual means limiting or perhaps denying the access of another needy individual. A classic scenario for these triage-like decisions is the allocation of the last remaining bed in an intensive-care unit. The decision about who will get the last bed is at the same time a decision about who will be denied it. To prevent such win-lose scenarios, nurses and other health care professionals need to use their clinical and ethical expertise to explore other options, such as transferring the least acutely ill person to another unit and requesting additional nursing care for the transferred patient. While nurses' micro-allocation decisions are not always so dramatic, their allocation of nursing-care time is an everyday challenge that can generate a great deal of moral distress (Hardingham, 2004; Varcoe & Rodney, 2009; see also chapter 8 here).

A number of criteria might be considered for making such selections. Edwards and Graber (1988b, pp. 709-710) group these under five main headings: *medical criteria, random selection criteria, constituency criteria, present and/or future quality of life criteria, and social worth criteria.* More than one type or group of criteria might be weighed together, or arranged serially in order of priority.[8] Some criteria are more controversial than others. Among the least controversial and most widely used is the likelihood of medical benefit. Social-worth criteria are ethically suspect for several reasons, but especially because assigning a higher value to one person's life over that of another offends against notions of equality and runs counter to nurses' ethical obligations (CNA, 2008). Random selection criteria (e.g., first come, first served; a lottery), by contrast, preserve equality, and are therefore favoured by some in the event that other acceptable criteria are insufficient to decide the issue (e.g., Childress, 1983; Rescher, 1988).

One criterion that Edwards and Graber do not list, and which has been generating debate for some time, is *personal responsibility for illness.* According to this criterion, it is morally appropriate if "persons in need of health services resulting from true, voluntary risks are treated differently from those in need of the same services for other reasons" (Veatch, 1988, p. 599). Smokers, for example, might be given a lower priority than non-smokers for access to treatment for heart disease based on the rationale that "they brought their sickness upon themselves." Again, though, in many cases judgements about whether a particular behaviour is the cause of a particular illness and, further, about whether the behaviour in question is truly voluntary, are highly controversial (Wikler, 1983).[9] Moreover, even if causality and voluntariness could be established beyond a doubt, those who emphasize equality or neediness will object to resource allocations based on such considerations — a position consistent with the guidance provided by the CNA (2008) *Code of Ethics*, which has it that nurses ought to allocate resources based on *need.*[10]

Notwithstanding the various challenges faced in this realm of decision-making, health care professionals ought to make micro-level resource allocation decisions based on what is best for the individual, while also taking into consideration the individual's preferences (CNA 2008; McPherson et al., 2004; Pellegrino, 1979, 1986). Still, what is best for the patient may not always be clear. The patient's perspective, the family's wishes, and what various health care professionals think is best can vary dramatically. (See the ethical decision-making models in the appendices for aids to working through these sorts of decisions.)

## 3. Meso-Allocation and Macro-Allocation

Decisions about who should get *access* to an already available resource, and how much of it they should get, are different from decisions about the availability and supply of resources. In a micro-allocation discussion we can distinguish the decision about who should get the last bed in intensive care from some prior decision bearing on how many beds should be available in intensive care in the first place. For example, given its allotted budget, the intensive-care unit might previously have decided to allocate its resources to purchase new equipment instead of providing additional beds. The options considered at this level, in turn, would have been constrained by resource allocation decisions made at higher levels of generality, ascending to the global budget for the hospital. Levels of generality beyond the meso level of the hospital reach to broader issues of public policy, and eventually to the total government budget for health spending as against other areas. A government decision to reduce health care expenditure by even a small percentage can have effects that eventually trickle down to the micro level, and at that point practitioners will find themselves with fewer resources to allocate to individuals.

Until recently, the ethical basis of meso- and macro-allocation decisions had not been widely recognized. Some of the principles behind such decisions are ethically suspect. Which group or constituency controlling or demanding resources has the most political clout? Who shouts the loudest or is best able to use the media to amplify their voice? Who is most effective at lobbying decision-makers? Diseases that catch the public's sympathy fare best in this competitive approach to allocating scarce resources. Less socially acceptable and little understood conditions, and the agencies and charities supporting them, are at a disadvantage. Television appeals for pediatric hospitals, for example, are well supported, but when did you last see a telethon for mental health services?

Ad hoc approaches to funding fall short of meeting the requirements of justice. To ensure a responsible and fair allocation of scarce resources, decision-making should be guided by ethical values and principles. But which ones? Should allocation decisions be guided primarily by concern for individual autonomy, or for equality, or the greatest good for the greatest number? What constitutes a reasonable balance between or among these values? What process should be used to make these choices?

These questions are being energetically debated today. Are we getting good "value" for our health care dollars? What are the benefits of so-called "high-tech" curative medicine as measured against more care-based approaches, and against health promotion and disease prevention? Although there is no consensus about the answers, there is agreement that more scrutiny needs to be given to the allocation practices that have evolved over time, and there is work being done to develop meso-level allocation decision-making models (Martin, Abelson & Singer, 2002; McPherson et al., 2004). Further, there is growing attention to the need for explicit attention to ethics in the development of the health and health care policy that affects what resources are available (Kenny & Giacomini, 2005). The nursing profession is well situated to contribute to such work.

## 4. Navigating Levels of Decision-Making

Each level of allocation involves different decision-makers. At the level of micro-allocation, decision-making is mainly the prerogative of physicians, although other health professionals, including nurses, may have control over or input into the control of some resource allocation decisions. At the meso level, trustees and administrators working in collaboration with health professionals make allocation decisions. At the macro level, political authorities or their designates (governments) make decisions based on information from many sources, including health care professionals and their organizations, the public, and health care researchers.

At every level decision-making is coming under increased public scrutiny, and decision-makers are expected to be more accountable.

The difficult questions that must be tackled are not for these decision-makers alone. In a democracy the authority to make these decisions is ultimately rooted in the will of the people, and the questions therefore are public questions. There is long-standing dissatisfaction with the existing mechanisms of decision-making about resource allocation and health care delivery. A major criticism is that these mechanisms do not adequately incorporate the community in decision-making.

## 5. Social Justice

The issues of justice concerning the distribution of resources for *health care* are different from issues concerning the distribution of resources required for *health* (Anderson et al., 2009; Sherwin, 2002; Rodney et al., 2004). As Daniels (2001)explains:

> If social factors play a large role in determining our health, then efforts to ensure greater justice in health outcomes should not focus simply on the traditional health sector. Health is produced not merely by having access to medical prevention and treatment, but also — to a measurably greater extent — by the cumulative experience of social conditions over the course of one's life. (p. 6)

Addressing these social conditions requires paying attention to the determinants of health.[11] Libertarianism tends not to view this approach and activity favourably, or at least not insofar as such change would involve governmental redistribution of resources or interference in individual liberty. For utilitarianism, the consideration of the determinants of health is a matter of being thorough in applying the principle of utility and ensuring that the utility calculations take into account all relevant options. For egalitarianism, addressing the determinants of health makes good sense in view of evidence that social inequalities are correlated with inequalities in health and health status (Wilkinson, 2005).

The view that broad social change is necessary to address the determinants of health and reduce inequalities of health is sometimes called *social justice* (Sherwin, 2002; World Health Organization, 2008). Social justice is receiving increasing attention in nursing theory and nursing research (Anderson et al., 2009). Indeed, the revised CNA (2008) *Code of Ethics* has a section devoted to "Ethical Endeavours" (pp. 20-21) that includes several statements aimed at promoting social justice. In this section, for example, the *Code* states, "Nurses should endeavour as much as possible, individually and collectively, to advocate for and work toward eliminating social inequities" (p. 20). One means of doing that is by "recognizing the significance of *social determinants of health* and advocating for policies and programs that address these determinants" (p. 20).

Nurses following this approach would attend to the intersections of health policy (e.g., allocation of health care services), social policy (e.g., poverty and homelessness), and educational policy (e.g., early childhood education) because all three policy sectors bear on health (see Clarke, 2010).

### Case 1: Access to Care versus Quality of Care

Nurses are concerned about the questions of justice that arise when emergency rooms are packed, patients are waiting for admission, and in-patient units are full to capacity. These are common problems across the country given that hospitals are typically at 97 per cent capacity and often at 100 per cent. The media stories about "log jams" in hospital and health care systems are well known to the public and nurses. Health care organizations are working to reduce wait times and delays in emergency rooms, and to increase access to community services. The problems of access and availability of care are complex and cannot be fixed rapidly. Creative, cost-effective, and systemic responses are and will continue to be implemented.

Nurses on the front lines in the community, long-term care facilities, and hospitals worry that the reduced access to and availability of care lead to a decline in its quality and safety. One of the most important factors bearing on quality is the ratio of professionals to patients. Beyond a certain critical ratio, the quality of care will suffer. Another factor is patient flow. Across Canada the majority of hospital patients are aged over seventy-five and have complex chronic health problems. These patients go to emergency departments with urgent needs, and it can turn out that for some of them a return home is not a safe option. The process of applying to a long-term care facility takes time. When stable patients cannot be discharged, the system gets overloaded. Emergency departments are often packed, perhaps with patients waiting for admission. In-patient units are pressured to discharge, and emergency departments are pressured to admit only those who cannot be treated as out-patients. When the demand is greater than the capacity, waiting lists inevitably form for elective treatments and admissions. How to grant access and how to provide access to those waiting are ethical questions. Rationing is unavoidable when access is limited. When their workload increases, nurses must make sure that they are still providing safe, quality care.

One possible response is to decrease access to care by reducing the admission rate. Admitted patients can then receive competent and compassionate care, but the opportunity cost is that persons with needs are denied access to care. Another response is to increase nursing staff, but that is difficult to do because of recruitment and retention issues. Early retirements, injuries, and sick time also reduce the pool of nurses. The number of spaces in nursing education programs does not meet the demand for nurses. There is a lack of nurse academics to meet the needs of nursing education programs. In the past, in response to economic constraints, health care organizations closed beds and units, and reduced nursing staff. These responses are common reactions to a lack of financial resources and may reoccur. Times have changed from the 1980s and 1990s: now there is a shortage of nurses in Canada, and the shortage is expected to become more and more serious.

When nursing resources fall short of the needs of patients, hard choices, including trade-offs, will have to be made about access to service, the quality of service, and how to respond to this recurrent problem. When patients are admitted to a system in numbers exceeding the capacity that can be cared for competently and in a timely way, access is preserved but quality of care is sacrificed. Alternately, if the service limits access in an effort to remain within the critical ratio needed to provide safe care, it will preserve quality, but at the expense of access. Nurses find that in many cases they are in a situation where access has been ranked above patient safety, and they must plan how to stretch themselves to meet the patients' needs. But they must also respond to the root causes of this chronic situation; and they must consider both short-term and long-term responses.

As a unit reaches the critical ratio, nurses strive to meet their professional duties and provide the care needed to each patient. Under such circumstances, one option will be to work harder and smarter. With great effort, this surge of nursing can rise to meet the needs of patients. Yet this solution can only be short-term. An unsatisfactory workload leads to fatigue, increased risk of errors, and job dissatisfaction. Moral distress may be another response, as nurses find that they cannot provide the type of care needed. The following case illustrates the ethical challenges related to supply and demand and workload demands.

*Amina Ali is the chief nursing officer in an urban teaching hospital. She has many staffing vacancies. Amina hears many complaints from permanent nursing staff about their inability to give quality and safe care. The administration is worried because the loss of nurses directly limits their ability to admit patients from the emergency department, and treat and discharge patients from the unit. The administrators and the hospital board members believe that the hospital's responsibility to the community is being compromised.*

*Given the loss of nursing positions and the increased demands on those nurses employed, most nurses are advocating that beds be closed. They want to limit the number of patients admitted in order to ensure that they can provide safe and competent care.*

*The chief nursing officer knows that determining who gains access to care is an ethical problem. The emergency room is open around the clock. Wait lists are long: six months for hip replacements, for example.*

## Commentary

Amina faces several ethical issues. First, she has to decide about whether to trade off access to a service for a diminished quality of care within that service. If a decision is made to close beds, she and the nursing staff can take comfort in knowing that the care provided will be both safer and of a higher quality. However, patients who need care may not be admitted, and their conditions will deteriorate along with their quality of life as they wait for more long-term interventions. The downstream results will include greater demand on emergency departments and an overburdened community health care system. The hospital's response of closing beds to maintain quality care will lead to a different set of problems. The public and their community partners will say the hospital is not meeting the community's needs. Amina is aware that "the form of efficiency that must be sought is one that takes into account effectiveness, impact on patient well-being, and long-term as well as short-term goals" (Varcoe & Rodney, 2009, p. 139).

Amina is asked to chair a committee established by the hospital board. Members include key stakeholders from the community, hospital, patient groups, and staff. She realizes that the process must be open, transparent, and accountable. The committee works with the public relations department to use different media to educate the community about the problems and options. Opinions are invited and there are various means to communicate with the committee, including town hall meetings, online discussions, toll-free hot lines, and email or postal correspondence. The responses are studied and major themes are identified.

Initially Amina thought the options were to recommend beds be closed or "carry on as best as we can," an option in which nurses and other staff are overworked and care is compromised. She knew that by choosing between these options, she will have to weigh in the balance the needs and interests of patients, nursing staff, other clinical staff, and the hospital. Like everyone else she knew that the option to "carry on" regardless was not viable because of the busy emergency departments, premature discharges, and lack of community services. Staff, families, and patients are less tolerant of waiting times and decreased access to care. They want change that addresses their concerns and meets their needs.

The feedback from the community and staff presented other options that the hospital and the committee had not considered. Amina was particularly impressed by the focus groups held with nurses who had concrete suggestions about improving efficiency, saving costs, working smarter, and shortening stays. The consultation process emphasized that the hospital was dealing with micro-, meso-, and macro-allocation issues. The committee published an executive report. In the introduction they reported that the community had sent a clear message that they wanted responses to be based on a fair consultation process and to be informed about how hard decisions were made and evaluated. The value of procedural and distributive justice based on need was supported. Recommendations were made for shortening length of stay; to create more transition and convalescent beds, increase community supports, and use technology to save duplication of tests, and more use of telephone follow-up care by nurses. The complement of beds would stay at the same level pending an evaluation of the measures taken to maintain access and availability of quality care.

Nursing organizations proposed that employing nurses was a priority. They explained that nurses had left for several reasons, and pointed out that ways of attracting and retaining nurses are noted in the RNAO "Best Practice Guidelines about Professionalism" and other research papers about the need for permanent employment with benefits. The hospital had relied on casual nurses and had offered few permanent or full-time positions. Amina agreed that employment practices had to change. Nurses on the front line must have more control over their employment conditions. New graduates must be mentored, not humiliated. Senior nurses should be respected, treated with respect, and recognized as expert resources.

Amina was struck by how her thinking about the problem had been "either-or," and thanks to the committee and the consultation process she was now seeing the problem as having many causes and needing many responses from different sectors. After participating in this process, she was no longer thinking in simple black and white terms such as the more people who are given access, the poorer the quality of care. Instead she was thinking: the poorer the quality of care, the smaller the benefit to patients in the service, or a little for everybody may mean not enough for anybody.

The committee continues to have the mandate to evaluate the quality improvements. The outcomes to be measured are: length of stay, wait times in the emergency room, return admissions, patient satisfaction, and admissions avoided because of community nursing care. Amina also wants to evaluate the nurses' assessment of their employment conditions, job satisfaction, time off related to injuries and sickness, and use of replacement staff.

Amina realized the importance of communication. They had not been sharing with their community how and why the hospital was responding to upstream budget decisions. An example of the major change she was championing was that the hospital and community partners would collaborate when preparing a budget for the next year.

Another recommendation was for the hospital to establish a fair process for establishing waiting lists. Once they have waiting lists, they need to decide how people are prioritized for access. She knows that medical need will put them on the list. Then wait time will be the second criteria. She thinks prognosis is hard to predict, so she wants this criteria not to be used. She is worried that age will be used as strict criteria. She knows too many high-functioning older persons to want to restrict access based on age. Amina knows that urgency is a major factor. If you have a person at the end of the list who is deteriorating, they should move up the list. A subcommittee was established to study this problem. The wait-list committee consults colleagues in cardiac care, who have developed a process that is highly regarded as fair. They put all people needing cardiac surgery on a central list that helps them to move people on the list based on the urgency of their situation and available resources. Another recommendation accepted was to have a major fundraising committee. With the new approach to partnering with the community and the appointment of an effective development officer, the situation changes dramatically.

Amina has learned many lessons on this journey. She thought the only options were to close beds or not. Through following principles of procedural and distributive justice, she has learned that resource allocation problems require innovative and values-driven problem-solving.

### Case 2: Allocation of Clinical Placements and Support for Clinical Education

For a decade or so technology-based education has been supporting clinical learning. More students are taking distance education and on-line courses. Working in a simulation lab and with interactive learning software are excellent learning methods. Still, the clinical practice environment remains necessary for optimal learning. In recent years the supply of clinical placements has decreased, and competition has increased, for this scarce resource. The problem affects nursing students and registered nurses seeking higher qualifications.

Colleges and universities (in undergraduate and graduate programs) work with health care organizations and their respective nursing education department to find clinical settings to provide students with the opportunity to meet their learning goals. Ideally colleges and universities negotiate as a collective and are not in competition for scarce places.

From the perspective of health care organizations, issues of justice arise. The goal of educating students for the benefit of future patients must be weighed alongside the burdens and benefits for the organizations. Educators appreciate the stress experienced by busy health care systems but find that the benefits far outweigh the inconvenience and workload for the institution. Put simply, the students are the future of nursing. There is a temptation for schools of nursing to tolerate less than desirable placements because of the shortage of and competition for places. From the perspective of students, their clinical placement is essential. They may find the experience rewarding, but sometimes difficult. The reception they receive from the unit staff can range from supportive and welcoming to cold and sometimes hostile. Overworked nurses can see student nurses as an inconvenience and a burden. One nursing study reported that nurses themselves identified how they contribute positively and negatively to the moral climate of their workplace. It noted that the nurses admitted that at times they were not supportive of patients or colleagues and were demeaning (Rodney et al., 2006). This attitude also permeates some nurses' relationships with students. The scarcity of resources and the need for high quality nursing education can be at odds, which can create tension and discord in the workplace.

*Jason Green is a faculty member at a university school of nursing. His students are in the first year of a four-year program. Their clinical experience focuses on the provision of basic nursing care, communication skills, and establishing therapeutic relationships. Jason needs to find placements for the students at the nearby hospital.*

*The school's placement co-coordinator met with the hospital's education co-coordinator at a planning meeting, and Jason learns that the hospital has accepted his request to have students placed in the hospital's continuing care unit, Unit A, which has a mixture of rehabilitation and chronic care patients. There are patients of all ages — some with MS and ALS and some young people who are paraplegics and quadriplegics as a result of traumatic accidents. Unit A is operating at a maximum capacity of forty beds. Following an energetic recruitment drive the unit is well staffed. Its nurse manager, Mike Brown, is proud of the quality of care being provided.*

*Jason is not alone in his request for placements. Another school of nursing, one school of occupational therapy, and one school of social work have also asked to have students placed in the hospital, and clinical supervisors from other programs have also approached Mike about Unit A. Susan Polanyi, the agency's education co-ordinator, deals with the requests. Susan has worked with the schools of nursing to make the process of allocating much-sought units more equitable. Mike hears from Susan that his unit will receive one group of nursing students, and one student each in social work, occupational therapy, physical therapy, speech pathology, and chaplaincy, in addition to medical students. He is pleased. The students bring enthusiasm and can share the latest research about care. The patients will benefit from having new people on the unit.*

*Still, Mike worries about how the hospital's nursing staff will respond. He has been told by some nursing staff that they support nursing education in principle, but that having students on the unit takes their time away from patients. Their workload increases, and they fear that the quality of their patient care will go down. Mike decides to have a meeting with Jason and the nursing staff to hear their views. He explains the benefits that the program brings to patients, unit staff, the hospital, and the nursing profession. He learns that many of the nurses are concerned about finding the time to help the students. Mike wants the nurses to be supportive to the students in their learning and receptive to them when they arrive. Mike knows that not all the staff shares his views.*

## Commentary

Depending on the circumstances, practitioners-in-training can be considered a burden or a blessing for institutions and patients. In this case, a health care organization can see an "oversupply" of students as more of a burden than a benefit. The main conflict is between the benefits of student education and the perceived corresponding burden on the institution, staff, and its patients. The faculty and the agency worked to find solutions. They discussed their respective needs and concerns and identified ways of reducing the burdens on the agency.

The benefits of clinical education for students are indisputable. On this side of the issue, the main objective will be to seek out clinical settings that will best facilitate the development of well-rounded, competent, and safe practitioners. This goal is in the interests not only of individual students, but also of the profession and society as a whole. From the perspective of the students, the process addressed their concern for a just distribution of beneficial learning experiences. For example, students do not want to always work with patients with a specific condition. Also, students appreciate that some placements are in short supply and that not all students can have a full range of clinical experiences. When they are on the particular unit, students would consider their learning experience to be inequitable if Jason were to assign one student to several clinically interesting individuals, and another to patients who provide little opportunity for learning and professional growth.

The other side of the issue involves a consideration of the benefit to the institutions in which students are placed and to the patients.

Beneficence (or, more precisely, nonmaleficence) requires that any burdens that arise out of such placements should be minimized, if not eliminated. With regard to the good of the institution and its staff, this means taking steps to ensure that students do not disrupt the smooth functioning of the unit that they are assigned to. To this end, the staff who work with the students must be involved in the nursing education process, and the students must understand what is expected of them on the unit, and where to go for help.

In most cases, faculty and students should be able to develop a good working relationship so that the nursing staff see the students as a benefit and not a burden. In any event, nursing staff, by virtue of their professional role, have a duty to participate in the education of future practitioners.

Concerns for the well-being of patients can be more difficult to address. Mike Brown's staff members are right to be concerned about the quality of care if the students are expected to provide care they are not prepared to give. Patients (and their families) are entitled to the best care possible, and do not want to be treated as "test cases" or "guinea pigs." Jason Green and the students have a responsibility to make sure that the students are not going beyond what is permitted in the entry year of a program. To some extent these concerns can be addressed by prevention measures, such as outlining, with students and staff, what the students can and cannot do, reviewing students' daily learning plans, and ensuring that the students are closely supervised and not given responsibilities beyond their level of competence.

In a teaching hospital, patients are informed that students from various health disciplines will provide care. Care that is needed must be given. For some patients, simply being interviewed (let alone touched, probed, and examined) is in itself a burden, and all the more so when the intervention is not necessary for therapeutic purposes, but is aimed at giving students practice. For every practice or skill acquired, there must be a first time: the first time a student changes a dressing, draws blood, or inserts an intravenous. With reason, most patients would prefer not to be a student's (albeit necessary) "first-time" experience. Students need to be supported by their faculty and nursing staff as they learn. All efforts need to be made to minimize or eliminate the burdens of student assignments, but if those burdens are indeed acceptable when balanced against the benefits, further considerations arise about justice in their distribution.

Respect for autonomy comes into play in the selection of individual patients. This teaching hospital requires the consent of patients before they become part of a student's learning experience. If a patient does not want a student, Jason and the student must respect this decision. The team also makes an effort to understand the patient's perspective, and to try to resolve any misunderstandings or concerns.

A key action to facilitate the change on the unit was Mike's decision to have a thorough discussion of the program with Jason and the nursing staff, and to hear their views. As a result of the meeting, the nursing staff developed a list of recommendations about orientation for students, how students are assigned patients, and how the nurses communicate with Jason. For his part, Jason follows these suggestions and as a result the staff feels part of the teaching-learning team. They see students as an asset to the clinical unit, rather than a burden. For their part, the students reported benefits. The hospital staff has worked together to give students a variety of experiences throughout the hospital. In the end the staff on the unit found ways of working with the students and their teacher and of making the experience a beneficial one for students, patients, and the nursing staff.

The questions and issues that arose in this case were explored and addressed with input from the various parties involved. It may be that the steps taken to address the concerns of both staff and patients need continuous review based on student, patient, and staff evaluations. This approach to providing quality learning environments while providing excellent patient care is an opportunity for students, staff, and faculty to reflect more deeply on the values of the health system in which they work.

Ideally, schools of nursing should develop open and transparent processes to find more clinical places and share those spaces equitably. Without an open and transparent process, some colleges and universities might conclude that they are being treated unjustly. Reasons as to why some agencies find it challenging to work with students need to be studied, and innovative solutions found. New ways of supporting nursing education may need to be developed and evaluated. Advances in technology provide new learning opportunities — for example, the use of simulation labs, which play a vital role in nursing education. Although these are valuable tools in teaching and learning clinical expertise, students still need clinical placements.

### Case 3: Equitable Allocation of Nursing Time and Care

Traditionally nurses tended to believe that they did not have much control over the allocation of resources at the micro level. In the community, in long-term care facilities and acute-care settings, nurses accepted their assignments and tried to meet expectations.

More recently nurses have realized that they ought to take action when they are unable to practise according to their professional standards. Through professional and labour organizations they can work to improve nurses' employment conditions. At the same time, many nurses are forced to make hard choices about how they allocate their time. One resource that individual nurses do theoretically have some control over is their own time and nursing care — but under present circumstances, that is becoming one of the scarcest resources in the health care system.

In such situations, nurses have to make difficult decisions about the competing needs and demands of various individuals.

*Jessica Robertson works in the pediatric intensive-care unit of a community hospital. The unit is now at maximum capacity, with three children: Sarah, a profoundly developmentally delayed three-month-old baby; John, a three-year-old trauma victim admitted the previous day; and Omar, a five-year-old who is post-surgery.*

*Sarah is awaiting transfer to a specialty hospital for cardiac surgery. John is on a ventilator and requiring constant care; he is not expected to survive. Omar is ready for the step-down unit as soon as a bed becomes available. He is extremely anxious about leaving the protective environment of the unit.*

*The unit is usually staffed by two nurses, but on one particular shift Jessica's colleague has gone home ill, and no critical-care nurses are available for relief. Even with two nurses, it is a challenge to attend to the needs of these three children.*

*Left on her own, Jessica anguishes over the question of how she should set priorities with her limited time. She is faced with the need for micro-allocation decision-making. Jessica decides to use the distinct criteria of need, equality, likelihood of benefit, and urgency.*

*Commentary*

Organizing her options in terms of these criteria will help Jessica to achieve clarity about the choices she must make.

First, regarding clinical need, she sees that all of the children require her care. They are all very ill children. Jessica has essentially two options. One option is to divide her time and care evenly among the three children. This option, however, is incompatible with considerations of need and likelihood of benefit, and indeed may not even be promotive of equality. The three children, after all, have unequal needs, and allocating them equal shares of her time will not be fair. A second option is to rank the children in terms of needs. Jessica knows that deciding who is most needy is hard to do. How will she decide? She decides that the child with the greatest need is the child that is most seriously ill, and she will distribute her time with each of them accordingly. In essence, this amounts to choosing among the three children.

After assessing the children, she decides that John is clearly the sickest of the children, and therefore needs the greatest amount of attention. Then she thinks about who will benefit the most. Although John would probably benefit the most in the short term, in the long term that care would probably not make much difference. Omar, who is on the road to recovery, requires very little truly "critical care," although he might benefit greatly from support and attention because he is so anxious. Jessica's attention to Omar would probably have little short-term gain, but could make a difference to him in the long run. Sarah's needs are great, yet what benefits can be expected down the road, and what "quality of life" can she expect?

Whatever comfort and satisfaction Jessica takes from being able to devote the lion's share of her time to one child will be spoiled by the painful knowledge that this care will be at the expense of one or both of the other children. The situation is a "zero-sum" game in which one person can win only at the expense of someone else losing. Who will be the loser in this decision?

If Jessica devotes the least amount of time to John, it may be that he will die sooner than he otherwise would have if given more care. Even if she is unable to provide him with lasting benefit, she could at the very least make his dying easier, and provide added comfort to his family. Omar's life is not in imminent danger, but in neglecting his need in favour of the others she may be contributing to his poor adjustment to hospitalization. Sarah's long-term prognosis may not be very good regardless of how much time Jessica gives her, but this patient is certainly very sick and would benefit from more attention. If Jessica decides to assign Sarah the lowest priority, will she be making a "quality of life" judgement and communicating to Sarah's family the message that Sarah's life is less valuable than that of the other children? Jessica understands that "some groups in society are systematically disadvantaged, which leads to diminished health and well-being" (CNA 2008, p. 21). She reflects that in some way it may be that she is evaluating whose life is more valuable than another's. She is uncomfortable with this process. She believes each child's life is equally valuable, no matter how long they will live and what disabilities the child has.

Given these limited and less than ideal options, the choice to be made is truly difficult. However, it is important to examine the situation Jessica has been placed in, and look for alternatives. She realizes that the situation is unsafe for all the children. When she ranks them, she notes that they all need care, and they all have urgent needs. She decides not to try to decide who is more likely to benefit and who is more entitled to care. She contacts the nursing supervisor on call and asks for help in determining a response. For example, would it be possible to transfer one or more of the children to another critical care unit? Can their parents be asked to come and spend the night with the children, because the rooms do have beds available for a parent? Omar, in particular, seems an ideal candidate to be transferred. Indeed, the kind of emotional support he needs could be provided by people with less training than Jessica, or, with guidance, even a parent or a volunteer. Alternatively, would it be possible to call on one or more staff nurses who, even without special training, could provide basic nursing care under Jessica's supervision? At the very least, Jessica should receive advice and professional support from supervisors and colleagues. Are there any hospital policies or guidelines that might give some guidance on this matter? Probably Jessica does not have time to check these documents, but the supervisor should be able to get ready access to the policies and practices.

The case raises other issues that go beyond Jessica's immediate problem. When a hospital admits a child to an intensive-care unit, some might argue that this step in itself constitutes an agreement to provide the child with a certain standard of care. Hospitals are obliged to take whatever additional steps are necessary to ensure that nurses or other health professionals are not forced into situations like the one that Jessica finds herself in — that is, of unilaterally renegotiating the standard of care. Jessica is concerned with matters of justice such as this. According to the CNA (2009), nurses need to work to address organizational and other factors that have an impact on patients' health and well-being.

Jessica and the nursing department will want to consider how typical and common this situation is. Their inquiries should answer questions, such as why, apparently, no provisions for backup resources are made for such emergency situations, what prior decisions contributed to this crisis in the first place, and what future decisions will minimize the possibility of such crises, or at the very least provide greater support and guidance for decision-making. Looking at the root causes of these situations, they may examine the policy of performing expensive and resource-intensive surgery on children who are going to require considerable care and support for life. To what extent does this policy contribute to these sorts of situations? How should considerations of "quality of life" enter into these decisions about appropriate and beneficial, as opposed to futile, treatment.

They might ask if a better administrative system can be developed for responding to children awaiting internal or external transfer. For the well-being of the nursing staff and the good of the children served by the unit, Jessica will later be obliged to see that these issues are raised and dealt with in a thorough manner. She will undoubtedly experience a sharp learning curve. Until this incident she did not know what other resources were available in the hospital. She asks her colleagues and manager and learns that she can work with the hospital nursing council and her professional practice leader, and consult the clinical ethics committee. Following that consultation they propose that the unit hold an education event designed to help everyone understand the issues, and plan how to respond. Another suggestion is to conduct a multidisciplinary health team meeting in the unit. Staff would work together to find ways of preventing understaffing. Jessica may consider following the hospital's policy regarding reporting unsafe workload situations. Management may track these reports and look for trends and ways of avoiding these events. All the nurses will benefit as a result of the lessons learned from Jessica's experience.

**Case 4: Triage and Rationing of Intensive-Care Beds during a Clinical Crisis**

Suzanne is an infection-control nurse for the Emergency, Trauma and Critical Care (ETCC) division. The infection-control and ECT staff all know that a pandemic influenza is overdue, and Suzanne has been having workshops with the emergency, trauma, and critical care staff about the use of a triage process to determine who will receive a ventilator and intensive care. They agree that in a crisis ventilators and intensive-care beds will be in high demand and that decisions will have to be made about who receives this specialized care. Whether there is a pandemic or not, the ETCC staff knows that the triage protocols can be used whenever demand for critical care exceeds supply (Christian et al., 2006).

*Suzanne summarizes the key points in an educational package.*

1. *Inclusion criteria: patients who are in need of respiratory support and may benefit when admitted to the Intensive Care Unit (ICU). Examples are refractory hypoxemia, respiratory acidosis, probable respiratory failure, and those who have hypotension (with signs of shock).*

2. *Exclusion criteria: (a) poor prognosis despite care in ICU — severe trauma, severe burns, cardiac arrest, severe cognitive impairment; (b) require resources unavailable during a pandemic — advanced and untreatable neuromuscular disease, advanced malignant disease; (c) advanced medical illnesses, underlying illness, and high likelihood of death — persons with severe and irreversible neurological conditions, immuno-compromised, and end-stage organ failure.*

3. *Minimum qualifications for survival: assess use of available medical resources that can be supplied to any person. The goal is to identify patients who are not responding to treatment and are expected to die. Give resources to those who will have the greatest benefit. The goal is to avoid using up resources on those who are not improving and who are likely to have a poor outcome.*

4. *Prioritization tool: ranks patients who should and should not be admitted to ICU and have access to ventilation, using colour-coding. The colours will be (a) Blue (or Black) — manage medically, palliative care as needed, no admission or if admitted then discharge; (b) Red — highest priority for ICU admission and access to ventilation; (c) Yellow — intermediate priority; (d) Green — well enough be without ICU or ventilation; they do not have significant organ failure.*

*Some nurses accept the protocol, but a number of thoughtful objections and concerns arise. James says that given his experience in international nursing, he cannot accept that Canada must ration ventilators. Another nurse says that she did not enter nursing to play God and decide who lives and dies. Suzanne recognizes that they did not prepare sufficiently for staff meetings. It was unwise to roll out policies without considering the values and decision-making that underpin the policy. Suzanne asks for a few days to respond to their concerns and questions.*

## Commentary

Good ethics requires strong evidence and sound clinical experience. Suzanne realizes that she needed to have a meeting with the ETCC staff to discuss the ethical values that are the foundation of the policy. Not all participants would accept the key principles, but they could have an informed debate.

Suzanne invites the hospital ethicist, nursing staff, and medical intensive-care experts. Following their advice, all ETCC staff are given the Canadian Nurses Association position paper, "Emergency Preparedness and Response" (2007), research papers, and an ethical primer to read before the meeting. These readings explain that internationally recognized medical practice supports foundational ethical principles, especially justice, and that triage protocols provide everyone with the opportunity to survive, but that not all persons have an equal opportunity to survive. The literature explains that during a crisis, strategic thinking used in the theatre of war is required. Survival of the most persons is the goal. Clear communication, established decision-making systems, and clear selection criteria are essential.

Now, when they meet, the group is properly informed. James says he now understands that rationing is needed in Canada. He adds that he is familiar with making decisions about who will benefit the most from treatment. The use of triage methods was required when he was working for aid agencies in war-torn and disaster zones. Then and now he sees the same principle of helping those expected to survive.

The panel leads a discussion about the values underpinning the triage system. The first point is that clinical resources are finite. The ethicist reviews different principles of distributive justice. Using the principle of equality, in which everyone receives an equal amount of health care, is not practical. Some persons would have access to intensive care that they would not need. The option of selling or trading your option would punish those who are very sick with the flu and those who are unaffected. Next the group considers the principle of distribution based on the libertarian principle that people should be allowed to spend their wealth or assets as they desire. In other words, intensive care is available in part or in full to those who can pay for the health care, through their own assets or an insurance policy they have purchased. Certainly the funds would be appreciated by the hospital and health care system. The staff agree that a core value for Canadians is universal access to needed health care. Ability to pay must not be considered. Next, with the ethicist they quickly agree that core values about justice will not condone allocation based on gender, age, ethnicity, sexual orientation, or socioeconomic status. Urgency is assumed to be a factor in the inclusion criteria.

Thus far the criteria are need and urgency. They know that would leave far too many people in the inclusion group. Finally, they see the need to consider the principle of utility, that is, to look for ways of receiving the maximum benefit from the use of ICU's resources. The ICU nurses understand the situation readily. They see immediately that how long the person will need the ICU resource has to be considered. They could not have the beds dedicated to only a few persons. Once a patient is admitted, progress would have to be monitored carefully. The opportunity cost of keeping ICU beds occupied by one person when that person is not improving is immense. At this stage in the process, the ICU nurses can understand why there has to be an inclusion and exclusion criteria and a determination of the fairness of the criteria. The goal is to save as many lives as possible of persons with the pandemic flu, and the protocol was designed to achieve this outcome.

Not all nurses agree. Some reject the concept that equals are treated equally and the unequal are treated unequally. They want every person to have the same chance of having an ICU bed. Assessing persons and basing allocations on prognosis are risky. The notion of predicting prognosis and acting on that prediction are morally uncomfortable. They believe that the options of living one day, a year, or a decade are equally valuable and provide no basis for selection. The ethicist confirms that they have a valid position, and suggests an approach called the lottery system: chance determines access. Selection is based on a first-come, first-admitted basis, or care could be assigned to various persons at random. Yet this approach is in total opposition to the fundamental principles of distributive justice that are central to the Canadian health care system. There is a duty not to waste resources and give care that is futile.

Other nurses ask why the principle of retribution is not also being used. They think that if they are putting themselves in the front lines of the fight against the pandemic flu, in the event that they became infected they would want access based on the condition that they had followed their ethical duty to serve during a pandemic. Suzanne and the ethicist agree that the nurses have raised an important point that they had overlooked. They are aware that a nurse who has pandemic influenza would most likely be included and triaged into the Red (highest priority) group. As a group they agree it is reasonable for them to be moved from the Yellow (intermediate) group to the Red group to err on the side of caution. There is a frank discussion about borderline cases and how patients would fluctuate from one priority group to another. Discussions about how and why decisions are made would be encouraged. The safety of patient, nurses, and other health professionals is closely linked. All "depend on a safe moral climate in which the required organizational, material and interpersonal resources are available and the values for safe, competent, ethical care are in place" (Rodney et al., 2006, p. 24).

They end their meeting by agreeing that the main goal of the triage protocol is to use resources effectively, ensuring that each person who receives the scarce resources can survive. They recognize that their approach is in accord with the expectation of the Canadian Nurses Association's *Code of Ethics* (2008) that nurses honour their duty to care when there are clinical crises, such as a pandemic. The ICU nurses recommend that all staff and the public should be informed of how and why the triage protocol was reached. Procedural justice demands communication with the public to allow everyone to reflect on the ethical and clinical arguments supporting the policy. They recommend the five procedural values proposed in "Stand on Guard for Thee" (Joint Centre for Bioethics, 2005):

1. reasonable; that is, supported by reasons and evidence;

2. open and transparent: the process for decision-making be available for public discussion;

3. inclusive: decisions made by all groups affected and provide continuous opportunity for consultation;

4. responsive: be able to respond to issues and evaluate decisions when the crisis is in progress;

5. accountable: persons making decisions are answerable for decisions made or not made.

The nurses put the matter in crystal-clear terms. Until the meeting with the expert panel, none of these procedural values were in place or respected. The public and their patients needed to benefit from the same principles of procedural justice.

## Conclusion

As our society comes to terms with the problems of fiscal constraints on health care delivery, and government funding decisions have made it difficult for many individual, families, and communities to get access to the resources they need for health, issues of justice have continued to become more acute. For the good of all concerned, processes at the macro, meso, and micro levels must be set into place to enhance and facilitate proper decision-making in health care delivery and health policy. At every level, nurses should seek to become more involved because they are players whose interests, expertise, and concern are necessary for just solutions. A clinician quoted in Jameton (1984) over twenty years ago still captures the feelings of many nurses about these matters:

> You know, sometimes I feel like this. There I am standing by the shore of a swiftly flowing river and I hear the cry of a drowning man. So I jump into the river, put my arms toward him, pull him to shore and apply artificial respiration. Just when he begins to breathe, there is another cry for help. So I jump into the river, reach him, pull him to shore, apply artificial respiration, and then just as he begins to breathe, there is another cry for help. So back in the river again, reaching, pulling, applying, breathing and then another yell. Again and again, without end, goes the sequence. You know, I am so busy jumping in, pulling them to shore, applying artificial respiration, that I have no time to see who the hell is upstream pushing them all in. (p. 261)

For some time now it has been obvious that justice requires nurses to make the time to walk upstream — against the current — and educate people about the dangers by the river, or teach them to become better swimmers. Working to promote justice requires that nurses also move even further upstream so that they can engage policy-makers at all levels to improve the resources that Canadians need to achieve equitable access to both health care and the resources for health.

# Notes

1   Such commentators usually assume that alcoholism is voluntary — although we now understand that alcoholism is a serious addiction or disease.

2   Several commentators (e.g., Armstrong & Armstrong, 2003; Commission on the Future of Health Care in Canada, 2002; Saul, 1997; Storch, 2010) have warned that this egalitarian foundation is under threat.

3   For an interesting critique of this assumption (i.e., an argument that the free market is not necessarily more efficient or more cost-effective), see Stein (2001) and Pauly (2004).

4   Even if persons can be held "responsible" for their illness — which is in itself a problematic assumption — the consequences of paying for their illness would be catastrophic for themselves and their family members.

5   In reversing the decentralizing trend, as of 2009, the Alberta government reorganized the Alberta health services under one centralized health region.

6   Buchanan (1989, pp. 294-295) points out that terms like "micro-allocation" and "macro-allocation" are too imprecise to capture decision-making in these matters. Even so, they do serve a useful purpose and we therefore employ them throughout this chapter and this text.

7   Compelling — and growing — evidence indicates that improving education and social welfare can *improve health* (Anderson et al., 2009; Daniels, Kennedy, & Kawachi, 2004; Marmot, 2004).

8   Gorovitz (1988, p. 573) and Curtin (1984, p. 8) each list five slightly different principles for decision-making in these contexts. Some authors have advocated for a decision method that combines various criteria in order of priority. Rescher (1988) was an advocate of this approach. See Kilner (1990) for a comprehensive and thorough overview.

9   For a more detailed discussion of the implications of "blaming victims," see Martin (2001).

10  Norman Daniels is an ethical theorist who has long been promoting an approach to resource allocation (at all levels) based on need. See, for example, Daniels (1985, 1996), Daniels and Sabin (1997), and Martin, Abelson, & Singer (2002).

11  The determinants of health include: "income and social status, social support, education and literacy, employment and working conditions, physical and social environments, biology, genetic endowment, personal health practices and coping skills, healthy child development, health services, gender and culture" (Public Health Agency of Canada, 2003 as cited in CNA, 2008, p. 24).

# References

Anderson, J.M., Rodney, P., Reimer-Kirkham, S., Browne, A.J., Khan, K.B., & Lynam, M.J. (2009). Inequities in health and healthcare viewed through the ethical lens of critical social justice: Contextual knowledge for the global priorities ahead. *Advances in Nursing Science* 32 (4), 282-294.

Armstrong, P., & Armstrong, H. (2003). *Wasting away: The undermining of Canadian health care* (2nd ed.). Don Mills, ON: Oxford University Press.

Beauchamp T.L., & Childress J.F. (1994). *Principles of biomedical ethics* (4th ed.). New York: Oxford University Press.

Buchanan, A.E. (1989). Health-care delivery and resource allocation. In R.M. Veatch (Ed.), *Medical ethics* (pp. 291-327). Boston: Jones & Bartlett.

Canadian Nurses Association (2008). *Code of Ethics for Registered Nurses.* Ottawa.

Childress, J.F. (1983). Who shall live when not all can live? In S. Gorovitz, R. Macklin, A.L. Jameton, J.M. O'Connor, & S. Sherwin (Eds.), *Moral problems in medicine* (2nd ed., pp. 640-649). Englewood Cliffs, NJ: Prentice-Hall.

Christian, M.D., Hawryluck, L., Wax, R.S. et al. (2006). Development of a triage protocol for critical care during an influenza pandemic. *Canadian Medical Association Journal* 175 (11), 1377-1381.

Clarke, H.F. (2010). Health and nursing policy: A matter of politics, power, and professionalism. In M. McIntyre & C. McDonald (Eds.), *Realities of Canadian nursing: Professional, practice, and power issues* (3rd ed.; pp. 68-90). Philadelphia: Wolters Kluwer/Lippincott Williams & Wilkins.

Commission on the Future of Health Care in Canada (Romanow Commission). (2002). *Building on values: The future of health care in Canada.* Ottawa.

Curtin, L.L. (1980). Is there a right to health care? *American Journal of Nursing* 80 (3), 462-465.

Curtin, L.L. (1984). Ethics and economics in the eighties. *Nursing Management* 15 (6), 7-9.

Daniels, N. (1985). *Just health care.* Cambridge: Cambridge University Press.

Daniels, N. (1996). Wide reflective equilibrium in practice. In L.W. Sumner and J. Boyle (Eds.), *Philosophical perspectives on bioethics* (pp. 96–114). Toronto: University of Toronto Press.

Daniels, N. (2001). Justice, health and healthcare. *American Journal of Bioethics* 1 (2), 2-16.

Daniels, N., Kennedy, B., & Kawachi, I. (2004). Health and inequality, or, why justice is good for our health. In S. Anand, F. Peter, & A. Sen (Eds.), *Public health, ethics, and equity* (pp. 63-91). Oxford: Oxford University Press.

Daniels, N., & Sabin, J. (1997). Limits to health care: Fair procedures, democratic deliberation, and the legitimacy problem for insurers. *Philosophy and Public Affairs* 26 (4), 303-350.

Edwards, R.B., & Graber, G.C. (1988). Introduction: Allocation of scarce or expensive medical resources. In R.B. Edwards & G.C. Graber (Eds.), *Bioethics* (pp. 699-715). San Diego: Harcourt Brace Jovanovich.

Gorovitz, S. (1988). Equity, efficiency, and the distribution of health care. In T.A. Mappes & J.S. Zembaty (Eds.), *Biomedical ethics* (2nd ed., pp. 558-579). New York: McGraw-Hill.

Hardingham, L. B. (2004). Integrity and moral residue: Nurses as participants in a moral community. *Nursing Philosophy* 5, 127-134.

Howlett J., Stadnyk, K., Ryan, B., Mitchell-Lowery, A., Merry, H., Cox, J.L. (2001). Differences in the quality of life of cardiovascular patients from a large population-based study. *Canadian Journal of Cardiology 17* (Supp C), 238C.

Jameton, A.L. (1984). *Nursing practice: The ethical issues*. Englewood Cliffs, NJ: Prentice-Hall.

Joint Centre for Bioethics, Pandemic Influenza Working Group. (2005). *Stand on guard for thee: Ethical considerations in preparedness planning for pandemic influenza*. Toronto: University of Toronto. <www.jointcentreforbioethics.ca/people/documents/upshur_stand_guard.pdf>.

Kenny, N.P., & Giacomini, M. (2005) Wanted: A new ethics field for health policy analysis. *Health Care Analysis* 13 (4), 247-260.

Kilner, J.F. (1990). *Who lives? Who dies? Ethical criteria in patient selection*. New Haven, CT: Yale University Press.

MacDonald, M. (2002). Health promotion: Historical, philosophical, and theoretical perspectives. In L.E. Young & V. Hayes (Eds.), *Transforming health promotion practice: Concepts, issues, and application* (pp. 22-45). Philadelphia: FA Davis.

Marmot, M. (2004). Social causes of social inequalities in health. In S. Anand, F. Peter, & A. Sen (Eds.), *Public health, ethics, and equity* (pp. 37-61).Oxford: Oxford University Press.

Martin, M.W. (2001). Responsibility for health and blaming victims. *Journal of Medical Humanities* 22 (2), 95-114.

Martin, D., Abelson, J., & Singer, P. (2002). Participation in health care priority-setting: Through the eyes of the participants. *Journal of Health Services Research & Policy* 7 (4), 222–229.

McPherson, G., Rodney, P., Storch, J., Pauly, B., McDonald, M., & Burgess, M. (2004). Working within the landscape: Applications in health care ethics. In J. Storch, P. Rodney, & R. Starzomski (Eds.), *Toward a moral horizon: Nursing ethics for leadership and practice* (pp. 98-125). Toronto: Pearson-Prentice Hall.

O'Brien, L. (1983). Allocation of a scarce resource: The bone marrow transplant case. In C. Murphy & H. Hunter (Eds.), *Ethical problems in the nurse-patient relationship* (pp. 217-232). Boston: Allyn & Bacon.

Pauly, B.M. (2004). Shifting the balance in the funding and delivery of health care in Canada. In J. Storch, P. Rodney, & R. Starzomski (Eds.), *Toward a moral horizon: Nursing ethics for leadership and practice* (pp. 181-208). Toronto: Pearson-Prentice Hall.

Pauly, B. (2008). Harm reduction through a social justice lens. *International Journal of Drug Policy* 19, 4-10.

Pellegrino, E.D. (1979). Toward a reconstruction of medical morality: The primacy of the act of profession and the fact of illness. *Journal of Medicine and Philosophy* 4 (1), 32-56.

Pellegrino, E.D. (1986). Rationing health care: The ethics of medical gatekeeping. *The Journal of Contemporary Health Law and Policy* 2, 23-45.

Peter, E. (2004). Home health care and ethics. In J. Storch, P. Rodney, & R. Starzomski (Eds.), *Toward a moral horizon: Nursing ethics for leadership and practice* (pp. 248-261). Toronto: Pearson-Prentice Hall.

Public Health Agency of Canada (2003). *What determines health?* Toronto.

Rawls, J. (1999). *A theory of justice* (revised edition). Cambridge, MA: Harvard University Press.

Rescher, N.P. (1988). The allocation of exotic medical lifesaving therapy. In T.A. Mappes & J.S. Zembaty (Eds.), *Biomedical ethics* (2nd ed., pp. 601-611). New York: McGraw-Hill.

Rodney, P., Burgess, M, McPherson, G., & Brown, H. (2004). Our theoretical landscape: A brief history of health care ethics. In J. Storch, P. Rodney, & R. Starzomski (Eds.), *Toward a moral horizon: Nursing ethics for leadership and practice* (pp. 56-76). Toronto: Pearson-Prentice Hall.

Rodney, P., Doane, G.H., Storch, J. & Varcoe, C. (2006). Workplaces: Toward a safer moral climate. *Canadian Nurse* 102 (8), 24-27.

Royal Commission on Aboriginal Peoples. (1996). *Report of the Royal Commission on Aboriginal Peoples*. Ottawa.

Saul, J.R. (1997). *Reflections of a Siamese twin: Canada at the end of the twentieth century*. Toronto: Penguin.

Sherwin, S. (2002). The importance of ontology for feminist policy-making in the realm of reproductive technology. *Canadian Journal of Philosophy* 28 (Suppl), 273-295.

Staniszweska, S. (1998). Measuring quality of life in the evaluation of health care. *Nursing Standard* 12 (17), 36-39.

Stein, J.G. (2001). *The cult of efficiency*. Toronto: Anansi.

Stephenson, P. (1999). Expanding notions of culture for cross-cultural ethics in health and medicine. In H. Coward & P. Ratanakul (Eds.), *A cross-cultural dialogue on health care ethics* (pp. 68–91). Waterloo, ON: Wilfrid Laurier University Press.

Storch, J. (2006). The Canadian health care system and Canadian nurses. In M. McIntyre & E. Thomlinson (Eds.), *Realities of Canadian nursing: Professional, practice, and power issues* (pp. 34-59). Philadelphia: Lippincott.

Storch, J. (2010). Canadian healthcare system. In M. McIntyre & C. McDonald (Eds.), *Realities of Canadian nursing: Professional, practice, and power issues* (3rd ed., pp. 34-55). Philadelphia: Wolters Kluwer/Lippincott Williams & Wilkins.

Varcoe, C., & Rodney, P. (2009). Constrained agency: The social structure of nurses' work. In B.S. Bolaria & H.D. Dickinson (Eds.), *Health, illness, and health care in Canada* (4th ed., pp. 122-150). Toronto: Nelson Education.

Veatch, R.M. (1988). Voluntary risks to health: The ethical issues. In T.A. Mappes & J.S. Zembaty (Eds.), *Biomedical ethics* (2nd ed., pp. 593-601). New York: McGraw-Hill.

Wikler, D.I. (1983). Persuasion and coercion. In S. Gorovitz, R. Macklin, A.L. Jameton, J.M. O'Connor, & S. Sherwin (Eds.), *Moral problems in medicine* (2nd ed., pp. 587-602). Englewood Cliffs, NJ: Prentice-Hall.

Wilkinson, R. (2005). *The impact of inequality: How to make sick societies healthier*. New York: The New Press.

Williams, J.R. (1989). Allocation of health care resources. *Synapse* 5 (3), 10-13.

World Health Organization Commission on Social Determinants of Health. (2008). *Closing the gap in a generation: Health equity through action on the social determinants of health*. Geneva.

Yeo, M., Emery, J.C.H., & Kary, D. (2009). The private insurance debate in Canadian health policy: Making the values explicit. SPP Research Paper: The Health Series, Vol. 2, Issue 3, School of Public Policy, University of Calgary.

Yeo, M., & Lucock, C. (2006). Quality v. equality: The divided court in *Chaoulli v. Quebec. Health Law Journal* 14, 129-150.

# STUDY QUESTIONS: JUSTICE

## Case 1: Access to Care versus Quality of Care

1. The nurses want a quality practice environment. What is meant by this phrase, keeping in mind the principle of justice? Identify and discuss the needed infrastructure and leadership. Also identify and discuss what is needed on a nursing unit to create and sustain a quality practice environment.

2. Nurses want and should be treated fairly by their employers and their peers. There is said to be a tradition in nursing of the old eating their young. Discuss ways of supporting new graduates to be valuable members of the team. Discuss ways of reducing and ending the unfair treatment of nursing colleagues. In your discussion, address the principle of justice.

3. Casual employment can be attractive to some nurses at certain times in their career. Discuss the moral basis for arguing that health care agencies should offer permanent employment to nurses, and the benefits of this for nurses and patients.

4. Amina Ali changes from being a "black and white," "either-or" problem-solver. Discuss the distributive and procedural principles of justice evident in her thinking as the committee chair.

5. Suggest values and principles that should guide the waiting list subcommittee.

6. Discuss whether you agree with this statement, and why: "Heavy workload and moral distress are related." What can nurses do to reduce moral distress related to this issue? What resources are available where you study or are employed? What role could you take in addressing this concern?

7. Amina asks the nursing staff to help her respond to the problem. Do you think their involvement was window dressing, or authentic? What needs to happen for nurses' voices to be heard at decision-making committees? What would be the moral basis for supporting nurses participating in this kind of decision-making?

8. Amina recognizes that for the process to be most effective she must involve the community. At your local hospital, what involvement does the community have in developing hospital policies? Do you think the involvement is based on the three aspects of procedural justice? If not, what processes can you identify or suggest for facilitating such involvement?

## Case 2: Allocation of Clinical Placements and Support for Clinical Education

1. What factors support student learning in a clinical placement? What factors should faculty and health care agencies consider when allocating clinical placements so that equity and justice for all stakeholders are considered?

2. What issues of justice arise for student nurses in the context of their clinical assignments? What issues arise for faculty? What concerns might nursing staff have about these?

3. What information are patients entitled to when nursing students are involved in their care? Is a patient who is admitted to a teaching hospital expected to contribute to the education of health professionals?

4. If you were a clinical teacher, how would you use principles of justice as a guide to ensure that students' access to learning opportunities is equitable?

### Case 3: Equitable Allocation of Nursing Time and Care

1. Some nurses working in neonatal intensive care units have mixed feelings about the surgical and technological innovations that make it possible to "rescue" infants who would otherwise die. Discuss this issue with reference to "quality-of-life" considerations, whether care is beneficial or futile, and considerations of justice.

2. In the course of caring for children, nurses understandably develop more positive relationships with some children and their families than with others. To what extent might and should this influence the nurse's allocation of his or her time among various children?

3. What bearing, if any, might Sarah's condition have on the decision about how much care she should receive relative to the others? Consider your position in relation to relevant principles of justice.

4. Allocation decisions of the kind with which Jessica is faced are extremely painful, and are bound to be emotionally charged. To what extent is emotion an obstacle to such ethical decision-making? To what extent might it be a precondition for it? What is the role of these kinds of situations in nurses' experience of moral distress?

5. What resources are available in your institution for students or nurses when they are faced with ethical dilemmas? How would the institution respond to requests for support? Or how had it responded in the past? What do you think would enhance organizational responsiveness to students' or nurses' needs or concerns?

### Case 4: Triage and Rationing of Intensive-Care Beds during a Clinical Crisis

1. Do you know what pandemic plan is in place in your organization? What process was used to formulate the plan, and can you identify the principles of justice underlying the plan?

2. Does your organization's pandemic plan provide sufficient safe-guards for its employees? Do you know your rights and responsibilities if a pandemic or emergency occurs? Explore websites from the Canadian Nurses Association and your regulatory body to review these issues. Which principles of justice would support your position if you felt that you needed to present an argument to ensure your safety as a health professional during such an event?

3. Look at the Canadian Nurses Association position paper on "Emergencies, disease outbreaks and disasters" and determine your role in preparedness that would contribute to capacity-building that maximizes a systems response if an emergency occurs.

4. What are your personal views about the rationing of resources? Would you have suggested another approach to Jessica's dilemma, and, if so, what principles would you base your position on? Has further thinking about resource allocation led you to view the challenges from a different perspective?

# 8 INTEGRITY

*At crucial moments of choice, most of the business of choosing is already over. We have chosen by how we have lived our lives up until this point. Then our lives choose for us.*

—NANCY OLIVIERI

---

*The nurse's own values sometimes come into conflict with respect for a patient's autonomy, the views and wishes of colleagues, the rules, policies, and expectations of the institution, the law, or even with rules or policies issued by the profession. In some cases the practice environment itself can be an impediment to what the nurse believes to be ethical practice. When tension exists between ethical ideals and experienced reality, the nurse's sense of integrity is challenged. In these cases nurses will experience "moral distress."*

*Case studies in this chapter include conflict between a nurse and other care providers whose patient is a member of a marginalized population; the challenge for a nurse who considers refusing an assignment because of concern for herself and her family; and the dilemma faced by a nurse in a forensic setting who considers whether to blow the whistle about practices that harm patients. These case studies provide an opportunity to reflect on the concept of integrity and the challenge of developing and practising with integrity.*

---

## Integrity Defined

Integrity has a unique place among the values that guide nursing practice. It is more fundamental than the other values involved in nursing. Indeed, when pushed to a limit any issue involving those other values — beneficence, autonomy, truthfulness, confidentiality, and justice — can also become an issue of integrity. As a concept rich in meaning, then, integrity can be distinguished by four constituent features: moral autonomy; fidelity to promise; steadfastness; and wholeness.[1]

## 1. Moral Autonomy

As adults, we are all moral agents.[2] Through our actions or passivity, through words or silence, we can influence matters for good or ill. Becoming a more fully autonomous moral agent means accepting responsibility and being accountable for what we do or fail to do. It involves a continuing passage from a state of subjecting ourselves, with unquestioning loyalty or conformity, to the moral authority of others to a state of asserting authorship of our own moral lives.

Reflection is essential to this process. Blindly following authorities, such as faith and community leaders, professional expectations, the law, or our peers, is pre-reflective reasoning. Through the process of reflecting on who we are and how we experience our world, we find that we have been instilled with various moral beliefs, values, and principles. So long as we adhere to these without giving them critical examination, we are pre-reflectively subject to the authority of the influences (e.g., family, friends, community, societal norms) that have shaped our moral lives.

As we question what we have inherited and the external authorities to which we are subject, we reject some things and accept and affirm others. We shape our own moral code, or make the code we have inherited more fully our own by assuming responsibility for it. In doing so, we become more autonomous, directing and taking responsibility for our own moral lives rather than being uncritically guided by others. Our integrity develops as we assume greater control over and accountability for our moral lives. We change and grow in the process of reflecting on the values and principles that have shaped us pre-reflectively. Through ongoing reflection and dialogue with others, the values and principles that guide us in our actions and relationships become considered and more freely taken up rather than being assumed or taken for granted. As we strive for integrity, and to maintain such integrity as we have, this process does not end.

## 2. Fidelity to Promise

Moral agency is partially bound up with our willingness to make promises, and to hold ourselves to promises made. Moral agents are expected to be true to their word — to make promises and keep them. Someone who cannot be counted on to keep a promise lacks integrity.

The moral values and principles to which, upon reflection, we commit ourselves are implicit promises. We project ourselves into the future as the sort of person whose actions will be guided by that which we now promise ourselves. More or less explicitly, we promise others who know us that we can be counted upon and relied on to act consistently with the moral values and principles we now profess, even as we remain open to listening to others and modifying our values and principles. Thus nurses assume the task of shaping their lives in faithfulness to promises made to patients and to themselves. Indeed, nurses are expected to make and should carefully reflect on three important promises: to respect patient values and choices, to protect private information and confidences, and to help and not harm patients.

## 3. Steadfastness

Integrity requires us to maintain our considered values and principles during both calm and turbulent times. Being true to our considered moral code and promises is sometimes difficult. Sometimes we have to work hard at it. Wanting a comfortable life and having valid fears can pull us in a direction contrary to what, upon reflection, we believe and think to be right and good. Sometimes doing what is right carries a price or involves a sacrifice. There can be powerful forces constraining what we can and cannot do, and it can take considerable courage to do what we think is right.

Steadfastness has to do with standing fast and speaking up for what, upon careful consideration and reflection, we believe is right, especially in the face of forces and considerations that pull against this. If they cannot achieve perfect outcomes in highly complex and conflicted situations, nurses can at least commit themselves to continuing to work toward better outcomes for patients, their families, and health care team members by addressing barriers in the practice environment that impede doing the right thing.[3]

Although people of integrity are unwilling to yield their considered principles and values even when the pressures to do so are great, such steadfastness should not be confused with perfectionism, rigidity, stubbornness, and uncompromising stands. Integrity involves continuing self-reflection and self-examination and is open to other people and to a future self who can be different than the present self. Having integrity means listening to and being open to others, and being open to counterarguments and to ways of looking at a situation differently than in your initial response. It sometimes means making compromises out of respect for other people and their sense of integrity, or to achieve the most benefit for patients possible under less than ideal circumstances.

## 4. Wholeness

A human life is multidimensional. We exist in many different relationships, roles, and settings. The task of becoming whole — a task we can never complete — requires us to integrate the various parts of our lives, which include our relationships with other people, under the guidance of the values and principles that we have promised for ourselves. This is a lifelong task as we reflect on our values and principles in view of changing circumstances and changing relationships with other people. There are always new challenges of integration, and the integration will sometimes mean modifying our values and principles in light of reflection and dialogue with others. To aspire to integrity is to endeavour to achieve consistency and continuity across the various dimensions of our lives, even while being open to others and to change, and above all to changing oneself.

Baylis (2007) is therefore right to question consistency and continuity as being valuable in their own right and to emphasize the interpersonal nature of integrity. After all, the wholeness that we strive for includes our changing relationships with other people, who often have moral views different from our own. However, Baylis additionally appears to hold that having "a particular rule set" is also essential to integrity, as if persons who did not have that rule set could not be persons of integrity (p. 199).

On the account of integrity we give here, it is entirely possible, and this possibility is constitutive of integrity, that persons having quite different and even contrary "rule sets" or moral commitments could equally be said to have integrity provided they are open to others and other viewpoints. Absent such openness, what might appear as integrity is dogmatism.

The opposite of wholeness is a kind of self-dividedness or moral "schism." Such division can exist between our professed ideals and our actual practices; hypocrisy is an extreme instance of this tendency. A division can also exist between the different roles or relationships in our lives. Some people are different at work than they are at home, or with one group of people than with another. Such differences can be appropriate to a point, but at the extremes they can amount to a betrayal in one role of the values promised in another role.

Integrity, by contrast, requires that we integrate our ideals into our lives across its various dimensions and through the roles and relationships in which we find ourselves. We endeavour to realize our values and principles in and throughout our practices, to make real the ideals to which we are promised. When this integration is absent, nurses experience a disconnect that results in moral distress. They know what they ought to do but find significant barriers or impediments to doing it. In such situations, nurses need to look for the root causes of the conflict, which can be complex and systemic. The practice environment itself might be the problem, and there could be no quick or easy fixes for it. Strategic planning with colleagues could help to address systemic or institutional barriers to practising in accordance with the considered values and principles.

## Personal and Professional Integrity

The analysis of personal integrity can also be applied to groups: a business, an institution, and, for our purposes, a profession. In the early history of nursing, the actions valued did not satisfy the conditions of moral agency; nurses were not in a position to make their own promises. Critical thinking and autonomy in nursing were not valued; they were capacities considered antithetical to the making of a "good nurse." An early textbook in nursing ethics illustrates the point eloquently: "Implicit, unquestioning obedience is one of the first lessons a probationer must learn, for this is a quality that will be expected from her in her professional capacity for all future time" (Robb, 1900, p. 57; see also Lamb, 2004). Such "unquestioning obedience" is inconsistent with moral autonomy.

The history of nursing has been in part a struggle for moral autonomy and integrity.[4] A decisive moment in this struggle occurred when nurses, against considerable resistance, committed themselves to a code of ethics. A code of ethics is a "professional promise" to patients and to the public in general. It publicizes the values and principles for which nurses will stand accountable (CNA, 2008a; Oberle & Bouchal, 2009). In essence, a code establishes the rules for nursing standards; nurses will be responsible for the exercise of independent judgement in view of the code.

Anyone who enters a profession assumes a duty to stand up for and act in accordance with the values of that profession. The values for which nursing stands, like those of other professions, are unlikely to conflict with personal values. Benefiting others, being respectful of autonomy, being truthful, and preserving confidentiality, being just: who could argue with such ideals? However, the scope of various professions includes practices that, while sanctioned by a code of ethics, can nevertheless be inconsistent with personal values. For instance, soldiers, under certain conditions, are expected to kill people — something pacifists would not condone during a time of either war or peace. Lawyers are expected to defend people whom they might find morally repugnant. In some instances, and for some people, questions of conscience arise in the execution of their duties as professionals.

In nursing, such questions often arise in matters of life and death. The nursing profession accepts abortions, for example, as a legitimate health service. But many nurses are opposed to abortion on principle. For nurses who see abortion as being morally wrong, assisting in them would represent a loss of personal integrity; they should therefore be careful as far as possible not to work in areas in which they would encounter patients who require an abortion. Still, even when assisting with abortions, as with any similar situation, comes into conflict with the nurse's ethical values, the nurses have certain obligations, as the Canadian Nurses Association (2008a) points out. First the nurse must inform the employer of the conflict and avoid employment that may require assistance with abortions. In the event that no other nurse is available to assist a patient having an abortion, nurses must provide care until a nurse is available to care for the patient. The duty to care is an ethical priority.

Similarly, nurses who believe that the removal of a ventilator is a matter of assisted suicide should not work in an intensive-care unit that has a routine practice of removing ventilators for patients who are not expected to recover. In other words, when nurses know they will have an irreconcilable moral conflict, they should take steps to avoid being placed in a role in which they will frequently face that conflict. At the same time they should find ways of supporting their colleagues who are able to provide the necessary care. They should work politically to address policies that they believe are morally objectionable or less than conducive to what they believe is good nursing care.

A less dramatic but equally important conflict can arise around the use of restraints for reasons of safety. Nurses in long-term care settings sometimes find that nursing practice contradicts nursing standards and evidence-based guidelines, along with their values about respecting the dignity of patients. Using restraints and seclusion to manage violence in mental health settings can raise ethical conflicts. In exceptional circumstances, keeping a patient safe can take priority over treating that person in the way that most individuals would expect. Some nurses find this kind of intervention difficult to defend, and it remains the subject of debate. In the meantime, nurses ought to institute preventative measures that make actions such as restraint and seclusion less necessary — such as having adequate activity programs for confused elderly patients, advocating for "sitters" to stay with agitated patients, and becoming expert in therapeutic measures that prevent aggression. The nursing profession also has a responsibility to continue to engage in research about practice problems that require more debate.

Like other professions, the nursing profession recognizes that some of its members will have moral objections to some of its endorsed practices. The profession is respectful of personal conscience. For example, the Canadian Nurses Association *Code of Ethics for Registered Nurses* (CNA, 2008a) states, "If nursing care is requested that is in conflict with the nurse's moral beliefs and values but in keeping with professional practice, the nurse provides safe, compassionate, competent and ethical care until alternative arrangements are in place to meet the person's needs or desires" (p. 19). Even so, it is incumbent upon nurses to avoid situations in which such issues of conscience will arise. The CNA qualifies this point by adding, "If nurses can anticipate a conflict with their conscience they have an obligation to notify their employer or, if the nurse is self-employed, persons receiving care in advance so that alternative arrangements can be made" (p. 19).

The act of reconciling the personal and the professional can pose other, less dramatic, issues than ones of conscience. There is a difference between paying lip service to the ethical ideals of your profession and making them real in your daily practice. Aspiring to ethical ideals is a difficult task. Some effort will be required to shape yourself in accordance with these ideals and to pursue them with commitment. For example, respect for autonomy may not come naturally, or maintaining a caring manner can be difficult when you are dealing with a patient whom you personally dislike. Nurses need to learn how to listen authentically to the concerns of *all* patients as well as their family members, whether we "like" them or not, if they are to cross such hard spots in practice (Hartrick Doane & Varcoe, 2005; Liaschenko, 1994). Nurses must thoughtfully reflect on their own biases and prejudices, regardless of their practice focus or role in the profession.

Overall, professional integrity requires each nurse to promote and stand up for the values of the profession. Nurses need to be aware that their practice and the practice of others reflect on the image and reputation of the profession. They are thus obliged to keep within the bounds of their own competence, and to intervene when they suspect unprofessional or incompetent conduct in colleagues. To be sure, the commitment to the good of the patient requires this much, but it also requires you to uphold the integrity of the profession. Sadly, despite the significant gains that nursing has achieved in reaching its professional status, the image of the profession continues to be undermined at times by the entertainment media and other uninformed persons. Maintaining the integrity of the profession will depend on identifying and challenging the established stereotypes (Buresh & Gordon, 2000).

## Integrity and Multiple Obligations

Although maintaining integrity can be a challenge for people in any profession, it is particularly so for nurses. Nurses have a history of subordination in health care settings, and they have often lacked the power to define their activity in the workplace.[5] In some nursing workplaces, nurses may not be able to practise as their scope of practice states, and are expected to be subservient, becoming what some would call oppressed (David, 2000). Under these circumstances, their moral autonomy is threatened. Because nursing has historically been a profession predominantly (although not exclusively) pursued by women, an examination of the moral work of nursing and nurses' integrity as moral agents calls for a disciplinary, social, cultural, political, and gender-based analysis. In other words, we will not be able to understand — and hence support — nurses' enactment of their moral agency if we think of nurses as isolated, rational individuals who are discharging their professional ethical obligations. Nurses' sociopolitical positions greatly influence what they are able to accomplish (Rodney, Brown, & Liaschenko, 2004, p. 162).

Yet times are changing, and the profession is making progress. Nursing is a profession with well-educated members. The scope of practice has expanded. Nurses have regulatory standards and codes of ethics to guide their decision-making, and they are accountable for their decisions and actions. To be accountable, they must reflectively and critically appraise instructions and "orders," even while recognizing the limits of their scope of practice. Nurses can and should raise questions about orders that they think are not in patients' best interests. When collaboration and discussion have not resolved the difference of opinion, nurses are not obligated to follow orders that they believe are harmful to patients. The process for refusing orders must be followed in these cases, and regulatory colleges and employers have guidelines about how to proceed (see, for example, CNA, 2008a; CRNBC, 2006).

To enact their integrity as moral agents nurses should continue to cultivate skill in analyzing and responding to the challenges they face. Conflicts can arise when nurses are expected, or even obligated, to do something inconsistent with their personal or professional values. Integrity can be at issue in any of four intersecting relationships: with patients; with the institution in which one practices; with other health professionals; and with the community.

## 1. Integrity and the Nurse-Patient Relationship

In some cases nurses experience a conflict between their respect for the patient's autonomy and their own moral autonomy. This can happen when a patient wants something that the nurses believe is contrary to their professional judgement or that is otherwise inappropriate. A patient who requires and asks for assistance to smoke tobacco, for instance, can put nurses in such a situation. More generally, integrity can arise as an issue whenever a patient puts nurses in a situation of dividedness with respect to values. For example, a patient diagnosed with cancer might request that this information be withheld from a partner. The nurses could possibly have developed a therapeutic relationship with the partner over time, but in any case the nurses might believe that the partner has a right to know and should be told. If so, it will be difficult for the nurses to maintain their integrity in dealing with both the patient and the partner.

More extreme situations can raise direct questions of conscience — for example, when respecting the patient's wishes would mean being complicit in something that the nurse believes to be morally wrong, or even illegal. Patients who would benefit from life-saving treatment and probably recover but who nonetheless decide to refuse treatment are a case in point. Some nurses may think that remaining involved in such a patient's care is inconsistent with their values about preserving life. These nurses are in a difficult position. Since they cannot refuse to care for the patient they might want to seek employment in a place where these kinds of value conflicts are not as likely to arise. For example, while nurses may refuse to care for patients having abortions, they have the duty to not seek or accept employment where it is reasonable to expect that they will be called upon to assist with abortions. Even if they have taken this step and they find that they are needed, they cannot abandon the patient until a qualified nurse arrives to relieve them of their duty to provide care.

## 2. Integrity and the Nurse-Employer Relationship

Most nurses are employed in health care institutions and do not contract directly with patients. Nurses must provide care within constraints laid out by the organization, which can limit them in their ability to practise according to the standards of their profession (Varcoe & Rodney, 2009). For example, nurses may know that there are legal and professional sanctions about the use of physical restraints. Even though their employer may have a least-restraint policy, they are expected to use physical restraints.

Integrity issues arise whenever their employer's expectations and power call for them to comply with policy and practices that are inconsistent with their own personal or professional values. Institutional policies or practices can require a nurse to act inconsistently with the professional promise to promote the autonomy and well-being of the patient. For example, policies about discharge planning can restrict patients' choice of the long-term care facility (nursing home) where they will be transferred and probably spend the rest of their lives. In these examples, safe, compassionate, and ethical care can be jeopardized by unsafe practices, economic pressures, and patient "flow" demands.

Problems of this sort sometimes come to a head in an assignment refusal. Examples include such things as refusing additional assignments because the workload is already too heavy and patients will be endangered, or because the assignment is beyond the nurse's professional competence. "When patients' needs compete with those of the employers," Carnerie (1989) wrote two decades ago, "nurses are trapped on the dangerous ground in the middle" (p. 20). This dilemma continues to occur today. Yet nurses should not accept the role of being oppressed and powerless. Nurses have a moral obligation to reflect on and subsequently address the root causes of these problems and work to improve the quality of patient care; advocating for a moral community in which they can live their values (Hardingham, 2010; Rodney & Street, 2004; Varcoe & Rodney, 2009). The CNA *Code of Ethics* (2008a) recommends that nurses be engaged in such ethical endeavours to improve the health of groups. Nurses can find this activism a difficult route to follow when they work alone. Finding like-minded peers is a good strategy. Professional, regulatory, and labour organizations can be resources to develop strategies to change policies and practices. To be silent, look the other way, and conform is equivalent to agreeing with and supporting actions that you believe are unethical, unsafe, and contrary to professional and legal expectations. Such problems reflect a troubling level of moral disengagement (Bandura, 2002) in which nurses abdicate the ethical foundations of their practice (Oberle & Bouchal, 2009, pp. 258-262).

Questions of professional integrity can also arise when a commitment to the patient is not directly at stake. A conflict between nurse and employer can threaten the integrity of the profession itself, or the nurse's integrity. The employing institution may treat nurses as being less than professional, not allow them to work to their scope of practice, and fail to respect their professional and moral autonomy. For instance, it has been well documented that when not enough support staff are present, nurses' time for patient care is disrupted by non-nursing tasks such as answering telephones and finding equipment (CNA, 2009; McDonald & McIntyre, 2010). Further, psychological and physical violence and sexual harassment in the workplace are far too common for nurses (Varcoe, 2010). Such problems occur (at least in part) because nurses often lack input into policy-making and control over the conditions of their practice. Again, complicity is not an ethical response. Nurses must be strong advocates for themselves, for their colleagues, for their profession, and for their patients and their patients' families and communities. This means that nurses must become proactive in finding ways of changing their practice environments.[6]

### 3. Integrity and the Nurse-Colleague Relationship

Similar issues can arise in relationships with colleagues. The classic example involves a conflict between the nurse's obligations to a physician and to a patient.[7] These conflicting obligations may put the nurse in a double bind. A number of years ago Johnstone (1988) pointed out, "Nurses are expected to obey doctor's orders, on the one hand, and yet are held independently accountable on the other" (p. 155). Today these words would be shocking to newer nurses. Nurses are not the stereotypical handmaidens of physicians and passive subordinates. Likewise, physicians and other health care professionals are aware that allied health care professionals are colleagues, and they are all expected to work respectfully together. Nevertheless, conflicts should and do arise. Healthy debate about obligations and treatment plans is desirable. How should nurses proceed when there are conflicts? To begin, nurses realize that the term "obey" at this point in their history is seldom used, at least in the Western world. Physicians write and give orders, and normally nurses follow those orders if there is no good reason to challenge them. Nurses are accountable for their actions, and even if another discipline has provided the order, that does not exempt them from accountability for the effects of that action or its moral good (CNA, 2008a).

A number of considerations can bear on the resolution of conflicts between nurses and other colleagues, but ultimately the question reduces to how much weight should be assigned to each obligation relative to the other. On this question, there has been a major shift in the professed values and principles of nursing. Owing to a wide variety of factors, the earlier belief that the nurse's primary loyalty is to the physician has been superseded by the current value that nurses' primary obligation is to the patient. Today this belief is enshrined in various statements by the profession. Nursing is now a profession and has come a long way from the days when unquestioning obedience was a virtue. However, in some practice environments nurses must contend with the culture shaped by this legacy. In the CNA Code (2008a) and many other professional documents, nurses can find direction about how to engage in ethical endeavours to promote the welfare of patients and themselves.

## 4. Integrity and the Nurse-Community Relationship

Although the majority of nurses are employed in institutions, recent years have also seen a shift to work locations outside hospital walls. As Côté and Fox (2007) argue, "Increased need for health services amongst a growing elderly population and other groups such as children and youth, those suffering from mental illness, people living in rural or remote areas, and First Nations and Inuit communities has resulted in increased demand for home and community care" (p. 4). Some nursing commentators believe that the community can become the dominant employment setting for nurses in the future.

The practice environment in the community is less structured than it is in institutions. Rules and norms governing professional behaviour are not as settled and codified. Nurses in the community have much greater latitude for the exercise of judgement and decision, and must work much more independently. The community environment can also pose considerable challenges for the nurses' commitment to ensure that they provide needed, quality care to patients. The seriousness of these challenges will depend on the extent to which the shift from institutional to community-based care is supported by a sufficient reallocation of resources. Economics, and in particular the expectation that money will be saved by a decreased reliance on institutions, is a major factor driving the shift to the community. If a considerable portion of the savings incurred as a result of deinstitutionalization is not redirected to developing infrastructures for care in the community, the shift to the community will amount to abandonment.

Nurses in the community can find themselves working in co-operation with patients' family members, volunteers, and other less highly skilled caregivers. Nurses recognize that less-skilled personnel can do many caring jobs, and they appreciate how valuable and important the work of family members and volunteers can be. But they also know that caring attitudes and good intentions alone may not be enough for effective, quality care. Given budget constraints, volunteers and underqualified personnel may be delegated tasks beyond their competence, and family members may be burdened with care responsibilities beyond their abilities (Peter, 2004). This tendency could have serious implications for the quality and safety of care.

Issues of integrity will arise for nurses in the community to the extent that supporting resources, and in particular human resources, are insufficient to ensure the kind of safe, quality care to which nurses are professionally devoted. These issues will be all the more pronounced the greater the responsibility of the nurse for the care of the patient — including the supervision or co-ordination of less-qualified or even underqualified caregivers (Peter, 2004).

**Integrity and Moral Distress**

Although the statement is over twenty years old, Mappes's (1986) account of the difficulty of acting with integrity remains pertinent: "It is well and good to say what nurses should do. It is quite another thing, given the forces at work in the everyday world in which nurses work, to expect nurses to do what they ought to do" (p. 131). The inhibiting "forces" to which she refers include such things as economic pressures, sexism, and power imbalances. In addition nurses might be internalizing these "forces" and thus inhibiting themselves from engaging in ethical practice (Oberle & Bouchal, 2009, p. 259; Varcoe & Rodney, 2009).

This tension between ethics and reality has long been a recurrent theme in the literature on nursing ethics. Early on Flaherty (1985), for example, voiced the ethical ideal and norm that "nurses are obliged by ethics and by law to question directives and policies about which they have concern" (p. 102). She acknowledged, however, that pressing realities may make it difficult to practise in accordance with this obligation. She warned that nurses "often find themselves in situations in which they have limited authority, and when they attempt to exercise their broad ethical and legal responsibilities to and for patients, they will feel powerless, excluded, and dependent if there is a lack of nurse/physician/administrator collaboration and co-operation" (p. 110).

These observations describe a common predicament. In each case, the ethical problem has to do not so much with deciding what is morally right, but rather with doing it in a constrained environment that is not conducive to the realization of professional values. Despite being supported by professional values, and even to some extent because of them, nurses sometimes find themselves in situations in which it is difficult or costly to do what they know to be right.

In such situations they will find it difficult to realize or uphold their promised values and principles — that is, difficult to maintain integrity. Varcoe and Rodney (2009) state that moral distress arises from the difficulty that nurses experience in enacting their moral agency: "As the enactment of moral agency is prerequisite to professional practice, the social structure of nurses' work (within current health care contexts dominated by corporatism and narrow definitions of efficiency) threatens the foundation of professional practice as well as the well-being of nurses" (p. 136).

Moral distress has long been a serious problem in nursing.[8] One area in which moral distress is particularly troublesome is care of the critically ill or dying. Rodney (1994) reported that "given the situational constraints they experience in their practice," nurses "often experience moral distress when they care for patients undergoing life-prolonging treatment" (p. 41). These constraints "go beyond the purview of bioethics (patient-centred problems) into professional and institutional problems such as communication conflicts, questionable competence, and excessive workloads" (p. 41). Moreover, the problems identified are likely to be compounded by "an overall problem of resource allocation" (p. 42). End of life issues continue to be a major source of moral distress for nurses and other members of the health care team, and the issues are confounded by worsening problems with resource allocation (Hamric, Davis, & Childress, 2006; Hamric & Blackhall, 2007; Storch, 2004).

Resource allocation problems have worsened because of the rise of a corporate culture in health care that too often emphasizes cost-saving and efficiency at the expense of quality of care (Stein, 2001). Corporate climates can stifle nurses' practice goals, with unfortunate consequences as nurses find they are expected to make do with less and accomplish, if not more, at least the same as they have in the past (Varcoe and Rodney, 2009). As a result nurses can feel defeated and frustrated as they experience a lack of control over their practice and the quality of their work. Some nurses respond to the moral distress they experience by attending only to patients' immediate physical needs and demeaning other nurses' attempts to attend to emotional needs (Varcoe and Rodney, 2009), reflecting a sense of moral disengagement.

Regardless of the particular conceptualization, the cumulative effects of moral distress are being recognized as a serious concern. Webster and Baylis (2000) argue that unresolved moral distress can lead to moral compromise and *moral residue* — moral residue being what we carry with us when we know how we should act in certain cases but were unwilling and/or unable to do so (see also Mitchell, 2001; Oberle & Bouchal, 2009). Webster and Baylis acknowledge that the experience of moral residue can encourage the moral agent to reflect on and improve his or her practice, but they also warn that the moral agent may move toward denial, trivialization, or unreflective acceptance of the incoherence between beliefs and action (pp. 224–226; Rodney, Brown, & Liaschenko, 2004, p. 163). Another outcome of the dissonance between nurses' moral values and their inability to act on them, along with a related sense of powerlessness, is decreased retention rates (Pendry, 2007). Organizations that respond to nurses' moral distress experience "higher levels of staff satisfaction resulting in a decrease in staff turnover" and influence "staff and patient satisfaction, quality of care and patient outcomes" (Pendry, 2007, p. 220).

Nurses in such situations will have to find ways of maintaining their integrity, but, once again, the problem also needs to be addressed in broader and more general terms. Probably the greatest challenge facing the nursing profession today is to work toward attitudinal and structural changes that will make the care environment more conducive to ethical nursing practice.

## From Conflict to Co-operation and a Moral Community

A generation ago, nurse ethicists Yarling and McElmurry (1986) wrote, "Professional nurses are conceived in moral contradiction and born in compromise" (p. 67). They saw a nursing world in which ideals were contradicted by realities; ethical promise was driven toward unholy compromise. "The fundamental moral predicament of nurses," Yarling and McElmurry charged, "is that often they are not free to be moral because they are deprived of their free exercise of moral agency" (p. 65). More recently a huge change has occurred in nursing education, regulatory and professional ethical expectations, and the scope of practice of nurses. A generation ago, these authors were correct in identifying the lack of autonomy as a problem, especially for nurses working in hospitals and other sometimes authoritarian environments. Today nurses are expected to be accountable for their decisions and actions. They are expected not only to have integrity but also to exercise moral autonomy. Doing so requires principles, education, and good communication skills. Nurses are expected to collaborate with an interdisciplinary team. A lack of collaboration and respect among health care disciplines should not be accepted; the issue should be addressed. It is important to be principled and willing to stand for one's principles and find ways of working as a team. Today's nurses learn that integrity should not be confused with self-righteousness. Likewise, steadfastness should not be confused with dogmatic rigidity, uncooperativeness, and closed-mindedness.

The process for discussing differences and reaching decisions should be respectful and fair. When systems and processes do not support respectful dialogue and decision-making, nurses should work to improve the practice environment. Certainly, a moral life is not developed in a monologue. Thoughtful dialogue and discussion can go a long way toward warding off or resolving conflict. There is a connection between promise and compromise (promising with others).[9] The difficulty is in deciding at what point adherence to promise is unreasonable, and at what point compromise becomes breach of promise. In some instances the line between being co-operative and being co-opted may be very fine indeed. Nevertheless, a line can and should be drawn.

Suggestions for helping nurses deal with conflict and moral distress include identifying the experience, acknowledging its existence, providing education in orientation and other workplace initiatives, and talking about it (Pendry, 2007). In many instances, holding ethics rounds, initiating an ethics consultation, and accessing chaplaincy services can also be helpful (Zuzelo, 2007).

Dealing responsibly with conflict and moral distress also requires that nurses work toward improving their work environment for practice. However, as the CNA (2008a) states: "Quality work environments are crucial to ethical practice, but they are not enough. Nurses need to recognize that they are *moral agents* in providing care. This means they have a responsibility to conduct themselves ethically in what they do and how they interact with persons receiving care" (p. 5). Furthermore:

Nurses in all facets of the profession need to reflect on their practice, on the quality of their interactions with others and on the resources they need to maintain their own well-being. In particular, there is a pressing need for nurses to work with others (i.e., other nurses, other health-care professionals and the public) to create the *moral communities* that enable the provision of safe, compassionate, competent and ethical care. (CNA 2008, p. 5; see also Rodney et al., 2006, p. 27).

Nurses must, then, ensure their own *fitness to practice*; that is, the "physical, mental, and emotional capacities to deal with the often stressful and demanding health care environment" (Oberle & Bouchal, 2009, p. 257). As individual moral agents, nurses live in community with others — other nurses, other health care providers, and the patients, families, and communities they serve. In the health care context, this community should be defined by the shared goal of providing safe, competent, and ethical care.

### Case 1: Integrity and Nurses' Relationships with Colleagues and Employers

Nurses, as employees of health care organizations, have a duty to accept assignments. The employers expect nurses to be non-judgmental and to develop therapeutic relationships with their patients. The groups, communities, students, and large populations they work with expect fairness.

On occasion nurses will find that an assignment, policy, law, or practice creates an ethical dilemma for them. They might be asked to do something that runs counter to the expressed values of the profession, such as not report an adverse event. Nurses might want or feel obliged to refuse assignments for one or more reasons. Examples are valid concerns about their safety or the safety of their patients; a policy that stigmatizes or neglects a vulnerable population; an assignment that puts them in conflict with a personal value, such as assisting with an abortion; or a placement that undermines student learning.

The reasons for refusing an assignment can be nurse-centred or patient-centred, based either on beneficence or respect for autonomy. Both nurse-centred and patient-centred reasons can be bound up with concerns related to professional integrity. For example, although nurses are not obligated to assist with abortions, those opposed to abortion do have an obligation to avoid employment in situations in which they will be asked to work with women having abortions; and they must not abandon patients in any circumstances.

The concern for professional integrity can arise directly when nurses come to believe that an assignment is inconsistent with their ethical values. In the following case, personal and professional values collide with the provision of care.

*Deborah, a twenty-five-year-old First Nations high-risk pregnant woman, comes to the hospital toward the end of her pregnancy. She is having contractions. Deborah tells the triage nurse in the emergency room about having taken street drugs during her pregnancy, and that she had been a sex-trade worker until just seven months earlier. In tears, she says that two years earlier she had a child who was taken away from her by the child protection services.*

Laboratory tests reveal that Deborah has no illicit drugs in her system, and she is quickly admitted to the mother and child unit. A drug screen shows that the baby boy does not have any drugs in his system.

Joan, an experienced nurse, is assigned to care for Deborah, who gives birth to a healthy baby boy. Joan is a mentor for Ashley, a novice nurse on the unit.

Deborah and her baby share a room together, and Deborah starts to nurse her son. The following day, Joan goes to a meeting with the unit social worker and a Children's Aid case manager. They talk about how Deborah is homeless and had been involved in drugs and the sex trade for five years. She also has a criminal record for assault. The daughter born to her two years earlier, and taken into care, has been adopted. The plan now is to take this new baby into protection.

Joan is asked to go to Deborah and take the baby out of the room. She is advised to say that the baby needs blood work done. After the baby is taken from Deborah, the Children's Aid case manager will inform Deborah about her baby being taken into care.

Joan agrees to the plan. She and Ashley will carry it out. Joan tells the social worker and case manager that as soon as she learned the women was First Nations she expected that the child would go into custody. The new nurse, Ashley, is not comfortable with the attitudes of her colleagues to Deborah, but does not feel able to intervene.

Deborah is devastated when she finds out that her child was taken into care. She pleads to keep her son. Joan tells her that all that matters is that her son is safe and the hospital has "done the right thing." Later that day Ashley tells Joan that she is extremely uneasy about having taken a baby away from its mother under these circumstances. It is a matter of integrity, she says. Joan tells Ashley that the unit manager expects them to take the babies away from high-risk mothers. "You had better get used to how we do things here." Ashley tries to console Deborah, who tells her to leave because she will never again be able to trust her. Deborah feels betrayed by all the staff and very alone in her tragic situation.

## Commentary

This case raises several ethical issues for Ashley as a novice nurse. She realizes that she lacked moral autonomy when working with Joan. Faced with the values and attitudes of her mentor and colleagues, she did not establish a therapeutic relationship with Deborah in which she could advocate for her. In remaining silent Ashley in effect condoned the negative attitude toward Deborah. From her point of view, the hospital staff is looking down on the woman because she is First Nations, used drugs, and had been a sex-trade worker. Ashley believes that the others made their decision to take the baby away without a full assessment of Deborah's capacity to care for the child.

Ashley also sees that she and Joan had a conflict of interest. By supporting Deborah through the first hours of motherhood, Ashley had implicitly promised Deborah that she would be true to her word. In this context, it meant a commitment to help Deborah be a good mother. Fidelity to her patient was tested when they "told a white lie" to get the baby away from Deborah and to avoid the possibility of a conflict and even a hostage situation. The root of the problem, Ashley decides, is that she had two patients: Deborah and her baby son. When they were asked to remove the boy, Joan and Ashley betrayed Deborah's trust. They had deceived Deborah when they told her that the baby needed blood work. Certainly, Ashley understands why this approach was taken. She knows that it would have been very hard to remove the baby from Deborah's arms if the mother was told that the boy was being taken into care. She knows that a hostile and violent situation could have developed. The best interests of the child supported removal of the baby before the news was given to Deborah. But Ashley was also rightly concerned about the best interest of the mother. If they had taken time to know Deborah, they might have learned that with support she would have been able to care for this child. It seems that recently her situation was changing. Postnatal care combined with social support could have been provided. Only if Deborah proved unable to care for her child would interventions and perhaps the extreme intervention of taking him into care be needed. As it turned out, Deborah — a new mother whose child had now been taken into custody without her consent — had needs that were not being met by her nurses. She experienced anger or grief, and probably felt victimized and judged because of her ethno-racial background and past. It would be hard for any nurse to gain her trust again.

To be morally responsive to Deborah, the nurses would ideally be working in an environment that enables them to provide care that reflects the professional values they hold. Rodney, Brown, and Liashenko (2004) argue that the moral situation of nurses is about "striving to do good when responding to the needs of the other" (p. 164); they use the term *relational matrix* to describe the connectedness of those working together in an organizational context. This type of environment helps nurses to develop a shared context that in turn validates their priorities for providing care. To weave professional integrity through their work with patients, nurses benefit from development of a critical perspective from which to examine and discuss the values and theories that guide their actions (Hardingham, 2004). If Ashley had learned while working with Joan that the norm was to raise moral concerns and discuss issues that threatened her integrity, she might then have felt comfortable interjecting suggestions about the approach to assessing Deborah's capacity as a parent or, if still indicated, removing her child. With either outcome, Deborah would be an active participant in the process and the plan of care would truly be patient-centred. This approach would consider the needs of both the child and parent.

Involving the mother in the process would mean that Deborah would have access to care after the decision about her parenting capacity was made. While Deborah would still have many needs to be met, she would more likely feel that she was able to count on the health care system for support. In the absence of this collaboration, Deborah would have a sense of being abandoned by her caregivers, placing her at considerable risk for engaging in the kinds of behaviours that had caused great difficulty for her in the first place.

This case demonstrates the moral strength that nurses need if they are going to be true to their ethical duties in the face of an established practice and culture of judging marginalized persons. If Ashley does not respond to the ethical dilemma, she will not have accord between her professional values and nursing practice. This lack of wholeness and harmony leads to moral distress. If this conflict is not resolved, Ashley could experience moral residue, which results from compromised integrity in a situation in which, because of organizational constraints, someone does not act in a way that reflects their professional values (Hardingham, 2004).

Instead, Ashley does decide to take action. She proposes to her manager a way of responding to this challenge to a nurse's integrity. First, the unit should identify high-risk mothers and remove the conflict of interest by assigning the baby and the mother to different nurses. If this is not feasible because of how work assignments are structured, high-risk mothers could be assigned to nurses who are able to provide patient-centred care to both mother and baby simultaneously.

Second, Ashley asks that nurses acknowledge the attitudes and values that rest behind certain judgements and consider the need for more information in such situations. She proposes that all staff be provided with diversity education in which they have the opportunity to examine, clarify, and share their personal and professional values. Given the high rate of First Nations babies being taken into custody, Ashley wants to learn more about why, and how, to reduce the need, or the perception of the need. All Ashley knows about First Nations persons comes from the media. She asks that representatives from First Nations social services agencies meet with their staff and that they start to work together. Ashley understands that this professional development process can be challenging, and for that reason she enlists the help of the manager and the unit educator. She also consults the hospital bioethicist for advice on the proper approach in making a suggestion for a change in the organizational environment.

## Case 2: Conscience and Assignment Refusal

Traditionally, as employees of health care organizations, nurses have believed in the impossibility of refusing an assignment. Today, with increased professional autonomy and guidelines from their professional organizations (CNA, 2008a; CNA, 2003), nurses now know that they can, under certain circumstances, refuse to take a certain job. Reasons for assignment refusal are bound up with concerns about professional integrity. Nurses might feel able to turn down an assignment because they recognize that they lack the knowledge, skill, and judgement to provide the expected level of care. Or it might be a matter of their personal beliefs and values, as in the case of refusal to assist with abortions.

Pandemics are yet another type of challenge. In the event of a pandemic, nurses might want to refuse an assignment because of worries about their safety and that of their families as opposed to giving care against their conscience.

> *Andrew has worked in the hospital for the past six years. He finds his work fulfilling. He is now an infection control nurse and involved in pandemic planning for the hospital. He supports the hospital policy that all nurses have a duty to care and must continue working unless it is unsafe for them to do so. During education sessions on pandemic planning with front-line staff, he learns that some nurses will not come to the hospital during a pandemic. Andrew explains that no one is expected to work when the environment is unsafe, and everything will be done to provide equipment and protection for the staff. Some staff members remain firm that they do not have a duty to come to work during a pandemic.*
>
> *Given the shortage of nurses, the employer wants to work with all staff to address their concerns. From the perspective of the nursing leadership and hospital management, the nurses should accept patient assignments during a pandemic unless they are sick or the environment is unsafe. Andrew is asked to help the nurses understand their ethical obligations to patients.*

## Commentary

Andrew could start by listening to the staff's fears. They may have worries about infecting their families. They may have worries about income loss if they become ill. They may have health conditions that cause them to be more vulnerable to infections. These concerns are valid. Hospital management must provide fair compensation for any staff or family members who are affected by pandemic conditions.

Andrew can help the staff understand the concept of professional integrity. One aspect of integrity is to be loyal to patients, peers, community, and society. To be loyal is to be dependable, trustworthy, and honest. By choosing to enter the profession, individuals have implicitly accepted that patient welfare is a priority. Nurses have moral autonomy and are therefore in a position to make decisions that they can act on and live with. The nurse-patient relationship is based on a power imbalance. Patients are vulnerable and depend on nurses for several reasons. They depend on nurses who have special knowledge and clinical experience to care for them, sometimes in life and death situations. Nurses have experience working in a complex health care system. They know how to advocate for patients, some of whom can lack the will or mental strength to speak for themselves. During a pandemic, access to health care will be rationed using a triage system. Patients with pandemic flu will rely on nurses keeping the promise to care for all patients regardless of age, gender, social class, sexual orientation, and nature of illness. Ethical principles underpinning pandemic planning include trust and equity (Joint Centre for Bioethics, 2005). While normally all patients have an equal claim to health care, during a pandemic decision-makers must make difficult decisions about implementing various control measures for public safety.

Nurses and other health care professionals, just by entering their professions, have accepted the duty to care. They might take this promise to be faithful to patients for granted until tested. Nurses' professional and ethical codes and guidelines state that they should advance the health and well-being of all patients, and during a pandemic this duty to care becomes paramount. In the event that nurses do not honour the duty to care, the results at the bedside and societal level can be tragic. Lives that could have been saved might be lost. Other people might suffer far longer than needed. If an unnecessary toll mounts during or after the pandemic, the public will understandably lose trust in the profession. People could possibly turn to nurses and tell them that they expected them to have cared with integrity, not just talk about it.

Andrew needs to be forthright and discuss the need for moral courage during a pandemic. Nurses can realize that they were socialized through their education to be guided by rules, policies, codes, and standards of practice. They may never before have needed to think about what it means to have integrity. Facing a pandemic can be a life-altering experience that prompts nurses to think about the values that form the foundation of their practice. A reliance on what was taught and "drilled into me" will not be enough. During a crisis nurses must reflect on what it means to have integrity and how this value is lived. Andrew can help nurses realize that integrity is translated into action when there is a coherence between what they value and how they provide care and lead their professional lives. Nurses have a duty to care, which is described as "a nurse's professional obligation to provide persons receiving care with safe, competent and ethical care" (CNA, 2008a, p. 46). When nurses have a carefully reasoned plan for accepting assignments to care for patients with pandemic flu, they will be enacting professional integrity.

Andrew should address the elephant in the room. It is reasonable to be afraid of contracting the pandemic flu and infecting loved ones. The relationship between nurses and patients is built on trust; and, similarly, the employer, nursing leadership, and health care system leaders must also meet their ethical responsibilities in respect to the health and well-being of nurses. In Ontario in 2003, with the SARS outbreak, many lessons were learned about how to support nurses. Of the forty-three persons who died from SARS, two were nurses.

Clear, accurate, and timely communication is essential. Nurses must be provided with a safe environment. As part of that, nurses must have knowledge about the latest developments in caring for patients during a pandemic. Education and staff development must keep up with any adjustments in practice required. Nurses must have high-quality equipment, and workplace hazards must be removed. When nurses are not supported through education, communication systems, and infection control departments, and lack a safe environment, they are justified in withdrawing care. But before they do so, if possible, nurses should advocate for improvements and offer recommendations for resolving issues.

The nurse's health and welfare are a priority. When they face serious risks nurses are justified in exercising moral autonomy to protect their health. In doing so, nurses are enacting professional integrity because they have assumed control over and accountability for their professional lives. These concerns need to be discussed at various levels within the organization so that the needs of all stakeholders are equitably considered and addressed. In planning for a pandemic, "all parties need to work together in a transparent and collaborative manner to analyze the issues and make appropriate policy decisions" (CNA, 2008b, p. 8).

The moral values and principles to which we commit ourselves are implicit promises. We project ourselves into the future as the sort of person whose actions will be guided by the promises made to ourselves. More or less explicitly, we promise others that we can be counted on to act in a way that is consistent with the moral values and principles we profess. To be sure, many factors and forces will influence this action, and at all times we must be mindful of those conditions. By taking initiative, Andrew can help nurses reflect on their professional values and help them keep in mind why they entered nursing.

## Case 3: Preserving Integrity

Nurses are sometimes employed in positions that place them in a conflict of interest. They become torn between loyalty to the patient and to their employer. One field of nursing in which these tensions are often experienced is forensic nursing. The needs and identity of patients can be blurred because in addition to requiring health care they are also serving prison sentences. Likewise, the roles of nurses can be blurred. Often the workplace bears no resemblance to a health care setting. In the following case, nurses have come to believe that their integrity is being undermined by the employer's expectations.

*Pierre is employed as a forensic nurse in a maximum-security correctional institute. Many prisoners have mental health and other persistent health problems. Pierre's responsibilities include counselling, administration of medications, and teaching about health. He is frustrated. Several patients tell Pierre that the guards use physical force to "settle things down." Pierre sees that the prisoners have unexplained bruises on their bodies. One evening Pierre sees for himself guards being rough in their treatment of inmates. He talks to a guard in the health clinic, who explains that force is needed to maintain order for prisoners and staff. Pierre disapproves of the guards' actions, yet knows that reporting the incident will be highly unpopular with his peers and management.*

*Pierre wants to deal with his concerns, but there are extraneous factors involved and he believes that he is in a difficult position. At staff meetings he has heard homophobic and racist comments. During his employment Pierre has protected his private life and has not told his colleagues that he is gay and that his partner is First Nations. He loves forensic nursing, but he finds the work environment unethical. He is uncertain how to respond to the situation, but he knows he must advocate for change.*

## Commentary

Pierre is experiencing the moral dilemma faced by all potential whistleblowers. He knows what he ought to do, but also knows that the consequences will be harsh. Colleagues might ostracize him. Employment conditions might become so stressful that he will need to resign; yet his partner and family are settled in the community. Changing employment would mean relocation and hardship for his children and partner.

The root cause of his dilemma is the ambiguity of his role and relationship with prisoners. Prisoners are reluctant to trust Pierre and his peers because they believe that their confidentiality will not be respected. Pierre is expected to report behaviour that raises safety concerns. Pierre's focus should be on the prisoners as patients, but he knows that his responsibilities also involve custodial duties. He relies on guards to maintain a safe environment, but he knows that there is a culture of looking the other way as long as physical force does not get out of hand. The health care clinic has accepted this culture. Thus Pierre's values and beliefs are in conflict with colleagues, peers, and management. It can be the case that prior to this point Pierre had attempted to model integrity with his professional colleagues and the guards, but now it is time for another kind of action.

Pierre knows that his priority should be the health and welfare of the prisoners. In this environment he is not able to honour his core professional values of respect for privacy, choice, dignity, and access to health care. He has made compromises to get along with the staff, but the physical violence has now tipped the scales. Pierre realizes that with many of the prisoners, who need excellent nursing care, he is not maintaining therapeutic relationships based on trust. Integrity involves wholeness of person. Instead, Pierre feels torn in many ways.

Pierre has some hard choices to make. As Huston and Brox (2004) put it: "To fight each and every injustice in the workplace is often not worth the emotional expense. However, some situations do demand action" (p. 269). He knows that he should intervene to stop what he sees as physical abuse of his patients. He thinks about how to proceed. He reviews standards of practice for therapeutic relationships, prevention of abuse, and neglect of patients. He reviews the code of ethics. He studies the policies of the health clinic. To be prudent, Pierre should seek support before he reports the abuse, but he should also determine that the actions of the guards are not ethically supported. If he has colleagues who share his concerns, that would be a start. He could seek the advice of his jurisdiction's College of Nurses and other professional nursing groups. His labour organization could be another source of support. He is enrolled in a legal protection plan through the professional organization, and so he can seek legal advice. Hardingham (2004) points out that "gaining and maintaining our integrity is a relational process in which we need to reflect within ourselves and have a dialogue with others to do the work that allows us to settle on our principles and values, and to be able to justify them to others" (p. 131). Along with his related beliefs and values, talking with others will help Pierre clarify the problem. These discussions will help him articulate his position when he decides the time is right to make his case.

Pierre's partner also supports his decision to report the abuse. This decision should not be taken lightly, because "nurses who blow the whistle can suffer a range of serious physical and mental health problems.... Their professional lives and careers can be left in tatters," particularly when colleagues and employers harass or intimidate them or employers threaten dismissal (Johnstone, 2005, p. 8). Pierre recognizes this danger, but he wants to be certain that the fallout is not more than he can endure in his personal life.

Pierre is realistic. He knows that his actions may not end patient abuse. He expects to be criticized by some peers and colleagues. But he has accepted that, for him, professional integrity is a priority. He cannot continue to be silent, because to do so is to be as responsible as the persons harming the prisoners/patients.

Pierre is demonstrating moral courage and deserves the support of his nursing colleagues. They may need time to understand his reasoning. Yet they should not penalize him for deciding that the prisoners are individuals who deserve respect and who need their nurses to be their advocates. If he fails to obtain a satisfactory response, he can go beyond the management of the institution. Certainly each further step taken would escalate the issue to a new level and would entail more serious consequences.

Pierre knows that, unfortunately, some members of the public and his colleagues can express a lack of concern for the welfare of prisoners. But Pierre does know that the trust of the public is essential to a profession. A profession earns this trust by publicly professing certain standards and values for its members, and accepting responsibility for ensuring that they are upheld. This responsibility encompasses not only technical standards, but also ethical rules, including those professed in a code of ethics. The behaviour of one nurse reflects, for good or ill, on her or his profession as a whole. If he failed to live up to professional standards he would put the reputation of the profession at risk. If sufficiently serious and frequent, such failures could undermine the confidence of the public in the profession. Not only Pierre's integrity but also the integrity of all nurses could be called into question.

Certainly, the challenge for Pierre and his colleagues in enacting the professional values of integrity and acting in good conscience is directly related to the tone of the moral climate within which they work. Hardingham (2004) rightly makes the point that it is difficult to expect individuals to act in a way that reflects their moral values and integrity "unless we provide an environment in which they are able to do so" (p. 133). The role of managers includes supporting nurses to collaborate with colleagues and other health team members in advocating for work environments that are "conducive to the health and wellbeing of clients and others in the setting" (CNA, 2008a, p. 18). It is only reasonable to expect nurses to practise with integrity and to advocate for patients in an organization and health care system in which policies and managers provide an environment that allows that to happen.

## Conclusion

In their professional role, nurses are moral agents and responsible and accountable for conducting themselves in accordance with personal and professional values and principles. To be responsible and accountable, they need to reflect on their values and principles and engage in dialogue with others about those standards. The challenge of integrity is to realize and uphold the values and principles, even and especially in situations in which countervailing forces pull in an opposite direction. As Mappes (1986, p. 129) emphasized a generation ago, "the nurse's moral obligation is no less real" when she or he is constrained or pressured by difficult realities. Indeed, nurses have made progress. For example, Varcoe and Rodney (2009) noted recently that, according to their research, nurses respond to moral distress by enacting moral resistance in both overt and covert ways. For instance, when faced with ethical problems, despite constraints, nurses "made efforts to 'get to know' their patients, to work with others as a team, and to negotiate better care" (p. 137).

Integrity requires nurses to take action on the basis of their professional values. When personal risks are associated with standing up for what is right, this can take courage; and the courage to take a stand is best enacted when nurses stand with, rather than against, others. As Andrew Jameton (1990), the ethicist who first defined moral distress, put it, "We want, as participants in institutional culture, to be able to notice our moral problems and to cope with them with sensitivity and integrity and to keep our health care institutions responsive to their moral goals" (p. 450).

## Notes

1   The following discussion of this breakdown borrows from but goes beyond Mitchell's (1982) helpful analysis of the concept of integrity.

2   Moral autonomy, which is the sense of autonomy mainly at issue in this chapter, is similar in meaning to autonomy as moral reflection (see chapter 4).

3   There is a compelling metaphor expressing this point that one of the authors (Rodney) heard at a conference over twenty years ago. The speaker, a

renowned nurse ethicist, stated, "Just because perfect asepsis isn't possible, it doesn't mean we have to do surgery in a sewer." In other words, we can commit to doing *better* without getting paralyzed by the despair of not being able to achieve "perfect [moral] asepsis."

4      For an account of this struggle from an ethical point of view, see "Nursing's Struggle for Autonomy," in Jameton (1984, pp. 36-57). Crowder (1974) and Lamb (2004) also have good discussions of the history of nursing ethics vis-à-vis various codes of ethics. These discussions also help us to understand how crucial the formulation of codes of ethics were in the development of nursing as a profession.

5      Davis (1983) provides a thought-provoking discussion of the challenges facing nurses who were working in hospital settings over twenty years ago. See also Chambliss (1996) and Varcoe and Rodney (2009) for more recent accounts.

6      For examples of how nurses at all levels of practice can come together with each other and their colleagues in other health care professions to begin to make positive changes in their practice environments, see Rodney and Street (2004) and Storch et al. (2009).

7      For thought-provoking discussions of the nurse-physician relationship, see MacIntyre (1983) and Storch and Kenny (2007).

8      Jameton (1984) first coined the term "moral distress" as it relates to nursing. Some of the subsequent literature and studies on moral distress are reviewed in Wilkinson (1988) and Rodney, Brown, & Liaschenko (2004). See also Austin (2007); Hamric, Davis, & Childress (2006); Hardingham (2004); and Corley et al. (2005).

9      For an early discussion of "integrity-preserving compromise," see Benjamin and Curtis (1986, pp. 105-108).

## References

American Nurses' Association. (1985). *Code for nurses with interpretive statements*. Kansas City.

Austin, W. (2007). The ethics of everyday practice: Healthcare environments as moral communities. *Advances in Nursing Science* 30 (1), 81-88.

Bandura, A. (2002). Selective moral disengagement in the exercise of moral agency. *Journal of Moral Education* 31 (2), 101-119.

Baylis, F. (2007). Of courage, honor, and integrity. In L.A. Eckenwiler and F.G. Cohn (Eds.), *The ethics of bioethics: Mapping the moral landscape* (pp. 193-204). Baltimore: John Hopkins University Press.

Benjamin, M., & Curtis, J. (1986). *Ethics in nursing* (2nd ed.). New York: Oxford University Press.

Bishop, A.H., & Scudder, J.R. Jr. (1987). Nursing ethics in an age of controversy. *Advances in Nursing Science* 9 (3), 34-43.

Buresh, B., & Gordon S. (2000). *From silence to voice: What nurses know and must communicate to the public.* Ottawa: Canadian Nurses Association.

Canadian Nurses Association. (2003). *Ethical distress in health care environments.* Ottawa.

Canadian Nurses Association. (2008a). *Code of ethics for registered nurses.* Ottawa.

Canadian Nurses Association. (2008b). *Nurses' ethical considerations in a pandemic or other emergency.* Ottawa.

Canadian Nurses Association. (2009). *Tested solutions for eliminating Canada's registered nurse shortage.* Ottawa.

Carnerie, F. (1989). Patient advocacy. *The Canadian Nurse* 85 (11), 20.

Chambliss, D.F. (1996). *Beyond caring: Hospitals, nurses, and the social organization of ethics.* Chicago: University of Chicago Press.

College of Nurses of Ontario. (2008). *Refusing assignments and discontinuing nursing services.* Toronto.

College of Registered Nurses of British Columbia (CRNBC). (2006). *Tools for resolving professional practice problems.* Vancouver <http://www.crnbc.ca/downloads/403.pdf>.

Conway, M.E. (1983). Prescription for professionalization. In N.L. Chaska (Ed.), *The nursing profession: A time to speak* (pp. 29-37). New York: McGraw-Hill.

Corley, M.C., Minick, P., Elswick, R.K., & Jacobs, M. (2005). Nurse moral distress and ethical work environment. *Nursing Ethics* 12 (4), 381-390.

Côté, A. & Fox, G. (2007). *The Future of Home Care in Canada: Roundtable Outcomes and Recommendations for the Future.* Ottawa: Public Policy Forum <http://www.ppforum.com/sites/default/files/Future_Homecare_Report_EN_0.pdf>.

Crowder, E. (1974). Manners, morals, and nurses: An historical overview of nursing ethics. *Texas Reports on Biology and Medicine* 32 (1), 173-180.

David, B.A. (2000). Nursing's gender politics: Reformulating the footnotes. *Advances in Nursing Science* 23 (1), 83–93.

Davis, A.J. (1983). Authority, autonomy, ethical decision-making, and collective bargaining in hospitals. In C.P. Murphy & J. Hunter (Eds.), *Ethical problems in the nurse-patient relationship* (pp. 63-76). Boston: Allyn & Bacon.

Flaherty, M.J. (1985). Ethical issues. In M. Stewart, J. Innes, S. Searl, & C. Smillie (Eds.), *Community health nursing in Canada* (pp. 97-113). Toronto: Gage.

Greenwood, E. (1983). Attributes of a profession. In B. Baumrin & B. Freedman (Eds.), *Moral responsibility and the professions* (pp. 20-32). New York: Haven Publications.

Hammond, M. (1990). Is nursing a semi-profession? *The Canadian Nurse* 86 (2), 20-23.

Hamric, A., & Blackhall, L.J. (2007). Nurse-physician perspectives on the care of dying patients in intensive care units. *Critical Care Medicine* 35, 422-429.

Hamric, A.B., Davis, W.S., & Childress, M.D. (2006). Moral distress in health care professionals: What is it and what can we do about it? *The Pharos* 69 (1), 16-23.

Hardingham, L. B. (2004). Integrity and moral residue: Nurses as participants in a moral community. *Nursing Philosophy* 5 (2), 127-134.

Hardingham, L. (2010). Ethical and legal issues in nursing. In M. McIntyre & C. McDonald (Eds.), *Realities of Canadian nursing: Professional, practice, and power issues* (3rd ed.; pp. 337-354). Philadelphia: Wolters Kluwer, Lippincott Williams & Wilkins.

Hartrick Doane, G., & Varcoe, C. (2005). *Family nursing as relational inquiry: Developing health promoting practice.* Philadelphia: Lippincott, Williams, & Wilkins.

Huston, J. & Brox, G. (2004). Professional ethics at the bottom line. *The Health Care Manager* 23 (3), 267-272.

Jameton, A.L. (1984). *Nursing practice: The ethical issues.* Englewood Cliffs, NJ: Prentice-Hall.

Jameton, A. (1990). Culture, morality, and ethics: Twirling the spindle. *Critical Care Nursing Clinics of North America* 2 (3), 443–451.

Johnstone, M.J. (1988). Law, professional ethics and the problem of conflict with personal values. *International Journal of Nursing Studies* 25 (2), 147-157.

Johnstone, M.J. (2005). Whistle blowing and accountability. *Australian Nursing Journal* 13 (5), 8-10.

Joint Centre for Bioethics. (2005). *Stand on guard for thee: Ethical considerations in preparedness planning for pandemic influenza.* University of Toronto.

Lamb, M. (2004). An historical perspective on nursing and nursing ethics. In J. Storch, P. Rodney, & R. Starzomski (Eds.), *Toward a moral horizon: Nursing ethics for leadership and practice* (pp. 20-41). Toronto: Pearson-Prentice Hall.

Liaschenko, J. (1994). Making a bridge: The moral work with patients we do not like. *Journal of Palliative Care* 10 (3), 83–89.

MacIntyre, A. (1983). To whom is the nurse responsible? In C.P. Murphy & J. Hunter (Eds.), *Ethical problems in the nurse-patient relationship* (pp. 79-83). Boston: Allyn & Bacon.

Mappes, E.J.K. (1986). Ethical dilemmas for nurses: Physicians' orders versus patients' rights. In T.A. Mappes & J.S. Zembaty (Eds.), *Biomedical ethics* (2nd ed., pp. 127-134). New York: McGraw-Hill.

McDonald, C., & McIntyre, M. (2010). Issues arising from the nature of nurses' work and workplaces. In M. McIntyre & C. McDonald (Eds.), *Realities of Canadian nursing: Professional, practice, and power issues* (3rd ed., pp. 283-302). Philadelphia: Wolters Kluwer, Lippincott Williams & Wilkins.

Mitchell, C. (1982). Integrity in interprofessional relationships. In G.J. Agich (Ed.), *Responsibility in health care* (pp. 163-184). Boston: D. Reidel.

Mitchell, G.J. (2001). Policy, procedure and routine: Matters of moral influence. *Nursing Science Quarterly* 14 (2), 109-114.

Nelson, M.J. (1982). Authenticity: Fabric of ethical nursing practice. *Advances in Nursing Science* 4 (1), 1-6.

Oberle, K., & Bouchal, S.R. (2009). *Ethics in Canadian nursing practice: Navigating the journey.* Toronto: Pearson-Prentice Hall.

Pendry, P.S. (2007). Moral distress: Recognizing it to retain nurses. *Nursing Economics* 25 (4), 217-221.

Peter, E. (2004). Home health care and ethics. In J. Storch, P. Rodney, & R. Starzomski (Eds.), *Toward a moral horizon: Nursing ethics for leadership and practice* (pp. 248-261). Toronto: Pearson-Prentice Hall.

Robb, I.H. (1900). *Nursing ethics: For hospital and private use.* Cleveland: Koeckert.

Rodney, P. (1994). A nursing perspective on life-prolonging treatment. *Journal of Palliative Care Medicine* 10 (2), 40-44.

Rodney, P., Brown, H., & Liaschenko, J. (2004). Moral agency: Relational connections and trust. In J. Storch, P. Rodney, & R. Starzomski (Eds.), *Toward a moral horizon: Nursing ethics for leadership and practice* (pp. 154-177). Toronto: Pearson-Prentice Hall.

Rodney, P., Doane, G.H., Storch, J. & Varcoe, C. (2006). Workplaces: Toward a safer moral climate. *Canadian Nurse* 102 (8), 24-27.

Rodney, P., & Street, A. (2004). The moral climate of nursing practice: Inquiry and action. In J. Storch, P. Rodney, & R. Starzomski (Eds.), *Toward a moral horizon: Nursing ethics for leadership and practice* (pp. 209-231). Toronto: Pearson-Prentice Hall.

Scherer, P. (1987). When every day is Saturday: The shortage. *American Journal of Nursing* 87 (10), 1284-1290.

Stein, J.G. (2001). *The cult of efficiency.* Toronto: Anansi.

Storch, J.L. (1988). Ethics in nursing practice. In A.J. Baumgart & J. Larsen (Eds.), *Nursing faces the future: Development and change* (pp. 211-221). St. Louis: C.V. Mosby.

Storch, J.L. (2004). End-of-life decision-making. In J. Storch, P. Rodney, & R. Starzomski (Eds.), *Toward a moral horizon: Nursing ethics for leadership and practice* (pp. 262-284). Toronto: Pearson-Prentice Hall.

Storch, J.L., & Kenny, N. (2007). Shared moral work of nurses and physicians. *Nursing Ethics* 14 (4), 478–491.

Storch, J., Rodney, P., Pauly, B., Fulton, T., Stevenson, L., Newton, L., & Makaroff, K.S. (2009). Enhancing ethical climates in nursing work environments. *Canadian Nurse* 105 (3), 20-25.

Thompson, J.E., & Thompson, H.O. (1988). Living with ethical decisions with which you disagree. MCN: *American Journal of Child Maternal Nursing* 13 (4), 245-248, 250.

Tunna, K., & Conner, M. (1993). You are your ethics. *The Canadian Nurse* 89 (5), 25-26.

Varcoe, C. (2010). Interpersonal violence and abuse: Ending the silence. In M. McIntyre & C. McDonald (Eds.), *Realities of Canadian nursing: Professional, practice, and power issues* (3rd ed., pp. 414-434). Philadelphia: Wolters Kluwer, Lippincott Williams & Wilkins.

Varcoe, C., & Rodney, P. (2009). Constrained agency: The social structure of nurses' work. In B.S. Singh & H.D. Harley (Eds.), *Health, illness and health care in Canada* (pp. 122-151). Toronto: Nelson Education.

Webster, G.C., & Baylis, F.E. (2000). Moral residue. In S.B. Rubin and L. Zoloth (Eds.), *Margin of error: The ethics of mistakes in the practice of medicine* (pp. 217-230). Hagerstown, MD: University Publishing Group.

Wilkinson, J.M. (1988). Moral distress in nursing practice: Experience and effect. *Nursing Forum* 23 (1), 16-29.

Yarling, R.R., & McElmurry, B.J. (1986). The moral foundation of nursing. *Advances in Nursing Science* 8 (2), 63-73.

Zuzelo, P.R. (2007). Exploring the moral distress of registered nurses. *Nursing Ethics* 14 (3), 344-359.

# Study Questions: Integrity

## Case 1: Integrity and Nurses' Relationships with Colleagues and Employers

1. If your team or you were working in this setting, caring for Deborah, what compassionate and ethical responses would you make to her expressed concerns about the situation she is in? How would you help the team to maintain or adjust their attitudes so a patient in a similar situation would receive care based on sound moral values?

2. If you were in Ashley's position, what factors would you experience as barriers to acting with integrity? How would you respond to these barriers? How would you approach Joan, a senior colleague with whom you expect to be working for some time?

3. Imagine that you do ask to discuss the case with Joan. Her response is that based on her experience she knows what is best for the mother and child. She adds, "With time you will see that the 'real world of nursing' is a far cry from the classroom. If you don't adapt to the clinical realities, you will burn out." Consider why Joan makes this statement. If you were Ashley, how would you respond to the situation at that moment, later in the day, and in the long term? What steps can Ashley take to prevent feeling that she has lost her sense of integrity and should leave the profession?

4. You have just been hired as an educator for the unit that is caring for Deborah, and you sense that some staff members are experiencing moral distress and moral residue. How would you learn the root causes of the staff's problems with providing ethical care? What factors contributed to the situation? How would you respond, and what strategies would help you to address this problem with the staff?

5. Ashley has been told that sometimes you have to tell a "white lie" to restore calm. Also, you may need to withhold information or be silent to protect the patient or yourself from a difficult situation. Are these types of deception morally defensible? Consider a situation in which you or a colleague has not been truthful or told a lie. What was the impact on your integrity?

6. Ashley believes that there is tension between her mentors. Joan may think that Ashley wants to "do everything according to the book" and does not know the real world of nursing. Ashley may think that Joan is an example of senior nurses "eating their young." What can both nurses do to reduce the tension and support each of them in their goal of being ethical?

## Case 2: Conscience and Assignment Refusal

1. What are your thoughts about the situation that Andrew is encountering? What would you feel, think, and do if you were in his situation as an educator?

2. What do you know about your employer's or clinical placement's plan for a pandemic? Do you agree with their position/policy? What moral principles form the basis for their policy? Could you continue to work during a pandemic under the policy of your organization? What recommendations for change would you make?

3. Discuss with colleagues their experience during a similar situation. What were their fears and loyalties, and how did these challenge their professional integrity? How did they deal with their concerns? How would you have dealt with those concerns?

4. You are concerned about patients who might be infectious coming to your organization, and you believe that staff are not being provided with enough protection to provide care under safe conditions. How and to whom in your organization would you express your concerns to ensure that they are heard and responded to in a timely

and appropriate manner? Look at the Canadian Nurses Association *Code of Ethics* (2008) and your regulatory college's statements about the duty to care during a pandemic and crisis. How do these provide guidance for your practice?

## Case 3: Preserving Integrity

1. Think of a situation in your own practice that was not acceptable from your perspective or that of your colleagues. What environmental factors were present that supported or interfered with your ability to maintain integrity in your work? How did or could you deal with these to make appropriate changes?

2. If you were Pierre's colleague, how would you advise him about his plan to bring the abuse of the prisoners to the attention of authorities? What resources would you suggest that could be especially helpful to him, and why?

3. If you were one of the forensic nursing managers, how would you respond to Pierre's concerns? How would you share his concerns with your colleagues while attempting to bring some resolution to the problem?

4. Put yourself in Pierre's shoes. His employer has policies about respecting diversity. The Canadian Nurses Association *Code of Ethics* speaks out against discrimination and calls for respect for all colleagues. Granted that Pierre has legal and professional protection if he experiences discrimination in the workplace, what would be his next step? What benefits and risks might he encounter if he moves in that direction?

5. Nurses come from all walks of life. Reflect on your nursing education program or your workplace. Although nurses and patients are protected by laws against discrimination and harassment based on sexual orientation, gender, and age, do you find that these values are translated into action?

# APPENDIX A
# An Ethical Decision-Making Framework for Individuals (2009)[1]

BY *Michael McDonald*, PhD, W. Maurice Young Centre for Applied Ethics, University of British Columbia (UBC)
ADAPTED BY *P. Rodney*, RN PhD (UBC School of Nursing) & *R. Starzomski*, RN PhD (University of Victoria School of Nursing)

*November 19, 2009 Version*

## 1. Collect Information and Identify the Problem(s)

a) Identify what you know and *what you don't know but need to know.* Be prepared to add to/update your information *throughout* the decision-making process.

b) Gather as much information as possible on the patient's physical, psychological, social, cultural, and spiritual status, including changes over time. Seek input from the patient, family, friends, and other health care team members.

c) Investigate the patient's assessment of their own quality of life, and their wishes about the treatment/care decision(s) at hand. This includes determining the patient's competency as well as determining what family members the patient wants involved in discussions about and/or decision-making in their treatment/care. If the patient is not competent, look for an advance directive. Identify a proxy decision-maker for patients who are not competent and seek evidence of the patient's prior expressed wishes. Regardless of the patient's competence (capacity), involve the patient as much as possible in all decisions affecting him/her.

d) Include a family assessment; their roles, relationships, and relevant stories.

e) Identify the health care team members involved, and circumstances affecting them.

f) Summarize the situation briefly but with all the relevant facts and circumstances. Try to get a sense of the patient's overall health and illness trajectory.

g) What decisions have to be made? By whom?

## 2. Specify Feasible Alternatives for Treatment and Care

a) Use your clinical expertise to identify a wide range and scope of alternatives. *Avoid binary thinking* (such as "treat/don't treat") and lay out carefully tailored alternatives for the problems you have identified.

b) Identify *how* various alternatives might be implemented (e.g., time trials).

## 3. Use Your Ethics Resources to Evaluate Alternatives

a) *Principles/Concepts*

*AUTONOMY*: What does the patient want? How well has the patient been informed and/or supported? What explicit or implicit promises have been made to the patient?

*NONMALEFICENCE*: Will this harm the patient? Others?

*BENEFICENCE*: Will this benefit the patient? Others?

*JUSTICE*: Consider the interests of all those (including the patient) who have to be taken into account. Are biases about the patient or family affecting your decision-making? Treat like situations alike.

*FIDELITY*: Are you fostering trust in patient/family/team relationships?

*CARE*: Will the patient and family be supported as they deal with loss, grief, and/or uncertainty? What about any moral distress of team members? What principles of palliative care can be incorporated into the alternatives?

*RELATIONAL AUTONOMY*: What relationships and social structures are affecting the various individuals involved in the situation? How can these relationships and social structures become more supportive of the patient, family members, and health care providers?

b) *Standards*
Examine professional norms, standards and codes, legal precedents, health care agency policy.

c) *Personal judgements and experiences*
Consider yours, your colleagues', and other members of the health care team.

d) *Organized procedures for ethical consultation*
Draw on the expertise of the resources in the health care agency. Consider a formal case conference(s), an ethics committee meeting, and/or an ethics consultant, especially if the situation is complex and/or conflicted. Survey relevant bioethics literature/reference materials.

## 4. Propose and Test Possible Resolutions

a) Select the best alternative(s), all things considered.

b) Perform a sensitivity analysis. Consider your choice(s) critically: Which factors would have to change to get you to alter your decision(s)? Then carefully consider whether you want to maintain or change your previous choice(s).

c) Think about the effects of your choice(s) upon others' choices: Are you making it easier for others (health care providers, patients and their families, etc.) to act ethically?

d) Is this what a compassionate health care professional would do in a caring environment?

e) Formulate your choice(s) as a general maxim for all similar situations. Think of situations where it does *not* apply. Consider situations where it does apply.

f) Are you and the other decision-makers still comfortable with your choice(s)? *If you do not have consensus, revisit the process.* Remember that you are not aiming at "the" perfect choice, but the best possible choice.

g) Ensure that there is a clear implementation plan. Ensure that the rationale for and details of the plan are clearly communicated to all those who will be affected (patient, family, and health care providers). Be sure that the implementation plan includes feedback from relevant individuals (the patient, family and friends, health care providers).

## 5. Make your choice

Live with it and learn from it! Seek feedback on the process from all those involved. Take the opportunity to reflect on how you will deal with other challenging situations in the future. Consider organizing follow-up debriefings and continuing education sessions and/or planning changes to related policies and procedures.

## Note

1    The authors thank Dr. Michael McDonald for his kind permission to use this version of his *"Ethical Decision Making Framework for Individuals."* An earlier version of this framework also appeared as an Appendix in: Storch, J., Rodney, P., & Starzomski, R. (Eds.) (2004), *Toward a moral horizon: Nursing ethics for leadership and practice* (pp. 512-514). Toronto: Pearson-Prentice Hall.

# APPENDIX B
## ETHICAL/STAKEHOLDER ANALYSIS (RESPECT)

Ethicists have formalized the process of ethical analysis in various decision procedures or guides. Often, these are organized sequentially in terms of steps in the decision-making process.

The ethical analysis and decision procedure offered here (acronym: RESPECT) incorporates the main features identified in most such procedures. The points are listed sequentially, but responsible decision-making need not follow this sequence exactly.

This analytic tool is oriented around the idea of stakeholders. A stakeholder is someone who will be affected by a given decision and who in virtue of this effect is entitled to have his or her interests and values considered and respected in the decision-making process. A stakeholder is also someone to whom one owes an account for one's decision.

1. **R**ECOGNIZE MORAL DIMENSION OF TASK OR PROBLEM

2. **E**NUMERATE GUIDING AND EVALUATIVE PRINCIPLES

3. **S**PECIFY STAKEHOLDERS AND THEIR GUIDING PRINCIPLES

4. **P**LOT VARIOUS ACTION ALTERNATIVES

5. **E**VALUATE ALTERNATIVES IN LIGHT OF PRINCIPLES & STAKEHOLDERS

6. **C**ONSULT & INVOLVE STAKEHOLDERS AS APPROPRIATE

7. **T**ELL STAKEHOLDERS THE REASONS FOR THE DECISION

It is important to understand that this is not a formula that can be mechanically applied to output "right" answers to moral questions. Rather, it is a process to be followed to ensure that all considerations relevant to a given moral issue or decision are carefully identified and weighed. Working through such a process will help ensure that the decision one reaches will be morally justifiable and defensible and that one will therefore be able to give proper account for it. The check marks beside each point can be viewed as reminders of the sorts of things one should consider and review in advance of making a moral decision or a decision with a significant moral component.

# ABOUT THE AUTHORS

**Michael Yeo, PhD**
Michael is an Associate Professor in the Department of Philosophy at Laurentian University. His two main areas of research are bioethics and ethics and public policy. He has done policy work for a variety of organizations, including the Canadian Medical Association, College of Family Physicians of Canada, Canadian Nursing Association, and Privacy Commission of Canada.

**Anne Moorhouse, RN, PhD**
Anne is a Professor in the Seneca-York Collaborative BScN Nursing Program, Toronto, and teaches bioethics at Ryerson University. She is a former member of the Canadian Nurses Association ethics advisory group and a consultant on ethical issues for the Registered Nurses Association of Ontario.

**Pamela Khan BN, MSc(A)**
Pamela is a Senior Lecturer at the Lawrence S. Bloomberg Faculty of Nursing and a member of the Joint Centre for Bioethics, both at the University of Toronto.

**Patricia (Paddy) Rodney, RN, MSN, PhD**
Paddy is an Associate Professor at the University of British Columbia (UBC) School of Nursing. She is also a Faculty Associate with the Mary and Maurice Young Centre for Applied Ethics at UBC and a Research Associate with Providence Health Care Ethics Services. Paddy is a member of the ethics committee at BC Women's Hospital in Vancouver and an ethics consultant on the BC Provincial Advisory Panel on Cardiac Health. Her research and publications focus on end-of-life decision-making and the moral climate of health care delivery.

# INDEX

Aboriginal people. *See* First Nations
  people
abortion, 24, 28, 45, 359
  conflict for some nurses, 45, 354,
    359, 368, 373
  "therapeutic," 112
abuse in the workplace, 108, 360. *See
  also* patient abuse
access to health care, 298, 307
  *vs.* quality of care, 316–21
Accord on Health Care Renewal, 84
accountability, 15, 24, 40–42, 298, 313
  for custody of health information,
    259
  nurses, 197, 357, 361, 376, 381
  provincial governments, 84
  for resource allocation decisions,
    304
acquired brain injury, 147
act utilitarianism, 55
active euthanasia, 171–73, 176, 195–96
adolescents, 157, 191. *See also* mature
  minor
  special ethical challenges for nurses,
    161
advance directives (or living wills),
  162–63
advocacy, 64, 89, 150–54
  autonomy-oriented, 151
  for better working conditions and
    patient care, 92
  "existential advocacy," 20
  nurses need to advocate for selves
    and profession, 92, 360, 381
  patient advocacy, 19

patient's advocate (nurse's role),
  18–20, 113, 151, 153, 180–85,
  197, 360
  social justice and human rights
    advocacy, 20
  for vulnerable and marginalized
    persons, 180–85
age of consent, 115
aging of population. *See* elderly
  people
AIDS, 264
Alberta, 82, 93
alcoholics, 294, 304
allocation of resources. *See* resource
  allocation and decision-making
alternative therapies, 120
Alzheimer's, 158
American Hospital Association
  "Patients' Bill of Rights," 15
American Nurses' Association, 212
  Code for Nurses, 23
Americanization of the Canadian
  health care system, 85
amyotrophic lateral sclerosis (ALS),
  175–77
Aristotle, *Nichomachean Ethics*, 56
assessment (in ethical analysis), 28–30
assessment of capacity. *See* capacity
  assessments
assignment refusal, 359, 368, 373
assisted suicide, 45, 171, 173–77, 196,
  355
at-risk babies, 110, 294
attention, 65–66
Augustinian sisters, 104
authority, 15
autonomy, 119, 143–97, 356, 392
  as advocacy and empowerment,
    150–53

public accountability, 15
repercussions from health care reform, 78
health promotion, 81, 128, 300
Hepatitis C virus (HCV), 130, 132
Hippocratic Oath, 128, 245
HIV, 130, 132
  confidentiality issues, 264–65, 267
home-care, 83–84, 91. *See also* community care
homeless persons, 128, 131
homicide, 171, 174
hospital closures or mergers, 78, 81
Hôtel-Dieu Hôpital, Quebec City, 174
human good, 57–58
human nature, 56
human rights advocacy, 20
hypocrisy, 353

ICN Code of Ethics for Nurses (International Council of Nurses), 23
impartiality. *See* fairness
implementation (in ethical analysis), 31
income level. *See also* poverty
  as determinant of health, 86
increased acuity/complexity of patients, 88
indirect euthanasia, 171
individual rights, 15, 114
information disclosure, 209, 358
  based on patient's own good, 208
  benefits of, 211
  change in attitude concerning, 208–09
  diagnosis of mental illness, 221–26
  disclosure without consent, 245, 255, 258–59 (*See also* breaches of confidentiality)

as exclusive prerogative of the physician, 219
  fears of negative consequences, 210–11
  legal requirements to disclose, 254–55, 273–75, 277
  "no-new-information" policy, 207, 218–19
  nurse/physician conflicts, 218–20
  ongoing dialogue, 217–18, 220
  therapeutic benefits, 209
  Western society, 229
information sharing
  "need-to-know," 252
  patient authorization and, 251
information technology experts, 258
informational privacy, 248
informed consent, 15, 128, 148, 151, 153, 191, 198n6, 212
  age of consent, 115 (*See also* mature minor)
  coercion or coercive pressure, 153–54
  competence and capacity to decide, 156–61 (*See also* capacity assessments)
  cultural factors and, 156
  knowledge aspect of, 154
  legal and professional duties mandating, 155
  nursing responsibilities regarding, 117, 147, 154–55
  in research and experimentation, 14
  rooted in principle of autonomy, 305
  substitute decision-making, 162–63
informed decisions, 217, 229
injection drug users (IDUs), 129–30, 132, 304
  barriers to treatment, 131

moral conflicts. *See* conflict and moral
distress

moral courage, 371, 375, 379

moral decision-making, 54, 58

moral distress, 73, 76, 94n1, 127, 175,
310, 317, 353, 363–64, 372, 381

moral education, 56

moral ideals, 38, 44, 46

moral judgements, 48, 50

moral justification, 49

moral life, 26, 55–57, 106

moral ought, 38

moral philosophy, 15, 24–26. *See also*
ethical theories; ethics

moral reasoning, 15, 24

moral reflection, 149–50

moral rights, 52

moral rules and principles, 55–56,
58–59

moral strength. *See* moral courage

morality, 40–41, 48

morally principled decisions, 40–42

multicultural society. *See* plurality of
cultures and points of view

Nancy B. case, 14, 173–74, 177

narrative ethics, 67

need, 302–03

needle sharing, 131

"need-to-know," 252

negative stereotyping (in emergency
room), 153

news media, 312, 357
on distribution of health resources,
294, 307
on emergency departments, 307

*Nichomachean Ethics* (Aristotle), 56

"no-new-information" policy, 207,
218–19

"non-compliant" patients, 145, 147,
156–57

nonmaleficence, 86, 104, 208, 210, 392

normative analysis, 28

North American Free Trade
Agreement (NAFTA), 94n4

nurse-employer relationship, 359–60,
368, 370. *See also* employment
conditions

nurse/physician conflicts, 218–20

nurse practitioners, 84

nurse recruitment programs, 79, 95n5

nurse researchers, 83. *See also* research
and experimentation
advocacy for better working
conditions and patient care, 92
influence on health policy, 92
social justice and, 315

nurse retention rates, 79, 365

nurse staffing cutbacks
increased patient morbidity and
mortality, 92

nurse-colleague relationship, 361, 366,
368, 370

nurse-patient relationship, 17, 40, 358
contractual model, 17–19
patient's advocate model, 18–20, 113,
151, 153, 180–85, 197, 331, 360
power imbalance, 228, 374

nurses' complicity in ethical problems,
88–89, 360

nurses' role as gatekeepers, 310

nursing education, 88, 90, 315, 354
baccalaureate degrees, 90–91, 122
clinical education, 322–27
continuing education, 90–91
ethics-specific education, 91
"everyday" nursing concerns
neglected, 87

universalizability, test of, 50–52
University of Toronto Joint Centre for
    Bioethics, 91
unregulated health care workers, 80
unsafe employment conditions, 108,
    332
Ursuline sisters, 104
user fees, 82
utilitarianism, 54–55, 59, 208, 296,
    300–01, 314
    in resource allocation, 295
utility, principle of, 54, 335

"value" for health care dollars,
    313
value judgements, 45–46
values, 21–22, 27, 29–30, 368. *See also*
    moral beliefs and values
values clarification, 21, 26
values dimension of nursing, 22
ventilators, 333–34, 355
virtue ethics, 55–58
    renaissance in contemporary ethical
        theory, 56
virtues, 56, 65
*voluntary* decision, 153
voluntary euthanasia, 170–71, 173

vulnerable and marginalized persons,
    117, 128, 158
    advocating for, 180–85
    policies that stigmatize, 368

watchdog, 154
weak paternalism (or limited
    paternalism), 165–66
Western, evidence-based health care,
    120
Western conception of autonomy, 156
Western society
    focus of decision-making on
        individual, 229
    full disclosure, 229
"When patients' needs compete with
    those of the employers," 359
whistleblowers, 378–79
wholeness, 352–53, 371, 378
"women's issues," 62. *See also* feminist
    ethics
workloads. *See under* employment
    conditions
World Health Organization (WHO),
    111

Zeliotis, George, 85

# from the publisher

A name never says it all, but the word "broadview" expresses a good deal of the philosophy behind our company. We are open to a broad range of academic approaches and political viewpoints. We pay attention to the broad impact book publishing and book printing has in the wider world; we began using recycled stock more than a decade ago, and for some years now we have used 100% recycled paper for most titles. As a Canadian-based company we naturally publish a number of titles with a Canadian emphasis, but our publishing program overall is internationally oriented and broad-ranging. Our individual titles often appeal to a broad readership too; many are of interest as much to general readers as to academics and students.

Founded in 1985, Broadview remains a fully independent company owned by its shareholders—not an imprint or subsidiary of a larger multinational.

---

If you would like to find out more about Broadview and about the books we publish, please visit us at **www.broadviewpress.com**. And if you'd like to place an order through the site, we'd like to show our appreciation by extending a special discount to you: by entering the code below you will receive a 20% discount on purchases made through the Broadview website.

Discount code: **broadview20%**

*Thank you for choosing Broadview.*

Please note: this offer applies only to sales of bound books within the United States or Canada.

FSC

www.fsc.org

MIX

Paper from
responsible sources

FSC® C013916